Group Travel Operating Procedures

Group Travel Operating Procedures

Saurabh Gupta

RANDOM PUBLICATIONS
NEW DELHI (INDIA)

Group Travel Operating Procedures

ISBN 978-93-5111-544-1

Published in 2015 in India by

RANDOM PUBLICATIONS

Reprint, 2017

4376-A/4B, Gali Murari Lal, Ansari Road
New Delhi-110 002
Phone : +9111-43580356, 011-23289044, 011-43142548
e-mail: sales@randompublications.com,
info@randompublications.com, randomexports@gmail.com

Type Setting by : Friends Media, Delhi-110089
Digitally Printed at : Replika Press Pvt. Ltd.

Preface

Group travel is the movement of people between relatively distant geographical locations, and can involve travel by foot, bicycle, automobile, train, boat, airplane, or other means, with or without luggage, and can be one way or round trip. Group travel can also include relatively short stays between successive movements. Reasons for traveling include recreation, tourism or vacationing, research travel for the gathering of information, for holiday to visit people, volunteer travel for charity, migration to begin life somewhere else, religious pilgrimages and mission trips, business travel, trade, commuting, and other reasons, such as to obtain health care or fleeing war or for the enjoyment of traveling. Group travel may occur by human-powered transport such as walking or bicycling, or with vehicles, such as public transport, automobiles, trains and airplanes. Motives to travel include pleasure, relaxation, discovery and exploration, getting to know other cultures and taking personal time for building interpersonal relationships. Travel may be local, regional, national or international. In some countries, non-local internal travel may require an internal passport, while international travel typically requires a passport and visa. A trip may also be part of a round-trip, which is a particular type of travel whereby a person moves from one location to another and returns.

I would like to thank my team for standing beside me throughout my career and writing this book. My special thanks go to "Random Publications" who have published the book.

– Saurabh Gupta

Contents

1

Groups

DEFINITION AND FEATURES OF GROUPS

Contrary to the conventional understanding, not every collection of people can be regarded a group. The Oxford English Dictionary defines group as "a number of persons or things regarded as forming a unit, on explanation of any type of mutual or general relation, or classified jointly on explanation of a general degree of parallel." From the sociological perspective, a group can be defined as two or more humans that interact with one another, accept expectations and obligations as members of the group, as well as share a general identity. Going by this definition, society can be perceived at the macro stage as a big group, while a social group (*e.g.* family, club, and team) which is considerably small may be viewed as small at the micro-stage.

According to Paul Hare, the defining feature of a group is social interaction. A true group exhibits some degree of social cohesion and is more than an easy collection or aggregate of individuals, such as people waiting at a bus stop. Features shared by members of a group may contain interests, values, ethnic or social background, and kinship ties. An aggregate is a collection of individuals who are present at the similar time and lay, but does not necessarily form a unit or have any general degree of parallel. Individuals standing at a street corner or the members of an audience at a music programme constitute aggregates, not groups.

Muzafer Sherif formulated a more technological definition.

According to Sherif a group has to be 'social unit consisting of a number of individuals interacting with each other based on sure elements:

- General motives and goals;
- An accepted division of Labour, *i.e.* roles,
- Recognized status (social rank, dominance) relationships;
- Accepted norms and values with reference to matters relevant to the group;
- Development of accepted sanctions (praise and punishment) if and when norms were respected or violated.

Based on the definitions one may consider a few criteria to call a group a group:

- Number of persons – more than one
- Interdependence
- Acceptance of roles and status
- Parallel of goals, motives
- Shared norms and values

Features

Several other definitions given by dissimilar social scientists have accentuated on the several characteristics of a group in several definitions.

Based on these one may arrive at the quintessential features of groups:

- *Interpersonal Interaction:* A group is defined as a collection of individuals interacting with each other; individuals are not a group unless they are interacting with one another
- *Perceptions of Membership:* A group may be defined as a social unit consisting of two or more persons, who perceive themselves as belonging to a group. Its members describe themselves and are defined by others as belonging to the group. Accordingly, the persons are not a group unless they perceive themselves to be part of a group
- *Interdependency:* Group may be defined as a collection of individuals who are interdependent. Usually, individuals are not a group unless an event that affects one of them affects them all. It is questionable that a group could exist without its members being interdependent.
- *Goals:* Group may be defined as a collection of individuals who join jointly to achieve a goal. According to this definition, the individuals are not a group unless they are trying to achieve a mutual goal. The primary defining feature of a group is the craving of its members to achieve a mutual goal.
- *Motivation:* Group may be defined as a collection of individuals who are all trying to satisfy some personal need through their joint association. Therefore, individuals are not a group unless they are motivated by some personal cause to be part of a group.
- *Structured Relationships:* A group may be a collection of individuals whose interactions are structured by a set of roles and norms. They share norms concerning matters of general interest and participate in an organization of interlocking roles. So, individuals are not a group unless their interactions are structured by a set of role definitions and norms.
- *Mutual Power:* A group may be defined as a collection of individuals who power each other. Accordingly, individuals are not a group unless they are affecting and being affected by each other.

Not all these features are equally significant and although it is impossible to gain consensus in the middle of social scientists as to which features are mainly significant. Though based on these features we may describe a group for the purpose of group work as: A group is two or more individuals in face to face interaction, each aware of his or her membership in the group as well as of others who belong to the group, and their positive interdependence as they strive to achieve mutual goals.

FACTORS INFLUENCING GROUP FORMATION

There are four major factors that usually power our decision to join and remain in a wide diversity of groups: attraction to members of the group; the behaviors, goals, or the task of the group; belongingness to the people in the group; and meeting needs or goals lying outside the group.

Attraction to the group mainly often grows out of proximity and the frequency of interaction. Your neighborhoods, classmates, roommates, and friendship are mainly determined by those who are in secure proximity and also accessible for interaction. Though, one necessity keep in mind that proximity makes only the potential for attraction. Several other factors usually approach into play when actually establishing a connection. Similarities, especially attitudinal parallel or vibes, appear to be as strong in group formation as in interpersonal attraction. Many other attributes of groups render them more attractive to prospective members and therefore contribute to group formation.

- Prestige of a group; *e.g.* members who have positions of higher power, aristocracy and eliteness
- Possibility of cooperative relationships and joint rewards heighten the attractiveness of a group the degree of positive interaction in the middle of members raising the range of personal and social needs being met.
- Size of the group; smaller groups offer higher possibility for interaction, for sharing similarities, and for meeting individual needs

The *task* of a group, as experienced in its behaviors and goals, is the second factor influencing group affiliation. You join a photography club because you enjoy taking pictures, discussing and sharing that action with others. You may even join a protest group to resist something that goes against your ideals; *e.g.* we join Green Peace to protest against environmental use by Corporations, or, we may even join students' movements to protest against the hike in tuition fees or cut down in transport concessions because you cannot afford to pay more.

Therefore, you are gaining rewards directly through group membership. The social swap theory to group formation predicts that we join and remain in groups when the rewards for doing so outweigh the costs, therefore yielding profits.

The third common factor of group formation is our *desire to affiliate* with the people in that group. We satisfy our need for affiliation through interacting with people, presently as we meet our need for attainment through the behaviors and goals of the group. The information that we affiliate for reasons of social comparison, in order to reduce anxiety, or to even to satisfy an innate craving, suggests that a group is a powerful forum for meeting our vital social needs and can yield a strong power on our Behaviour.

Group *membership* may help us meet needs that lie outside the group - therefore, group membership may be a stepping stone to achieve an external goal, rather than a source of direct satisfaction. A college professor may regularly attend meetings of a professional association to enhance the probability of promotion. A candidate for political office may join a host of society organizations to enhance his or her chances for election.

PLAUSIBLE EXPLANATIONS IN RELATION TO THE GROUP FORMATION

Based on the several factors influencing group formation, the following may be hypothesized:

- People join groups in order to satisfy sure individual needs.
- Proximity, get in touch with and frequent interaction give an opportunity to satisfy sure needs.
- Interpersonal attraction is a function of physical attractiveness, perceived skill of the other person (success or failure), need compatibility as well as several similarities - attitudinal, personality, economic, ethnicity, shared goals, etc.
- Individuals join groups if the behaviors of the group attractive or rewarding.

KINDS OF GROUPS

All of us are simultaneously members of several kinds of groups. We are members of a family, members of friendship groups, members of work organizations and members of fan club or a even a religious group. Sociologists have attempted to classify is several kinds of groups as follows:

VOLUNTARY VS. INVOLUNTARY GROUPS

We may join a political party or a scrupulous association (typical of a job).Such groups we join through our own choice and effort are *voluntary* groups. In contrast we are forced to join or are automatically incorporated as members of sure groups without choice; *e.g.* we are automatically classified in groups as members based on sex, age, nationality, religion and ethnicity. These latter groups in which we become members by birth or without any choice are *involuntary* groups.

OPEN VS. CLOSED GROUPS

Open groups are those groups characterized by changing membership. Here, virtually anyone can become a member. As sure members leave, new members are admitted, and the group continues. For instance, anyone can join the Hrithik Roshan fan club. On the other hand, there are some groups that uphold exclusiveness by restricting the membership and create it much harder to join. Only a few qualify to become members in such clubs. Such groups with restrictive membership criteria are closed groups; *e.g.* the mafia (underworld), Royal Enfield motorcycle clubs, night clubs, etc. Closed groups typically have some time limitation, with the group meeting for a predetermined number of sessions. Usually, members are expected to remain in the group until it ends, and new members are not added.

There are some advantages to open groups that incorporate new members as others leave, one of which is an increased opportunity for members to interact with a greater diversity of people. A potential disadvantage of open groups is that rapid changing of members can result in a lack of cohesion, particularly if too several clients leave or too several new ones are introduced at once. So, it will be better to bring in new members one at a time as and when opening occurs.

VERTICAL VS. HORIZONTAL GROUPS

There are sure groups, whose membership consists of individuals from all walks of life; *e.g.* religious groups may have members from all classes. Such a group may be regarded as a *vertical* group. On the other hand, a *horizontal* group consists predominantly of members from one social class. Occupational groups of doctors (*e.g.* IMA); guilds or associations of persons of a deal *e.g.* electricians, carpenters, non-gazatted officers for instance are composed mainly of members from the similar social class.

PRIMARY VS. SECONDARY GROUPS

Cooley described *primary* groups as collectivities of individuals – as in the case of play groups, neighborhood or village – "characterized by intimate, sympathetic face-to- face association and cooperation." A *primary* group is a group in which members develop secure, personal, intimate and enduring relationships; *e.g.* family, neighbors, work associates, etc.

Here, the members know each other very well, are greatly influenced by one another and feel closely related. On the other hand, *secondary groups* are characterized by contractual relationships and 'communication on indirect media'. These are 'relatively superior, relatively temporary, anonymous'; they are also 'formal, impersonal groups, in which there is little social intimacy or mutual understanding' and 'based on some interest or action', and whose 'members interact on the foundation of some specific roles.'

NATURAL VS. SHAPED GROUPS

Natural groups consist of members coming jointly in a spontaneous manner, on the foundation of naturally occurring events, interpersonal attraction or the mutually perceived needs of members. Family, peer groups and street gangs are examples of natural groups. On the other hand, *shaped* group are those groups constituted by any power or intervention external to the group. Such groups are usually shaped for a scrupulous purpose. Therapy groups, encounter groups, committees and teams are examples of shaped groups.

FORMAL VS. INFORMAL GROUPS

Formal groups are those groups that require someone to determine a task that needs to be accomplished, which requires some type of organizational organization, made up of several job roles, for which individuals are recruited. Here, task is what matters, and everything else—particularly the individuals and the roles they inhabit—may be changed. Informal groups work the other method round. A group of individuals meet: if they form a group, then they will informally allocate roles depending on individual preferences, and/ or on talents. This collection of roles creates an organization possible, and so occasionally they may undertake a task jointly, such as organizing a trip, or a night out or a party. It is the preferences of the Individuals which are paramount; tasks are incidental.

TREATMENT VS. TASK GROUPS

Treatment groups signify groups whose major purpose is to meet the socio-emotional needs of the group members. Such groups often aim at meeting the members' need for support, education, therapy, growth and socialization. Treatment groups contain growth groups (*e.g.* encounter groups for couples, value clarification groups for adolescents, or educative groups for society women); therapy groups (psychotherapy groups, support groups for de- addicted or the sober); socialization groups (YMCA, half-method homes). In contrast, *task* groups approach in subsistence with the purpose of accomplishing a goal that is neither intrinsically nor immediately connected to the needs of the group members, but rather, of broader constituency.

The classic instance for *task* groups in social work practice setting are Medical Teams, Treatment conferences convened to monitor treatment as well as Staff Development (Progrmmes).

Some of the major variation flanked by treatment and task groups contains the following:

- Members in treatment groups are bonded to their general needs, where as in a task group, the members are working towards accomplishing a task or a mandate which eventually might lead to bonding

- Roles develop through interaction in treatment groups, while in task roles are usually defined based on competencies
- Communication is open in treatment groups, while communication in task groups are focused approximately a scrupulous task
- Procedures in treatment groups are flexible, while it is formal and based on agendas in task groups
- Self-disclosure is high in treatment groups, whereas it might not at all happen in task groups
- Proceedings are confidential and kept within the context of the treatment groups, where as in task groups it may be open to public scrutiny
- Success of treatment groups is evaluated on the foundation of the group meeting the members' treatment goals, where as in task groups it is based on the attainment of task or a mandate

The kind of group that we discussed last – shaped groups as well as treatment groups – are of great interest to group work, as the groups that we approach crossways in group work predominantly belong to this kind of groups.

Other kinds of groups contain the following:

- *Reference Group:* Individuals approximately universally have a bond Towards what are recognized as reference groups. These are groups to which the individual conceptually relates him/her, and from which he/she adopts goals and values as a part of his/her self identity.
- *Peer group:* A peer group is a group of almost the similar age, social status, and interests. Usually, people are relatively equal in conditions of power when they interact with peers.
- *Clique:* An informal, tight-knit group, usually in a High School/College setting, that shares general interests. There is a recognized yet shifting power structure in mainly *Cliques*.
- *Club:* A club is a group, which usually requires one to apply to become a member. Such clubs may be dedicated to scrupulous behaviors, such as sporting clubs.
- *Household:* all individuals who live in the similar home
- *Society:* A society is a group of people with a commonality or sometimes an intricate net of overlapping commonalities, often - but not always - in proximity with one another with some degree of stability in excess of time. They often have some organization and leaders.
- *Franchise:* this is an organization which runs many instances of a business in several locations.
- *Gang:* A gang is usually an urban group that gathers in a scrupulous region. It is a group of people that often hang approximately each other. They can be like some clubs, but much less formal.

- *Mob:* A mob is usually a group of people that has taken the law into their own hands. Mobs are usually a group which gathers temporarily for a scrupulous cause.
- *Posse:* A posse was initially an American term for a group of citizens that had banded jointly to enforce the law. Though, it can also refer to a street group.
- *Squad:* This is usually a small group, of approximately 3-8 people, that would work as a team to accomplish their goals.
- *Team:* similar to a squad, though a team may contain several more members. A team works in a similar method to a squad
- *Learning (groups):* Drs David and Roger Johnson of the University of Minnesota (the gurus of group work and co-operative learning research) identify three kinds of groups that can promote collaborative learning:
  - *Informal learning groups:* Ad hoc, transient, short term groups that can be quickly shaped and utilized in even a big lecture situation. Formal learning groups - The sort of groups that we would use to work on superior collaborative projects. This kind of group work is more structured and requires much more scheduling. Formal learning groups usually contain multiple opportunities for reflection on the group's progress.
- *Base groups (revise group):* Self-selected groups of students who work jointly independently of specified class time or assignments.

GROUP COMPOSITION

Whether a group should be homogeneous (consisting of members from similar age-groups, sex and socio-economic background) or a heterogeneous in membership, depends on the group's goals. In the context of social group work, given specific target population with specific needs, a group composed entirely of members of that population quite similar in features is more appropriate than a heterogeneous group.

For instance, let us consider a group composed entirely of elderly people. Such a group would be able to focus exclusively and deal more uniformly on the specific troubles that characterize their developmental era, *e.g.* loneliness, separation, loss in income and eventually social location, rejection, deterioration of the body, atrophy in power and so forth. This parallel in the middle of the members can lead to a great degree of cohesion, which in turn offers the possibility for an open and intense exploration of their life crises, leading to universalisation (as a principle) of their troubles. Members are more likely to express feelings that have been once kept private. Moreover, their life circumstances make a bond with one another. Likewise, self-help groups (SHGs) for women also benefit greatly from the homogeneity of the composition of their group, enabling them to pursue the general goal of credit management (thrift-savings) or self-development in a concerted fashion. Alternately, where it is desired to give diverse, socially demanding growth experiences, a microcosm of the outside social structure is desired. In such an event, a heterogeneous group is best. Personal-growth groups and sure therapy groups tend to be heterogeneous. Therefore, participant members are allowed to experiment with new Behaviour and develop interpersonal skills with the help of feedback from a rich diversity of people in an environment representative of everyday reality.

Group Size

There has been contesting views concerning the desirable size for a group. The answer depends on many factors: the age of clients, experience of the leader, kind of group, and nature of the troubles to be explored. For instance, a group composed of elementary school children might be kept to 4 to 6, whereas a group of adolescents might be made up of 8 to 12 people. For a weekly ongoing group of adults, in relation to the 10 to 12 people with one leader may be ideal. A group manageable in size is big enough to provide ample opportunity for interaction and small enough for everyone to be involved and to feel a sense of "group."

FREQUENCY AND DURATION OF MEETINGS

Another bone of contention is concerning the periodicity of group meetings. Questions regularly posed contain:

- How often should a group meet?
- For how extensive should a group meet twice weekly for 1- hour sessions? Or is 1½ to 2 hours once a week preferable?

With children and adolescents it may be better to meet more regularly and for a shorter era to suit their attention span. If the group is taking lay in a school setting, the meeting times can correspond to regularly scheduled class periods. For groups of college students or relatively well functioning adults, a 2-hour weekly session might be preferable. A 2-hour era is enough to allow some rigorous work yet, not so extensive that fatigue sets in.

You can choose any frequency and duration that suit your approach of leadership and the kind of people in your group. For an in-patient group in a mental health centre, it is desirable to meet on a daily foundation for 45 minutes. Because of the members' psychological impairment, it may not be realistic to hold their attention for a longer era.

GROUP LIFE-CYCLE

Other questions that have often intrigued us are:

- What should be the duration of a group?

- Is it wise to set a termination date?

For mainly groups (in the social work perspective) a termination date should be announced at the outset, so that members will have a clear thought of the time frame within which they would be operating. Groups in educational organizations typically run for in relation to the 15 weeks. This would be extensive enough for trust to develop and for work Towards behavioral changes to take lay. But it should not be so extensive that the group appears to be dragging on interminably. A major value of this kind of time limited group is that members are motivated to realize that they do not have forever to attain their personal goals. At dissimilar points in this 15-week group, members are challenged to review their progress, both individually and as a group. If they are dissatisfied with their own participation or with the direction the group is taking, they have the responsibility to do something to change the situation.

Some groups compose of the similar members who meet for years. Such a time structure allows them to work through issues in some depth, and offers support and challenge in creation life changes. These ongoing groups do have the potential for fostering dependency, and therefore it is significant that both the leader and members evaluate the impact of the group on the clients' daily livelihood.

LAY FOR GROUP MEETINGS

Other questions concern the environment and ambience for group meetings. Several spaces will do, but privacy is essential. Member's necessity is assured that they will not be overheard by people in adjoining rooms. Groups often fail because of their physical setting. If they are held in a day hall or ward full of distractions, productive group work will not happen. You would require a room that is not cluttered up with chairs and tables and that allows for a comfortable seating arrangement. Member's necessity is able to sit in a circle. This arrangement lets all the participants see one another and allows enough freedom of movement that members can spontaneously create physical get in touch with.

DISPERSAL AND TRANSFORMATION OF GROUPS

Two or more people in interacting situations will in excess of time develop stable territorial relationships. These may or may not develop into groups. But stable groups can also break up in to many sets of territorial relationships. There are numerous reasons for stable groups to malfunction or to disperse, but essentially this is because of loss of compliance with one or more elements of the definition of group provided by Sherif. The two mainly general causes of a malfunctioning group are the addition of too several individuals, and the failure of the leader to enforce a general purpose, though malfunctions may happen due to a failure of any of the other elements (*i.e.*, confusions concerning status or of norms).

In a society, there is obvious need for more people to participate in cooperative endeavors than can be accommodated by separate groups. The military has demonstrated best as to how this is possible by its hierarchical array of squads, platoons, companies, battalions, regiments, and divisions. Private companies, corporations, government agencies, clubs, too have all urbanized comparable (if less formal and standardized) systems when the number of members or employees exceeds the number that can be accommodated in an effective group. Not all superior social structures require the cohesion that may be establish in the small group. Consider the neighborhood, country club, or the diocese, which are basically territorial organizations who support big social purposes. Any such big organizations may need only islands of cohesive leadership.

For a functioning group to effort to add new members in a casual method is a sure prescription for failure, loss of efficiency, or disorganization. The number of functioning members in a group can be reasonably flexible flanked by five and ten, and an extensive-standing cohesive group may be able to tolerate a few part-timers. The key concept is that the value and success of a group is obtained by each member maintaining a separate, functioning identity in the minds of each of the members. The cognitive limit to this span of manages on individuals often set at seven. Rapid shifting of attention can push the limit to in relation to the ten. Beyond ten, subgroups will inevitably start to form with the attendant loss of purpose, dominance order, and individuality, with confusion of roles and rules. The average classroom with twenty to forty pupils and one teacher is a rueful instance of one supposed leader juggling a number of subgroups.

Weakening of the general purpose once a group is well recognized can be attributed to: adding new members; unsettled conflicts of identities (*i.e.*, territorial troubles in individuals); weakening of a settled dominance order; and weakening or failure of the leader to tend to the group. The actual loss of a leader is regularly fatal to a group, unless there was lengthy preparation for the transition. The loss of the leader tends to dissolve all dominance relationships, as well as weakening dedication to general purpose, differentiation of roles, and maintenance of norms. The mainly general symptoms of a troubled group are loss of efficiency, diminished participation, or weakening of purpose, as well as an augment in verbal aggression. Often, if a strong general purpose is still present, an easy reorganization with a new leader and a few new members will be enough to re-set up the group, which is somewhat easier than forming an entirely new group.

BENEFITS OF GROUPS

Affiliation to groups carries sure implications, both constructive and detrimental. Given below are some of these:

- In mainly circumstances, the productivity of groups is higher than that of the individuals. This synergy is best demonstrated in the form of team work whether it be in cricket, football or at work.
- Groups are likely to create effective decisions and solve the troubles better than individuals working alone. When troubles are discussed in groups, there is a better probability for clarification out of which a diversity of solutions emerge. It is for this very cause that we constitute committees.
- It is through group membership that we inculcate values of altruism, kindness, compassion, responsibility and so forth. Family and peer groups are such primary groups responsible for engraving into us a wide range of such human values.
- The excellence of emotional life in conditions of friendship, love, excitement, joy, fulfillment and attainment is richer in groups and helps in personal growth. A person who does not have any connection with others will not be able to experience mainly of the emotions. The excellence of everyday life is better in groups because of the advantages of specialization and division of Labour.
- Conflicts are absorbed better considering the possibility of sharing. Likewise, conflicts are supervised more productively in groups owing to the peer support and a diversity of ideas to problem solving.
- A person's identity, self-esteem and social competencies are easily clarified and shaped by the groups to which he/she belongs. Being a member of dissimilar types of groups gives you with an identity, *e.g.* a student, family member, caste, etc. Friendship (groups) offer opportunities to experiment with dissimilar types of Behaviour without the threat of rejection thereby helping to develop the self-esteem.

Even while groups give a lot of benefits, social scientists have also pointed out characteristics of groups that are not very constructive. For one, people in groups are for reasons of anonymity and security, are more likely to take more extreme positions and engage in impulsive and antisocial behaviors. Another negative aspect is the tendency of groups to force their members to conform, in extreme cases even threatening the identity of the individuals. Social scientists also point out that sometimes group affiliations become so strong that group members turn hostile on nonmembers and other groups. Intense group Behaviour may precipitate many conflicts in the society.

Though, a proper understanding of groups and its proper application in dealing with groups within the context of social work will help us reap the immense benefits from by groups. Experiments mannered by social scientists have proved time and again the strengths of by groups for the development of the individual and society. That is the cause why an understanding of groups is crucial to the practice of group work. In the context of group work, groups contribute immensely to the personality development of individuals.

UNDERSTANDING GROUPS

There have been in common two approaches that may have enhanced our understanding of groups. The first came from social scientists that experimented on groups in laboratories or observed groups functioning in society setting. The alternate approach came from group work practitioners who examined how groups function in practice settings such as social work, education, group therapy sessions and recreation. Such an understanding has led to improved methods of working with a diversity of dissimilar kinds of groups.

Social Psychology as a subject addresses to the vital research question that was asked by social scientists concerning the extent to which being a part of a group, powers the individual group member. Early findings suggest that the attendance of others did indeed have an important power on an individual group member; groups tended to generate forces that force individuals to conform to the standards of behavior and judgments of individual members. Le Bon recognizing that people in groups react differently from individuals, referred to the forces generated by group interaction as 'group contagion' and 'group mind'. Another aspect that might interest us is cohesion. *Cohesiveness* of a group is the extent to which members are attracted to the group. Cohesiveness is the 'total field of forces which act on members to remain in the group'. In easy words, it is the measure of interpersonal attractiveness in the middle of the members of the group. Studies demonstrate that the 'satisfaction that members derive from associating with one another is only one reward that binds them to a group and so only one dimension of cohesiveness. Review of literature distinguishes other two kinds of rewards – *social interdependence* and *instrumental interdependence*. Social interdependence occurs where members are attracted to one another basically because of the perceived advantage involved in being with and interacting with other members of the group. Instrumental independence occurs where individuals are attracted to one another in order to jointly achieve some goal; *e.g.* teaming up to win a race or game, participation in struggles to displacement resulting from development, working in an orchestra.

The nature of the group too may power the participating individuals. Allport for instance, establish that attendance of others improved task performance. The concept of a *primary* group was also a significant contribution to the revise of groups. Cooley defined a *primary* group as 'a small informal group, equivalent to the family or a friendship group, which wields tremendous power on member's values, moral standards and even normative Behaviour'. The primary group was so viewed as essential in understanding the socialization procedure and the development of the individuals involved. Faris E asserts three properties atypical of primary groups – faceto- face dealings, temporal priority and a feeling of wholeness. As against this *secondary groups* are characterized by contractual relationships and 'communication on indirect media'. Weber attributed the development of secondary groups to the increased stages of bureaucratization, depersonalization and reutilization happening in the society. Ferdinand Tonnies observed an "irreversible" moving absent from the warmth of tribal life as experienced in small isolated societies to the cold urban anonymity. Accordingly, the *gemeinschaft* was on the wane and would be superseded by contractual relationships of the *gesellschaft.*

HISTORICAL DEVELOPMENT OF GROUPS

THE CONTEXT

Group work was seen as a movement before it became a field. From a field, it became a method, and back to a field. Group work played a significant role in dealing with a number of shifts happening in the U.S. in the late-19th century and early-20th century: the industrialization of the U.S.; big population shifts from rural to urban centers, and; the enormous wave of immigration, mainly to U.S. urban regions.

The history of social work may be measured in scrupulous focus is on three major phases:

- The formation of a group work association, 1930s;
- The merger into the National Association of Social Workers, 1950s; and
- The rebirth of group work, 1970s.

The entire similar one may consider some growths occurring flanked by 1910 and 1920; those who were concerned with adult education, recreation, and society work began to realize the full potential of group work. They understood better that groups could be used to help people participate effectively in their societies, to enrich people's lives and to support those persons whose primary connection were not satisfying or dysfunctional. So did they become aware of the potential of groups for helping people acquire social skills as well as problem-solving skills?

They began to make good use of groups in preventing delinquency and in rehabilitating those maladjusted. The organizations that built the base of group work were by nature self-help, informal and recreational ones; they were present in the form of resolution homes, neighborhood centers, Y's, the Scouts, Camp Fire Girls, Jewish Centers Camps and for that matter even in Labour union organising in industries. Later designated as 'group work agencies', the novel element that united these services and appealed mainly were involvement in small groups, the democratic method of life, society responsibility and perceived membership in behaviors with implications at national or even global.

Early in 1920, Mary Richmond realized the potentials of working with groups and wrote on the importance of small group psychology. Mary P Follett, a political scientist in 1926 wrote in the book "The New State", that solutions to social troubles would 'emerge from the creation of groups in neighborhood and approximately social interest'. Follett strongly whispered in the power of the small groups shaped in societies to solve social troubles that neighbors had in general. John Dewey, who proposed and urbanized the thought of progressive education also establish the usefulness of small groups as early as 1933. Dewey perceived social group work method as an application of the principles of progressive education to small informal groups in leisure time settings. Dewey, through his progressive education movement, advocated working with small leisure-time groups. The powers of Follett and Dewey leading thinkers in group work reinforced an individualist perspective that became engrained in group work.

FORMATION OF CLUBS

The first form of group setting could be traced back to Sir George Williams, who organized the hard working laborers of Bridgewater draper shops, towards the Christian method of livelihood. The success of such groups inspired the extension of such group setting to other draper shops or other young men, thereby giving birth to London's Young Men's Christian Association in 1844. Soon the ripples of YMCA reached the women and girls of Germany and England, encouraging them for Christian companionship. In England, similar movements, having less association with the church, originated in 1855 simultaneously in two spaces. These were directly led by women - Emma Roberts, who started a prayer union in the middle of her friends, and Mrs. Arthur Kennard, who started the Common Female Training Institute in London for the nurses returning from Crimean war. The successful working of these two organizations motivated Mrs. Kinniard and Miss Roberts to amalgamate both the organization under one head. Therefore, the YWCA came into subsistence in 1877. Giving due consideration to the less fortunate woman, the privileged women in United States initiated many programmes in excess of the years. One such notable movement was the formation of Union Prayer Circle by Mrs. Marshal O in 1858. This was transformed as boarding home in 1860, and later renamed as the Ladies Christian Union in 1866. Rooms were rented on top floor of the warehouses and equipped to meet the needs of the wage earners in New York.

In America, the Boston YWCA began as an effort of thirty women in 1866 focusing on temporal, moral and religious welfare of their fellow beings. Now both YMCA and YWCA have recognized themselves as pioneering organizations with active involvement in educational, recreational and religious behaviors for young men and women. It remnants an information that the publications from these associations that have significantly contributed towards literature of social group work. The contribution from these associations in providing skilled volunteers while practicing group work is tremendous.

THE RESOLUTION MOVEMENT

Social disorganization, the child of industrial revolution, demanded the formation of an organized body to meet the welfare needs of the people bearing the brunt of industrialization. The settlement movement owes its origin to Jane Addams, the founder of the Hull Home in Chicago in 1889. The movement focused on the causes of poverty and functioned through three thrust regions–Research, Reform and Residence.

Jane and the other pioneers, who whispered in the group approach, set the objectives of the movement as follows:-

- The residents of the region could share their learning's of cultural and religious in the middle of the needy.
- The identification of resolution workers with the local region
- The responsibility of the group for social reform.

The congested immigrant population became the target of mainly of the resolution workers. There they could observe the changing circumstances and needs of the people while matching the several possessions to satisfy the needy. They provided a diversity of services including educational, health and legal services, and also advocated changes in social policy. According to Rameshweri Devi and Ravi Prakash settlements have also served as centers for classes in English and citizenship, as well as for clubs which gave both older and younger immigrants the best of American culture.

Stanton Coit concentrated his behaviors in the formation of clubs in the neighborhood, which would unknowingly develop deep bonding in the middle of the society members. He was the founder father of the Neighborhood Guild, the first American resolution in 1886. Picnics and other recreational behaviors were taken up so that more youth would participate and develop the settlements to a structured informal association. Woods and Kennedy in the Resolution Horizon have commented that the settlement movements have provided ample opportunities for 'the actual interplay of association'.

THE PLAYGROUND AND RECREATION MOVEMENT

The part played by recreation movement towards group livelihood is noteworthy. The socialization procedure begins in a child when he starts to associate and accept another child to play with him. Even though the first municipal play ground of U.S. was the English Village Green, group games were not entertained until the nineteenth century. In 1868, the first church of Boston came up with a vacation play ground, while the Washington Park in Chicago was opened for team games in 1876. But it was in 1885, with the beginning of a sand park in

Boston by Marie Zakrzewska, that the play ground was chosen as a movement in the history of social group work. She got the inspiration for such a concept observing the children playing in sand piles in public parks. Soon playgrounds and summer camps mushroomed under the initiative of settlements, churches and schools. It is the success of play ground movements and the need for more tax supported play grounds that resulted in the beginning of the Playground and Recreation Association of America in 1906. Schools and other social agencies supported the movement highlighting the importance of such a group experience in the social and emotional growth of a child.

The World War Society Service organized during Word Wars I and II had greatly accelerated the recreation movement. Taking its origin from the privately owned small playground for the poor, the growth of recreation movements was distant beyond imagination. It has grown to the extent that now it contributes the major source of the country's wealth.

THE WORLD WARS AND AFTER

Post World War I, social scientists also began to focus on groups operating in the society. One of the earliest to do so was Frederic Thrasher who studied gangs of delinquents in the Chicago region. He studied groups by befriending gang members and observing the internal operations of gangs. Thrasher observed that every member of a gang had a *status* within the group linked to the functional role that the member played for the gang. Thrasher also highlighted the role of culture that urbanized within a gang, suggesting there was a general code that may be followed by all members. The code was enforced by group opinion, coercion and physical punishment. This work beside with others have influenced the methods group work is practiced with youths in resolution homes, neighborhood centers and youth organizations. Some later group workers relied on naturalistic observations of groups of boys in a summer camp to demonstrate how cohesion and inter-group hostility develop and operate. Social scientists also learned more in relation to the people's behavioral in groups from studies done in industry and in the United States Army.

Characteristically, workers in industries knit themselves into informal organizations in and in relation to the work, develop expectations that their jobs and work dealings be limited to persons of a type – gender, age, ethnic qualities, education and social class. Such assemblages manifest it in spaces such as cafeterias where the employees sort themselves based on the rank, sex, age and lay in the plant.

THEORETICAL BASES

The 1930s witnessed the power of small group theory especially the differentiation done by Cooley with regard to the Primary and Secondary groups. The proposition by Tonnies to differentiate flanked by *gesselschaft* and *gemeinschaft* also aided a better understanding in relation to the groups. The 1950s witnessed an explosion of knowledge and development of theory concerning small groups. The major researchers incorporated the likes of Bales, Homans, Bion, Lewin, Weber, etc., to mention a few. The major themes that urbanized in the first half of the twentieth century contain conventionality, communication and interaction patterns, leadership, interpersonal preference and social perception that are significant components while dealing with group procedure in social work. It is also significant to mention the contribution of psychoanalytic theory, learning theory, field theory, social swap theory and the system theory that explains group functioning.

A GLIMPSE OF PROFESSIONALISATION AND THE DEVELOPMENT ON LITERATURE IN SOCIAL GROUP WORK

Although it is often whispered that group work is considerably younger than casework, group work agencies actually started only a few years after casework agencies recognized their forte. The first course of group work was offered by Clara Kaiser, in the School of Social Work at Western Reserve University in Cleveland. When she left for New York in 1935, Grace Coyle sustained to develop the course. Group Work was taught partially as a method and partially as a field of practice. By 1937 in relation to the 10 schools offered specialised courses in social work. Though, as Schwartz points out, the real historical differences flanked by the two is that casework soon became recognized with social work profession, where as group work did not begin to become formally connected with the profession, until much later throughout the National Conference of Social Work in 1935.

This remained somewhat informal until 1955 and the founding of the National Association of Social Workers. A small cadre of group workers met in New York Municipality in the early 1930s to have informal discussions. This group proposed a gathering of group workers at the NCSW. In 1936, the American Association for the Revise of Group Work was founded with the intention of clarifying and refining both the philosophy and practice of group work. This group created the National Association for the Revise of Group Work under the leadership of Arthur Swift. It was a 'missionary spirit' which motivated this early group. By 1939, group work began to be treated as a separate subject, markedly with the National Conference of Social Work. The identification of group work with social work profession became stronger throughout the 1940s although group workers sustained to uphold loose ties with recreation, adult education, and mental hygiene until the 1950s. In 1955, group workers joined hands with six other professional groups to form the National Association of Social Workers (NASW).

In information, group work was very closely associated with society organization method and its concept of citizen's participation. Later, throughout the 1940s and 1950s group workers began to use groups more regularly to give therapy and remediation in mental health settings. This was significantly influenced by the increased interest in psychoanalysis and ego psychology and also partly due to the World War II, which created a severe shortage of trained workers to deal with mentally disabled war veterans. It was spurred on by the sustained interest in the use of groups in psychiatric settings throughout the 1950s. Although there was an increased emphasis in the 1940s and 1950s on utilizing groups to improve the social functioning of individual group members, interest remained in by groups for recreational and educational purposes, especially in Jewish society centers and in youth organizations such as Girls Scouts and the YWCA. Throughout the 1940s and 1950s groups were also used for purposes of society development and social action in many dissimilar neighborhood centers and society agencies. At the similar time, there was an accompanying augment interest in the revise of small group as a social phenomenon.

The years post-World War II saw an immense rise in group work literature. Gertrude Wilson's "Social Group Work Practice", Harleigh B. Trecker's "Social Group Work", Grace Coyle's "GroupWork with American Youth" and Gisela Konopka's "Therapeutic Group Work with Children" all appeared in a time span of hardly two years. All these books set out to clarify the orderly procedure of social group work as part of the helping function of social work on the wide scope of applications ranging from the healthy to sick, individuals and groups. The decade of the 1960s witness the decline in the popularity of group services. The skills of group worker were then viewed as being more important in the region of society organization in organising youths and adults approximately significant social concerns. Also, throughout the 1960s, the push towards a generic view of practice and the movement absent from specializations in casework, group work and society organizations, weakened group specializations in professional schools and reduced the number of professionals who were trained in group work as their primary mode of practice.

The interest in group work waned still further throughout the 1970s. Fewer professional schools offered advanced course in group work and fewer practitioners used group work as a practice method. The late seventies saw the reemergence of a professional journal, Social Work with Groups in 1978. Additionally, in 1978 social group workers shaped a committee to host a symposium in Honour of Grace Coyle which paved the method for an annual conference in subsequent years. The conference scheduling committee was transformed into the membership driven organization, "The Association for the Advancement of Social Work with Groups". In order to augment practioners awareness in relation to the potential benefits of groups, group workers throughout the US and Canada came jointly and held the first Annual Symposium for the Advancement of Group Work in 1979. Each year since then, the annual symposium on group work as a practice method has been convened religiously without fail.Group work has also made inroads into the south-east Asia, especially India and China. Social work education in China has experienced a very rapid expansion in excess of the past decade.

Top Chinese leaders have advocated strongly for social work and in 2006, the government launched a series of new social policy initiatives aimed at professionalizing social work. This has provided an opportunity for researchers and educators to think in relation to the possible impact and future challenges confronting the civil affairs sector and social work educators. Group work has survived through hard times. Its' resiliency is a testament to the persistence of the core of people as well as the strength of the method. What kept group work going throughout the "quiet" years were the attendance of individuals and legendary teachers and proselytizers of the like of Schwartz Bernstein, the Abels, and Ramey". The people who came jointly to begin AASWG, with their "wonderful spirit of inclusion, validation and humanity that is imbedded in group work ideology" determined that group work should survive.

Group work ideology has stood the test of time because it is rooted in a clear understanding of the realities of human lives and the human condition. Concepts of citizenship, participation, society, mutual aid, and democracy are still powerful.

According to Ephross:

- "We were right then, we're right now." Middleman and Goldberg remind us that "it is group work that has anchored and continues to anchor social work in its custom of social reform and concern for oppressed people..."

IMPORTANT GROUP WORK LITERATURE THROUGHOUT THE LAST TWO DECADES

Carrell, S 1993 has written on group exercises for adolescents. The book also contains a manual for therapists. The exercises are useful for school social workers and group workers involved in life skills training. Morganett has written a book on life skills and group counseling for young adolescents. Rose, S. and Edilson, J. have also written a book on specific group work exercises for children and adolescents. Toseland, R is well recognized for his book on Group work with elderly and family care givers. Hurley has urbanized therapeutic group exercises for the elderly. Pehroozi has presented models of Group Work in his book Social Work with Group. Berecher has urbanized an innovative concept described Telephonic Group Work. Breton has urbanized the concept of Empowerment Oriented Group Work in his book Social Work with Group. Brown, A and Mistry, T have focused on Group Work with mixed membership group highlighting on race and gender based issues. Coxe and Parsons, R have urbanized their theories on empowerment oriented Group Work practice with elderly. Glassman, U and Kates, L have written on the Humanistic Approach in Group Work. Nosko, A and Wallace, R have highlighted on gender based issues in Social Work Group.

Throughout the last decade the following books on GroupWork have contributed significantly to the understanding of Group Work An introduction to GroupWork practice by Ronald Tosland and Robert Rivas.

Encyclopaedia of Social Group Work with groups:

- By Alex Gifferman, Robert Salmon.
- By Group Work by Spot Doel.
- Social Work with group by Helen Northen and Roselle Kurland.
- Perspectives on Social Group Work Practice, Alissi Albert, S.
- The Essentials of Group Worker by Doel, Spot and Sawda, Catharine.
- A Hand Book of Social Work with Groups by Gravin, Charles D, Lorriae M. Gulier (Ed).

PRESENT TRENDS IN GROUP WORK

TECHNOLOGY MEDIATED GROUP WORK

Several support groups are forming group on row. For instance women suffering from breast cancer have online support groups. Mainly of these support groups offer information on the problem and in relation to the treatments methods. They also give accounts of people who have dealt with the disease successful.

GROUP DYNAMICS

MODELS OF GROUP DEVELOPMENT

In this section we will briefly review following models of group development:

- Tuckman's five stage model
- Punctuated equilibrium model
- Tubb's model
- Fisher's model
- Poole's model
- Boss and Ryterband model
- Schutz's three stage model

Tucknan's five stage model

An alternative, and more popular, model by Tuckman identifies four main successive stages of group development and relationships: forming, storming, norming and performing.

- Stage 1 Forming: The initial formation of the group and bringing jointly of a number of individuals who identify. tentatively, the purpose of the group, its composition and conditions of reference. At this stage consideration is given to hierarchical structure of the group, pattern of leadership, individuals roles and responsibilities, and codes of conduct. There is likely to be considerable anxiety as members effort to make and impression, to test each other, and to set up their personal identify within the group.

- Stage 2 - Storming: As members of the group get to know each other better they will put forward their views more openly and forcefully. Disagreements will be expressed and challenges offered on the nature of the task and arrangements made in the earlier stage of development. This may lead to disagreement and hostility. The storming stage is significant because, if successful, there will be discussions on reforming arrangements for the working and operation of the group, and agreement on more meaningful structures and formations.
- Stage 3 - Norming: As disagreement and hostility start to be controlled members of the group will set up guidelines and standards, and develop their own norms of acceptable behaviour. The norming stage is significant in establishing the need for members to co-operate in order to plan, agree standards of performance and fulfill the purpose of the group. This co-operation and adherence to group norms can work against effective organizational performance. It may be remembered, for instance, that, in the bank wiring room experiment of the Hawthorne studies, group norms imposed a restriction on the stage of output of the workers.
- Stage 4 - Performing: When the group has progressed successfully through the three earlier stages of development it would have created structure and cohesiveness to work effectively as a team. At this stage the group can concentrate on the attainment of its purpose and performance of their general task if likely to be at its mainly effective method.
- Stage 5 - Adjourning: This is last stage of the group development formation. At this stage wrapping up becomes the priority instead of high performance. At this stage some members feel upbeat due to task accomplishment and some feel depressed because this is the time members disband and friendship urbanized throughout the group work will have to part. But this stage occurs only in the life of temporary groups. For permanent groups performing is the last stage of development.

These five stages are dynamic stages of group, several times group may regress to lower stages after progressing to higher stages. This is the mainly cited model of group development. Reaching to performance is mainly often measured desirable as groups are expected to be high performing in performing stage. But this is not true. Some time when disagreement stimulation is necessary, storming stage will also produce high performance in groups.

Punctuated equilibrium model

This model is applicable to temporary groups having specified deadlines. Studies suggest that such groups have their unique pattern of action and inertia. Behaviour of such groups have general pattern: a. the first meeting sets group's direction, b. this first stage of group action lacks urgency, symbolizes the stage of inertia, c. transition takes lay at the end of the first stage, this mainly often happens when groups have consumed exactly half of its allotted time, d. transition introduces major change, symbolizes intense action stage, e. second stage of inertia follows the action stage, and f. group's last meeting is marked again by accelerated ace of behaviors. Essentially, this model suggests that temporary groups with defined deadlines display extensive periods of inertia intercepted by brief intense action, sweeping changes stimulated primarily by members' consciousness concerning time and deadlines.

Tubbs's small group development model

This model is conceptualized into four stages:

- Orientation: In this stage, group members get to know each other, they start to talk in relation to the problem, and they look at the limitations and opportunities of the project.
- Disagreement: Disagreement is a necessary part of a group's development. Disagreement allows the group to evaluate ideas and it helps the group avoid conventionality and groupthink.
- Consensus: Disagreement ends in the consensus stage, when group members compromise, select ideas, and agree on alternatives.
- Closure: In this stage, the final result is announced and group members reaffirm their support of the decision.

Fisher's small group development

This model is again a four stage model of development:

- Orientation: Throughout the orientation stage group members get to know each other and they experience primary tension, the awkward feeling people have before communication rules,and expectations are recognized. Groups take time to learn in relation to the each other and feel comfortable communicating with new people.
- Disagreement: The disagreement stage is marked by secondary tension, or tension nearby the task at hand. Group members disagree with each other and debate ideas. Keep in mind that disagreement is measured well, because it helps the group achieve desired results.

- Emergence: In the emergence stage, the outcome of the group's task and its social structure become-apparent.
- Reinforcement: In this stage, group members look at their final decision from several perspectives by supportive verbal and nonverbal communication.

Poole's small group development model

Poole suggested that group development is a complicated formation and moves back and forth flanked by three tasks: task,' topic and relation. The three tracks can be compared to the intertwined strands of a rope.

- Task track: The task track concerns the formation by which the group accomplishes its goals,
- Topic track: The topic track concerns the specific thing the group is discussing at the time,
- Relation track: The relation track deals with the interpersonal relationships flanked by the group members. At times, the group may stop its work on the task and work instead on its relationships. When the group reaches consensus on all three tracks at once, it can proceed in a more unified manner.

Breakpoints

Breakpoints happen when a group switches from one track to another. Shifts in the conversation, adjournment, or postponement are examples of breakpoints. Bass and Ryterband's model. This model consists of four separate stages in group development: mutual acceptance and membership; communication and decision creation; motivation and productivity; and manage and organization.

- *First stage:* developing mutual acceptance and membership: Members have an initial mistrust of each other and a fear of inadequacies. They remain suspicious and limit their behaviour through conventionality and ritual. The priority is with questions of likes and dislikes, and power of dependency of group members.
- *Second stage:* communication and decision-creation: Once members have learnt to accept each other they begin to express their feelings and conflicts. Norms of formation are recognized and there is acceptance of legitimate power in excess of the group. Member develop a liking, or at least a sense of caring for each other. There are more open communications and reactions. More constructive problem-solving and decision-creation behaviour strategies develop.
- *Third stage:* motivation and productivity: Troubles of members' motivation have been resolved. Members are involved with the work of the group. They co-operate with each other instead of competing.

Members are motivated by intrinsic rewards to achieve a high stage of productivity.

- Fourth stage - manage and organization: The final stage of group development. Work is allocated by agreement and according to the members' abilities. Members work independently and the organization of the group is flexible and adaptable to new challenges.

Schutz's three Stage model. This model suggests that each group irrespective of its nature given enough time goes through the three interpersonal phases of inclusion, manage, and affection in the similar sequence. The three stages are described briefly:

- Inclusion. In this stage the question is where they fit, in-or out. It starts with formation of groups. People attempt to know each other through discussion on issues that never closes. Question that is answered: do I belong ? The stage deals with the issues like attention, acknowledgement, recognition, identity, and participation. Once the issue of boundary problem or belongingness is resolved, the group moves to manage issue.
- Manage. At this stage issue is whether I am at top or bottom, Here people decide concerning sharing of responsibility, sharing of power and manage. Typical behaviour at this stage is leadership struggles, competition, and methods of decision creation, sharing of responsibility for the group's work. Each member tries to set up a comfortable interchange and degree of initiation with respect to manage, power and responsibility.
- Affection.. Ta third and last stage, the issue is 'close to or distant'. Members have already recognized their power and manage dealings. Now they want to set up emotionally secure and intimate connection. Positive behaviour are intimacy, personal confidence. Negative response is hate, hostility, and emotional rejection.

The three issues are always present: in the group. They may surface again as for some members the issues are not still resolved. The dealing with these needs have been compared with changing of tires where bolts are tightened Again and again. Likewise, in group development, the need regions are worked on until they handled satisfactorily. Later they are returned to be more satisfactorily worked upon if the similar was left out in the first cycle.

SOCIOMETRY

Originally urbanized by Moreno, sociometry (also described social network mapping or organizational network analysis) a is a method of indicating the feelings of acceptance or rejection in the middle of members of a group. A sociogram is a diagrammatical illustration of the pattern of interpersonal connection derived from sociometry. The sociogram depicts the choices, preferences, likes or dislikes, and interaction flanked by individual members of a group. It can also be used to display the structure of the group and to record the observed frequency and/or duration of contacts in the middle of members.

The foundation of sociometry, though, is usually 'buddy rating' or 'peer rating'. Each member in the group is asked to nominate or to rate, privately, other members in conditions of some given context or feature, for instance with whom they communicate, how influential or how likeable. Questions may relate to either work or social behaviors. For instance: who would you mainly prefer or least prefer as a work-mate ? or who would create a good leader of the group? Or with whom would you choose and not choose to go on holiday?

Positive and negative choices may be recorded for each person, although sometimes positive choices only are required. The choices may be limited to a given number or they may be unlimited. Sometimes individuals may be asked to rank their choices.

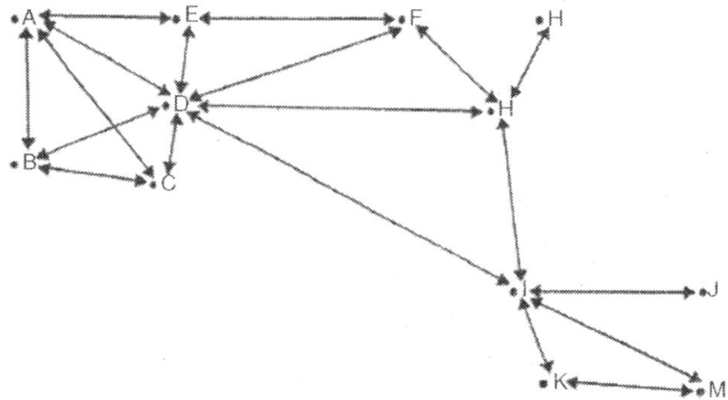

- D is a star and is most often chosen by members
- J and G are unpopular chosen least by members
- D serves a bridge by belonging tow cliques ABCD and DEFH
- ABCD clique has all channel communication

Constructing a Sociogram

In constructing the sociogram the aloofness flanked by the points may be arranged to indicate the degree of positive attraction. If two people, choose each other the points on behalf of these individuals will be closer jointly than if neither person chooses the other. If both positive and negative choices are recorded some distinguishing characteristic, such as dissimilar colors or the use of solid and broken rows, can be used to differentiate clearly flanked by selection and rejection.

Members' choices could be tabulated, but the advantage of the sociogram is that it gives a visual account of the sociometric structure of a group. It designates cliques and sub-groups, compatibility, and members who are popular, isolated or who act as links. Though, sociograms can become complicated and unwieldy especially for superior groups or where there is an unlimited number of nominations, if rankings are given, or where both positive and negative choices are recorded. Individuals express desired choices and may indicate what they feel should happen. This does not always correspond with actual patterns of behaviour.

Colleagues' rating is used sometimes ad part of a staff selection formation, usually as a foundation for Judgement of candidates "sociability' rating. This method can only be used, of course, if a group of candidates have been jointly extensive enough to become well acquainted with each other. Within sociometry, we use following terminology to identify several types of interaction:

- Social networks, A specific set of linkages in the middle of defined set of people Cluster. Existing groups within social network
- Prescribed clusters. Formal groups with in network such as departments, task forces, committees etc.
- Emergent clusters. Informal groups like friendship group, interest group
- Coalitions. Clusters of people who temporarily align jointly to attain sure objectives
- Cliques. Relatively permanent informal groups involving friendship Stars. Individuals with mainly linkages in a network
- Liaisons. Individuals who connect two or more clusters but are not members of any cluster
- Bridges. Individuals who function as linking pins by belonging to two or more clusters
- Isolates. People who have no connections in social network

Understanding concerning emerging clusters, cliques, coalitions, stars, liaisons, and bridges etc. may be useful in putting people on several projects, or identifying informal leaders, or identifying people who can break peace if there is disagreement in the network.

MORE APPARATUS FOR OBSERVATION AND ANALYSIS OF GROUPS

Bales Interaction Formation Analysis

The vital assumption behind interaction analysis is that behaviour in groups may be analyzed from the viewpoint of its function. This approach has urbanized mainly from the work of Bales on methods for the revise of small groups. This aim is to give methods of describing group formation and indications of factors influencing the formation.In Bales' 'Interaction Formation Analysis' every act of behaviour is categorized, a it occurs, under twelve headings. These differentiate flanked by `task' functions `socio-emotional' functions. The categories apply to both verbal interactions non-verbal interaction.

Major Categories	Subcategory	Illustrative Behaviour
Social-Emotional area (A. Positive& Mixed Reaction	1. Seems friendly	jokes, raises other' status, gives help, rewards, friendly
	2. Dramatizes	laughs, shows satisfaction,
	3. Agrees	shows passive acceptance, understands, concurs, complies.
Task Area B. Attempted Answers	4. Gives suggestion	direction, implying autonomy for others.
	5. Gives opinion	evaluation, analysis, expresses feeling, wish
Task Area	6. Gives information	information, repeats, clarifies, confirms
	7. Asks for information	requests orientation, information, repetition, confirmation.
C. Questions	8. Asks for opinion	requests opinion, evaluation, analysis,
	9. Asks for suggestion	requests suggestion, direction, possible
	10. Disagrees	Passively rejects, resorts to formality, withholds help
Social& Emotional Area	11. Shows tension	Asks for help; Withdraws, daydreams
D. Negative(& Mixed) Reactions	12. Seems unfriendly	Deflates other's status, defends or asserts self, acts hostile

Fig. Categories for Interaction Process Analysis.

Symlogs

Bales devised another organization of coding and observing group interaction described Symlog which stands for Organization for the Multiple Stage Observation of groups.

Here Bales argues that three structural dimensions underly differences in the middle of individuals in groups: dominance versus submission (or status), friendliness versus unfriendliness (or attraction), and instrumental manage versus emotional expressiveness (or role orientation). When individuals are classified as either high, neutral, or low on these three dimensions, their location in the group's structure can be recognized. Bales's model yields the 26 separate positions recognized by the labels listed in Forsyth.

Formation observers' Checklist

John Brilhart provided a comprehensive checklist of questions related to formation flow. These can be used for observing groups:

- Are there clear and accepted goals? Has the committee a clear understanding of its charge? Is there an understanding of the kind of output required?
- Are all members are aware and accepting the limits of their regions of freedom?
- Are any environmental troubles disrupting the group such as poor seating arrangement, noise, and other distractions?
- Do members appear to be adequately prepared with information?
- Are information and ideas being evaluated, or accepted at face value?
- Has some formation or agenda for the discussion been provided or urbanized by the group? If so, how well this being followed? Does it help chooses group?
- Distinguished problem solving discussion, has the group defined and clarified the rows, can b thoroughly, or has it started working on solution too soon'?

- How creative is the group in generating potential solutions to the problem? In interpreting information?
- Has Judgement been deferred until the solutions have been listed and understood by all members?
- Do members share values and criteria of decision creation or there is clarification sought on these issues?
- When evaluating decisions does group uses information previously accessible to it?
- How are decisions being made?
- If needed, has group made adequate plans to implement its decisions including members responsibilities, possessions future meetings etc.
- Are periodic summaries needed to help members recall previous discussions and to move to new issues without much repetition?
- If needed, are decisions properly recorded?
- If there is a designated leader, what approach does he adopt and whether that is appropriate for the group?
- Does the role structure give all the inputs? Are any needed behavioral function's missing?
- Are special procedural techniques such as brain storming etc being used in methods that are productive? Could procedural changes benefit the group?

National Training Laboratory Approach

National Training Laboratory,USA trains people in group formation. The following framework presents two observation sheets, one covering six kinds of leader-member task-function behaviour and the other covering six kinds of leader-member group structure and maintenance function behaviour.

Task Functions

- Initiating Proposing tasks or goals; defining a group problem, suggesting a formation or ideas for solving a problem.
- Information or opinion seeking: Requesting facts, seeking relevant information in relation to the a group concern, asking for suggestions and ideas.
- Information or opinion giving: Offering facts, providing relevant information in relation to the group concern; stating a belief; giving suggestions or ideas.
- Clarifying or elaborating: Interpreting or reflecting ideas and suggestions; clearing up confusions; indicating alternatives and issues before the group, giving examples.
- Summarizing: Pulling jointly related ideas, restating suggestions after group has discussed them; offering a decision or conclusion for the group to accept or reject.

- Consensus testing: Sending up 'trial balloons' to see if group is nearing a conclusion; checking with group to see how much agreement has been reached.

Group Structure and Maintenance Functions

- *Encouraging:* Being friendly, warm and responsive to other, accepting others and their contributions, concerning others by giving them an opportunity for recognition.
- *Expressing group feelings:* Sensing feeling, mood, relationships within the group, sharing one's own feelings with other members.
- *Harmonizing:* Attempting to reconcile disagreements, reducing tension through 'pouring oil on troubled waters', getting people to explore their differences.
- *Compromising:* When own thought or status is involved in a disagreement offering to compromise own location, admitting error, disciplining oneself to uphold group cohesion.
- *Gate-keeping:* Attempting to stay communication channels open, facilitating the participation of others; suggesting formation for sharing opportunity to talk about group troubles.
- *Setting standards:* Expressing standards for group to achieve, applying standards in evaluating group functioning and manufacture.

Use of Dissimilar Frameworks

Dissimilar frameworks use a dissimilar number of categories for learning behaviour in groups, The interaction analysis method can become intricate, especially if non-verbal behaviour is incorporated. Several of the categories in dissimilar frameworks may at first sight appear to be very similar. It is significant, so, to stay the framework easy, and easy to understand and complete. The observer's own personality, values and attitudes can power the categorization of behaviour. For these reasons it is preferable to use trained observers, and wherever possible and appropriate to use more than one observer for each group.

S.No.	*Project* *Class hour* *Date*	*1*	*2*	*3*	*4*	*5*	*6*	*7*	*8*
1	Seems friendly								
2	Dramatizes								
3	Agree								
4	Gives suggestion								
5	Gives opinion								
6	Gives information								
7	Asks for information								
8	Asks for opinion								
9	Asks for suggestion								
10	Disagrees								
11	Shows tension								
12									

Fig. Bales FORN Group Report

The observers can then compare the stage of consistency flanked by their categorizations.Observation sheets can be intended to suit the scrupulous necessities of the group situation and the nature of the action involved. Bales Interaction Formation Analysis subcategory can be good observation schedule

F=Frequntly, O=Occasionally, R=Rarely, N=Never General comments on the GroupInstructions: On each scale indicate the degree to which the group accomplished each identified behaviour. Use follwoing for your evaluation:

1- Poor, 2=Fair, 3=Average, 4=good, 5=Excellent

Likewise, problem solving part of formation observation can be undertaken through Brilhart's schedule.

S.No.	*Item*	*1*	*2*	*3*	*4*	*5*
1	The concern of each member was identified regarding the group problem.					
2	This concern was identified before the problem was solved					
3	In the problem analysis, the present condition was carefully compared with specific condition desired					
4	Goal was carefully defined and agreed by members					
5	Valid (and relevant) information was secures when needed					
6	Possible solution were listed and clarified before they were evaluated					
7	Criteria for evaluating proposed solutions were clearly identified and accepted by the group					
8	Predictions were made regarding the probable effectiveness of each proposed solution, using available information and criteria					
9	Consensus was achieved on the most desirable solution					
10	A detailed plan of implementation chalked out					
11	The problem solving process was systematic and orderly					

Fig. Problem Solving Process Scale (Brilhart)

SEVERAL ROLES IN GROUP FORMATION

If the group is to be effective, then, whatever its structure or the pattern of interrelationships in the middle of members, there are two main sets of functions or processes that necessity be undertaken task functions and maintenance functions.

- Task functions are directed towards problem-solving, the accomplishment of the tasks of the group and the attainment of its goals. Mainly of the task-oriented behaviour will be concerned with 'manufacture' behaviors, or the swap and evaluation of ideas and information.
- Maintenance functions are concerned with the emotional life of the group and directed towards structure and maintaining the group as an effective working unit. Mainly of the maintenance-oriented behaviour will be concerned with relationships in the middle of group members, giving encouragement and support, maintaining cohesiveness and the resolution of disagreement.

Task and maintenance functions may be performed either by the group leader or by members. In non-hierarchical groups both sets of functions are accepted out interchangeably by several members and the right balance is achieved flanked by them.

The appropriate combination of task-oriented behaviour and maintenance-oriented behaviour is essential for groups to be effective. In addition to these two kinds of behaviour members of group may say or do something in effort to satisfy some personal needs or goals.

The display of Behaviour in this method is termed self-oriented behaviour. This provides classification of three main kinds of functional behaviour which can be exhibited by individual members of a group: task-oriented, maintenance-oriented and self-oriented.

While discharging task and maintenance functions members of groups assume three types of roles: Task roles, group structure and maintenance roles and self oriented roles.

A popular organization for the classification of these role is devised originally by Benne and Sheats which further classifies the three roles into many sub-roles:

- *Task roles:* These assume that the task of the group is to select, describe and solve general troubles. Any of the roles may be performed by the several members or the group leader.
- *Initiator-contributor:* Suggests tasks and goals for the group, identifies troubles that need to solve and suggests formation to approach them, generates new ideas.
- *Information-seeker:* Asks for information in relation to the task, clarifies issues, checks factual accuracy.
- *Opinion-seeker:* Asks for the input from the group in relation to the it's values, seeks expression of opinions and concerns of all members to ensure full participation and variation opinion expressed..
- *Information-giver:* Provides facts, ideas, information concerning group troubles and proposes many alternatives to solve the problem.
- *Opinion-giver:* States his or her beliefs and values in relation to the troubles at hand.
- *Elaborator:* Builds on others ideas and explains ideas within the group, offers examples to clarify ideas.
- *Coordinator:* Tries to identify general meeting points in the middle of flanked by ideas, synthesizes ideas.
- *Orienter:* Shifts the direction of the group's discussion.
- *Evaluator-critic:* Events group's actions against some objective average. Energizer: Stimulates the group to a higher stage of action. Procedural-technician: Performs logistical functions for the group. Recorder: Keeps a record of group actions
- *Group structure and maintenance roles:* The analysis of member-

functions is oriented towards behaviors which build group-centered attitudes, or uphold group-centre behaviour. Contributions may involve a number of roles, and members or the leader may perform each of these roles.

- *Encourager:* Appreciates the ideas of others.
- *Harmonizer:* Mediates and reconciles differences flanked by group members, reduces tension, ensures that differences in the middle of members are brought to surface and resolved satisfactorily.
- *Compromiser:* When own thought or status is involved in a disagreement offering to compromises own location, admits error, disciplines, oneself to uphold group cohesion.
- *Gatekeeper/expediter:* Keeps communication channels open, makes legroom where others can contribute, suggests formations to share ideas.
- *Average Setter:* Suggests standards or criteria for the group to achieve.
- *Group observer:* Keeps records of group behaviors and uses this information to offer feedback to the group.
- *Follower:* Goes beside with the group and accepts the group's ideas.
- *Individual roles:* These are directed towards the satisfaction of
- personal needs. Their purpose is not related to either group task or to the group functioning,
- *Aggressor:* Attacks other group members, deflates the status of others, and other aggressive behaviour.
- *Blocker:* Resists movement of the group.
- Recognition seeker: Preoccupied in catching the attention of group to him or her.
- *Self-confessor:* Seeks to disclose nongroup related feelings or opinions.
- *Dominator:* Controls the group by manipulating the other group members. Help seeker: Tries to gain the sympathy of the group.
- *Special interest pleader:* Uses stereotypes to assert his or her own prejudices.
- By discouraging self oriented in groups and by actively performing task and group structure and maintenance, groups are capable of achieving twin goals of high performance and member satisfaction and morale.

GROUP PROCESSES

Group processes refer to what happens within groups including communication, decision creation, leadership, motivation and cohesiveness, norms, roles, power and manage dynamics, synergy, social loafing or free riding, social facilitation effect etc. Issues of communication, decision-creation, and group think, group shift, disagreement management norms, roles, power etc have been taken in other units. Here we will take up the issues of group cohesiveness, synergy, social loafing and social facilitation effects.

Group Cohesiveness

Group cohesiveness refers to extent to which members of the group are attracted towards each other demonstrated through unity in the group, conventionality to the norms of the group and willingness to continue in the group. Attraction, cohesion, and willingness to conform to the norms are interrelated concepts. The higher the attraction in the middle of members towards each other, the higher will be cohesion. The higher the cohesion, the greater will be the power of members to conform to the group norms.

Cohesiveness is an significant concept as it is related to group performance and productivity. But it may work as double edged sword. It may enhance or depress group productivity depending on whether group's goals (performance norms) are aligned with organizational goals. Studies uniformly suggest that connection flanked by productivity and group cohesiveness is moderated by the nature of performance norms in the group. If the group is highly cohesive, more members will follow its goals. If group's performance norms are high (aligned with organizational goals: high productivity, high quality, customer orientation towards outsiders and nonmembers) and cohesiveness is high, more members will attempt to perform to their best so that group attains its goals. Contrary to that, if group's performance norm is low, and cohesiveness is high more members will collude to suppress the productivity. This happens when. cohesive workers union decides not to perform optimally or resort "work to rule". When group cohesiveness is low, and performance norm is high, there may be a moderate improvement in productivity. When group cohesiveness is low, performance norm is also low, there may not be a important effect on productivity.

Gibson and his Colleagues have suggested one or more of following steps can be used by managers if they are interested in enhancing group cohesiveness:

- Create the group smaller.
- Encourage agreement with group goals
- Give opportunity to members to spend more time jointly 1.
- Augment the status of the group and also create eligibility of group membership hard.
- Stimulate competition with other groups
- Reward groups, not individual members
- Physically isolate groups

Synergy

Group processes can facilitate as well as hamper group effectiveness. When communal effort of the group members produces much better outcome for the group than what is possible through easy addition of contributions of individual members. The concept of synergy has been derived from biology that refers to an interaction of two or more substances that generates an outcome which is dissimilar from the individual addition of the substances. Synergy is observed in groups when through interaction and group formation arrive at creative break through decisions or solutions to the problem.

Social Loafing or Free Riding

We are reminded of a story. A Yajan was to.happen in un Asharam. The rishi of the Asharam requested each household to contribute one bowl of milk in the kunda tomorrow morning. Households thought that so several people will contribute milk, if I contribute one bowl of water, it will not be detected. In the morning the whole kunda was full of water only. Moral of the story is that when individual contribution is not recognized, individuals tend to reduce their contribution. Social loafing or free riding is tendency of individuals to reduce their effort or contribution in the group situation than when working individually. This happen when individual efforts are not identifiable or not rewarded. Free riders consider that group is working anyway, if I take the benefit, what is the harm. As a result of social loafing, group outcome is less than easy addition of contribution of persons working alone. Therefore social loafing is a case of negative synergy. Social loafing happens because of diffusion of responsibility. It may also happen when all the members are looking towards others for initiative and effort.

Social Facilitation Effect

Social facilitation effect is a phenomenon in which individual's performance improves or deteriorates in attendance of others. This may not be measured entirely a group formation, as other may or may not be a group member. Though, group gives a social context where such phenomenon occurs. You have privately prepared a presentation, and you are comfortable with it but when you actually present it, it gets messed up. It usually happens in initial presentations when things are not learnt thoroughly. Contrary to that, some time you create extempore presentation, and you deliver it beyond your expectations. The studies on social facilitation suggests that if the task is easy and routine, task is performed more efficiently in attendance of others. If the task is intricate requiring more focused attention, performance appears to deteriorate in attendance of others.

Another trend is if the task is well learned., performance improves in attendance of others whereas if the task is not well learned performance declines in attendance of others.

From group effectiveness point of view synergy and social facilitation on well learned tasks may augment process gains and social loafing and social facilitation on poorly learned task may generate formation losses. Likewise group cohesiveness and task and group structure roles may contribute positively to formation gains while self oriented behaviour may contribute to processes losses. The formation gain or loss will actual group effectiveness.

INTER-GROUP PROCESSES

Schein suggests that groups working in organizations face two major troubles. One they perform effectively, *i.e.*, contribute positively to organizational goals and fulfill their members needs. Second, how to make and sustain circumstances flanked by groups which enhances the productivity of each without hampering inter group dealings and coordination. This problem emerges as groups become more committed to their own goals and norms and start competing with one another and undermining rivals's behaviors. Consequently, they become liability for organization as a whole. Challenge before managers is to develop collaborative intergroup dealings where task interdependence or the need for unity becomes precondition for organizational effectiveness. What happens in intergroup competition with in and flanked by competing has been first studied by Sherif and his colleagues. The similar experience is observed in other replications in dissimilar types of groups at several locations. The experiences can are described in conditions A. what happens with in each competing groups, B. What happens flanked by competing groups, C. What happens to the winner and D. what happens to the loser.

Preventing Inter-group Disagreement

Managers who are responsible for coordination and integration of performance of several groups may consider by some of the following steps:

- *Emphasize total organizational effectiveness:* Departments and sections should be assessed and rewarded for their contribution to overall goal of the organization rather that individual effectiveness.
- *High interaction and frequent communication:* Opportunity should be created for working jointly on projects requiring intergroup cooperation, groups may be rewarded on the foundation of help extended to other groups.
- Frequent rotations of members in the middle of groups and departments. People having experience of working in multiple departments have more understanding and empathy than people who have no such opportunity. Therefore frequent rotations and transfers of members will develop more empathy and prevent disagreement.
- *Avoid win-lose situation:* Managers may emphasize pooling of scarce possessions for organizational effectiveness rather than driving the groups to win-lose situation. Groups/departments should be rewarded equally for organizational attainment.

Reducing Negative Consequences of Inter-group Competition

- *Locating the general enemy:* When groups are competing within organizations and power is being wasted, manager need to canalize it fight the general enemy. Two departments manufacture and sales are fighting in the middle of themselves, if they exhorted to fight the competing company, there may be reduction in the departmental disagreement. Now disagreement has shifted to a higher stage and power is being used to fight general enemy.
- *Bringing leaders, of competing groups jointly:* Working jointly generates understanding of each other. Leaders of competing groups if brought jointly may convince each other who inturn may power their group members. Frequent contacts and dialogues of group representatives may reduce disagreement.
- *Locating super ordinate goals:* When survival of the competing group is stake or competing groups have recognized- which is beneficial to both parties, groups will agree to collaborate: When there is aggressive takeover bid from a foreign competitor, companies competing earlier may join hand to abort take overbid. Likewise, when Mohammedan Sporting and Mohan Baghan are playing with in the country, they are arch rivals, but when the members the two team working jointly and on behalf of India, they forget the identity of Mohan Baghan or Mohammedan, and play for the country.
- *Experiential intergroup training:* Experiential training to reduce intergroup disagreement has been tried by organizations. If organization is aware of the problem and recognize that it needs to do something to deal with the problem and also ready to share this problem to an external consultant, then Blake and Mouton's experiential workshop approach can be used for reducing disagreement

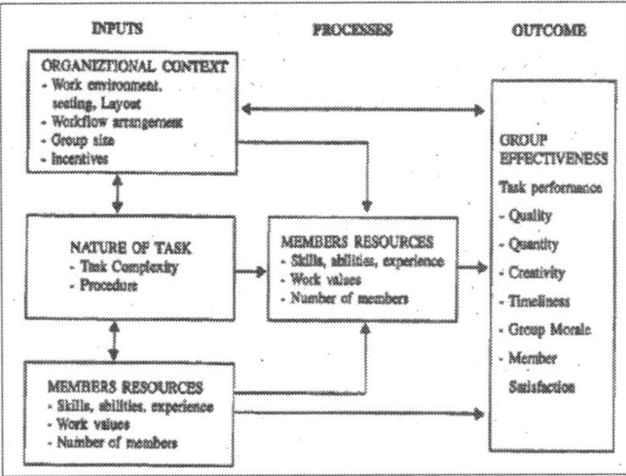

Fig. A Model of Group Effectiveness

IMPROVING GROUP EFFECTIVENESS

Group effectiveness is influenced by multiple factors. A simplified model of group effectives has been conceptualized in conditions of Input-processes-and outcomesIn input variables the in the model incorporated organizational context: environment, structure, layout, technology, incentive organization:, nature of task: task complexity, formation, and group members possessions: skills and abilities, work values, number of members. Likewise, Formation variables incorporated cohesiveness, norms, roles, decision creation, synergy, social facilitation etc. At outcome stage, the model comprises quality, quantity, and timeliness of performance, group morale and members' satisfaction.

Based on several researches following suggestions are made to improve group effectiveness:

- Groups exist within superior organizational context, orgazational structure, strategy, power connection, selection formation, motivational structure, organizational layout, and workflow etc will power group productivity. Where organizational climate is supportive, possessions are abundant, and company follows meritocracy, group is likely to perform well. Managers should so, seem the group performance in context and attempt to give supportive context.
- Stay the groups smaller usually having five or seven members perform better performance due to better adherence to group norms and cohesiveness. Smaller groups also more satisfied members.
- In order to collaborative norms organizations should reward group performance rather than individual performance.
- Intricate tasks require more focused interaction compare to easy tasks. Therefore group will require more frequent and more intense interaction for solving intricate troubles.
- Group members if having requisite skills to tackle the problem, group's effectiveness will be high.
- If group's goals are aligned with organizational goals, and cohesiveness is high, group performance will be high. Therefore managers need to encourage groups to internalize organizational goals.
- Groups necessity use decisions techniques that minimizes the possibility of group think.
- Managers need to encourage shared leadership concept where members can interchange the task and groups structure roles. Self oriented behaviour should be minimized.
- To minimize social loafing develop task structure, dedicated roles and some measure to assess individual contribution to group attainment.
- When the task is interdependent, use effective communication and minimize disagreement to enhance high productivity.

- Groups within an organizations should not pitted against each other to compete for scarce possessions, instead emphasis should be on pooling and sharing of possessions and work for super ordinate goals of organization.
- Educate and train group members in group formation and group dynamics.

GROUP DEVELOPMENT AND ITS STAGES

WHAT IS GROUP DEVELOPMENT?

Group development is a procedure of the growth and progress of a group towards full maturity in excess of a era of time with primary focus on the relationships in the group. In Social Group Work through guided group experience, the group is helped to develop responsibly and with maturity. From the stage of forming the group, to its termination, through cautiously and well planned programme behaviors, the group is helped to achieve its potential. "Regular meetings of the group, a wider interaction in the middle of the members, a free flowing conversation, laughter, common spirit of cooperation and accommodation, are signs of a positive environment in a group, reflecting a clear sign of group development" Group development, therefore, is an index of the specific stage of growth, task accomplishment and emotional integration of the members which goes through dissimilar stages. Understanding the stages of group development helps in developing appropriate methods of intervention in the group procedure so as to bring in relation to the group's growth and induce behaviours that help in achieving group goals.

INDICATORS OF GROUP DEVELOPMENT

- Attendance
- Punctuality
- Definite meeting time and attendance
- Development of a formal organization
- Willingness on the part of the members to undertake initiative and responsibility
- Increased innovation and motivation
- Controlled behaviour of the members
- High stage of participation
- Emergence of leader
- Shift from 'I' and 'Me' to 'We' and 'Us'

STAGES OF GROUP DEVELOPMENT

The attainment of the goals is the objective of any professional encounter; the tasks are done with a purpose. The Social Group Work procedure is conceived of as one that is systematic and proceeds through stages also referred to as phases. A group can pass through several stages of development; from the initial stage where it may appear as a mere assembly of individuals, it can go on to become a group with a strong 'we feeling'. The stages and the behaviors associated with it give structure and direction to the procedure. The dissimilar stages are but a reflection of the procedure of maturity of the group. Theoretically, we may segregate dissimilar stages of group development for conceptual clarity but in reality they are intertwined. Throughout the stages there are two concerted concerns of the Social Group Worker, namely, structure and sustaining a collaborative connection and working on the tasks directed at achieving goals. The tasks and behaviors chosen reflect the Social Group Worker's ideas in relation to the what is necessary at dissimilar points in time to bring in relation to the change.

Another author Ken Heap has described the stages of group work as comprising of group formation and scheduling; the first meetings; the working stage; use of behaviors and action; and the termination of group. Toseland and Rivas have more basically described the stages as scheduling stage, beginning stage, middle stage, and ending stage. On the foundation of the classification by dissimilar experts we can say that a group can have maximum six stages as discussed by Trecker or a minimum three stages of development, as explained by Bales. The several models describe the progressive stages in group development which may range from three to even six

- *Bales:* Orientation Evaluation Decision creation
- *Tuckman:* Forming Storming Norming Performing Adjourning
- *Klein:* Orientation Resistance Negotiation Intimacy Termination
- *Trecker:* Beginning Emergence of group feeling Development of Bond strong group Decline in Group Feeling Ending
- *Garland, Jones and Kolondny:* Preaffiliation power and manage Intimacy differentiation Separation
- *Northen and Kurland: Inclusion:* Orientation uncertainty exploration Mutuality and Goal Attainment Separation- Termination stages.

Drawing from the several models, for our purpose, we have classified the stages as follows:

- *First stage:* Forming the group (Beginning)
- *Second Stage:* Exploration (Initial sessions)
- *Third Stage:* Performing (Action Stage)
- *Fourth Stage:* Assessment (Evaluation)
- *Fifth Stage:* Termination (Separation)

Before we present a discourse on the dissimilar stages of group development, we need to understand that group work as practiced in the Indian context may be at variance with practice in the western countries. As the thought of joining a group voluntarily for therapeutic or recreation purposes may be an alien concept to the target population, the social group worker practicing this method in the Indian settings following the Western theoretical framework may discover it an uphill task. The importance of group work as a therapeutic method of social work intervention is being slowly realized in our country. In our discourse on the several stages of development of group, we shall create a conscious effort not to lose sight of the Indian context of practice.

FIRST STAGE: SCHEDULING AND FORMING THE GROUP (BEGINNING)

Social agencies, in conventionality with their objectives help people form groups so as to give them opportunities for a satisfying group experience. Individuals join groups to seek avenues of self expression and social creativity besides satisfying their needs of being loved, wanted and accepted by others. The first stage of this procedure comprises efforts of the group worker that primarily focus on the scheduling and the forming of the group.

THE BEGINNING

This stage marks the beginning of the procedure of group development and is also described the pre-group or pre-affiliation stage by some experts. In India the groups have to be shaped by the group worker in mainly cases. S/he may form the group from in the middle of the existing clientele of the social welfare agencies/NGO's or from in the middle of the open society settings. Before forming a group, the group worker necessity revise the target population beside the following points:

- Geographical site
- Age/sex
- Socio-economic background
- Needs
- Interests
- Reasons for joining the group
- Any other relevant details

This information helps the group worker to form the group on some general ground and accordingly determine the group goals. Careful scheduling should precede the formation of the group which comprises decision in relation to the target population, needs and goals, the possessions accessible etc. An accurate understanding and analysis of the needs of the target population is significant at this stage so that there is no gap flanked by the member's and the worker's perception of the felt needs of the group. Though, the procedure of the revise and scheduling is a continuous one; it enables the group worker to steer the group through the dissimilar stages of development.

The members may have to be influenced to join the group as they may be ignorant of the usefulness of being a part of a group and may not have had any such experience in the past. "Groups in India are initially conceived by an organization or welfare agency, as people themselves usually do not take such initiatives. Both the voluntary and the government organizations have establish working with the group a useful strategy.

The worker in India so, has to carry the thought of forming a group for an already defined objective to the people. S/he has to educate the potential members in relation to the needs and issues the group will address and how it is likely to benefit them. The worker usually meets the members for the first time and several members have little or no experience of working with such groups. The formation stage therefore, will require careful scheduling. There are two sets of plans that a worker necessity prepare. The first part of the scheduling concerns how the formation of the group will be accomplished, and second, what issues will arise once the group gets going and how these will be dealt with."

The other details that have to be focused while scheduling and forming the group are:

- *The size of the group:* The decision in relation to the size of the group is dependant on several factors such as the needs of members, purpose of group, nature of group membership etc. for instance self help groups may be big in size but therapeutic groups work best when they are small. Though there is no ideal size, a group size ranging from eight to fifteen members may be a good size.
- *Composition of the group:* Scheduling in relation to the composition of the group has to be in keeping with its purpose. Whether it is a self help group, task group or treatment oriented group, it may be either homogenous or heterogeneous. Before deciding the nature of membership, the group worker should familiarize herself with the client group beside the points such as their socio-economic background etc.
- *Frequency of the sessions and their duration:* Though there is no hard and fast rule, frequency of the sessions may be decided in accordance with the needs and purpose of the group. There should not be too extensive gaps flanked by the sessions, lest the group gets disintegrated. Recreation groups, therapeutic groups, task groups should meet at least once or twice a week.
- *Time and lay of meetings:* The lay where the group is to meet at the designated time has to be decided in consultation with the members. The guiding factors are the convenience of the members, availability and adequacy of legroom and possessions.
- *Duration of the group:* Whether the group will exist for a extensive or short term may again have to be in keeping with the needs and goals of the group. The group can be terminated after achieving its

objectives and a tentative time may be earmarked for it. There should though be an element of flexibility in deciding the time-frame.

SECOND STAGE: EXPLORATIONS (INITIAL SESSIONS)

EXPLORATION

In the initial sessions the group may appear more as a constellation of dissimilar individuals than an organized entity. This stage is usually characterized by a low group consciousness. There may be shyness, hesitation, indecision and lack of participation. Some members may be hyper active, and some may be insecure and nervous, not having had such an experience in the past. Though, this stage marks the beginning of the development of a feeling of belonging and oneness in the middle of the members. Tuckman has used the term 'storming' to explain this procedure of exploration. In the initial meetings a semblance of order has to be restored so as to ensure a free flow of ideas and actions. This stage involves the following steps.

ORIENTATION AND INDUCTION

The initial stage is significant as it lays the base of the success or failure of the group work Programme. The worker should introduce the members to the group by outlining her/his role and the purposes for which the group has been shaped, the members should be encouraged to speak in relation to the themselves, their hopes and aspirations. In the initial sessions the members have to be inducted into the group with a sure sensitivity so as to raise their stage of comfort and sense of ease. The members may be unfamiliar with each other and may be interested in finding out in relation to the agency, the worker, other members and the purpose of the group.

The group worker helps members become part of the group. This does not happen overnight but is a gradual procedure as in this procedure the members may have to provide up some of their individuality as also their biases and prejudices. They may have to exercise more self manage and discipline. Some people relate more easily than others, all nevertheless, start creation efforts to adjust which may not be always easy. Some may be easily accepted and accept the group, others may take more time. Slowly the members start speaking the similar language as the other members and accept the group goals and consider them as their own As the individual starts developing a sense of belonging there may be a change in his/her behaviour patterns.

PREPARATION OF THE PROFILE OF THE MEMBERS

Presently as there is a need for the members to know each other, the worker too should revise and observe the members closely. The worker should prepare a profile of each member giving his/her age, family background, physical features, habits, interests, stage of confidence, any peculiar habits or traits etc. It would help if this is based on the facts gathered and his/her observations in the initial sessions. This would not only help her/him understand the group connection stages and interaction patterns better but also begin from where the group is. Further this may help her/him map the development in excess of a era of time, especially at the stage of evaluation.

SETTING SPECIFIC OBJECTIVES

While there may be superior goals which a group may strive to ultimately achieve, specific interim goals also need to be explored, which can form the foundation of Programme scheduling. Here the worker has to help the group determine the desired stage of behaviour or social change. Although in the first stage the group has been shaped keeping in mind some purpose, It is at this stage that goals have to be specifically delineated. Here the group worker encourages the active participation of the group members and helps the group assume the responsibility to determine the stage of change they desire to achieve in their behaviour or social situation. *e.g.* kicking up the habit of smoking/ chewing tobacco, giving up by abusive language.

Objectives are nothing but statements of what the group worker is trying to achieve through the group work procedure. They provide meaning to the procedure. "Objectives serve the similar purpose as a compass; they guide the agency and the worker to a determined destination". They should be clear and specific and later reviewed at the stage of evaluation in conditions of their accomplishment. At this stage there is a need to spell out the specific objectives which delineate the actual outcomes expected from the group worker's intervention. For instance in the case of a group of school dropouts, some of the objectives could be

- To develop an interest in studies by simplifying the methods of teaching and learning
- To motivate them to resume studies by creation them understand the benefits of formal schooling
- To remove the fear of subjects like maths, etc.

Here the worker should pay attention to the feasibility on one hand and the needs and aspirations of the members on the other. S/he should focus on the specific benefits the members are likely to get and refrain from imposing her/ his point of view. The objectives have to be interpreted to the members, and their doubts and queries are to be encouraged.

DEVELOPING A STRUCTURE

As the group is now ready to settle down, it can be structured at this stage. The members necessity now be prepared and encouraged to assume roles and responsibilities. They are to be told in relation to the expectations of the group from them in conditions of tasks, on the foundation of their capabilities and talents. In the Indian context the members may have to be closely assisted till they learn to assume responsibilities on their own. Some may need constant help of the group worker to carry out their roles. The worker at this stage necessity constantly encourage the members to use their latent talents and capacities.

A functional organization necessity emerge at this stage so as to enable the members to assume an active role and create responsible decisions. "Every group that aspires for independence and self-determination necessity arrange its constituent members in such a method that they can say to be "organized." The form of organization is in itself of minor importance ....if a group is to develop and carry out its Programme, it necessity have methods of assigning or delegating responsibility, methods of getting the whole group to participate in the scheduling, carrying out, and evaluation of the behaviors that create up the Programme and methods of handling routine relationships with the agency and other groups." With the emergence of a formal organization the group starts giving proof of its flexibility and maturity. After the group is geared to assume responsibility, it is ready to move into the after that stage.

THIRD STAGE: PERFORMING (ACTION STAGE)

ACTION STAGE

After some sessions, the signs of group development start emerging as the group progresses into its active stage. The focus of this stage is on the provision of Programme experiences intended to offer opportunities for adjustment and growth. The Progrmmes may be of a extensive or short term depending on the immediate and extensive term objectives. This stage is the peak time in the group procedure as the members start taking the group seriously. The sessions become regular, the attendance is likely to be high and so is the involvement and participation of the members. This stage is likely to be characterized by a flurry of action as considerable time is devoted to Programme scheduling and implementation, *e.g.*, a group of youth in a society, who may have been spending their leisure time aimlessly are shaped into a group. The group worker after observing their talents for singing and acting encourages them to put up a musical drama.

The group is encouraged and helped to write its own writing, compose the songs and choreograph the dances.Then with the help of the society support the group puts up the first illustrate and slowly becomes an recognized theatre group. In the active stage the scripting, composing followed by continuous frantic rehearsals for the illustrate may consume the maximum time and efforts of the members. Face by face they may also be busy mobilizing and utilizing the possessions to put up the illustrate. This is but one instance, there may be many others. Throughout this stage the development gets more pronounced and may be reflected in high attendance, regular meetings, and members taking more responsibility. More and more responsibility is transferred by the worker to the group. The group starts surging ahead; setting its Progrmmes, moving constantly to its destination. The accent is now on 'we' and 'us'. The members get comfortable with each other, anxiety declines, leadership emerges, and members start taking initiative and are ready to assume leadership roles and responsibilities. They may be more forthcoming with their talents and more ready to take on demanding and intricate Progrmmes. This is the mainly active stage of the group work procedure and spans in excess of a major part of the working life of the group. The group may now well be on its method to achieving its goals. Scheduling and development of the Programme, its execution and monitoring are the defining characteristics of this stage.

PROGRAMME SCHEDULING AND EXECUTION

Programme is a series of behaviors based on the detection of interests and needs of the members and an significant component of Social Group Work procedure; the method it is planned even more significant. It may range from art and craft to music, dance, social events to picnics excursions. At this stage the Programme interests are likely to emerge from within the group. The members who may be initially be at a loss from where to begin necessity now be encouraged to take in excess of. The members are stimulated to discover and use their own possessions. The Programme scheduling and development procedure by itself is an significant tool in helping the group to realize its potential "Programme should evolve from easy to more intricate, with movement coming as a result of group growth in skill and readiness. Movement from initially 'personal' to 'social' or 'society concerns' should be an ultimate objective if our Progrmmes are to have greater social significance"

TASK ACCOMPLISHMENT

"When the group begins to illustrate signs of readiness to move ahead, the worker should help the members realize their wishes for dissimilar and more demanding experiences. When group members begin to express desires to correct inadequacies and improve their work, they have reached an advanced point in their development.

Progrmmes that may have been self-centered shift in emphasis to the superior agency and society concerns. Dedicated interests may be revealed, and there may be an interest in a diversity of small group behaviors within the superior group. Here the worker is described upon to use his knowledge of agency and society possessions. His role becomes that of an interpreter to the group, especially in regard to future possibilities. Evaluation occupies a superior share of time as the group becomes confident of its capacities"

As the group strives to accomplish its goals and related tasks, it may face several barriers which may obstruct change. Besides members' own anxieties and fears, there may be dysfunctional behaviours or dysfunctional processes within the group that may impede progress and pose barriers to goal accomplishment. Non-availability or restrictive access to possessions or services may require the group worker to assume the role of a mediator or advocate.

MONITORING PROGRESS

The group worker at this stage steps down and allows the group to take in excess of. Though s/he needs to constantly monitor and stay a track of the methods the Programme is being mannered. As work towards the group goals gathers momentum it is significant to monitor the progress on a regular foundation. The Programme can be monitored on the foundation of specific indicators such as interaction patterns, self improvement, emotional integration with the group, leadership and communication skills etc. Based on the information gathered, Progrmmes can be customized and consolidated. If an intervention or Programme is not producing the desired effect, the worker after analyzing reasons can negotiate a dissimilar approach or strategy.

FOURTH STAGE: ASSESSMENT (EVALUATION)

EVALUATION

After the action stage is in excess of, the group should be ready to evaluate the outcome of its efforts in a free, frank and objective manner. "Evaluation is that part of Social Group Work in which the worker attempts to measure the excellence of a group's experience in relation to the objectives and functions of the agency. Evaluation may centre upon individual growth, Programme content or worker performance because all these characteristics tend to power the common attainment of the group."

Evaluation is continuously done throughout the group work procedure, but, after the group behaviors are in excess of, before the termination stage; a comprehensive assessment of the whole experience is a necessity.

If you recall, throughout the exploration stage a profile of the members was prepared; at this stage a comprehensive summary statement of each member and group as a whole, reflecting the individual and overall stage of development and achievements is to be prepared. The overall purpose and objectives of the experience should not be lost sight of while creation this assessment.

IMPERATIVES OF EVALUATION

Evaluation helps the agency and worker to reorganize their practice and vary their objectives in the light of the outcome findings of evaluation. To create the procedure of evaluation a positive and conclusive exercise and in order to create an unbiased, objective evaluation it is imperative that there exist sure predetermined indicators on the foundation of which the assessment can be done.

INDICATORS

Individual growth

From the members' perspective, evaluation presents an opportunity to discover out the outcome of their actions from the beginning to the end of the procedure.

It aids the procedure of development and helps in assessing some of the following characteristics:

- The stage of growth in each member in conditions of confidence, decision creation, etc.
- The extent of the use of the opportunities provided to the members for the expression of their creativity and talents
- The stage of their participation and involvement in the group Progrmmes
- The development of 'we feeling' and a sense of belonging
- Resolution of disabling conflicts and development of capability to foster cooperation and sharing
- Development of a social consciousness and the skill to take up responsibility and leadership in the society.
- Enhancement of communication, organizational and interaction skills

Worker performance

Evaluation presents to the group worker a mirror of his/ her professional competence or incompetence as the case may be.

The worker can be evaluated beside the following points:

- Skill to identify indicators for judging the growth and development of the group
- Effectiveness in scheduling and conducting the group sessions
- Extent of success in helping the group achieve its objectives and goals
- Mistakes and shortcomings
- Skill to use professional knowledge and skills.

Agency's purpose

Evaluation provides the agency the information it needs to uphold the excellence of its services and bring in relation to the improvements in its policies and Progrmmes beside the following rows:

- Lay down objective standards for the appraisal of its personnel
- Ensure circumstances under which effective group work can be done
- Improve its organizational and administrative procedures
- Reformulate objectives for groups and agency in row with its needs
- Review the Programme content and method

RECORD KEEPING

Another imperative of evaluation is proper record keeping. Cautiously maintained records are a great aid to the evaluation procedure. Records are integral to the whole group work procedure but are mainly useful at the point of evaluation. The worker should uphold detailed records of each member and action. Well maintained records help to objectively assess the growth of the members; their strengths and shortcomings. In the middle of other things, it helps the worker understand which strategies worked and which did not. According to Trecker, it is doubtful whether evaluation of the Programme, individual growth or worker performance can be satisfactorily made without records. Evaluation is a type of research or information finding which involves data collection and data analysis. The source of data could be the records or progress reports made by the worker, any task files maintained by the members, other agency personnel, and feedback- verbal or written of the members, their family members, video tapes etc. For this s/he should develop some formats for recording the happenings in the group.

Although partial judgments can be made on the foundation of memory, thorough evaluation is possible only if adequate records have been kept. The worker at this stage necessity go back to her records and prepare an analysis and summary. S/he should not only review the growth and development of the group but also his/ her role and connection with the group; and how well s/he understood the changing interests and evolving needs of the members. Though not very popular in India, attitudinal and personality measurement levels to measure the changes in the member's behaviour, knowledge and attitudes could be put to effective use to create the assessment more authentic and scientific.

Feedback

Though some type of feed back at the end of each session may be taken, a detailed exercise is usually done at this stage. Effective use of praise and constructive criticism are the defining characteristics of the feedback exercise. The group worker can give her feedback to the members on several characteristics such as participation, Programme development and implementation, leadership, teamwork, how well the members adhered to and worked for the attainment of the group objectives etc. The worker too should solicit feedback concerning how her/his behaviour affected the procedure S/he necessity welcome criticism and respond to it positively as it illuminates the pathway to growth and creates the worker aware of her/his strengths and weaknesses. The resultant feedback helps the group worker to be more aware of their positives and negatives which they necessity stay in mind for future.

The members should be also trained by the group worker in giving and getting feedback:

- Positive feedback should be given first
- It should be specific
- Criticisms should be given as a suggestive alternative
- Initially the members may be encouraged to provide a written feedback
- The worker may prepare some formats for the purpose.

FIFTH STAGE: TERMINATION (ENDING STAGE)

TERMINATION

There comes a time/point in the life of every group when it comes to an end, which could be a positive or negative experience as the case may be.

The group is deemed to be terminated on a positive note, when it is said to have achieved its goals and the group worker has ensured its smooth closure through a proper procedure. Sometimes the groups may have to secure on a negative note, when the members drop out prematurely; fail to develop strong relationships; the relationships are marked by bitter conflicts or the worker cannot continue with the group any longer. When the Group worker leaves the group for whatever cause, the group may not sustain for extensive. Should the date of termination be set in the beginning? Some experts are of the view that a termination date should be announced at the outset so that the members know the time at their disposal to achieve their objectives.

The duration should though be extensive enough for the group to develop and allow behavioral change. The group should review its progress from time to time and accordingly take decisions for the future course of action.

Presently as the group worker has done in the previous stages of development; at this stage she has to ensure that the group is terminated in a proper method. "Despite highly satisfactory experiences, groups sometimes reach a era in their natural life when interests diminish and decline is noticeable.

The group appears to have "served its time" attendance falls off members withdraw and become related to other groups.......this is a era which calls for careful thinking and analysis on the part of the worker. The agency.......should operate as a helpful agent for the proper closing of the group which has fulfilled its function in the lives of the members.

By arranging satisfying terminal experiences with groups it is possible to create the conclusion of group life a vestibule for further group experience. Those members who wish to continue may be helped to form a new group"

Ending the Group

The group has to end in a planned manner. Members may react differently to the termination of the group.

The worker has to stay the group informed in relation to the ending time and should not break the news suddenly. While nothing much may be done when the group comes to an end abruptly, in other cases the ending of the group can be accepted out in a planned method.

The last Sessions

Towards the end of the social group work procedure the worker has to help the members approach to conditions with the information that there may be no more regular meetings and guide them how to face the challenge of filling up the vacuum that the termination might make.

The worker has to prepare the group:

- For the termination stage
- Share with the group the final evaluation.
- Examine how distant they were successful in accomplishing some of the goals and failed to achieve others, as the case may be.
- provide the members an opportunity to express their happiness, anxiety, fears, good/ bad experiences, talk in relation to the their accomplishments
- Talk about their future plans

"Developing leadership in the middle of the group members, capability structure of members and developing systems to carry on the functioning of the group can create the termination smooth"

ROLE OF GROUP WORKER IN GROUP DEVELOPMENT

FACTORS AFFECTING GROUP DEVELOPMENT

The development of the group is influenced by a diversity of factors, depending on which groups develop at varying pace. This explains why some groups organize very well and are able to achieve their goals without facing several hurdles, while others fail to accomplish their tasks and achieve their goals.

- Group structure
- Communication and interaction patterns
- group goals
- expectations from the group
- leadership
- group norms and culture
- group discipline
- The role played by the group worker

Our primary focus here is on one significant ingredient that ensures the development of the group through the successive stages, namely the role played by the Social Group Worker at each stage.

ROLE OF GROUP WORKER

The role of the worker is very significant and varies at each stage of development, the bottom row being that the worker has to understand the stage of the group at each stage and proceed at the pace of the group. For this s/he necessity revise and examine to understand where the members are in their development. The worker plays a diversity of roles, sometimes as an enabler, helper, guide and facilitator, sometimes as a trouble shooter, mediator and educator and at other times as an advocate or a leader. S/he gives direction to the group members in scheduling the group behaviors and then executing them. S/he enables the members to create choices and helps them to become self-directing as early as possible. Through all stages the worker has to develop and exhibit a professional behaviour.

It is not possible to have a average blue print of the role and tasks of a group worker as it is affected by a diversity of factors. Trecker rightly said that the worker's role will vary with dissimilar groups as the situations operating within groups are so dissimilar, that the worker has to first understand the group and the circumstances nearby it before attempting to describe the specific characteristics of his job with it.

In the Initial Stage

At the initial stage the group worker helps the members build a sense of belonging, which is an emotional experience. The ability and understanding in initiating in them a sense of belonging is a crucial task of the worker. She has to foster those circumstances under which this belongingness is fostered. For this s/he needs to accept as well as get acceptance from the group. " the greatest single element in the beginning stages of work with the group is the worker's skill to accept the group as it is, with both strengths and limitations, positives and negatives...... In the beginning the worker should lay emphasis on warmth and friendliness rather than on group organization or scheduling."

With the sense of belonging comes a feeling of pride, warmth, affection, sharing and commitment; a sense of respect for other members as well as a respect for group objectives. Real belonging builds up a sense of companionship and accelerates the psychological procedure of growth in human dealings. The group may go through several stages of belonging. All members may not experience the similar intensity of belonging especially at the early stages. Initial stages may need more worker time as well as an active role on her/his part.

In the initial stage, where exploration is central, the Social Group Work needs to focus her attention on the following:

- Pay attention to the orientation and induction and provide the members a clear thought of what the agency stands for.
- Spend time in trying to gain information in relation to the each member and the needs of each.
- Helps the group determine its objectives and goals
- attempt to relate the purpose of the group to the overall purpose of the agency.
- Seem for methods to strengthen the ties in the middle of the members.

The group worker can create the following efforts at this stage, in the middle of others:

- Set up rapport
- Help the members to get well-known with each other by organizing ice breaking sessions
- Take up easy behaviors with the substance of helping the members open up and start talking and sharing
- If the members already know each other, inform them in relation to the purpose of the group
- Help the members deal with their anxieties, apprehensions or misconceptions, if any
- Explain the vital rules to be followed throughout the group behaviors.

IN THE MIDDLE STAGE

Subsequently the worker's responsibility is to help the group make a kind of functional organization that will create possible the sort of Programme the group wishes to conduct. S/he does not structure the group but helps it to structure itself; the bottom-row is to stay the structure as easy as possible. The worker while helping the individuals in groups to make and uphold satisfying constructive relationships should encourage role allocations on the foundation of merit.

Programme is an significant tool in the hands of the worker and at this stage, the worker has the task of helping the group to plan, develop and execute the Programme. Her/his main role in Programme development is to consciously stimulate and guide the procedure of interaction for individual and group development. S/he helps the group to understand its capacities and limitations and guides the interaction in relation to the procedure of group development. S/he not only helps to stimulate the group to action but also helps it to discover and use the agency and society possessions and those within the group. S/he constantly encourages the members to take initiatives in performing the group tasks and develop leadership in the group by identifying the potential leaders and creating opportunities for them to take up leadership roles. The group worker may at this stage be described upon to address the power issues that arise in the group. Some members may attempt to control and manage the group which may not presently lead to disagreement and groupism albeit generate hostility in the middle of the members and even towards the group worker. The worker has to deftly resolve the power issues which s/he can do by encouraging and developing a sense of cooperation, partnership and a mutual respect for each other. The worker will be especially helpful in working with the leadership that has grown out of the group.

In the active stage of group development the worker should vary her role. Rather than being active she necessity now allow the members to assume responsibility. Remaining in the background, her primary task should be to monitor the changes and progress that are taking lay in the group. S/he will guard against too rapid progression and ensure that the groups do not take on more than they are prepared to handle successfully. Throughout this stage, programmes of longer duration and more involved organization may be encouraged

IN THE LAST STAGE

The role at the final stage begins with reviewing the group experiences and dealing with feelings of separation. It is significant that the worker plans for this stage and handles it skillfully and sensitively. The manner in which group procedure is concluded will strongly power how the members continue to uphold the progress they have achieved. The worker should develop proper formats for recording all the happenings in the group. Records have both short term and extensive term goals and usage. An significant task of the Social Group Worker is to uphold the records with keen observation and sensitivity. S/he should uphold full records of the behaviour of the members and their responses and in doing so be careful in the selection, organization of the material, and examine and summarize from time to time. The last stage calls upon the worker to primarily assess whether individual and group goals have been successfully obtained and plan for the maintenance of change and sustained growth after termination.

Though the actual write up and interpretation and utilization of the records is done at dissimilar stages of development, it assumes special significance in the concluding stages. Records are mainly useful at the point of evaluation and termination as realistic judgments cannot be made on the foundation of memory. The worker at this stage has to create realistic evaluation of the Programme, individual growth and how her/his role has changed and evolved through the several stages of group development. S/he has to review the whole procedure and understand all that has happened in the group and retrace the role played by her/him in bringing in relation to the group development. S/he has the crucial task of cautiously and objectively evaluating the outcomes of interventions and share this information with the group; helping them to assess their achievements and failures. This review is particularly significant if the group is terminating or being handed in excess of to a new worker. If the group decides to end, the worker should ensure a smooth termination and if it decides to continue sans the worker, s/he can continue to monitor the functioning of the group and stay the get in touch with alive.

In the last stage the worker should make situations within the group where the members can act out the changed behaviours independently. This helps the group to approach to conditions with the scenario where the group support may be no longer accessible. Successful termination involves preparing the members adequately for separation from the group and enhancing the transition of the members from being dependant on the group to being on their own.

CONCLUSION

Social Group Work, whereas a method for the group worker, is a important new experience for the members, intended to provide them an opportunity to approach jointly and fulfill their needs and desires through a group procedure. In Social Group Work through guided group experience, the group is helped to develop responsibly and with maturity. From the stage of forming the group to its termination, through cautiously and well planned programmes, the group is helped to achieve its potential. The stages and the behaviors associated with it give structure and direction to the procedure. Theoretically we may segregate dissimilar stages of group development for conceptual clarity but in reality these stages are intertwined with each other. On the foundation of the classification by dissimilar experts we can say that a group can have maximum six stages as discussed by Trecker or a minimum three stages of development, as explained by Bales.

We have discussed the stages as follows:

- *First stage:* Forming the group (Beginning)
- *Second Stage:* Exploration (Initial sessions)
- *Third Stage:* Performing (Action Stage)
- *Fourth Stage:* Assessment (Evaluation)
- *Fifth Stage:* Termination (Ending stage)

Before forming a group the group worker necessity revise the target population. The details that have to be focused while scheduling and forming the group are the size of the group, its composition, frequency of the sessions and their duration time and lay of meetings and duration of the group. The exploration stage involves the following steps, namely orientation and induction; Preparation of the profile of the members; setting specific objectives; developing a structure. Scheduling and development of the Programme, its execution and monitoring are the defining characteristics of the performing stage which is the mainly active stage. After the action stage is in excess of, the group is ready to evaluate the outcome of its efforts in a free, frank and objective manner.

In the last sessions the worker prepares the group for the termination stage. Here s/he shares the final evaluation with the group and analyzes how distant they were successful in accomplishing some of the goals and failed to achieve others, as the case may be. The role of the worker varies at each stage of development, the bottom row being that the worker has to understand the stage of the group at each stage and proceed at the pace of the group.

Though the importance of group work as a therapeutic method of social work intervention is being slowly realized in our country, the information remnants that it is still primarily practiced by the students of social work as a part of their field work training and thereafter the scope of by this method is usually limited. In India the groups have to be shaped by the group worker in mainly cases. S/ he may form the group from in the middle of the existing clientele of the social welfare agencies/NGO's or from in the middle of the open society settings.

PROCEDURE OF GROUP FORMATION – TASKS UNDERTAKEN BY THE TRAVEL OPERATORS

We mentioned in the forgoing discussion that the worker has to discover answers to sure significant questions while embarking on the use of a group to help the target group. Now we will outline the actual tasks the worker has to engage in to initiate the procedure of group formation.

- Once the use of group has been accepted as the best possible option (after considering dissimilar alternatives) for helping the designated population group, the group worker has to formulate a tentative purpose for the group. The worker identifies a general need or concern of the target group and translates that need into a tentative purpose of the prospective group. The following situations may illustrate the rationale for selecting group work as a better option to help:
  - Many people facing similar situation can benefit from sharing their experiences (parents of mentally challenged children);
  - Persons belonging to similar stage of development like adolescents who can benefit from positive group experiences;
  - When individuals have troubles with power figures, in relating to others or having problem of separation;
  - When the target for change is in the social environment like sanitation, educational or health services and the need is for enhanced civic amenities;
  - When people wish or need to avail of the benefit of some beneficiary-oriented scheme of the govt. which requires formation of a group, like self-help groups for procuring micro credit.
- If the worker is required to work with an already existing group, s/

he needs to comprehend its purpose before s/he begins work with the group.

- Achieving optimally effective composition of the group is a crucial task throughout the formation procedure. Will the group constitute only of women or young girls, only of men or male youth, of children, of able-bodied or differently-abled persons; will it be a mix of persons belonging to dissimilar regions, religions, words and cultural background, with dissimilar educational and socio-economic status? This decision will mainly be based on the tentative purpose formulated, anticipated member behaviour and emotional response to prospective members and the knowledge of the patterns of habitual social intercourse prevailing in the superior population group. For instance in Indian society, groups with the mix of genders are socially not very acceptable, unless the group's purpose is task-oriented (for instance in the corporate sector) which may benefit by a combination of diverse skills and perspectives; or a group composed of all aggressive or all withdrawn persons may not benefit from interaction with each other. Who is selected to be the member of the proposed group has lasting impact on the individual member and the group as a whole. If persons are placed in groups that are unsuitable for them, they may be harmed by the membership or may drop out of the group. Dissimilar results flow from different combination of people. What is significant is to see that there is a good fit flanked by any one person and the other group members. The size of the group should be determined by the nature of interaction in the middle of the members and their participation necessary for achieving the purpose of the individual members and the group as a whole.
- The worker identifies potential members from the designated population group on the foundation of dissimilar criteria mentioned earlier.
  - The worker may select members from students of a class; from a list prepared on the foundation of a survey of the families below poverty row or of children afflicted with some specified disability; from the census statement; from membership of previous groups; from the list of persons who may have applied for a scrupulous course or training; or the official records of courts, hospitals, therapists, psychiatric clinics etc.
  - The worker may need to advertise (by word of mouth, leaflets, posters, ads in the newspapers, letters to the organizations like schools from where the potential members can be drawn), state the purpose of initiating the group and invite members to join.
  - In a society-based agency, the worker talked to the society

leaders, local MLA and Municipal Councilor, visited the potential members personally and explained the purpose of the group and its likely benefits for them.

- In an epilepsy clinic for children, parents accompanying their wards were contacted by the travel operators and the purpose, content and structure of the proposed group was explained to them personally.
- In a residential 'Home' for destitute children, the worker, though recognized to the inmates on explanation of her dissimilar responsibilities, explored the strengths and liabilities of the prospective members in conditions of the purpose envisaged, the contribution expected of the members for the proposed group and informed all potential members in relation to the group to be launched and its purpose and structure.

- Pre-group contacts form a important part of the worker's tasks throughout the group formation procedure. The aim of these contacts is to secure appropriate members for the group being planned and their preparation for participation in that group. Through these contacts, the people in the target population get to know the availability and nature of the group based service, their eligibility for that service, ascertain if their goals are similar to others to be met through the group and prepare them for entry in the scrupulous group. The tasks may require more than one visit or meeting. The worker informs the potential members the tentatively planned group structure, the duration and the frequency of the sessions. In case of a group of children or young adults, pre-group contacts also entail meeting the parents/ family members to apprise them of the proposed group, its purpose, the benefits it will offer and its structure. Pre-group contacts may happen throughout a meeting of the society residents and society leaders or throughout some social/ religious event throughout which the worker gets an opportunity to introduce the group to be launched.
- Pre-group interview (one or more than one) with potential member helps clarify and alleviate member's anxiety in relation to the group's structure, expectations of the group in conditions of his role, response of other members towards his membership. It brings out valuable data in relation to the member's attitudes, perception of his need, life situation or difficulty; and his capability to relate to and to communicate with others; In therapy groups, Intake interviews are held with individuals to arrive at an in-depth assessment of the nature and severity of the problem, difficulty or situation; on the foundation of which their compatibility or incompatibility to group membership may be decided.

- Even when the potential members are influenced of the purpose of the group, they may be anxious to know as to what exactly is expected of them, how the group work and what will the other members will be like.
- Pre-group get in touch with also initiates worker – member connection, whether mannered through an individual interview, a visit to the locality of the potential members, or in a meeting held in the society.
- Sure rules and norms that the members are expected to observe initially, the issues of confidentiality, democratic participation, antidiscrimination, and the manner of modifying the norms need to be shared with the potential members throughout pre-group contacts.

Right from the point of worker/ agency agreeing to plan the group; spelling out its purpose, structure, membership; undertaking publicity; selection and recruitment of potential members, worker has to perform numerous significant tasks which have extensive lasting impact on the group's success in conditions of attainment of its goal – individual member's and the group. Scheduling the whole procedure of group formation before the group has its first meeting is vital for the group's success.

GROUP LEADERSHIP

Leadership is the capability to motivate a group of individuals towards fulfillment of group's objectives. The capability to motivate could derive from power that is both formal and informal for formal and informal power is significant in leadership. It is widely accepted that leadership can transpire from within a group as well as by formal appointment to lead a group. In social group work, one discovers and encourages emergence of leaders from within the group.

Some type of leadership is present in every group, though it is not definite whether the group is aware of this information. It is also observed that the kind of leadership has an effect on the group. Depending on the objectives, nature, size and composition of the group, leadership needs to evolve.

UNDERSTANDING LEADERSHIP STYLES

While there are several leadership styles, it is usually agreed that leadership styles is in accordance with the circumstances – the skill of members, urgency of the situation and several such crucial factors. The following are a few significant leader behaviours:

DIRECTIVE

When the task to be accomplished is unclear or hard to be achieved, the leader ensures its successful accomplishment through clearly defining individual tasks and role expectations of members. His intervention is meaningful in such instances. Though, this approach may not be appropriate where the tasks in question are well defined and easy to attain.

SUPPORTIVE

The leader shows high concern towards group members and their needs. This approach is appropriate for groups working on well defined tasks. Members under the supportive leader are establish to be happy and highly satisfied.

PARTICIPATIVE

Here, the leader involves the group members in decision creation and in all functions of the group. Discussions, consultations and group consensus are stressed upon. Though, this calls for members who are responsible and who understand the importance of their contribution to the group's success.

CHARISMATIC

Medha Patkar pioneer of the *Narmada Bachao Andolan* (Save the Narmada Movement) is measured to be a charismatic leader for the following reasons:

- skill to inspire followers towards goals that appears incredible to the general man
- vision in relation to the future
- understanding followers' needs and limitations.

TRANSFORMATIONAL

"This highlights on leaders who inspire followers to transcend their own self-interests and who are capable of having a profound and extraordinary effect on followers. Seven features were establish: sincerity of the leader; bonding – effort to develop the organization as a family by personalized relationships; consultation and participation; collectivization and teamwork; empowerment and support; serving as a role model; bringing in changes continuously while maintaining stability and being innovative".

LEADERSHIP AND DECISION CREATION

Indecisiveness is a silent killer that robs the group of efficiency, resulting in dismantling of the group and its purpose. It is very significant for the group to approach to a consensus, and decide on its key issues to enable successful accomplishment of its goals. A decision could be arrived at through group's brainstorming, discussion and dialogue depending on the time accessible, the complexity of the problem and the group members' capability. A leader has to create the group understand that it is significant to finalize goals that are achievable and apposite to the groups' capability and possessions. Being pushy can lead to unrealistic targets that could lead the group to collapse.

Decision creation is necessary to assign responsibilities to group members. It also is an significant aspect of problem solving processes. A leader's uphill task lies in ensuring completion of assignments that the members had agreed to. While persuading her group members to arrive at a decision, the leader has to exercise the ability of appropriateness; the sense of timing – realizing when to take hold of an issue and when to let go. Realizing that the group is in a location to go ahead, the leader shall seize the opportunity to press hard for a decision. There could also be occasions when the ideal thing to do could be to motivate the group to ascertain further facts prior to the decision.

"The leader allows himself to be put in a hard location whenever he uses steamroller tactics to secure a scrupulous course of action. By doing this against the group's better Judgement, he assumes full responsibility for the possible failure of action. The group members learn from this that it is all right for them not to take responsibility. Moreover, if failure results, they learn that the leader is untrustworthy, and their motivation to participate in the after that action sinks. Finally, the (often unconscious) resentment of the leader, which certainly is to be expected, is likely to sabotage the action so that it will be a failure. To put it another method, the leader's job is to set and maintain the circumstances required for the group's maximum intelligence to assert itself. If everyone leaves a meeting with the justifiable feeling that he could have reached a better decision in five minutes all by himself, then leadership has failed".

LEADERSHIP AND COMMUNICATION

A leader is expected to communicate effectively with everybody. While one to one communication is also significant, the leader's capability to communicate with the group as a whole is mainly vital. This is one ability that is indispensable for a good leader. The leader is a good interpreter and proud voice for her group. She is ready, able, and willing to explain clearly its purpose to persons who may not be well-known with it. She can do it in easy language and in so doing increases his own ability in social communication. The leader is expected to persuade the not so vocal members to converse freely. Some members will discover it hard to partake in discussions for very several reasons. This could be fear of speaking in the middle of a group of individuals, being unsure as to how their ideas would be received; difficulty in choosing the appropriate words and inexperience in putting forth their ideas. Managing poor participation of members (due to their troubles in communicating) is a important aspect the leader will have to tackle through persuasion and also by setting a personal instance.

In meetings, the leader is expected to create people comfortable and at ease with one another. By doing so, she facilitates easy flow of interaction and positive exchange of ideas flanked by the members. Throughout discussions it is significant for the group leader not to put forth her views before the other members have done so. For, too early a viewpoint from the leader would perhaps be opposed or accepted by all members present – keeping with the trend of 'safely supporting the leader'. Listening is an significant aspect of communication. The leader needs to be a good listener, who through her effective listening encourages members to speak without hesitation or inhibitions. Experience designates that the time accessible before and after the conduct of group meetings is a key opportunity for getting a true picture in relation to the status of issues and the group's functioning.

BONDING AND CONNECTION

The leader has an affirmative outlook of the group. Bonding and connection structure are vital ingredients to successful accomplishment of group goals.

The following are some methods in which a leader can bond her team:

- Focusing on the positive characteristics of the group members and also the situation instead of spreading despair through looking at the negative face of issues
- Firmly believing in the democratic approach in group dealings; for finding solutions and for arriving at decisions
- Zealously learning from other people and amending her methods of thinking on the foundation of combined experience and thinking of the group members
- Sensitivity to the differences in capacities, ideas, approaches of individual group members thereby enabling their optimum contribution to the group's functioning.
- Acknowledging that groups are dissimilar and that she needs to develop understanding of group members and helping each individual to become a part of the group.
- Following the principle 'praise in public and reprimand in private' to the fullest extent; prompt and constant appreciation for the good work of all members that ensures motivation and satisfaction in the middle of the members
- Handling troubles of individual behaviour and personal relationships without letting it hamper the groups' functioning
- Impressing on the group that individuals are diverse and that their diversity is the group's mainly priceless plus
- Finding and maintaining circumstances that facilitate optimum contribution of each group member Leadership then is concerned with the detection and coordination of member possessions, on the assumption that individuals are not equal and that their differences are the group's mainly valuable asset.

ROLES OF THE TRAVEL OPERATOR

A travel operator plays two vital roles while working with groups: as a member and as a leader switching roles as and when tasks emerge. Membership and leadership skills are viewed jointly due to the following rationale: For the group's efficient functioning, the leader and his members need to be dealt with skillfully. Similar concerns of individualistic communication emerge for leaders and members.

A travel operator has to perform several functions which are broadly grouped into:

- Job oriented functions that facilitate the group to converge and concentrate towards fulfilling group's objectives
- Individual oriented functions to cater to the personal needs of group members that ensure healthy group cohesiveness and
- Maintenance oriented functions that ensure the consistency of group members' contribution.

SKILLS AND TECHNIQUES OF GROUP TRAVEL

According to Trecker skill is the cap skill to apply knowledge and understanding to a given situation. Trecker also has specified skills for social group travel as follows.

- *Skill in Establishing Purposeful Relationships:*
  - The travel operator necessity be skillful in gaining the acceptance of the group and in relating himself to the group on a positive professional foundation.
  - The travel operator necessity be skillful in helping individuals in the group to accept one another and to join with the group in general pursuits
- *Skill in Analyzing the Group Situation:*
  - The travel operator necessity be skillful in judging the developmental stage of the group to determine what the stage is, what the group needs, and how quickly the group can be expected to move. This calls for skill in direct observation of groups as a foundation for analysis and Judgement.
  - The travel operator necessity be skillful in helping the group to express ideas, work out objectives, clarify immediate goals, and see both its potentialities and limitations as a group.
- *Skill in Participation with the Group:*
  - The travel operator necessity be skillful in determining, interpreting, assuming and modifying his own role with the group.
  - The travel operator necessity be skillful in helping group members to participate, to locate leadership in the middle of themselves, and to take responsibility for their own behaviors.
- *Skill in Dealing with Group Feeling:*
  - The travel operator necessity be skillful in controlling his own feelings in relation to the group and necessity revise each new situation with a high degree of objectivity.
  - The travel operator necessity be skillful in helping groups to

release their own feelings, both positive and negative. He necessity be skillful in helping groups to examine situations as a part of the working through of group or inter-group conflicts.

- *Skill in Programme Development:*
  - The travel operator necessity be skillful in guiding group thinking so that interests and needs will be revealed and understood.
  - The travel operator necessity be skillful in helping groups to develop Progrmmes which they want as a means through which their needs may be met.
- *Skill in By Agency and Society Possessions:*
  - The travel operator necessity be skillful in locating and then acquainting the group with several helpful possessions which can be utilized by them for Programme purposes
  - The travel operator necessity be skillful in helping individual members to create use of dedicated services by means of referral when they have needs which cannot be met within the group.
- *Skill in Evaluation:*
  - The travel operator necessity have skill in recording the developmental processes that are going on as he works with the group.
  - The travel operator necessity be skillful in by his records and in helping the group to review its experiences as a means of improvement. Therefore, the social travel operator has several skills to master.

SKILLS IN STRUCTURE GROUP COHESIVENESS

The travel operator necessity know his group members – their strengths, capacities, fears, troubles and roles they can play in the group's progress.

The following are the other factors the worker needs to concentrate upon in structure himself within the group:

- Effective rapport structure with the group members; to get on the similar wave length with people easily and quickly
- Winning the confidence and trust of people by accepting members as they are and enabling them to see the worth of every job that has to be done in the group big or small
- Establishing a good working connection, based on friendship and mutual confidence that would facilitate power in excess of the group members
- Skill to avoid splinter groups, especially sub groupism by empathizing and thinking for all the group members. The travel operator has to be careful to interpret the silence of the group members. Silence always does not denote negative characteristics; it could presently indicate the individuals' hesitation.

- Skill to remain cool and composed while listening to the distasteful – understanding and internalizing the information that two people can seem at the similar thing and seem at it differently. It is significant that the worker has to strengthen his inner self without getting upset or hitting back at unpleasantness of the group. He needs to understand that this is in light of the superior good of the group.
- Cap skill to get the group to willingly shoulder responsibilities rather than taking up all the burden on himself – the skill to segregate works that can be delegated and executing those which are best done by the worker.

FACILITATION SKILLS

This involves the travel operator helping the group to stay focused on the goals to be achieved, to ensure that the group members work towards a general direction. Facilitating skill, also sometimes described the "here-and-now" of group interaction is often missed by the travel operators. This is because group processes take a back seat when group interactions are intense. Also, at times the travel operator may hesitate to intervene throughout a lively yet dispersed discussion.

Though, the travel operator has to acquire this skill to enable spirited group accomplishments. To help a group accomplish the goals it has set for itself, the worker will often discover it helpful to guide the group's interaction in a scrupulous direction. By limiting or blocking a group member's communications, by encouraging another member to speak or by linking one group member's communication to those of other group members, the worker can guide the group's interaction patterns. This method has been referred to as selecting communications patterns purposely. Helping the group uphold its focus can promote efficient work by reducing irrelevant communications and by encouraging a full exploration of issues and troubles. The travel operator does this by minimizing unwanted interactions and by stirring optimum search investigation of concerns and tight spots.

SKILLS OF INFORMATION COLLECTION AND EVALUATION

Information is power and this is true in working with groups too. It is handy in impacting communiqué designs in the group. Through information gathering and evaluation skills, the travel operator bridges the gap flanked by the procedure-oriented approach of facilitating group processes and the task oriented approach of by action skills to achieve goals and satisfy members' needs. Without effective data gathering and assessment skills, workers' interventions are not ground in a complete understanding of the situation. This can result in the use of premature, oversimplified, or previously attempted solutions that have not been cautiously analyzed and weighed.

REQUESTING INFORMATION, QUESTIONING AND PROBING

By skillfully questioning and probing the travel operator may gather data effectively. A broad outlook to the task in question and to the pursuits of the group could be added that could benefit the group immensely. Skills are needed in properly wording the questions – leading questions; double questions etc should be avoided. The questions need to extract information that is clear and precise. Care should be taken while dealing with sensitive issues and concerns.

ANALYZING SKILLS

Once the data have been gathered and organized, the worker can use analyzing skills to synthesize the information and assess how to proceed. *Analyzing skills contain:*

- Pointing out patterns in the data,
- Identifying gaps in the data, and
- Establishing mechanisms or plans for obtaining data to complete an assessment.

SYNTHESIZING SKILLS

Another useful data gathering and assessment skill is blending verbal and nonverbal communications.

Examples of synthesizing skills contain:

- Creation connections in the middle of the meanings behind a member's actions or words, expressing hidden agendas
- Creation implicit feelings or thoughts explicit
- Creation connections flanked by communications to point out themes and trends in member's actions or words Synthesizing skills can be useful in providing feedback to members in relation to the how they are perceived by others.

LISTENING SKILLS

We convey our listening skills verbally and Non- verbally. By appropriate feedback and playback the travel operator conveys verbally whereas through his eye get in touch with, gestures and body language he conveys it Non-verbally. Egan suggests that, in addition to body location and eye get in touch with, skills that indicate that a worker has heard and understood a member are part of effective listening.

Research has shown that effective listening skills are an significant feature of successful leaders. Effective listening skills contain repeating or paraphrasing what a member says and responding empathically and enthusiastically to the meaning behind members' communications. They also contain what Middleman has referred to as 'scanning' skills. When scanning the group, the worker creates eye get in touch with all group members, which lets them know that the worker is concerned in relation to the them as individuals. Scanning also helps reduce the tendency of workers to focus on one or two group members.

REFRAMING AND REDEFINING

Often, one of the greatest obstacles to the work of a group or an individual is failure to view a problem from dissimilar perspectives that block attempts to discover a creative solution. Redefining and reframing the problem can help members look at the problem from a new perspective. Therefore, a worker may want to reframe or redefine an issue or concern facing the group.

ACTION SKILLS

This comprises modeling, role playing and rehearsing situations in the group. Action skills can be helpful in both task and treatment groups. Modeling refers to the worker or a member demonstrating behaviors in a scrupulous situation so that others in the group can observe what to do and how to do it. Role playing refers to having group members act out a situation with each other's help. The two primary purposes of role playing are to assess members' skill in responding to an interpersonal situation and to help members improve scrupulous responses. Responses can be improved through feedback, rehearsal of a new response, or coaching. Role playing can be a very useful tool when trying to help members improve responses to stressful situations.

Rehearsing refers to practicing a new Behaviour or response based on the feedback received after a role play. Because it is hard to learn new behaviors or to diminish less adaptive but habituated Behaviour patterns, a member may have to practice a new response many times.

CONFRONTATION SKILLS

From handling conflicts and resistance to enthusing group members, confrontation skills could be a valuable tool for the travel operator. Confrontation is the skill to clarify, look at, and challenge behaviors to help members overcome distortions and discrepancies in the middle of behaviors, thoughts, and feelings. Though, one has to vigilantly judge the state of affairs and in relation to the accept skill of his interventions throughout confronting situations. He has to be fully aware that confrontations are forceful, emotionally charged and also expect strong responses. Since confrontations often involve indicating members' mistakes and limitations, the worker has to prepare the group for a candid examination on these rows by underlining the information that ultimately such discussions aid in identifying potentials and abilities of the group.

SKILLS OF DISAGREEMENT RESOLUTION

Disagreement resolution skills are needed to smoothen out frictions within the group and also with those outside the group – inclusive of social systems.

There could be many grounds for conflicts in the middle of the members. The travel operator should facilitate the group to consider conflicts as a factor nourishing the group's development. Conflicts, if constructive and issue based, help the group to get a clearer vision of its goals and discover individual strengths and weaknesses. It is well recognized that conflicts are bound to happen; through efficient group facilitation, conflicts could be minimized and antagonistic disagreements avoided.

CRITIQUING SKILLS

Constructive criticism is an significant skill for the worker, for lots of learning happens while critiquing the group's progression and behaviors. It enables retaining the focus on the group's primary purpose. It also means appropriate questioning of the leader's inputs and interventions, contribution of members and patterns of group's functioning. Critiquing by members is healthier and several a times anticipates and prevents flaws.

LEADERSHIP SKILLS

This is a vital skill that is disputed by researchers – is leadership a trait or a Behaviour? Is a leader born or made? Despite differing views, it has been proved beyond doubt that leadership skill can be learned. Though, there is no 'one size fits all' solution to mastering leadership skills. Group leaders have to constantly remind themselves that they are working with human beings each with dissimilar viewpoints, personalities and methods of functioning.

The key skill of the leader is communicating and keeping communication channels open within the group at all times. This means the leader has to involve all members in discussions – the quiet ones, the ones who may not be comfortable talking in groups or those who can be easily silenced.

The other key skills of leadership are:

- Consensus seeking
- Gate keeping
- Setting standards
- Self understanding that leads to enhanced communiqué
- Inter-personal understanding that leads to understanding members' viewpoints
- Preventing disruptive behaviour such as diverting, blocking, dominating, silence, attention seeking, sympathy seeking etc

HOW TO ACQUIRE GROUP TRAVEL SKILLS?

Reach out and ascertain the qualities of individuals who are successful in working with groups. By checking yourself against this list of traits you could perhaps figure out where you stand with regard to working with groups. The mainly significant point to be kept in mind is that no one individual shall possess all the qualities and that all of us can endeavor to imbibe them. Keenly observing democratic leadership styles in action and understanding reasons behind all the reverence and power these individuals possess in excess of their groups. Experience shows that it is worthwhile observing good presiding officers and good discussion leaders. Do not stop with observation, but do take hold of the skills of competent leaderships.

Reading relevant material from libraries, authenticated Web sites, journals, reports etc will stay you updated on the latest in the field. Maintaining a dairy of everyday work with the group provides a written documentation for reference. It designates the regions for improvement, when reviewed periodically. It is a tool for self evaluation if done methodically and with honesty. Interacting with social work fraternity and with travel operators in professional forums such as workshops, seminars, conferences, training programmes etc facilitates interchange of ideas and experiences in working with groups. It is a practical knowledge bank and feeds the travel operator with skills mainly demanded in the field. Gain hands on training through observing a group or by becoming a member of an existing group.

Lastly, by lending a hand to others to acquire group travel skills, one can constantly check and reinvent oneself in relation to the skills needed in working with groups.

2

Group Insurance

INTRODUCTION TO EMPLOYEE BENEFIT PLAN

Employee benefit schemes are plans sponsored by employers, under which benefits are paid if the employee dies, falls sick, is disabled or retires. Thus, employee benefits include benefits covering the risks of premature death, disability, superannuation and unemployment. In other words, the employer provides some financial security to the employees and their dependents through these employee welfare schemes.

Employees in the organised sector thus have a clear advantage over their less fortunate brethren in the unorganised sector and those engaged in rural occupations related to agriculture. Employee benefits differ with the type and scale of the organisation.

Generally large progressive organizations in addition to their statutory obligations offer many employee benefits. Such benefits are included with the total employee compensation package. While designing these benefits the employer should keep in mind his objectives, employee's needs, options available and their costs.

DEVELOPMENT OF EMPLOYEE BENEFIT SCHEMES

Employers, having recognised their responsibility towards their employees besides paying salaries and wages, started providing additional rewards for their service. These benefits besides provident fund, gratuity and life assurance also included vacation benefits, employee discounts on the firm's products etc.

The employer provided such benefits with the objective of promoting a sense of security among the employees, to improve their morale and to enhance their productivity.

This also resulted in better employer-employee relationship, improved the industrial relation climate and prevented strikes and lockouts. It helped the employer to reduce labour turnover and promoted employee loyalty. Some of the benefits were made compulsory by law while some were introduced by mutual agreements between the employer and the employees.

GROUP INSURANCE FUNDAMENTALS

MEANING OF GROUP INSURANCE

Many employees were aware of the economic security provided by insurance-oriented service benefits. The employers on the other hand also appreciated group insurance as an easy method of providing life insurance to the employees. Group insurance developed in India in the early 1960s. It is the coverage of many persons under one policy. Under group insurance, the insurer drafts a single policy known as a *master policy* for the insured group.

Under employee group insurance, the contract of insurance is between the insurer and employer. So it is the employer who pays the premium. Further it is the employer who can decide upon the members and the extent to which they shall be insured. The employer nominates employees for the pension scheme based on different criteria like their earnings potential, their seniority, age and post.

Employees have no say in choosing the extent of their cover. However, the employer while introducing the group insurance scheme for the first time may give an employee the option to join or not to join the scheme. This is necessary, especially when the employees have to contribute for the plan or forego another benefit in order to be covered under a group insurance plan. Certain features of group insurance differentiate it from individual insurance. Let us now discuss the distinguishing features of group insurance.

FEATURES OF GROUP INSURANCE

Group policy

Under group insurance a single policy known as a master policy is issued to the group policyholder who may be the employer or the authorised person representing the group Certificates and summary evidence of insurance is given to the members of the group insured. The master policy is a detailed document that states the contractual relationship between the insurer and the group policyholder. A list of persons eligible for coverage with relevant information such as age, occupation etc is sent by the employer or nodal agency to the insurer. The insurer examines the list, quotes the premium payable and confirms coverage for the listed persons when the premium is paid.

Underwriting group

This is the most important distinguishing feature of group insurance. In group insurance, the insurer underwrites the group as a whole. Therefore group characteristics are important rather than the individual characteristics of group members. This means the underwriter considers the size, age composition, occupation and stability of the group as a whole rather than health and other insurability aspects of the individuals. For the reasons stated above, insurers prefer to underwrite larger groups rather than smaller ones to avoid the possibility of adverse selection. Underwriters favour a regular flow of new employees, as the old ones will be replaced with the younger ones, so that the average age group remains more or less constant. Further, actively and efficiently working employees can be assumed to be in average health.

Cost effective

Group insurance generally costs less than individual insurance. This is because the group insured generally needs no medical examination. Secondly, the acquisition cost for the insurer is also low. The insurer pays less commission to agents of group insurance than to the agents of individual insurance. Moreover, the employer offers administrative services such as collection of premiums, where the employees share the premiums. The cost of administrating the scheme for the employer is minimal. So the group coverage is provided to customers at prices lower than that of individual insurance.

Experience rated premiums

The insurer charges experience rated premiums when the group is too large. In group insurance, the premium reflects the loss. In simple words, the group is charged higher premiums if the loss experienced in the previous year is higher than expected losses. Where the loss experience is considerably less than expected loss experience over a period of time the saving is passed on by the insurer to the master policyholder by way of reduction in premium.

ADVANTAGES OF GROUP INSURANCE

Some of the advantages of group insurance are as follows:

- With group insurance, persons with less or no life insurance are also able to get some measure of insurance protection.
- Coverage is also available to those employees who are otherwise uninsurable.
- Life insurance companies can reach a vast number of clients at less cost within a short span of time.
- It is a tax effective tool. The employer gets tax relief for the premium paid by him on behalf of the employees. Employers are also entitled to tax relief for premiums paid by them if the scheme is partly contributory.

LIMITATIONS OF GROUP INSURANCE

There are also some limitations to the group insurance schemes, which are discussed below:

- The nature of group insurance is temporary. It means once the member is out of the group, the coverage ceases. The employee also loses insurance coverage in the event of termination of the group plan.

- The master policy issued by the insurer is not very flexible. It does not meet the individual needs for insurance. The insurer under group insurance cannot focus on the financial needs of the individual, which is possible in individual insurance.
- A few members who could have been charged fewer premiums if individual insurance had been taken, have to pay higher premiums because the premium is fixed for the group as a whole.

GROUP ELIGIBILITY

A group to be insured under the group life insurance scheme has to fulfill the following conditions:

- The group, which should be homogenous, should have been formed for purposes other than to seek insurance.
- The group should allow new comers to enter into the group for the continuity of the group.
- The method of determining the amount to be insured should preclude individual selection.
- Safeguards should be established to produce a normal distribution of risk and to avoid the inclusion of undue proportion of the total insurance of the group upon unhealthy lives or on a few lives or on the lives of advanced ages.
- A universal administrative organisation referred to as nodal agency in our country, must be in existence that is able and willing to act on behalf of the insured.
- Besides the insured members there should be some party who can pay a proportion of the total cost.

ELIGIBLE GROUPS

Earlier, group insurance was taken only for the employees of an organisation.

Later on, other groups were also included like groups of professionals, co-operative societies, debtors of one creditor, etc. Let us now discuss some of the groups that are eligible for group insurance.

Individual employer groups

Employees may be working with a single large company, a sole trader or in a partnership firm. The employees of any of the above are referred to as individual employer groups. So far, individual employer groups have been the most common groups insured.

This was due to the favourable characteristics of such groups, which are mentioned below:

- The employer can represent the employees as a single person dealing with the insurance company.
- Authentic employee data is readily available
- Payment of premiums is easy and regular.
- The employer has the required machinery to collect the claim money from the insurance company and pay it to the beneficiaries.
- The employer would have already screened the employees at the time of employment through a pre-recruitment medical examination. Besides, such employees also enjoy medical facilities offered by employers and therefore enjoy better health. So, it is convenient for the insurer to grant a cover without medical evidence.

Multiple employer groups

Employers may be financially or in any other way, connected to each other as associated companies. Such employers can form a group and take a group policy covering the employees of each employer of the group. There is a principal company who is a policyholder and deals with the insurance company. It collects the required data and premium from other employers as per the agreement.

Labour union groups

Under labour union groups, the insurer covers the members of a labour union by issuing a contract directly to the union. It is the union that pays the premium. The union may be meeting the premiums wholly out of the union funds or jointly with the members. It should be ensured in such cases that the coverage benefits individual members rather than the union or its office bearers.

Creditor-debtor groups

In creditor debtor group insurance, lives of the debtors are covered through a group policy issued to the creditor. The creditor, such as a bank or a finance company, insures its debtors as collateral security against the credit given to the debtors.

In the event of the death of the borrower, the insurer pays the benefit to the creditor. The creditor sets off the outstanding loan and any balance of the policy proceeds is paid to the legal heirs of the debtor.

Miscellaneous groups

Different other groups can also be insured under a group insurance scheme. Such groups include associations of public and private employees, associations of professionals such as lawyers, doctors, accountants, teachers, unit holders, veteran associations, religious groups, retail chains etc.

GROUP INSURANCE SCHEMES

The two main types of group insurance are *group life insurance and group accident and sickness insurance.* The group life insurance allows the members to name the beneficiaries of their choice. The employee/member has a special privilege to convert the policy on termination from the group. This can be highly beneficial, especially for an uninsurable person. Group accident and sickness policy have different components. And the technicalities differ from company to company. Let us now discuss the various schemes available to an employer.

GROUP LIFE INSURANCE

Three types of group life insurance are common in India – the group term insurance scheme, group gratuity scheme and group superannuation scheme. Group life insurance is the most common group insurance provided to employees. Group life insurance is a simple and economic way of providing life insurance to employees. Under this policy, generally a fixed sum is paid to the dependants of a covered employee on his death. It is also possible to offer what is known as graded cover that offers different covers to different categories of employees within the same group.

This scheme is renewable every year. As the premium rates are very low when compared to individual insurance, the employees and the weaker sections find it convenient and helpful. It helps their dependents in reducing debt burdens.

Definition

Group life insurance is that form of life insurance covering not less than 25 employees with or without medical examination, underwritten under a policy issued to the employer, the premium on which is to be paid by the employer or by the employer and employees jointly and insuring all of his employees or all of any class or classes thereof determined by conditions pertaining to the employment for amounts of insurance based on some plan which will preclude individual selection. Where the group is small, say less than 100, the insurer may insist on 100per cent participation of employees in the scheme, if the scheme involves contribution from employees also. For very large groups however, the insurer generally accepts the scheme if 75per cent of the employees participate.

Group gratuity scheme

The group gratuity scheme is an insurance scheme covering the employer's liability to pay gratuity under the Payment of Gratuity Act, 1972. The amount of gratuity to be paid is at the rate of 15 days wages based on the wages last drawn, for each completed year of service. However this is subject to a maximum limit. The Act requires that the gratuity be paid to those employees who have served the employer continuously for at least five years.

Group superannuation scheme

After retirement, employees need financial security. The provident fund and the gratuity provided by the employer may not be sufficient in an inflationary economy. Secondly such lump sum payments are often utilised by the employees to meet their current contingent liabilities. The employers observed that the employees actually also need a periodical payment over and above the normal terminal benefits. Such payment is made in the form of pensions by creating a superannuation fund. Superannuation scheme aims at providing old age pensions to employees after retirement.

Group insurance scheme in lieu of EDLI

Group insurance scheme in lieu of ELDI is also a type of group insurance scheme offered by life insurance. All employers who come under the Employee's Provident Fund and Miscellaneous Provision Act 1952, have a statutory liability to subscribe to the Employee's Deposit Linked Insurance Scheme, 1976, to provide for the benefit of life insurance to all their employees.

Under the scheme in effect from 24th June, 2000, the insurance benefit is equal to the average balance to the credit of the deceased employee in the provident fund during the last 12 months, provided that where such balance exceeds ₹ 35,000, insurance cover would be equal to Rs.35,000 plus 25per cent of the amount in excess of Rs.35,000, subject to a maximum of Rs.60,000. Hence if the length of service is inadequate and/or the salary is low, the benefit to the family of the employee in the event of his death would be meagre.

Where the employer provides for a better insurance benefit through an alternative insurance plan, he may be exempted from participating in this scheme. LIC's group insurance scheme in lieu of EDLI has been recognised as one such scheme.

Benefits to the employer:

- The premium payable by the employer in general is lesser than the total contribution, which has to be made under the EDLI scheme, especially when the salary level of the employees is high and the average age of the employee group is low.
- Settlement of claim for this scheme is quicker; the insurer just asks for the death certificate and the claim form from the employer.
- The premium paid by the employer is admissible as normal business expenses for income tax purposes.

Benefits to the employee:

The coverage offered by LIC scheme is higher than that offered under EDLI scheme by the Provident Fund authorities.

Group savings linked insurance scheme

Group savings linked insurance scheme is a group insurance scheme, which is very popular since it offers a survival benefit in addition to the death benefit available under a group term assurance policy.

Where life insurance benefits are not linked to any statutory requirement, there is often a demand to link it with a survival benefit, particularly when the employees come forward to make contributions.

The central government employee's group insurance scheme is an example of such a combination.This scheme was introduced with the objective of providing, low cost insurance on a wholly contributory and self-financing basis, with a survival benefit to help the families of the government employees in the event of death of the employees while in service, and a lump sum payment to the employees on cessation of employment.Insurance companies now offer a similar scheme, which was originally formulated to suit the requirements of large public sector organisations like BHEL, HHAL, HMT, LIC, GIC, etc.

The scheme has since been extended to reputed private companies and educational institutions. The group savings linked insurance scheme can be a contributory or non-contributory scheme. Part of the premium collected is the savings premium that is accumulated at the rate declared from time to time; a part is utilised to provide life cover in case of death.

Main features:

- The employer acts as a facilitator and coordinator in maintaining the scheme and in making monthly deductions from salary.
- Contribution consists of risk premium and the savings portion. The savings portion earns interest at the declared rate, compounding yearly.
- As per regulations, the life cover premium and contribution for savings should be in the ratio 1:2 respectively.
- Employees are grouped into several agreed categories based on their salary and therefore the contribution and coverage depend on the category to which the employee belongs.

Benefits:

- In the event of death of the employee, the nominee gets an assured sum with accumulated savings and interest on the same.
- On retirement/resignation/termination, only the accumulated savings portion with interest is payable. Monthly contribution of employees is exempted under Section 88, of IT Act, 1961.

Requirements

The number of members joining the scheme has to be atleast 75per cent of the total number of employees.

The scheme has to be made compulsory for all the new employees. The premium payable is based on weighted mean of the ages of the members. Contribution is uniform for each category.

AVAILABLE GROUP INSURANCE SCHEME S IN THE INDIAN MARKET

GROUP INSURANCE SCHEMES OF LIC

LIC offers life insurance protection under group policies to various groups such as employee - employee, professionals, co-operatives, weaker sections of society, etc.

It also provides insurance coverage to people at subsidized rates under Social Security Group schemes. Besides providing insurance coverage, the Corporation also offers group schemes to employers, which provide funding of gratuity and pension liabilities of the employers.

GROUP TERM INSURANCE SCHEMES

Employer-Employee groups may be offered group insurance schemes providing uniform or graded cover.

Group insurance schemes providing uniform cover can be granted to associations of professionals, members of co-operative banks, welfare funds, credit societies and weaker sections of society.

GROUP INSURANCE SCHEME IN LIEU OF EDLI

The Employees' Deposit Linked Insurance scheme is applicable to all establishments and undertakings contributing to Employees" Provident Fund under the EPF and MP Act, 1952, with effect from 1.8.1976, unless exempted under Section 17 (2A) of the Act. The scheme provides for an insurance cover to an employee, which is linked to his balance in the PF Account, subject to a maximum of ₹ 60,000/-. Under LIC's scheme, the insurance cover starts from ₹ 5,000/- and depends on the service put in by the employee and the current monthly salary on each Annual Renewal Date. The cover provided is at least ₹ 2,000/- more than the cover given by the EDLI scheme.

GROUP GRATUITY SCHEME

Gratuity is a statutory liability of most of the employers, which accrues to an employee for every year of service put in by him. In the event of the premature death of an employee, his dependants are entitled to the amount of gratuity payable on retirement of the employee at the age of superannuation had he survived.

GROUP SUPERANNUATION SCHEME

The Group Superannuation Scheme is designed to provide pension to employees on their retirement from service. A decreasing group insurance cover in conjunction with superannuation benefits may also be provided under the scheme.

The scheme is of two types:

- Money Purchase Scheme
- Benefit Purchase Scheme

GROUP SAVINGS LINKED INSURANCE SCHEME

The Group Savings Linked Insurance Scheme (GSLI) offers insurance cover together with a savings element. The scheme is allowed to select Employer-Employee groups.

Under the scheme, out of the contributions received in respect of each employee, a portion is utilized for the insurance cover and the balance known as contribution for savings, is accumulated till exit, at an optimal rate of interest. In case of death during service, the amount for which the member was covered at the time of death is also paid along with the accumulated savings with interest.

GROUP ANNUITY SCHEME

Employers who have a privately administered Superannuation Fund, where moneys are invested by Trustees as per Income Tax Rules can purchase pensions for employees as and when due under 'Group Annuity policies from LIC.'

GROUP LEAVE ENCASHMENT SCHEME

According to Accounting Standard (AS-15) of January, 1995 and amended Section 209 (3) of the Companies Act, 1956, it has become necessary for employers to provide for the liability of leave encashment facility available to employees in the annual books of accounts.

The Group Leave Encashment Scheme (GLES) is designed to fund such liabilities of employers.

GROUP MORTGAGE REDEMPTION ASSURANCE SCHEME

This scheme covers the borrowers of Housing/Vehicle Loans from financial institutions where loans are recovered in EMI. Insurance cover allowed to borrower upto the outstanding loan excluding the EMI interest, subject to conditions applicable to the scheme.

GROUP INSURANCE SCHEME FOR DEPOSIT HOLDERS OF BANKS

This scheme covers account/deposit holder of a Bank. The cover allowed is ₹ 1,00,000/- per member with/without double accident benefit.

UNIT-LINKED GRATUITY PLUS

With effect from June 2006, LIC has brought out a Unit-Linked Group Gratuity Plan, called "Gratuity Plus" for management of Gratuity Funds.

It is a market-linked plan, which offers greater flexibility and transparency. The hallmark of the scheme is its competitive cost structure. Over and above low fund management charges and administrative expenses, it provides for life insurance cover at a minimal cost.

GROUP SOCIAL SECURITY SCHEMES

In many developed countries, insurance coverage either under individual plans or under group insurance is not available to persons belonging to the weaker sections of the community who are engaged in various occupations in the unorganized sector. For such people, social insurance is the only answer for providing a certain minimum of insurance cover. Therefore social security insurance is the growing concern of many nations. In most of the developed countries, insurers actively participate in social welfare measures. In our country also, insurance companies provide protection to weaker sections under group term insurance policy. The poorer section groups include handloom workers, rickshaw pullers, rural artisans, landless agricultural labourers, barbers, tailors co-operative milk producers etc. In the event of death of the member, a fixed sum is paid to the dependents. In case of an accident, the dependents can get double the sum.

GROUP DISABILITY INCOME INSURANCE

Workers compensation provided to employees in the event of work-related disability is often inadequate. These benefits also fail to cover disability due to accidents that are not work- related. The group disability income insurance available in most of the foreign countries (but not in India) provides economic security to the employees in the event of disability. Group disability income insurance is of two types - short term plans and long-term plans.

SHORT-TERM DISABILITY INCOME INSURANCE

This plan is also known as the sick leave plan. It pays benefit to the employees for a short period of about six months. The employees are credited with a certain number of sick days for each month worked. If the employee takes more sick days than he actually earned, then his salary is reduced accordingly.

Such plans also have an elimination period, generally for a week. It means that the benefits are not paid for the first week of illness or disability. By imposing such a condition, the employer tries to reduce the moral hazards like malingering and excessive absenteeism. Under short-term plans, only disability that is not work-related is covered. The amount to be ascertained as disability income benefit depends upon the earnings of the employee. The short-term plan may or may not be insured.

LONG-TERM GROUP DISABILITY INCOME PLAN

The long-term group disability income plan pays benefits for a minimum period of two years and upto a maximum age of 65 years. Such benefits are normally paid on a monthly basis. Long- term benefit plans also require a waiting period of about 3 months or more. These benefits are generally offered to fulltime employees only. Under long-term disability plans, benefits are given to the employees for both workrelated and non-work-related injuries or disability. Disability in this context generally means total disability.

MARKETING OF GROUP INSURANCE

Life insurance has been from the beginning marketed through agents. Group insurance is no exception. But the agents have to take special permission for canvassing group insurance from the office. However the percentage of group insurance sold through agents is Meagre. This is due to the lack of expertise on the subject among agents. Group insurance is a technical subject that requires special knowledge. Also, the commission rates paid by the insurer for group schemes to the agents are very low. Further, the agents are required to deal with high level executives and the senior officers of the companies. The average agent therefore finds it rather difficult to enter the area of group schemes selling.

A large number of group schemes were directly sold by the executives of pension and group schemes department of LIC. These departments were originally located only in the metropolitan cities. However, now they have been established in all the divisions of LIC. Marketing officials of the pension and group schemes department market the product directly.

Occasionally schemes are also sold through approved agents. But the agent's role here also is restricted to that of a spotter. Efforts to educate the agents on group insurance scheme and develop a cadre of group insurance agents has not been successful except in the metros where the experiment was a limited success. It is often said that life insurance is always sold, never bought. But group life insurance is sometimes bought because progressive employers are interested in employee welfare schemes. They aim at reducing taxes and promoting employee loyalty to reduce employee turnover. Group insurance schemes, group gratuity scheme, group insurance in lieu of EDLI and group superannuation scheme, are often purchased by the employers on their own initiative.

While in India, group insurance is mostly marketed either directly or through agents in foreign countries, group insurance is marketed by career agents, brokers and independent benefit consultants. In some of the foreign countries banks are also now permitted to market group insurance.

EMERGENCE OF NEW INSURANCE INTERMEDIARIES

In the present market in India there are new insurance intermediaries like brokers and institutional agents, particularly banks. Such intermediaries are better placed to market group schemes.

ALTERNATIVES OF FUNDING GROUP INSURANCE

Employers examined the alternatives of funding the benefit plans with the following objectives:

- To control and use reserve funds
- To reduce or eliminate payment of premium taxes
- To enjoy better tax benefits

After examining various conventional alternatives of funding and the present demands of employers, the following methods of funding a group insurance plan were developed.

FULLY INSURED PLAN VARIATIONS

Retrospective premium arrangements

Under this arrangement, the insurer retains the right of charging additional premiums if the costs or losses are higher than expected. Thus, instead of keeping a margin for contingency while calculating premiums, the premiums are calculated on the basis of actual costs and expected claims. The additional premium that an insurer is allowed to collect is normally restricted to a level so as to equate the premium schedule that includes margin for contingencies.

Cost plus funding

Under this method the employer shares the risk of the insurer and pays lower premium, so that the employer can use the reserves, which were otherwise used by the insurer. The employer here also bears a part of the administrative costs on a monthly basis.

Extended grace period

The employer can also retain the funds available to him by adopting this method. The insurer extends the grace period for payment of premium from 31 days to 60 or 90 days. With the extended grace period the employer can retain and use the two or three months' premium in other channels.

Release of reserves

The master policyholder also can appeal to the insurer to release the reserve it holds on his contract. This way the employer can use a portion of the reserve for his other requirements.

Flexible funding life insurance

It is also a cost-plus approach to group insurance funding where the employer's monthly premium equates the claims paid in the previous month including reserve adjustments, premium taxes and other expenses of the insurer.

The employer or the group policyholder can accept liability for all claims or restrict his liability to the extent of a conventional fully insured plan.

SELF FUNDING BENEFIT PLANS

An alternative to the insured plan is self-funding by the employer. It is a conventional method that was most commonly used for workers' compensation benefit. The employer can opt for self-funding considering the size of the group and the cost of self-funding compared to insured plans. When the employer chooses a self-funding plan additional staff is required for administration of funds. The organisation may appoint an outside claims administrator, but this means it has to forego the benefits of expertise of the insurance company in claim settlement and other aspects like cost containment. An efficient employer therefore considers all these points in addition to the cash flow requirements of the employer before selecting from among the alternative of funding employee benefits plan.

However these alternatives exist only in the foreign countries. These are not in vogue in our country.

FUNDING ALTERNATIVES IN INDIA

In India also, the employers have alternatives of funding available, which range from fully funded plan to a fully insured plan. When the employer opts for a fully funded plan he also has to decide whether to self-administer the plan or to retain an external administrator. The following are the funding alternatives of different schemes practiced by employers in India.

Funding gratuity scheme

The employer may choose either of the following ways of meeting his gratuity liability:

- Pay as you go method: He can pay the gratuity out of current revenues as and when it's due. The gratuity value generally varies from one financial year to another. This is because the number of employees may change every year and also the level of gratuity liability increases with the increase in service of the existing employees. A prudent employer generally does not follow this method.
- Creation of reserve method: He can create a reserve in the books of accounts to provide for his gratuity liability. Such a reserve is not a separate fund but merely an accounting provision in the books. The management needs to be very rigid and disciplined to ensure that the organisation does not use such reserves for meeting current requirements.
- Setting up a Trust Fund: Alternatively the employer, to safeguard the interest of the employees, can set up a gratuity trust that is

irrevocable. The trustees may opt to manage it themselves or enter into a group gratuity scheme with an insurance company.

Advantages of group gratuity scheme with the insurer:

- The employer can benefit from the expertise of the insurance company in the investment of funds that the trustees may not have.
- The insurer has a large portfolio. This enables the insurer to secure optimum benefits from the market. The insurer enjoys a better spread and is protected from fluctuations.
- The actuarial skills of the insurer in evaluating the adequacy of fund are unmatchable.
- They can also update it from time to time.
- The insurer ensures that the dependents of an employee covered under the scheme get the same gratuity even if an employee dies young.

Due to these factors, employees generally insist on the insured scheme rather than a trustee administered fund. Moreover, employees feel insecure if the funds are in the hands of the employer. Therefore insured schemes are generally preferred.

Funding superannuation scheme

The employer may agree to pay pensions to his employees. He selects the categories of employees who should be covered under the scheme. The employer grants pension to all these employees of the selected category with the intention of providing financial security to them even after their retirement. Under the superannuation scheme, the following two alternatives for funding are available to the employer.

Payment by employer

The employer need not make any reserve for such pensions. If the 'pay as you go' method is adopted, any amount due can be paid out of the current revenues of the employer at that time. However this is not advisable, as the payment of pension under this method depends on the future earnings of the organisation. This again involves uncertainty as to the level and continuation of the payment of premium.

Funding through trust

The employer can establish a trust fund with his contributions and the contributions of employees if any. The employer appoints trustees to administer the fund. These trustees are entrusted with the responsibility of investing the funds as per investment pattern prescribed by the government to secure the pensions of the employees. As per the provisions of Schedule IV Part B of the Income Tax Act, 1961 the approval of such a fund by the income tax commissioner is obligatory. In this way, the employees covered under the pension scheme are granted complete financial security after their service.

The appointed trustees can exercise either of the two options available to them for managing the fund. They themselves can administer the fund or can take an insurance scheme with any insurance company. Let us discuss these options in detail.

Trustee administered fund

Where the trustees administer the fund, they have to accumulate the contributions as per the requirements of the Central Board of Direct Taxes. The trustees can buy annuities from an insurance company for the member employees when the pensions become due.

The trustees of the fund carry out the following functions:

- Collecting contributions
- Buying and selling of securities
- Collecting interest
- Obtaining tax exemption certificates
- Purchasing the annuities from insurance companies
- Maintaining the books of accounts

Insured schemes

Where the trustees obtain a group superannuation scheme with the insurer, the trustee's duties of management and administration of the fund are transferred to the insurer. The trustees pay the contributions to the insurance company as premiums and the insurance company issues a master policy to the trustees. The insurance company pays the premium as and when they fall due. So, all the members of the group are insured under a single policy.

The contributions made by the employer and the employees may be predetermined as a certain percentage of the salary pensions and are then paid accordingly. Alternatively, the pension may be agreed upon beforehand and accordingly the contribution rate can be determined on an actuarial basis. Where the rates are fixed on the actuarial basis, it is to be noted that such rates have to be reviewed periodically. This helps in maintaining the relationship between the contributions and pensions at the appropriate level so that the insurance company has sufficient funds to provide the benefits to the members of the scheme.

TRUSTEE-ADMINISTERED FUND VS. INSURED SCHEME

An insurance company is well experienced and efficient in administering the pension plan. Trustees may lack such expertise. Therefore a prudent employer may prefer to entrust the administration and management of the pension scheme to the insurance company. This way, the employer can concentrate on other promotional activities of the business. It is observed that the costs involved in insurance schemes are high when compared to a trustee-administered scheme. To choose between these two alternatives, employers in our country keep in mind the expected yield on contribution and the size of the group. Where the number of employees is large the employer may go for the trustee-administered fund. In such organisations, experienced and trained staff can efficiently administer and invest the large contributions. On the other hand, the employer selects an insured scheme where the number of employees covered under the pension scheme is small. This is because with small contributions, the trustees cannot follow the suggested investment pattern and they also lack the expertise required for managing the pension scheme. With a trustee- administered fund, employees are provided with a wide range of benefits.

Such benefits include disablement pension, discretionary pension, early retirement pension and ill health retirement pension. On the other hand, in an insured scheme the benefits available for the employees are limited to pensions that are dependent on life. The insurance schemes available to the employer are standardized and not tailormade. The rate at which a fund is built may be changed if required under a trustee-administered fund. This is not possible in an insured scheme.

The most favourable characteristic of an insured scheme is that it makes sure that the employees get their pensions regularly and without any difficulty. It relieves the trustees from the responsibility of administering the fund and at the same time, offers financial security to the employees. The insured pension scheme also has the advantage of offering a reasonable pension in the event of the premature death of a member, if the employer adopts a gratuity insured scheme in conjunction with the superannuation scheme

3

Communication and Knowledge-sharing Errors in Groups Travel Operations

Working in groups can be difficult. Group members must decide who knows what, coordinate who will do what, share knowledge, and accomplish their individual and collective tasks. Research indicates that groups do not often handle these tasks as well as they should, and, as a result, almost always perform worse than expected based on the sum of members' individual knowledge and abilities. Groups composed of people who know each other well or who have worked together in the past often work together better than comparable groups of strangers. One explanation for why group performance improves over time is that experienced groups develop a transactive memory that enables them to make better use of each individual's expertise. Transactive memory systems theory, a theory of group-level cognition, explains how people in collectives learn, store, use, and coordinate their knowledge to accomplish individual, group, and organizational goals. It is a theory about how people in relationships, groups, and organizations learn "who knows what " and use that knowledge to decide "who will do what," resulting in more efficient and effective individual and collective performance.

Cognitive interdependence and the norm of reciprocity drive the creation of transactive memory – each member takes responsibility for different knowledge areas, and members rely on one another for information outside of their responsibility. Although experienced groups often share knowledge more effectively and perform better than newly formed groups because of their more developed transactive memory system, they still rarely achieve their theoretical maximum. This chapter investigates why this might be the case, and what groups can do to improve their knowledge sharing among members. It explores sources, processes, and outcomes of knowledge-sharing problems through the theoretical lens of transactive memory theory. We will present a conceptual framework for understanding knowledge-sharing errors in groups, and investigate the role of communication in creating, correcting, and reinforcing errors. It is important to note the assumption that underlies this conceptualization: namely that, taken together, members have sufficient knowledge, skills, and resources to perform group tasks. In addition, we will focus our attention on the organizational context, but these concepts could also apply to groups in other contexts, such as families, friendship groups, support groups, etc.

TRANSACTIVE MEMORY

As originally formulated, transactive memory theory indicates that group members utilize one another as storehouses of information, and assign information based on notions of relative expertise. The resulting system of labels and locations provides the group with access to a large body of knowledge while at the same time reducing the cognitive load for remembering information across group members. Brandon and Hollingshead extended Wegner's initial conceptualization in a paper describing the development of transactive memory systems in organizations by adding task to labels and locations as a defining element of the cognitive representation of the system. That is, task is viewed as a macro-organizing feature defining the overall structure of transactive memory, and as a micro-element defining the connections between expertise and people, in the form of task–expertise– person units.

TRANSACTIVE MEMORY DEVELOPMENT AND TEP UNITS

Brandon and Hollingshead argued that transactive memory evolves from three iterative, independently operating, but reciprocally influential cyclical processes:

- Satisfaction of conditions leading to perceived cognitive interdependence among group members,
- TEP unit and individual mental model development, and
- shared mental model development – *i.e.*, reconciling perceptions across group members.

At the very beginning of transactive memory development, groups are likely to proceed linearly through the model; however, the model is dynamic and can be non-linear. Group activities at later points in the model may induce changes in all three processes. We will revisit the dynamic aspects of the model later in the chapter.

CONDITIONS FAVORING TRANSACTIVE MEMORY DEVELOPMENT

Perceived cognitive interdependence is a prerequisite for the development of transactive memory, as it motivates members to attend to what other members know in the group, and to begin developing a conceptual map regarding "who knows what." Without it, a transactive memory system is not likely to develop.

Perceived cognitive interdependence occurs when members perceive that each member's outcomes are dependent on the knowledge or information held by other members of the group. It can be stimulated by group reward structures, divisible task structures, a general need for cognitive simplicity, a close relationship, or some combination of these factors.

Some examples of conditions that might foster perceived cognitive interdependence include:

- A team must divide up a large project into subparts and assign each part to a different team member;
- Members of a project team are rewarded based on overall team performance rather than on each member's individual contribution to the project; and
- Co-workers who also have a close personal relationship may rely on one another for information, advice, and help.

It is important to note that perceptions of cognitive interdependence are more important than the reality of it, although they are likely to be positively associated.

CONSTRUCTION AND ORGANIZATION OF TEP UNITS

Once members perceive cognitive interdependence, the group is likely to move into the next phase of transactive memory development – the creation of TEP units. The addition of TEP units to transactive memory theory evolves from a general view that task perceptions are fundamental to the transactive memory system. Understanding that the task of building a home requires areas of expertise such as architectural design, plumbing, etc., helps the construction team identify the subtasks, the expertise, or information needed for each subtask, and the responsible person. Further, the perceived structure of the task will likely define the major labels and locations of the transactive memory system – for example, architecture, plumbing, electrical, and carpentry will likely be the top-level hierarchical labels for expertise. What TEP units provide are connections between the hierarchically organized domains of knowledge and locations to a conception of the group task. Brandon and Hollingshead suggest that task perceptions link easily to labels and locations because task perceptions also have an easy-to- use hierarchical organization of simplified labels for task components to provide a basic reference system for the task.

A complete reference for transactive memory then results by knowing, for example, that installing the hot water system in a house requires a plumber named Hakuho. Partial TEP units – where task, expertise, or person information is missing – are less useful. It is not that helpful to know that Asashoryu is a fine chef when the task is building a house, or to know that the design of the home requires design blueprints until one knows that group member Akebono is an architect. While TEP units therefore provide a complete reference for transactive memory, task perceptions can also be a source of error for a group if task representations are a poor fit to the actual task, or if there is disagreement among group members about the structure of the task. Brandon and Hollingshead describe TEP units as constructed via an ongoing, iterative process of three related cycles: construction, evaluation, and utilization. In the construction cycle, full or partial TEP units evolve from each member's notions about task, expertise, and people.

Once constructed, full or partial TEP units do not represent certainty, but rather hypotheses a group member has about the distribution of task-relevant information within the group. Wegner states that one quality of transactive memory systems is the modification of crude notions of expertise via group communication to more refined and accurate conceptions, which suggests a dynamic quality to TEP units. Thus, in the second cycle of TEP development, hypothesized full TEP units, components of TEP units, or partial TEP units are tested, confirmed, and/or revised using available information in the evaluation phase.

After construction and evaluation cycles are satisfied, group members make use of TEP units for transactive memory tasks in the utilization cycle, such as requesting or passing along information. Results from the utilization feed back to the earlier cycles for further TEP development, as needed. For example, a group building a home may initially construct a TEP unit that links carpentry to Kitanoumi, due to his certification as a master carpenter.

However, when Kitanoumi repeatedly fails to remember information related to the home's wall framing, group members will begin to reassess their TEP units, and perhaps start to allocate information related to carpentry elsewhere. Over time, ongoing iterations of TEP development cycles will produce more accurate representations of who knows what about the group task. The TEP units and their labeled reference systems and representations comprise the individual's mental model of the transactive memory system. Such a structure meets definitions of mental models as organized structures of objects and their relations and as an individual's view of a system that is dynamic, system specific, and gained through experience.

MENTAL MODEL DEVELOPMENT

In the third phase of transactive memory development, group members begin to form similar mental models and arrange their TEP units in a similar fashion. Blickensderfer, Cannon-Bowers, and Salas define shared mental models as "the extent to which individual team members' mental models overlap – the extent to which team members share the same understanding of the task and the team," which in the case of transactive memory means not only similar TEP units, but also similar macro-organization of those units.

While some differences in representations among group members are likely, a premise of transactive memory theory, and a tenet of mental model research, is that groups will seek to reduce these differences via communication and negotiation. We expect that mental models will be most similar between group members who interact frequently.

Ultimately, transactive memory functions best when mental models are:

- Accurate in their representations of expertise,
- Shared across group members, and
- Validated – that is, group members' actions meet members' expectations about their areas of expertise and responsibility.

When all these factors are high, the group has an effective or convergent transactive memory system. One concept that may seem notably absent in our figure is team performance.

Although the presence of a transactive memory has been positively linked with team performance in previous research, knowledge-sharing errors can sometimes produce positive outcomes. We will discuss the complex relations between knowledge-sharing errors and performance at the end of the chapter.

DIMENSIONS OF TRANSACTIVE MEMORY ERRORS

The conceptual framework we propose for understanding errors is adapted from Brandon and Hollingshead's dimensions of transactive memory effectiveness.

Transactive memory systems can vary in terms of accuracy, sharedness, and validation Transactive memory systems will be most effective when knowledge assignments are based on group members' actual abilities, when all group members have similar representations of the system, and when members fulfill expectations. It is important to note that each of these dimensions should be thought of as a continuum rather than a dichotomy.

ACCURACY ERRORS

Effectiveness of transactive memory depends on the extent to which group members recognize one another's expertise accurately. Inaccurate recognition of expertise directly affects the expertise–person relations in the TEP unit. Accuracy errors occur when members are unaware of one another's expertise or inaccurate in their judgments of expertise. Actual expertise can be different from people's stereotypes about relative knowledge based on diffuse characteristics such as gender, race, or age and communication Behaviour such as talkativeness and frequency of speech.

Inconsistency between actual and inferred expertise can result in:

- Unexpected ignorance of a group member who was initially assumed to be an expert but turned out to be a non-expert or
- Uunexpected expertise which can be discovered later in a member who was not perceived as an expert initially.

Changes in team environment, such as instability of membership and task structures, can increase the likelihood of accuracy errors.

Sources of Accuracy Errors

When a team meets for the first time, it is challenging for group members to identify one another's knowledge, skills, and abilities accurately without direct experience on which to base their judgments. Therefore, people often rely on various signals to form perceptions of expertise. Those signals include diffuse characteristics such as gender, race, and age. Diffuse characteristics often carry social status and are associated with beliefs that a high status person is expected to be more competent than a low status person even when there is no evidence to support the expectation. Some social stereotypes include expectations about domains of expertise. For instance, female members are expected to be more knowledgeable about cooking than male members, and Asian members are assumed to be better at math than white American members.

The effects of diffuse characteristics tend to be smaller for groups that have longer tenure and equal distribution of power. Communication behaviors can also serve as indicators of expertise. Speaking forcefully without hesitation, a greater frequency and longer duration of talking, and a high proportion of group participation are positively associated with perceptions of expertise. However, such communication Behaviour may not be closely related with true expertise. For example, individual members with expertise may hesitate to participate and display a lack of assertiveness when speaking with a higher status person. This may be especially true in vertical cultures, which value hierarchy. Many Asian cultures value modesty, and may view explicitly communicating one's competence as egregious self-promotion. In certain situations, experts may not want to let their expertise be known to their group – to avoid additional work assignments, for example. Self-censorship may further exacerbate knowledge-sharing problems. Another way that communication can influence accuracy errors is through third parties. Valued colleagues and friends often provide opinions, experiences, and insights about other people. Sometimes these insights can lead to inaccurate perceptions about relative knowledge.

SHAREDNESS ERRORS

Some degree of sharedness errors – a lack of agreement among members about "who knows what," "who is to remember what," and "who is doing what" – seems an inevitable part of transactive memory development. Whatever the origin of the error, the consequence for the group in part or whole is reduced efficiency in the allocation and retrieval of information, often with subsequent impacts on group processes and outcomes. Sharedness errors fall into one of three categories: omission, redundancy, and expediency. Failure to complete tasks due to group members assuming that others are doing the work is an example of an omission error. Such errors arise when the "person" component of a TEP unit is faulty – *i.e.*, there is failure to connect notions of task and expertise notions to a specific group member.

Two related categories of errors, each involving self-assignment into TEP units, are redundancy and expediency. Redundancy errors involve group member repeating tasks already completed by another group member. Redundancy errors can result when there are multiple members who have expertise in the same area, and failure to clarify the "person" component of the TEP unit leads to duplicated work. In expediency errors, group members take on tasks, regardless of their level of expertise, out of perceived urgency to complete the work. Shared micro- and macro-organization of TEP units are critical to the development of an effective transactive memory system. The notion of similarity in memory organization is common across transactive memory research, although under a variety of terms such as "shared representations," "shared mental models," or "convergent expectations". While variation in mental models across group members is expected for newly formed groups, over time those differences can be reduced via group interaction. In terms of measurement, mental model sharedness will range along a continuum described by completely idiosyncratic to completely shared.

Sources of Sharedness Errors

Few if any groups will tread an idealized path to completely shared mental models and, subsequently, a convergent transactive memory system; all groups will tread in the waters of idiosyncrasy for at least some time. New groups, particularly where tasks are unfamiliar and members are not acquainted, are likely to have low sharedness. Mental models will be transferred more quickly when newcomers are already familiar with their new group and demonstrate adaptability and commitment to the group, and when old-timers socialize newcomers via direct and indirect feedback. Regarding group factors most likely to influence sharedness, the quality and frequency of communication is likely the most critical element. Transactive memory research has already indicated the importance of communication- related variables on transactive memory, such as communication channels and interpersonal training. In general, low levels of communication and feedback from other group members can prevent individual members from generating or revising TEP units.

VALIDATION ERRORS

Validation errors occur when group members fail to take responsibility for actions in their perceived areas of expertise and, as a result, fail to participate in the transactive memory system. Examples include a group member not providing an answer to a question, or failing to execute a task in an area of perceived expertise. Validation errors can sometimes be made unintentionally. For instance, group members interacting electronically may fail to contribute because of an undetected technological glitch in the network. A single validation error is not likely to completely invalidate the transactive memory system.

For instance, when a group member fails to contribute on one occasion, others may attribute that failure to factors outside the control of the group member and thus continue to perceive the group member as the relative expert if there are high levels of trust in the group. Complete invalidation of the system would occur when all group members fail to take responsibility on every occasion that they are asked questions on their perceived expertise or are required to execute a task in their area of expertise.

Sources of Validation Errors

Validation errors arise from many sources that can be grouped into two broad categories – motivational and contextual sources. Group members may not be motivated to contribute to a team because they place a low priority on their team membership, because they do not receive any incentives for contributing to that team, or because other members are not contributing or have not in the past. There are also features of the work, communication, and team context that can lead to validation errors.

For example, team members may fail to take responsibility because they are experiencing work overload. This is most likely to occur when work responsibilities are unevenly divided in the group. Work overload can result from attending to one's own work, or from backing-up an overloaded co-worker. Validation errors can be caused by problems imposed by the communication environment: failures in the communication network, misinterpretations of group members' messages due to the lack of richness offered by electronic communication, or time zone differences. Members may not contribute because of status differences among members of the group, and the evaluation apprehension that can accompany it. It is important to note that inaccurate attributions about why a member is not contributing can exacerbate validation errors. For example, a team member may attribute the consistently delayed responses of a member in another time zone to personal characteristics rather than to the situation. This, in turn, can lead to resentment and a negative group climate.

OTHER PRECURSORS OF KNOWLEDGE-SHARING ERRORS

Knowledge-sharing errors can also stem from characteristics of the task, team, or team members as well as from the team's external environment.

TASK VOLATILITY

Tasks can change over time either because they are not well structured at the onset or because of changes in the task specifications by the client or customer. The performance benefits of a transactive memory system can materialize only if there is a match between task knowledge available within the team and the requirements of the task. In addition, some tasks, such as disaster relief work, are by nature volatile. The impromptu teams that respond to such events are also likely to experience transactive memory errors of sharedness and validation, as the expertise required by the task may not be available, and members may lack the time to develop a shared understanding of the task and the expertise required; even when the expertise is known and available, team members may lack resources to take action based on their expertise.

MEMBERSHIP CHANGE

Many organizational groups experience dynamic membership changes due to turnover, transfers, and change of organizational roles. While a newcomer's novel areas of expertise could potentially contribute new knowledge to the transactive memory system, such membership changes can sometimes have a negative effect on group performance, at least in the short run. When newcomers join a group, they often fill predetermined roles by adapting their specialization to preserve the stability of the original group structure. Without deliberate examination of the newcomer's area of expertise, the emphasis on the maintenance of the old structure may override the need to assimilate the newcomer's expertise into the system.

GROUP SIZE AND WORK ALLOCATIONS

There is much evidence that large groups may be more likely to suffer from knowledge-sharing errors than small groups. A review of the literature on the effects of group size by Moreland, Levine, and Wingert indicates that large groups experience more coordination problems, including confusion about task assignments, miscommunication, and scheduling difficulties. They are more likely to have motivational problems with social loafing, free-riding, and efforts to avoid exploitation. Cooperation is less likely in large groups, and negative behaviors such as stealing, cheating, and not helping people in need are more likely.

Members in large groups tend to participate less, and are less satisfied with their group. Of course, these are just generalizations, and there are many exceptions. All of these factors can contribute to the likelihood of accuracy, sharedness, and/or validation errors.

Lack of Teamwork Skills

There is much evidence that large groups may be more likely to suffer from knowledge-sharing errors than small groups. A review of the literature on the effects of group size by Moreland, Levine, and Wingert indicates that large groups experience more coordination problems, including confusion about task assignments, miscommunication, and scheduling difficulties. They are more likely to have motivational problems with social loafing, free-riding, and efforts to avoid exploitation. Cooperation is less likely in large groups, and negative behaviors such as stealing, cheating, and not helping people in need are more likely. Members in large groups tend to participate less, and are less satisfied with their group. Of course, these are just generalizations, and there are many exceptions. All of these factors can contribute to the likelihood of accuracy, sharedness, and/or validation errors.

Lack of Teamwork Skills

Group climate can influence the frequency and severity of knowledge-sharing errors. Acute stress in the group has been positively associated with breakdowns in the transactive memory system. High levels of relationship conflict negatively influence the relation between group agreement on where the expertise is located in the team, and performance. Thus, even in situations of high sharedness, relationship conflict can increase the incidence of validation errors. Group members can refuse to participate in the transactive memory system by intentionally withholding their knowledge. Further, a competitive climate may lead to knowledge hoarding in that group members only complete their part of the task but do not verbalize their expertise while doing so. Nor do they answer questions related to their expertise once their part of the work is complete.

OUTCOMES OF ERRORS

In the previous sections, we have argued that accuracy, sharedness, and validation errors present unique obstacles to reaching convergence of transactive memory in groups. In this section, we discuss consequences of these errors at the individual, group, and organizational levels, and how the errors affect transactive memory development and group outcomes. Many empirical research findings on the positive relations between transactive memory systems and group performance imply that transactive memory errors would negatively affect the quality of performance at the group level.

Our previous discussion on the three dimensions of transactive memory errors specify the mechanisms through which those errors can negatively affect group performance:

- Accuracy errors create ambiguity about the content, reliability, and depth of group members' expertise and reduce use of available knowledge resources
- Sharedness errors increase coordination costs, omission, and redundancy of some tasks; and
- Validation errors lead to the lack of group members' participation in the memory system.

Each type of error is likely to lead to performance losses. At the individual level, group members may experience negative emotions and interpersonal conflicts due to transactive memory errors. When group members find that their expertise was not accurately assessed by fellow members, they may feel that their expertise and contributions are unnoticed, devalued, and minimized, which in turn lowers their level of trust Towards other members and satisfaction about their group processes. Also, when there is no agreement on who knows what and who is responsible for what, group members may experience role conflicts, and much time may be spent trying to reach consensus about subtask assignments. These coordination problems may negatively affect the group members' perceptions about their group effectiveness.

Transactive memory errors may also lead to both performance and financial loss at the organizational level. Validation errors in particular are directly related to and reflective of knowledge management processes in organizations. The lack of participation in maintaining and contributing to a knowledge repository costs organizations a loss of time, effort, and money.

When organizational members foresee the transactive memory system failing in the future, they may be more likely to pursue working alone as opposed to actively participating in sharing knowledge. While the consequences we have addressed so far are pessimistic, transactive memory errors may not always lead to catastrophic outcomes in the long term. When we consider that transactive memory systems constantly change over time until the system approaches full convergence, errors are a natural part of the process of constantly updating the system. For instance, there may be unexpected gains when a new expert is discovered in a group and that expert can contribute to the group task in a more meaningful way. By aligning the new expert's roles more accurately with the person's expertise, the group is better able to update the TEP units, redefine member roles, and get closer to the fully converged transactive memory system.

The dynamic nature of transactive memory systems is important when considering changes in group membership, member learning, task types, and structures over time. Positive outcomes from knowledge-sharing errors can occur, but may not be common. Because of such changes, an error at one point may not be an error at a different point. For instance, when a group member is incorrectly assessed as an expert in computer programming at an early stage, it would be an incidence of accuracy error. However, that member, who was initially not an expert in computer programming, is likely to acquire knowledge and become an expert over time as task experience accumulates. Similarly, while membership changes increase the likelihood of accuracy and sharedness errors, having a new member in some cases may help the entire group reassess relative expertise of all group members and reconfigure areas of responsibilities. When errors go undetected and the transactive memory system is not updated by the group, errors may be harmful to group process, group performance, or the individual members who are trying to repair the damage done by those errors.

ERROR PREVENTION

As mentioned earlier, transactive memory systems are unlikely to develop unless members perceive that they are interdependent with other members in the group. This motivates members to attend to other members' knowledge and abilities, and to participate in the system. The team leader and team members must do their part to make everyone feel that they are valuable, everyone's contributions matter, they can rely on others for information and assistance, and they are accountable to others for their actions. Team-based rewards can also help create feelings of cognitive interdependence among group members. The likelihood of using transactive memory errors to change and update the system may be higher when group members are vigilant in identifying potential sources of errors.

This is likely to be easier to do when there is frequent task-related communication and interpersonal trust among members. Training members in groups and cross-training in different jobs gives group members an opportunity to learn about others' knowledge, abilities, and job requirements. Previous research has considered two interrelated factors to improve accuracy of transactive memory: time and communication. Team tenure seems to be positively related to minimizing the errors, because time allows extensive social relationships, socialization processes, mutual learning, and continuous observation of each other's performance. Communication facilitates familiarity with group members and their expertise over time. Although communication in general is critical to mitigate accuracy errors, group members are not always diligent or motivated to communicate their expertise or learn others' expertise, especially in autonomous and short-term groups.

Therefore, specific communication procedures that facilitate the expertise recognition will likely reduce accuracy errors. Self-disclosure and feedback in the early stage of group development can facilitate group learning, through which group members introduce themselves and explicitly exchange their areas of expertise to better align their roles to their expertise. This process can be even more beneficial for heterogeneous groups because early verifications of each member's unique characteristics may help the group to better leverage them, especially when they reflect unexpected expertise. In situations where errors can have grave impacts, such as air traffic control, team familiarity and experience are especially important, as they increase the likelihood that members will request and accept back-up when needed.

CONCLUSION AND CONNECTIONS

We conclude by reorganizing our framework of knowledge-sharing errors to fit the 7C model. Consistent with some other chapters in this book, the norm of reciprocity is the "cause" or mechanism that leads to the development of transactive memory. Team-based rewards, divisible tasks, close relationships, and a cooperative group climate are conditions of a supportive climate that gives rise to perceived cognitive interdependence, the condition necessary to jumpstart the transactive processes of evaluating members' knowledge and capabilities, delegating knowledge responsibilities, and information processing, which involve learning, storing, and sharing knowledge. The subprocesses of creating, testing, and revising TEP units and of individual and shared mental model development influence how members evaluate other members' knowledge, delegate knowledge responsibilities, and process information.

Member knowledge, motivation skills, and abilities are important to measure and control as covariances, as these aspects of group composition naturally have a strong and significant impact on the fidelity of the transactive memory system. Contingencies such as task and membership change, group size, group diversity, and acute stress can lead to consequences such as knowledge-sharing errors, which in the short term may have a negative impact on individual and team performance. In the long term, these knowledge-sharing errors may lead to improved performance under some conditions. Knowledge-sharing errors are a natural and unavoidable process as team members learn and adjust to one another's capabilities. Managers, team leaders, and team members themselves can reduce the negative impacts of these errors by creating conditions that facilitate effective knowledge sharing, and through vigilance. However, these steps alone do not guarantee that knowledge-sharing errors will be corrected, let alone detected What leads some teams to learn from their mistakes, and others to continue down the same ill-advised path? Future research should address this important issue.

MANAGING COMMUNITY RISKS THROUGH A COMMUNITY-COMMUNICATION INFRASTRUCTURE APPROACH

The risk communication literature offers a number of commonly held assumptions about individuals' perceptions of risk, their processing of risk messages, and likely responses to communication strategies. Not all of these assumptions have been empirically tested, especially in the context of community risk-management activities, although new advances in communication sciences are beginning to be integrated into systematic research Progrmmes designed for community-communication risk-management initiatives. A select sampling from that body of research includes: knowledge management, cultural factors, community dynamics, decision-making styles, relationship building resilience, inclusion/exclusion, information flow directions, collaborative process, media preferences, informal networking, and threat mitigators.

These initiatives, when integrated with knowledge management strategies, will create a more in-depth understanding of how local communities deal with information and communication in the context of risks and crises. A keystone to the management of risks and disasters is an understanding that these events occur at the local or community level. This chapter focuses on community risk communication by leveraging insights from these areas of research and applying them within a local community knowledge management perspective. Specifically, a community-communication infrastructure approach will take center stage as a means for increasing community resilience against a backdrop of continuing and emerging community vulnerabilities.

A community-communication infrastructure is the process of placing attention on a diverse body of stakeholders who are encouraged to participate in the sharing of ideas regarding risks and threats in their communities. Collaboration is established when multiple layers of scientists, practitioners, and the public manage knowledge at levels that are accessible to most of those concerned. Within this context, communication processes can create awareness, educate, and coordinate and evaluate efforts Towards managing community knowledge about risks. This chapter isolates knowledge processes involved in preparing the public, media, and risk managers for risks and threats associated with emergencies and disasters in support of a community-based risk communication infrastructure model.

We believe that a community-communication infrastructure approach stands above other ideas for conceptualizing and operationalizing risk and crisis communication in local communities. Because communities are unique and their members and organizations respond differently to communication stratagems, a model or framework such as the one proposed here assimilates the diverse knowledge bases of a community's unique profile, and recommends appropriate policies and plans. This approach is compatible with those that emphasize a synergy of different knowledge management perspectives, as advocated by Murphy and Eisenberg in Chapter 15 of this volume.

ORGANIZATIONAL KNOWLEDGE AND COMMUNITY RISKS

As a means of positioning our arguments we engage the 7C model, where knowledge in risk communities can be seen within a causal process. Figure 13.1 provides an explanation of this method where process assumes a central position, and contexts provide a backdrop for the problem under study. The causes within the framework specify challenges of the current system, and consequences serve to identify outcomes from knowledge management processes. To begin, by specifying community as a context for research, we aim to heighten awareness on organizational knowledge issues that contribute to community-communication infrastructure building. In marked contrast to other paradigms of research, a community science approach includes staples of inquiry that presume a multi-layered framework from which to study. Communities must be studied in their environment, encumbered with their own peculiarities that emanate from the social, cultural, political, and geographical influences in which they live. The set of circumstances or facts that surround a particular event matters, so a sub- stantial challenge for community research is finding an appropriate mechanism for examining community problems where theory and methods are applied within the context of the community framework. Preparedness is often linked to levels of community motivation, and research findings have offered glum reports regarding the low priority placed on a community-centered approach directed Towards risk management. Communities are often characterized as socio-political entities composed of multiple semi-autonomous organizations competing for scarce resources. Portraying communities in this manner signifies processes of conflict rather than consensus, and the products of these practices marginalize opportunities for resilience.

Depicting communities as compositions of self-interested networks and organizations paints a bleak picture for developing knowledge management Progrmmes that are effective and lasting. Community-communication infrastructure capacity building creates space for considerations of resource dependency issues, turf battles, and disincentives for collaborative action. It is within this infrastructure that knowledge interpretation about risk policies can transpire. Media accounts of communities failing to protect residents are commonplace, and point to complexities inherent in identifying and managing risks. An additional issue to be considered is that communities are complex systems with multiple levels of analysis begging to be measured, compared, and triangulated for generating "big picture" explanations. A systems approach to analysis involves collecting data at individual, neighborhood, organizational, network, and community levels. We are invoking "conditions" in specifying how context is better understood. Explanations for community phenomena are often elusive when investigators focus only on a certain level that is inextricably nested within other levels. Take the example of tornado warning research that seeks to understand sheltering Behaviour based only on survey responses from community members.

Unknown to investigators are community norms for sheltering based on previous experiences, community warning systems, protocols, and the influence of media on community-based practices in severe weather contexts. An important consideration, then, is developing and implementing evidence-based solutions or practices within the community. In knowledge ecologies such as communities, a primary goal of research is finding mechanisms for translating research findings into practical guidelines for problem management. Communities and their stakeholder-practitioners are not empty vessels simply waiting for researchers to pour knowledge into their vacuous holding tanks. Trust and credibility play large roles in making the knowledge transition a less arduous process. Ensuring that knowledge transfers are unpacked for public consumption, and are evidence-based, are key steps that involve the collaboration of scientists, practitioners, and community members. A second condition of the context involves community risk perceptions, the social-cultural context, and knowledge networks. Despite ongoing debates, recognition of the social and cultural dimensions of communication is now a part of the knowledge processes in communities, government, and industry. Decades of research suggests that anxieties, fears, and responses are based upon factors other than "objective" risk itself. For example, Dake and Wildavsky's study of individual differences in community risk perception and risk-taking preferences found that risk perceptions have little to do with knowledge, are modestly related to personality, and are more strongly related to political orientation and cultural biases than objective risk perception.

These overviews are built on economic conceptualizations of risk that distinguish uncertainty from risk, and argue that risk is an ordered application of knowledge to the unknown. From a different perceptive, anthropologist Douglas and her associates highlight the different ways of approaching risk that are culturally defined; risk perceptions are developed through the filter of shared expectations and conventions. Making sense and making decisions are issues of culture, and culture is a principle contributor to the risk community-communication process. The perspective that emerges from this work is one in which risk issues are embedded in a "tangle" of perceptions, associations, and, sometimes, unrelated agendas. In order to make sense of such issues, people draw on shared interpretive resources.

The risk communication process is talked into existence interactively, in ways that reflect and re-form political agendas, cultural agendas, values, and power relations. In the wake of multiple disasters in the past five years, most people assume they live in an uncertain, if not risky, environment. This phenomenon has created multiple models that integrate individual risk forecasting, information management processes, and media access and demonstrated that people cope by blocking information from their awareness and strive for a "new normalcy". Knowledge networks expand and contract during risk information seeking and play key roles in risk management processes, including access, veracity, and usability. For instance, when risk probability is low, risk messages are unlikely to resonate with individuals who will have little motivation to seek or process information from media sources.

When risk probability is heightened, individuals become curious, process risk messages more directly, and may seek additional information from the government and media. As the threat of risk becomes more salient, individuals become more immediate in their desire for information and will intensify their media exposure. When threat seems imminent, the process of information seeking becomes acute and media access becomes vigorous, if not frantic Thus, a challenge to any risk communication process is to understand information that leads a knowledge network to more accurate cognitions and risk perceptions, and then to protective actions. These perceptions are not shaped only by the objective state of risk, but also by social, cultural, and political factors.

CHALLENGES OF PRESUMED COMMUNICATION STRUCTURES

Community preparedness officials are expected to perform their responsibilities in accordance with federal mandates such as the National Incident Response System in the United States. NIMS is based on the classic Incident Control System, drawing heavily from the centralized and hierarchical concept of "command and control." NIMS and the command and control structure hail from a military background that is often inappropriate for those community organizations that operate in a much less hierarchical and scalar fashion in which flexibility, collaboration, and open communication are expected. Moreover, because a typical response to an adverse event evokes a "panic" frame of mind centralization of authority and responsibility ensue, confirming that citizen participation is curtailed and services at the local level are usurped. This is unfortunate, since research has demonstrated that more effective response efforts result from localized units who are most familiar with the community. Glaser's framework component, cause, becomes operational in this regard.

Due to statutory requirements and years of normative Behaviour, many researchers challenge the notion of a top-down command and control approach to disasters. A notable exception to this assertion is the 9/11 Commission Report suggesting that this type of approach operated somewhat effectively at the Pentagon on that fateful day primarily due to the Incident Command System that overcame difficulties in coordinating the response efforts of local, state, and federal agencies. Beyond that example, most reports by government and independent organizations have taken issue with the command and control paradigm that pervades many response agencies, FEMA being the most visible. As a result, the top-down approach to disaster prevention, preparation, response, and mitigation faces a number of challenges that are becoming more salient each year. First, the public has expressed its concern with the ineffectiveness of command and control approaches that lack competent inter-organizational communication. This scrutiny reached a fever pitch in the United States following Hurricane Katrina. Second, media coverage and editorializing before, during, and after disasters will only become more prominent. Response organizations must engage in strategic relationship management with the media prior to disasters to develop the collaborative working relationships necessary during these catastrophic events.

The command and control approach offers less of a chance of making that type of partnership work. Third, information and communication management will become more complex as advances in technology outstrip human capacity to assimilate information. Information overload is difficult to manage from a command and control perspective. Thus, there are challenges in the way the federal government is organized for dealing with disasters. The US Government Accountability Office has issued numerous reports recommending approaches that are more localized and efficient. Although perhaps living up to the parameters for which they were originally institutionalized in the 1950s, command and control structures are no longer meeting the preparedness, response, and recovery expectations a half century later, thereby inhibiting information exchange. It is not so much that the command and control system should be entirely supplanted by new and unproven initiatives.

The command and control system, in fact, has evidenced a noteworthy record of rapidly moving federal financial resources, human resources, and materiel in emergencies in ways that remain pertinent. Governmental entities need to continue command and control activities within a more complete system of organizational knowledge. This means that in addition to a constant iterative improvement of the command and control function, the larger resilience system enables all levels of society to prepare, respond, relieve, recover, and mitigate in a massively parallel and flexible manner that cannot be accomplished by federally directed top-down command and control systems. Following Ronan and Johnston, we must think more in terms of an integrated risk-crisis environment – one that recognizes and leverages local organizational knowledge assets not as unwieldy and independent phenomena, but as sources for potential interdependency. Such interdependency has the best chance of succeeding when multi-organizational response networks are recognized and legitimized through collaborating processes.

COLLABORATION PROCESSES AND BOUNDARY SPANNING

Collaboration is a process through which autonomous stakeholders can constructively explore mutual benefits, interdependence, reciprocity, concerted action, and joint production. Research has shown that the collaborative process gathers professionals from organizations that differentiate responsibilities and their orientations Towards the problem. It promotes diversity in stakeholders, and embraces the natural complexities that produce a more comprehensive outcome. The process brings forth goals, values, and priorities that articulate the overall purpose of the alliance, and begins to identify knowledge resources necessary to manage a risk. All too often, however, collaboration efforts fall short, resulting in inefficient or even disastrous results.

The tsunami disaster and Hurricane Katrina are noteworthy illustrations of the failure of risk networks to operate conjointly. The developmental phases for establishing inter-organizational collaboration move from selecting key stakeholders, to committing to work together, to attending to the problem domain, to finally managing implementations of ideas and recommended proposals. Flexibility, adaptability, and ongoing information sharing are key aspects of collaboration. A process of sustained and systematic communication strategies are enacted by relationship partners seeing themselves through collective identities where they share ownership for their relationships and the resultant knowledge structures. Collaborative networks also evolve through the structures and relationships among organizations in communities.

These networks are often structured based on statutory requirements at the federal, state, and/or local levels. In many other instances, inter-organizational networks emerge as semi-formal configurations due to common interests in risk awareness and communication issues. For example, most disasters bring together scientists, public officials, policy analysts, and practitioners as members of risk analysis networks. Risk messages exchanged among these constituents create a communication network essential to the community infrastructure. The interdependency of their relationships is important to understand. Scientists depend on policy-makers to facilitate their work and promote their results among practitioners. Practitioners and scientists depend on public officials to fund their risk communication initiatives. Collaboration among these diverse audiences requires constant interaction between scientists, managers, and other stakeholders that improves the policy-making process and builds robust consensus.

When collaboration processes are championed and embraced by community stakeholders, multiple benefits are often observed:

- effectiveness gains;
- efficiency gains;
- resource gains;
- capacity gains;
- legitimacy gains;
- social development benefits.

Boundary spanning is a process that is highly related to collaboration, and is viewed as the coordination of experiences, values, context information, expert insight, and the actions of two or more independent organizations. Learning organization literature offers a plentiful stream of studies related to boundary spanning, with many having a focus on knowledge management. General conclusions drawn from this research indicate that boundary spanning includes working together with organizations, coordinating activities, and mobilizing resources in the community. Knowledge networks often have the responsibility to formally or informally establish and maintain communication patterns across organizations.

Not only do individual participants belong to multiple communities of practice; "their multiple memberships provide a mediating mechanism that permits the spanning of boundaries between these communities". At this level, boundary-spanning information systems integrate information-flow and coordinate work across "islands" of knowledge. The creation of shared knowledge is feasible when organizations share and improvise local practices through membership in the same workgroup. By belonging to a community of organizations, mutual engagement in joint enterprise utilizes a shared repertoire of resources. When inter-organizational groups are formed to address community safety, boundary spanning allows for interactions with outside stakeholders, and enables members to effectively deal with ambiguities of external threats. Knowledge is constructed across organizational groups through collaborative processes such as conversation and joint work. Collaboration between organizations exists in part because there is a belief in the power of many versus one in successfully addressing a shared problem among large and/ or diverse organizations. Community partners who participate in boundary spanning require sensitivity to and an understanding of the dynamics of power. In order to remain autonomous yet cope with dependency relationships, partners are mindful of who benefits in the relationship, what the perceived advantages and disadvantages of the relationship are, and what the partners compete for as they collaborate.

ENVIRONMENTAL SCANNING

Community organizations of all types would benefit from inter-organizational communication concepts related to information seeking and coordination. One of the key concepts is environmental scanning. Environmental scanning is the acquisition and use of information about events, trends, and relationships in an organization's internal and external environments. Assessing risks utilizing ES creates uncertainty and the need for change. However, through the search for important cues about how the world is changing, environment scanning helps inter-organizational domains create a risk management framework that will lead knowledge networks Towards a strategic assessment of future events. Dutton and Jackson and Galbraith determined that scanning activity is inherent in the identification of and formation of strategic issues and the analysis of alternative courses of action. The keys to successful scanning are active and open exploration of communities incorporating diverse sources of information and diverse viewpoints. Environmental scanning represents a process where "information seeking is seldom an end in itself, but instead is part of the processes of decision making and problem solving".

The more organizations utilize a systemic approach, the more likely it is that they will avoid blind spots while scanning. Scanning is an opportunity to take an objective look at community needs by:

- Detecting important economic, social, cultural, environmental, health, technological, and political trends, situations, and events;
- Identifying the potential opportunities and threats implied by these trends, situations, and events;
- Gaining an accurate understanding of strengths and limitations; and

- Providing a basis for analysis of future strategies.

This results in preliminary information needed to select priority issues for which specific plans will be developed. Environmental scanning includes both looking at information and looking for information. It is through environmental scanning that organizations, and thus communities, can better plan and prepare for potential crises. Environmental scanning offers the opportunity for a more formal system of information collection and appraisal, and provides community members the mechanism to devise and implement a strategically designed risk management plan. Several studies have reported the positive influence of ES on performance. The most significant influencing factors are shared vision, strategic planning, and management process, which encourage people to regularly participate in face-to- face discussions on planning issues that could be used proactively to cope with external change. Collaboration processes, boundary spanning, and environmental scanning constitute mechanisms that encourage organizational knowledge. These can readily be seen as "processes" within the 7C framework. Channels are means of understanding these efforts, and are taken up in the following section.

RISK COMMUNICATION CHANNELS

Risk communication systems, knowledge networks, organizational structures, and channels and technology serve what Pigg refers to as community information infrastructure – places and opportunities to access and exchange risk information in all formats. Community members have a wide variety of risk message sources to choose from, including broadcast radio and television, cellular, print, Internet, and ham radios. Accordingly, our focus herein is on the most salient channels that enhance community information processes and theories that explain channel use with a specific emphasis on risk knowledge development and management. Our purpose is not exclusively on technological channels, but on identifying processes that develop pathways for knowledge management and collaboration and the support of communication infrastructure. Diffusion of information research, a theoretical offshoot of Rogers' diffusion of innovation theory has examined how and when people have learned of major events, from the Kennedy assassination to the September 11 attacks.

This research indicates that interpersonal communication plays a larger role when the event is more significant. For any given event, when and how people get the news depends largely on where they are at the time of the event. For example, during the Tylenol poisonings in 1984, Carrocci found that 70 percent of respondents learned the news through radio or television, but more than 70 percent reported telling others – a higher percentage than typically found in other diffusion studies. They mainly told family and close friends. Respondents also reported seeking out additional information from the news media, a process explained by media dependency theory. Media dependency theory holds that people in modern societies increasingly rely on mass rather than interpersonal communication for information, that this reliance intensifies in times of crisis or uncertainty, and that those who are more dependent on the media will be more likely to be influenced by it. Hindman and Coyle found increased dependency on the radio after flooding in Grand Forks, North Dakota, and dependency was linked to volunteer mobilization. Lowery found Memphis residents who were more threatened by the September 11, 2001 attacks reported greater media dependency in the months after the attacks – but threat also was positively related to reliance on interpersonal communication. Group or community identification can moderate the effects of dependency on attitudes. These processes highlight the essential nature of knowledge transfer at informal levels within local communities.

The interplay and perhaps inherent nature of interpersonal communication and media use point to the need for additional research in this area. Online communities are an increasingly common channel of risk and crisis communication. Online communities cross geographic lines and offer additional activities that are critical for both risk and crisis communication plans. For instance, online communities serve to create awareness for community vulnerabilities and potential risks within the community, they contribute to the platform of ideas during debates over community values, and they create "gathering spaces" for community members as they sort through a host of issues attached to the emotional conditions of crises.

Online community forums dedicated to risks and crises come in a variety of forms. Some are specifically dedicated to certain types of disasters, such as Scipionus which provides hurricane maps or are communities devoted to diseases. Participation in online forums is presumed to enhance the responsiveness of communities in the face of risks and crises. A bold initiative was advanced by Scheiderman and Preece for an online community concept called a "community response grid". Based on popular social network computing platforms such as Facebook and MySpace, community response grids would integrate multiple channels and media for linking and informing members of breaking news and up-to- date information about risks, and provide space for discussions over community issues.

Designed to be both synchronous and asynchronous, CRGs offer optimal flexibility for community members' needs, and would coordinate with public and private organizations who serve as members of the risk community. Many of the challenges in making CRGs truly functional, reliable, and, perhaps most importantly, attractive involve costs. In an increasingly congested electronic environment with many options, CRGs and similar online community risk forums must compete for the attention of a cognitively loaded target. Investments of this size, estimated in the millions of dollars per community, pose formidable challenges for champions of these communication challenges.

However, done properly, the communication opportunities afforded from a CRG are virtually limitless, bringing together the advantages of interpersonal ties, network ties, and media dependence to effectively reach dispersed and diverse audiences. More research is required regarding how the Internet can be combined with traditional media for delivering a more effective campaign. The next section takes the notion of community information structures a step further, with a discussion of community-communication infrastructures.

COMMUNITY-COMMUNICATION INFRASTRUCTURE AND RESILIENCE

We do not take lightly the task of employing a community-based approach to risk and crisis communication. Larger perspectives such as communication infrastructures should be embraced for understanding communities as meta-systems whose component systems have become complex, autonomous, and tentative for securing interdependence as a community goal. Kim and Ball-Rokeach characterized communication infrastructure as a system of storytelling, particularly among urban residents, that is a means for understanding and supporting community resilience. Situated in a communication action context, this framework focuses on civic engagement as a mechanism for developing a sense of collective efficacy and participation within the community. Heath and colleagues have taken a different perspective on defining communication infrastructure where attention is placed on a diverse body of stakeholders who are encouraged to participate in the community of ideas regarding risks and threats in their communities. "Zones of meaning" are created when multiple layers of scientists, practitioners, and the public manage knowledge at levels that are accessible to most of those concerned.

Although not characterized specifically as infrastructure, the Center for Disease Control and Prevention has developed a framework for their emergency communications system that resembles what others might characterize as infrastructure. Included within their communication system are stakeholders such as clinicians, veterinarians, the media, academia, health educators, businesses, and the transportation industry, as well as processes of a communication nature – for instance, the management of hotlines, press briefings, health alerts, and Web-based content. Our own conceptualization of community-communication infrastructure borrows from previous ideas, synthesizes available research on communities, and offers new prospects for how communities can leverage important resources in order to maximize resilience.

The risk environment of today requires multiple intersections among disciplines, and opportunities must be created to engage research from related fields in focusing on common community risk challenges. Multidisciplinary research initiatives offer the potential to address social problems that extend beyond the capacity and resources of single-investigator projects. This is accomplished through infrastructure support and participation among multiple stakeholders. Knowledge accurately acquired, developed, communicated, and managed within communities with the proper stakeholders through the most appropriate and effective channels offers the promise of a more clear and supportive community-communication infrastructure, an approach to the current web-like knowledge network of community stakeholders as seen in Figure 13.2, allowing for community risks to be more adequately and efficiently managed. Residents of communities have come to expect that adequate risk management systems are in place to protect them from adverse events, and citizen discontent is certain when prevention, response and recovery mechanisms fail to achieve their touted goals. In order to effectively and efficiently manage risks, a community communication infrastructure approach creates opportunities for information sharing and knowledge transfer.

If a community has put in place communication, social, and institutional infrastructures, response time and crisis recovery should be positively affected. Increasing community involvement and participation in risk management spawns positive civic and social effects often referred to as resilience. Resilience is a community infrastructure notion, advanced by Grotberg, that refers to the thoughts, feelings, and even the spirit of individuals Towards their community and its members.

- It is perceived as an ideal state where communities and members possess an optimistic, pliable, and hardy perspective Towards both normal and crisis conditions. Resilience is a community's level of sustainability despite the presence of risk factors. Resilient communities are those that enjoy strong relationships within and outside the family, understand the need for vibrant community services, and are energetic in developing a community climate that is compassionate, empathic, respectful, and communicative.

Resilient communities are known to exhibit four common characteristics: collective self-esteem, cultural identity, social humor, and collective honesty. It is through resilient acts that communities and their members construct strategies that productively approach risk and uncertainty. One of the centerpieces of understanding and building community infrastructure is enhancing community resilience.

Determining community resilience levels is an essential process in developing an understanding of how members of the risk analysis network communicate with their communities. Returning to the 7C model, resilience serves as a "consequence" of the knowledge flow process. Risk communication, trust, and community involvement are not new phenomena; previously, a National Research Council committee recommended that deliberative and participative community processes should be engaged to inform public policy choices. The committee argued that these processes lead to a more informed public and more support for decisions. Project Impact, established in 1997 by FEMA, was meant to actively engage communities in the process of disaster resistance. Research from Project Impact discovered that communities were better able to secure resources from support organizations, and were better positioned to understand their community's relative risk and plan for managing these risks. In essence, these communities became more resilient from building community infrastructure. Several subsequent studies have verified the positive effect of community involvement during risk policy decision-making in a variety of contexts.

Even community members who do not directly participate in the planning and deliberating process have more positive views of the policy decision, based on their perception that the process was fair and inclusive of community members' viewpoints. In sum, public meetings that genuinely involve citizens in dialogue and stress the importance of interactive exchange have greater chances of success. These types of meetings not only increase perceptions of participation, but also build relationships important in the trust and credibility areas. A community-based approach to managing risks and promoting resilience allows community members to address the ripple effect that follows a crisis. Initially, a community must deal with the physical/structural damage, such as buildings, streets, and homes.

Depending on the structural issues, public health may be jeopardized as hospitals often experience surges in patients and quickly exceed capacity in a crisis. Even after a community has mobilized recovery processes, many citizens may experience psychological ramifications of the crisis, such as anxiety and fear. A community with a strong social network, communication infrastructure, and appropriately coordinated public and private services and institutions can not only recover from a crisis, but also move forward and develop from the experience.

4

Pressure Groups Prick Conscience of the Tourist Industry

Advocacy groups (also known as pressure groups, lobby groups, campaign groups, interest groups, or special interest groups) use various forms of advocacy to influence public opinion and/or policy; they have played and continue to play an important part in the development of political and social systems. Groups vary considerably in size, influence, and motive; some have wide ranging long term social purposes, others are focused and are a response to an immediate issue or concern. Motives for action may be based on a shared political, faith, moral, or commercial position. Groups use varied methods to try to achieve their aims including lobbying, media campaigns, publicity stunts, polls, research, and policy briefings. Some groups are supported by powerful business or political interests and exert considerable influence on the political process, others have few such resources. Some have developed into important social, political institutions or social movements. Some powerful lobby groups have been accused of manipulating the democratic system for narrow commercial gain and in some instances have been found guilty of corruption, fraud, bribery, and other serious crimes; lobbying has become increasingly regulated as a result. Some groups, generally ones with less financial resources, may use direct action and civil disobedience and in some cases are accused of being a threat to the social order or 'domestic extremists'. Research is beginning to explore how advocacy groups use social media to facilitate civic engagement and collective action.

An advocacy group is a group or an organization which tries to influence the government but does not hold power in the government. A single-issue group may form in response to a particular issue area sometimes in response to a single event or threat. In some cases initiatives initially championed by advocacy groups later become institutionalized as important elements of civic life (for example universal education or regulation of doctors — see below for details). Groups representing broad interests of a group may be formed with the purpose of benefiting the group over an expended period of time and in many ways, example as Consumer organizations, Professional associations, Trade associations, and Trade unions.

ACTIVITIES

Advocacy groups exist in a wide variety of genres based upon their most pronounced activities:

- Anti-defamation organizations issue responses or criticisms to real or supposed slights of any sort (including speech or violence) by an individual or group against a specific segment of the population which the organization exists to represent.
- Watchdog groups exist to provide oversight and rating of actions or media by various outlets, both government and corporate. They may also index personalities, organizations, products, and activities in databases to provide coverage and rating of the value or viability of such entities to target demographics.
- Lobby groups Lobby for a change to the law or the maintenance of a particular law and big businesses fund very considerable lobbying influence on legislators, for example in the USA and in the UK where lobbying first developed. Some Lobby groups have considerable financial resources at their disposal. Lobbying is regulated to stop the worst abuses which can develop into corruption. In the United States the Internal Revenue Service makes a clear distinction between lobbying and advocacy.
- Legal Defence funds provide funding for the legal Defence for, or legal action against, individuals or groups related to their specific interests or target demographic. This is often accompanied by one of the above types of advocacy groups filing an Amicus curiae if the cause at stake serves the interests of both the legal Defence fund and the other advocacy groups.

TYPES

Organizations can be categorized along the lines of the three elements of commerce: business owners, workers, and consumers:

- Employers' organizations represent the interests of a group of businesses in the same industry.
- Occupational, or labour organizations promote the professional and economic interests of workers in a particular occupation, industry, or trade, through interaction with the government, and by preparing advertising and other promotional campaigns to the public. Such groups will also provide member services such as career support, training, and organized social activities. These goals are distinct from those of the regulatory body of a self-governing profession, which licenses and supervises its practitioners with the mission of serving the public interest. The advocacy organization does not interact directly with employers in the way a trade union does.

- Consumer organizations exist to protect people from corporate abuse, promote fair business practices, and enforce consumer rights.

INFLUENCE

In most liberal democracies, advocacy groups tend to use the bureaucracy as the main channel of influence – because, in liberal democracies, this is where the decision-making power lies. The aim of pressure groups here is to attempt to influence a member of the legislature to support their cause by voting a certain way in the legislature. Access to this channel is generally restricted to groups with insider status such as large corporations and trade unions – groups with outsider status are unlikely to be able to meet with ministers or other members of the bureaucracy to discuss policy. What must be understood about groups exerting influence in the bureaucracy is; "the crucial relationship here [in the bureaucracy] is usually that between the senior bureaucrats and leading business or industrial interests". This supports the view that groups with greater financial resources at their disposal will generally be better able to influence the decision-making process of government. The advantages that large businesses have is mainly due to the fact that they are key producers within their countries economy and, therefore, their interests are important to the government as their contributions are important to the economy. According to George Monbiot, the influence of big business has been strengthened by "the greater ease with which corporations can relocate production and investment in a global economy". This suggests that in the ever modernising world, big business has an increasing role in influencing the bureaucracy and in turn, the decision-making process of government.

Advocacy groups can also exert influence through the assembly by lobbying. Groups with greater economic resources at their disposal can employ professional lobbyists to try and exert influence in the assembly. An example of such a group is the environmentalist group Greenpeace; Greenpeace (an organisation with income upward of $50,000,000) use lobbying to gain political support for their campaigns. They raise issues about the environment with the aim of having their issues translated into policy such as the government encouraging alternative energy and recycling.

The judicial branch of government can also be used by advocacy groups to exert influence. In states where legislation cannot be challenged by the courts, like the UK, pressure groups are limited in the amount of influence they have. In states that have codified constitutions, like the USA, however, pressure group influence is much more significant. For example – in 1954 the NAACP (National Association for the Advancement of Coloured People) lobbied against the Topeka Board of education, arguing that segregation of education based on race was unconstitutional. As a result of group pressure from the NAACP, the supreme court unanimously ruled that racial segregation in education was indeed unconstitutional and such practices were banned. This is a novel example of how pressure groups can exert influence in the judicial branch of government.

Advocacy groups can also exert influence on political parties. The main way groups do this is through campaign finance. For instance; in the UK, the conservative parties campaigns are often funded by large corporations, as many of the conservative parties campaigns reflect the interests of businesses. For example, George W Bush's re-election campaign in 2004 was the most expensive in American history and was financed mainly by large corporations and industrial interests that the Bush administration represented in government. Conversely, left-wing parties are often funded by organised labour – when the labour party was first formed, it was largely funded by trade unions. Often, political parties are actually formed as a result of group pressure, for example, the Labour Party in the UK was formed out of the new trade-union movement which lobbied for the rights of workers.

Advocacy groups also exert influence through channels that are separate from the government or the political structure such as the mass media and through public opinion campaigning. Pressure groups will use methods such as protesting, petitioning and civil disobedience to attempt to exert influence in Liberal Democracies.

Groups will generally use two distinct styles when attempting to manipulate the media – they will either put across their outsider status and use their inability to access the other channels of influence to gain sympathy or they may put across a more ideological agenda. Traditionally, a prime example of such a group were the trade-unions who were the so-called "industrial" muscle. Trade-unions would campaign in the forms of industrial action and marches for workers rights, these gained much media attention and sympathy for their cause. In the USA, the Civil Rights Campaign gained much of its publicity through civil disobedience; African Americans would simply disobey the racist segregation laws to get the violent, racist reaction from the police and white Americans.

This violence and racism was then broadcast all over the world, showing the world just how one sided the race 'war' in America actually was. As a result of the Civil Rights Campaign, institutionalized racism in the USA has all but been eradicated, up to the point that the USA now has an African American for President.

Advocacy group influence has also manifested itself in supranational bodies that have arisen through globalisation. Groups that already had a global structure such as Greenpeace were better able to adapt to globalisation. Greenpeace, for example, have offices in over 30 countries and has an income of $50 million annually. Groups such as these have secured the nature of their influence by gaining status as nongovernmental organisations (NGOs), many of which oversee the work of the UN and the EU from their permanent offices in America and Europe. Group pressure by supranational industries can be exerted in a number of ways: "through direct lobbying by large corporations, national trade bodies and 'peak' associations such as the European Round Table of Industrialist".

INFLUENTIAL ADVOCACY GROUPS

There are many significant advocacy groups through history, some of which could be considered to operate with different dynamics and could better be described as social movements.

Here are some notable groups operating in different parts of the world:

- American Israel Public Affairs Committee (AIPAC), the American Israel lobby, which is described by the New York Times as the "most influential Lobby impacting US relations with Israel."
- British Medical Association, which formed at a meeting of 50 doctors in 1832 for the sharing of knowledge; its lobbying led to the Medical Act 1858 and the formation of the General Medical Council which has registered and regulated doctors in the UK to this date.
- Campaign for Nuclear Disarmament, which has advocated for the non-proliferation of nuclear weapons and unilateral nuclear disarmament in the UK since 1957, and whose logo is now an international peace symbol.
- Center for Auto Safety, an organization formed in 1970 which aims to give consumers a voice for auto safety and quality in the United States.
- Drug Policy Alliance, whose principal goal is to end the American "War on Drugs".
- Electronic Frontier Foundation, an international non-profit digital rights advocacy and legal organization based in the United States.
- Energy Lobby, an umbrella term for the representatives of large oil, gas, coal, and electric utilities corporations that attempt to influence governmental policy in the United States.
- Financial Services Roundtable, an organization representing the banking lobby.
- Greenpeace, an organization formed in 1970 as the Don't Make a Wave Committee to stop nuclear weapons testing in the United States.
- National Rifle Association, an organization that formed in New York in 1871 to protect the rights of gun-owners.
- Oxfam, an organization formed in 1942 in the UK as the 'Oxford Committee for Famine Relief'.
- Pennsylvania Abolition Society, which formed in Philadelphia in 1775 with a mission to abolish slavery in the United States.
- People for the Ethical Treatment of Animals, an animal rights organization

that focuses primarily on animal treatment on factory farms, in the clothing trade, in laboratories, and in the entertainment industry.

- Royal Society for the Protection of Birds, founded in Manchester in 1889 to campaign against the 'barbarous trade in plumes for women's hats'.
- Sierra Club, which formed in 1892 to help protect the Sierra Nevada.
- Stop the War Coalition, an organization against the War on Terrorism which included a march of between 750,000 and 2,000,000 people in London in 2003.
- Suffragettes, which sought to gain voting rights for women through direct action and hunger strikes from 1865-1928 in the United Kingdom.
- The Affiliated Residential Park Residents Association Incorporated (ARPRA), which was established in 1986 to represent residents of residential parks in New South Wales, Australia.
- Sunday School movement, which formed in about 1751 to promote universal schooling in the UK.
- Tories, which formed in 1678 to fight the British Exclusion Bill and developed into one of the first political parties, now known as the Conservative Party.

CORRUPTION AND ILLEGAL ACTIVITY

In some instances, advocacy groups have been convicted of illegal activity. Major examples include:

- Jack Abramoff Indian lobbying scandal Corrupt and fraudulent lobbying in relation to Native American gambling enterprises
- Tobacco Master Settlement Agreement between the Attorneys General of 46 states and the four largest US tobacco companies who agreed to pay $206 billion over the first twenty-five years of the agreement.

ADVERSARIAL GROUPINGS

On some controversial issues there are a number of competing advocacy groups, sometimes with very different resources available to them:

- Pro-choice movement vs Pro-life movement (abortion policy in the United States)
- SPEAK campaign vs Pro-Test (animal testing in United Kingdom)
- The Automobile Association vs Pedestrians' Association (now 'Living Streets') (road safety in the United Kingdom since 1929)
- Tobacco Institute vs Action on Smoking and Health (tobacco legislation)
- Flying Matters vs Plane Stupid (aviation policy in the United Kingdom since 2007)

BENEFITS AND INCENTIVES

The general theory is that individuals must be enticed with some type of benefit to join an interest group. Known as the free rider problem, it refers to the difficulty of obtaining members of a particular interest group when the benefits are already reaped without membership. For instance, an interest group dedicated to improving farming standards will fight for the general goal of improving farming for every farmer, even those who are not members of that particular interest group. Thus, there is no real incentive to join an interest group and pay dues if the farmer will receive that benefit anyway. Interest groups must receive dues and contributions from its members in order to accomplish its agenda. While every individual in the world would benefit from a cleaner environment, an Environmental protection interest group does not, in turn, receive monetary help from every individual in the world.

Selective material benefits are benefits that are usually given in monetary benefits. For instance, if an interest group gives a material benefit to their member, they could give them travel discounts, free meals at certain restaurants, or free subscriptions to magazines, newspapers, or journals. Many trade and professional interest groups tend to give these types of benefits to their members. A selective solidary benefit is another type of benefit offered to members or prospective members of an interest group. These incentives involve benefits like "socializing congeniality, the sense of group membership and identification, the status resulting from membership, fun and conviviality, the maintenance of social distinctions, and so on. A solidary incentive is one in which the rewards for participation are socially derived and created out of the act of association.

An expressive incentive is another basic type of incentive or benefit offered to being a member of an interest group. People who join an interest group because of expressive benefits likely joined to express an ideological or moral value that they believe in. Some include free speech, civil rights, economic justice, or political equality. To obtain these types of benefits, members would simply pay dues, donating their time or money to get a feeling of satisfaction from expressing a political value. Also, it would not matter if the interest group achieved their goal; these members would merely be able to say they helped out in the process of trying to obtain these goals, which is the expressive incentive that they got in the first place. The types of interest groups that rely on expressive benefits or incentives would be environmental groups and groups who claim to be lobbying for the public interest. Some public policy interests are not recognized or addressed by a group at all, and these interests are labeled latent interest.

THEORETICAL PERSPECTIVES

Much work has been undertaken by academics in trying to categorise how pressure groups operate, particularly in relation to governmental policy creation. The field is dominated by numerous differing schools of thought:

- Pluralism: This is based upon the understanding that pressure groups operate in competition with one another and play a key role in the political system. They do this by acting as a counterweight to undue concentrations of power.
- However, this pluralist theory (formed primarily by American academics) reflects a more open and fragmented political system similar to that in countries such as the United States. Under neo-pluralism, a concept of political communities developed that is more similar to the British form of government
- Neo-Pluralism: This is based on the concept of political communities in that pressure groups and other such bodies are organised around a government department and its network of client groups. The members of this network co-operate together during the policy making process.
- Corporatism: Some lobby groups are backed by private businesses which can have a considerable influence on legislature.

SOCIAL MEDIA USE

A study published in early 2012 suggests that advocacy groups of varying political and ideological orientations operating in the United States are using social media to interact with citizens every day. The study surveyed 53 groups, who were found to be using a variety of social media technologies to achieve organizational and political goals. Facebook was the social media site of choice with all but one group noting that they use the site to connect with citizens. Twitter was also popular with all but two groups saying that they use Twitter. Other social media being used included YouTube, Linkedin, wikis, Flickr, Jumo, Diigo, Tumblr, Foursquare, Identi.ca, Picasa and Vimeo. As noted in the study, "while some groups raised doubts about social media's ability to overcome the limitations of weak ties and generational gaps, an overwhelming majority of groups see social media as essential to contemporary advocacy work, and laud its democratizing function."

5

Travel Agency

An Introductionustomers on behalf of suppliers such as airlines, car rentals, cruise lines, hotels, railways, sightseeing tours and package holidays that combine several products. In addition to dealing with ordinary tourists most travel agencies have a separate department devoted to making travel arrangements for business travellers and some travel agencies specialize in commercial and business travel only. There are also travel agencies that serve as general sales agents for foreign travel companies, allowing them to have offices in countries other than where their headquarters are located.

ORIGINS OF TRAVEL AGENCY

The British company Cox and Kings is sometimes said to be the oldest travel agency in the world, but this rests upon the services that the original bank, established in 1758, supplied to its wealthy clients. The modern travel agency first appeared in the second half of the 19th century. Thomas Cook, in addition to developing the package tour, established a chain of agencies in the last quarter of the 19th century, in association with the Midland Railway. They not only sold their own tours to the public, but in addition, represented other tour companies. Other British pioneer travel agencies were Dean and Dawson, the Polytechnic Touring Association and the Co-operative Wholesale Society. The oldest travel agency in North America is Brownell Travel; on July 4, 1887, Walter T. Brownell led ten travellers on a European tour, setting sail from New York on the SS Devonia. Travel agencies became more commonplace with the development of commercial aviation, starting in the 1920s. Originally, travel agencies largely catered to middle and upper class customers, but the post-war boom in mass-market package holidays resulted in travel agencies on the main streets of most British towns, catering to a working class clientèle, looking for a convenient way to book overseas beach holidays.

SCOPE IN TRAVEL AGENCY

Travel and Tourism as one of the world's largest foreign exchange earner among industries, provides employ-ment directly to millions of people worldwide and indirectly through many associated service indus-tries. As a very large industry, it includes Government tourism departments, Immigration and customs services, travel agencies, airlines, tour operators, hotels etc and many associated service industries such as airline catering or laundry services, guides, interpreters, tourism promotion and sales executives etc. Travel and tourism enterprises include major internationals with thousands of workforce, though small private travel agent have handful of employees.

Work in the travel and tourism industry is essen-tially concerned with providing services for people who are away from home, on business or holiday. Travel can be leisure travel involv-ing package tours, pilgrim travel, adventure travel etc or for purely business. Work at every functional level in the industry involves dealing directly with people. Travel company personnel must be up-to-date on current rules and regulations and documentation required, in areas like cargo, ticketing and passports, visas etc. so as to correctly advise their clients, and to take care of the paperwork when necessary. Besides this, all tourism staff in marketing, counter sales, or guide services, should be knowledgeable about the places their clients visit, in terms of general background, how to get there, connections by air, rail and road and the facilities available. In India, Travel and tourism, as an industry, has been somewhat slower to take off than in many other places. However, with increasing worldwide interest in travel, and with the Government's encourage-ment of its activities, it is undergoing massive expansion and improve-ment. This forecasts a bright future for all those who choose to make a career of travel and tourism. Young people with drive and a capacity for hard work can rise to top positions very quickly in travel and tourism or even head their own agencies. A job in the industry gives good returns as well as perks including opportunity to see many locales at low prices. Now a days working in an airline, whether on the ground or in flight is an exciting option for many people. In the airlines, one can work as Traffic Assistance, Reservation and Counter Staff, Airhostess and flight pursers, Sales and Marketing staff and customer services. A course in travel and tourism or a qualification on Hotel management helps to get in. The jobs in airlines though challenging are glamorous and afford the possibility of traveling to exciting destinations.

Free tickets for the family offered by some airlines are an added advantage. Domestic and international Airlines such as Air India, Indian airlines, Jet airways, Air Sahara, Aeroflot, British Airways, Cathay Pacific, Emirates, Singapore Airlines etc offer employment opportunities with attractive salaries and numerous benefits. Opportunities are plenty in travel agency business.Many resorts, travel groups use travel agents to promote their tour packages to travellers. They deal with almost everything connected with travel including the shortest route to the destina-tion, travel mode, obtaining important documents that are required like visa, passport, vaccination certificates etc, suitable places to stay, current exchange rates, tourist attractions to visit, climate and they will plan the trip keeping in mind the clients' preferences, budgets and special needs.In travel agencies there are openings for reservation and counter staff, Sales and Marketing staff, Tour escorts and tour operators, cargo and courier agencies etc. A short tem course or a diploma in travel and ticketing for few months duration will help gain entry into an agency. Several large travel agencies also offer short-term training programme-mes, and tend to absorb most of the candidates. Some agencies take in fresh graduates and train them on the job. Most travel agencies demand persons with a pleasing personality and the ability to deal with custom-ers. A knowledge of destinations and procedures help a great deal. Now sky is the limit in the field of travel and tourism.

DEFINITION OF TOUR OPERATOR

A tour operator typically combines tour and travel components to create a holiday. The most common example of a tour operator's product would be a flight on a charter airline plus a transfer from the airport to a hotel and the services of a local representative, all for one price. Niche tour operators may specialise in destinations, *e.g.* Italy, activities and experiences, *e.g.* skiing, or a combination thereof. The original raison d'etre of tour operating was the difficulty of making arrangements in far-flung places, with problems of language, currency and communication.

The advent of the internet has led to a rapid increase in self-packaging of holidays. However, tour operators still have their competence in arranging tours for those who do not have time to do DIY holidays, and specialize in large group events and meetings such as conferences or seminars. Also, tour operators still exercise contracting power with suppliers (airlines, hotels, other land arrangements, cruises, etc.) and influence over other entities (tourism boards and other government authorities) in order to create packages and special departures for destinations otherwise difficult and expensive to visit.

The three major tour operator associations in the U.S. are the National Tour Association (NTA), the United States Tour Operators Association (USTOA), and the American Tour Association (ATA). In Europe, it is the European Tour Operators Association (ETOA), and in the UK, it is the Association of British Travel Agents (ABTA) and the Association of Independent Tour Operators (AITO). The primary association for receptive North American inbound tour operators is the Receptive Services Association of America (RSAA).

DIFFERENCE BETWEEN TRAVEL AGENCY AND TOUR OPERATOR

Travel Agency is like a Retailer selling from all suppliers. He Can reserved a Hotel, rent a car for you or book your airport transfers. For tour packages he would use your choice and accordingly book a Coach tours are a Tour itinerary designed according to your wish with a Car Travel and Sightseeing + Hotel Reservation + Air Tickets/ Rail Tickets etc directly from the respective suppliers or a Tour Operator. Tour Operator is one who has already made some of his own itineraries and based on the category and budget choice of the Traveller (Who approaches him directly) or Travel agent (Indirect approach with respect to the Customer) make the full arrangement.

FUNCTIONS OF TRAVEL AGENCY

Travel agency is a retail business, that sells travel related products and services to customers, on behalf of suppliers, such as airlines, car rentals, cruise lines, hotels, railways, sightseeing tours and package holidays that combine several products. In addition to dealing with ordinary tourists, most travel agencies have a separate department devoted to making travel arrangements for business travellers and some travel agencies specialize in commercial and business travel only. There are also travel agencies that serve as general sales agents for foreign travel companies, allowing them to have offices in countries other than where their headquarters are located.

As the name implies, a travel agency's main function is to act as an agent, that is to say, selling travel products and services on behalf of a supplier. Consequently, unlike other retail businesses, they do not keep a stock in hand. A package holiday or a ticket is not purchased from a supplier unless a customer requests that purchase. The holiday or ticket is supplied to them at a discount. The profit is therefore the difference between the advertised price which the customer pays and the discounted price at which it is supplied to the agent. This is known as the commission. A British travel agent would consider a 10-12per cent commission as a good arrangement. In some countries, airlines have stopped giving commission to travel agencies.

Therefore, travel agencies are now forced to charge a percentage premium or a standard flat fee, per sale. However, some companies still give them a set percentage for selling their product. Major tour companies can afford to do this; because if they were to sell a thousand trips at a cheaper rate, they still come out better than if they sell a hundred trips at a higher rate. This process benefits both parties. Other commercial operations are undertaken, especially by the larger chains. These can include the sale of in-house insurance, travel guide books and timetables, car rentals, and the services of an on-site Bureau de change, dealing in the most popular holiday currencies. The majority of travel agents have felt the need to protect themselves and their clients against the possibilities of commercial failure, either their own or a supplier's. They will advertise the fact that they are surety bonded, meaning in the case of a failure, the customers is guaranteed either an equivalent holiday to that which they have lost or if they prefer a refund. Many British and American agencies and tour operators are bonded with the International Air Transport Association (IATA), for those who issue air tickets, Air Travel Organisers' Licensing (ATOL) for those who order tickets in, the Association of British Travel Agents (ABTA) or the American Society of Travel Agents (ASTA), for those who sell package holidays on behalf of a tour company. A travel agent is supposed to offer impartial travel advice to the customer. However, this function almost disappeared with the mass-market package holiday and some agency chains seemed to develop a 'holiday supermarket' concept, in which customers choose their holiday from brochures on racks and then book it from a counter. Again, a variety of social and economic changes have now contrived to bring this aspect to the fore once more, particularly with the advent of multiple, no-frills, low-cost airlines.

FUNCTIONS OF TOUR OPERATORS AND TRAVEL AGENTS

Sometimes there is confusion over the difference in functions of tour operators and travel agents. Tour operators are the organisers and providers of package holidays. They make contracts with hoteliers, airlines and ground transport companies then print brochures advertising the holidays that they have assembled. Travel agents give advice and sell and administer the bookings for a number of tour operators. It is estimated that there are some 7,000 travel agency shops ranging size from the multiples, with several hundred outlets each, to the individual shop.

Some travel agents also undertake tour operating - be it on a small scale, eg a local agent packaging a group holiday for a local club, or on a larger scale - most famously by the legendary Thomas Cook, who was the first tour operator, and Sir Henry Lunn (Lunn Poly) who is widely credited with "inventing" skiing as a leisure activity. Agents can also sell the 'components' (flights, ferry bookings, car hire etc) for those who travel independently.

Although most package holidays are sold through travel agents a significant and growing percentage are sold direct to the consumer through advertising - Teletex, TV Travel Shops and the internet. ABTA - The Travel Association - represents both travel agents and tour operators. The Federation of Tour Operators represents only tour operators- its members have c.70per cent of the market. All current FTO members are also members of ABTA, and the two organisations work closely together - with the FTO particularly active with overseas governments and suppliers.

OPERATIONS

As the name implies, a travel agency's main function is to act as an agent, that is to say, selling travel products and services on behalf of a supplier. Consequently, unlike other retail businesses, they do not keep a stock in hand. A package holiday or a ticket is not purchased from a supplier unless a customer requests that purchase. The holiday or ticket is supplied to them at a discount. The profit is therefore the difference between the advertised price which the customer pays and the discounted price at which it is supplied to the agent. This is known as the commission. A British travel agent would consider a 10-12per cent commission as a good arrangement. In Australia, all individuals or companies that sell tickets are required to be licensed as a travel agent.

In some countries, airlines have stopped giving commission to travel agencies. Therefore, travel agencies are now forced to charge a percentage premium or a standard flat fee, per sale. However, some companies still give them a set percentage for selling their product. Major tour companies can afford to do this, because if they were to sell a thousand trips at a cheaper rate, they still come out better than if they sell a hundred trips at a higher rate.

This process benefits both parties. Other commercial operations are undertaken, especially by the larger chains. These can include the sale of in-house insurance, travel guide books and timetables, car rentals, and the services of an on-site Bureau de change, dealing in the most popular holiday currencies.

The majority of travel agents have felt the need to protect themselves and their clients against the possibilities of commercial failure, either their own or a supplier's. They will advertise the fact that they are surety bonded, meaning in the case of a failure, the customers are guaranteed either an equivalent holiday to that which they have lost or if they prefer, a refund.

Many British and American agencies and tour operators are bonded with the International Air Transport Association (IATA), for those who issue air tickets, Air Travel Organisers' Licensing (ATOL) for those who order tickets in, the Association of British Travel Agents (ABTA) or the American Society of Travel Agents (ASTA), for those who sell package holidays on behalf of a tour company.

A travel agent is supposed to offer impartial travel advice to the customer. However, this function almost disappeared with the mass-market package holiday and some agency chains seemed to develop a 'holiday supermarket' concept, in which customers choose their holiday from brochures on racks and then book it from a counter. Again, a variety of social and economic changes have now contrived to bring this aspect to the fore once more, particularly with the advent of multiple, no-frills, low-cost airlines.

COMMISSIONS

Most travel agencies operate on a commission-basis, meaning that the compensation from the airlines, car rentals, cruise lines, hotels, railways, sightseeing tours and tour operators, etc., is expected in form of a commission from their bookings. Most often, the commission consists of a set percentage of the sale. In the United States, most airlines pay no commission at all to travel agencies. In this case, an agency usually adds a service fee to the net price.

TYPES OF AGENCIES

There are three different types of agencies in the UK: Multiples, Miniples and Independent Agencies. The former comprises a number of national chains, often owned by international conglomerates, like Thomson Holidays, now a subsidiary of TUI AG, the German multinational. It is now quite common for the large mass-market tour companies to purchase a controlling interest in a chain of travel agencies, in order to control the distribution of their product. (This is an example of vertical integration.) The smaller chains are often based in particular regions or districts.

In the United States, there are four different types of agencies: Mega, Regional, Consortium and Independent Agencies. American Express and the American Automobile Association (AAA) are examples of mega travel agencies. Independent Agencies usually cater to a special or niche market, such as the needs of residents in an upmarket commuter town or suburb or a particular group interested in a similar activity, such as sporting events, like football, golf or tennis. There are two approaches of travel agencies. One is the traditional, multi-destination, out-bound travel agency, based in the originating location of the traveller and the other is the destination focused, in-bound travel agency, that is based in the destination and delivers an expertise on that location. At present, the former is usually a larger operator like Thomas Cook, while the latter is often a smaller, independent operator.

CONSOLIDATORS

Airline consolidators and other types of travel consolidators and wholesalers are high volume sales companies that specialize in selling to niche markets. They may or may not offer various types of services, at a single point of access. These can be hotel reservations, flights or car-rentals, for example. Sometimes the services are combined into vacation packages, that include transfers to the location and lodging. These companies do not usually sell directly to the public, but act as wholesalers to retail travel agencies. Commonly, the sole purpose of consolidators is to sell to ethnic niches in the travel industry. Usually, no consolidator offers everything, they may only have contracted rates to specific destinations. Today, there are no domestic consolidators, with some exceptions for business class contracts.

CRITICISM AND CONTROVERSY

RACKING

Travel agencies have been accused of employing a number of restrictive practices, the chief of which is known as 'racking'. This is the practice of displaying only the brochures of those travel companies whose holidays they wish to sell, the ones that pay them the most commission. Of course, the average customer tends to think that these are the only holidays on offer and is unaware of the possible alternatives. Conversely, by limiting the number of companies that a travel agency represents, this can bring a better and more profitable, working relationship between the agency and its suppliers. Travel agencies can then obtain special benefits for their customers, from a supplier, by concentrating their bookings with that supplier. Some examples of these special benefits would be room upgrades or the waiver of change and cancellation fees.

THE INTERNET THREAT

With general public access to the Internet, many airlines and other travel companies began to sell directly to passengers. As a consequence, airlines no longer needed to pay the commissions to travel agents on each ticket sold. Since 1997, travel agencies have gradually been disintermediated, by the reduction in costs caused by removing layers from the package holiday distribution network. However, travel agents remain dominant in some areas such as cruise vacations where they represent 77per cent of bookings and 73per cent of packaged travel.

In response, travel agencies have developed an internet presence of their own by creating travel Web sites, with detailed information and online booking capabilities. Several major online travel agencies include: Expedia, Travelocity, Orbitz, CheapTickets, Priceline, CheapOair. Travel agencies also use the services of the major computer reservations systems companies, also known as Global Distribution Systems (GDS), including: SABRE, Amadeus CRS, Galileo CRS and Worldspan, which is a subsidiary of Travelport, allowing them to book and sell airline tickets, hotels, car rentals and other travel related services. Some online travel websites allow visitors to compare hotel and flight rates with multiple companies for free. They often allow visitors to sort the travel packages by amenities, price, and proximity to a city or landmark.

Travel agents have applied dynamic packaging tools to provide fully bonded (full financial protection) travel at prices equal to or lower than a member of the public can book online. As such, the agencies' financial assets are protected in addition to professional travel agency advice. All travel sites that sell hotels online work together with GDS, suppliers and hotels directly to search for room inventory. Once the travel site sells a hotel, the site will try to get a confirmation for this hotel. Once confirmed or not, the customer is contacted with the result. This means that booking a hotel on a travel Web site will not necessarily result in an instant answer. Only some hotels on a travel Web site can be confirmed instantly (which is normally marked as such on each site). As different travel websites work with different suppliers together, each site has different hotels that it can confirm instantly. Some examples of such online travel websites that sell hotel rooms are Expedia, Orbitz and WorldHotel-Link. The comparison sites, TripAdvisor and SideStep search the resellers site all at once to save time searching. None of these sites actually sell hotel rooms. Often tour operators have hotel contracts, allotments and free sell agreements which allow for the immediate confirmation of hotel rooms for vacation bookings. Mainline service providers are those that actually produce the direct service, like various hotels chains or airlines that have a website for online bookings. Portals will serve a consolidator of various airlines and hotels on the internet.

They work on a commission from these hotels and airlines. Often, they provide cheaper rates than the mainline service providers as these sites get bulk deals from the service providers. A meta search engine on the other hand, simply culls data from the internet on real time rates for various search queries and diverts traffic to the mainline service providers for an online booking. These websites usually do not have their own booking engine.

CAREERS

With the many people switching to self-service internet websites, the number of available jobs as travel agents is decreasing. Most jobs that become available are from older travel agents retiring. Counteracting the decrease in jobs due to internet services is the increase in the number of people travelling. Since 1995, many travel agents have exited the industry, and relatively few young people have entered the field due to less competitive salaries.

However, others have abandoned the 'brick and mortar' agency for a home-based business to reduce overheads and those who remain have managed to survive by promoting other travel products such as cruise lines and train excursions or by promoting their ability to aggressively research and assemble complex travel packages on a moment's notice, essentially acting as a very advanced concierge. In this regard, travel agents can maintain competitive, if they become "travel consultants" with flawless knowledge of destination regions and specialize in topics like nautical tourism or cultural tourism.

TRAVEL TECHNOLOGY

Travel technology is a term used to describe applications of Information Technology (IT), or Information and Communications Technology (ICT), in travel, tourism and hospitality industry. Travel technology may also be referred to as tourism technology, hospitality automation, travel tracking and flight tracking.

DEFINITION

Since travel implies locomotion, travel technology was originally associated with the computer reservations system (CRS) of the airlines industry, but now is used more inclusively, incorporating the broader tourism sector as well as its subset the hospitality industry. While travel technology includes the computer reservations system, it also represents a much broader range of applications, in fact increasingly so. Travel technology includes virtual tourism in the form of virtual tour technologies. Travel technology may also be referred to as *e-travel/ etravel* or *e-tourism/ etourism* (eTourism), in reference to "electronic travel" or "electronic tourism". Travel technology is increasingly being used to describe systems for managing and monitoring travel, including travel tracking and flight tracking systems. In other contexts, the term "travel technology" can refer to technology intended for use by travellers, such as light-weight laptop computers with universal power supplies or satellite Internet connections. That is not the sense in which it is used here.

APPLICATIONS OF TRAVEL TECHNOLOGY

Travel technology includes many processes such as dynamic packaging which provide useful new options for consumers. Today the tour guide can be a GPS tour guide, and the guidebook could be an audioguide, podguide or I-Tours, such as City audio guides. The biometric passport may also be included as travel technology in the broad sense. XML-based technologies have become increasingly important for the travel industry. XML can be used to support air reservation booking or to implement optional services and merchandising functions in the booking process. Another important application of XML is the establishing of direct connections between Airlines and Travel Agencies. In order to create a generally accepted XML-standard, the Open Axis Group was founded.

HISTORY OF TRAVEL TECHNOLOGY

Certainly travel technology was born on the coat-tails of the airline industry's use of automation and their need to extend this out to the travel agency partners. It should be kept in mind that there was an online world before the advent of the world wide web in the form of private and commercial online services, via packet switched network using X.25. Travel technology played a significant role in the so-called dot-com boom and bust, circa 1997-2001.

6

The Business of Inbound Tour Operators

INTRODUCTION

This manual was designed as a reference and toolkit accompanying a training course for companies that have newly begun an inbound tour operator business or are considering starting one. If you do not have much background in the travel business, parts of this manual will be difficult to understand or use without some introductory level training. Contact the Association of Croatian Travel Agencies abut information on attending a course for new tour operators.

The course and these materials should help new inbound tour operators gain a better understanding of:

- The structure of the international travel industry, trends in specialty travel and new product demand;
- Market segmentation, using specific information on traveller interests, motivations and expectations, identifying potential market niches and buyers.
- Steps of new product development in organizing and selling new high value niche market tourism products.
- Sales and distribution channels, and developing strategies for their effective use
- Running a tourism business, as you all know, is complex. It is not possible to include within this publication everything that a tourism director or manager needs to know. It is not designed to be an introduction to the global tourism industry. Nor is it designed for those tour operators and travel agents involved in domestic and outbound tourism, although some of the contents may be relevant. Its aim is to provide a few tips to lead to a more successful business.

THE TOURISM BUSINESS

The role of the tour operator is to essentially sell accommodation, transport, activities and transfers in a combined all-inclusive package. The Tour operators' product is different to that sold by other businesses in many ways and understanding this will go a long way to being successful. What you are selling is an intangible product that must be bought blind because it cannot be seen, touched or experienced by the consumer before use. Instead, tour operators prepare brochures which represent their products in words and pictures. These brochures cannot accurately give an impression of how any one particular client will experience the product, so sellers are often described as selling dreams. Buying a holiday is like buying a bar of chocolate; only memories are left after the product is consumed.

You are selling a discretionary product, meaning that the clients do not have to buy it in the same way that they do food or fuel. When finances are tight or during a recession, they may choose to spend their money that would have gone on a holiday on other consumer durables such as a compact disc player or new washing machine.

It is not a heterogenous product. You could buy a refrigerator like your neighbour's and expect it to look identical and operate in exactly the same way, but holidays are by their very nature varied. Anyone coming to Croatia on a food and wine tour will have a different experience whether they come in July or October, even if they went with the same operator, stayed in the same hotels and ate at the same restaurants.

It is a perishable product. Holidays are only saleable up to the date of the flight departures, especially if you organize fixed date trips. Package holidays suffer from inseperability. The behaviour of everyone involved in the product, from the hotel porter to the vehicle driver can have an effect on the outcome of the experience. If we purchase a washing machine, our enjoyment of the product will not be reduced by an irritating plumber who installs it.

STRUCTURE OF THE TRAVEL TRADE

The travel industry is highly structured, and businesses within the industry tend to specialize in one or a small number of functions driven by their core business. Understanding the structure of the travel trade is important for a company in developing its core business strategy, making marketing decisions, and investing for growth. The structure of the travel trade is largely driven by how consumers travel and how they identify and select the travel services they purchase. As we review the most widespread types of businesses in the travel trade, it is useful to keep in mind some common distinctions made when describing travel companies and their markets.

DEFINITION OF TERMS IN THE TRAVEL TRADE

Inbound and Outbound

When a company focuses primarily on serving travellers coming from other destinations, we refer to them as inbound operators. They generally offer services for clients coming from other countries or regions. Examples of these include Adria Tours and General Tourist. When a company focuses on serving travellers in their domestic or regional market seeking to travel to foreign destinations, we refer to them as outbound operators. Examples of these would include the large number of agencies advertising package tours to other countries. The inbound operator seeks to understand foreign markets and develop products and services that will attract customers from overseas to their destination, and will focus on researching the travel motivations and preferences of target markets outside their own country. The outbound operator continually monitors demand for travel services within its own market, and will focus on identifying travel opportunities and creating products and services for these travellers going to other countries. Some companies may serve a local market, and they can attract both domestic and international travellers. A good example of this would be a ski resort. These are generally referred to as local operators without any distinction being made as to inbound or outbound.

Short Haul and Long Haul

Short haul refers to travellers coming from a nearby market, while long haul refers to travellers coming from far away. Usually, if the traveller's destination is further away than one day's driving distance, they are considered to be long haul. Typically, companies will serve both short and long haul markets, but will have a greater focus one or the other. The quality of the experience offered usually dictates whether or not a product can be sold to a long haul market. A low to medium quality attraction will generally not attract many long haul customers.

The cost of getting to that attraction is simply too high for the quality of experience to be gained. Only top destinations offering unique products and services are successful at attracting long haul customers. For example, you may drive one or two hours to the local aquarium or ski resort, since the effort of getting there is minimal for a day of fun. However, it is unlikely that a person from another country would plan a long trip to see the same attractions. They may only visit these attractions as part of a trip that has a greater focus: visiting Croatia for its historical or cultural attractions, or as part of an adventure travel vacation that involves multiple activities.

Operators and Resellers

Operators are companies that supply their own services or products, while resellers are marketing and selling the products and services of others, usually charging a mark-up or taking a commission. In practice, many travel companies do both. A tour operator will offer many of its own services but may also sell services of other suppliers as part of a package. A travel agency is mainly a reseller, but may for example employ its own guides or translators and sell these services directly.

Package Travel, Group Travel, and Independent Travellers (FIT)

Package travel refers to travel services sold as a package, where many services are bundled together for the convenience of travellers who don't wish to spend time making their own arrangements. Package travel may be sold both to group travellers and independent travellers. Group travel refers to package holidays that have a set itinerary and an allocation of seats or spaces. Customers purchasing the package joint the group. Independent travellers usually prefer not to travel with a group, unless it is a self formed group.

They prefer to have flexibility in their travel arrangements and may have done some research and have specific interests which dictate what they want to do and see on a trip. Sometimes they prefer not make to many advance plans, but in other instances they may carefully plan a custom tour that fits their own interests, working with either a travel agent or tour operator before leaving home. Independent travellers may purchase package travel services, but they will choose their own dates or request a private departure rather than traveling with a group.

TYPES OF TRAVEL OPERATIONS

Now as suggested, review the different types of travel operations that are the main players in the travel trade.

Travel Agencies

Travel agencies are perhaps the most visible companies in the travel trade. Their primary businesses is to resell accommodations, transportation services (including airplane and train tickets, car and bus transfers) individual services including guide and translator services, and package services such as sightseeing tours. Within each agency, there is often a focus on either inbound or outbound trade, with the outbound agencies focusing either on ticketing services and accommodation bookings, or on package holidays. Travel agencies generally serve a mix of long and short haul markets, although some specialize in long haul markets.

The majority of travel agencies seek to appeal to a large domestic market, so they focus mainly on products and services with a mass market appeal: beach and ski holidays, cruises, and package tours to well known and popular destinations. A small number may have a focus on specialty travel, and will offer products and services that cater to special markets. Examples would be agencies that specialize in custom travel arrangements, outdoor sports, or adventure holidays.

Most travel agencies that focus on outbound travel resell the products of both outbound and inbound operators, but they can also find products to retail from other travel resellers or from travel portals. Most travel agencies offer ticketing services for international travel, and can assist their customers with obtaining information on travel requirements such as visas and vaccinations, as well as obtaining travel insurance.

Outbound Tour Operators

Outbound tour operators create and market travel products to customers in their own markets that are usually long haul travellers seeking a specific experience in a foreign destination. They may design and operate their own trips, working with partners in the destination, or they may choose trips already designed by inbound operators and simply market these to their own clients.

Outbound operators generally have an in depth knowledge of what their customers are looking for and what their travel requirements are, and are thus able to design travel products that meet those needs. In the past, most outbound operators focused on group travel arrangements, but increasingly they are offering package travel for independent travellers. Outbound operators usually offer trips to a variety of destinations, and many focus on a small number of specialty travel segments, leaving the mass market travel arrangements to travel agencies.

Inbound Tour Operators

Inbound tour operators create and market travel products and services to customers mainly in long haul markets. Customers in countries far away generally do not have in depth knowledge of a destination or the service providers in that destination, may not speak the language, and may not feel comfortable making their own arrangements. Inbound tour operators serve these customers by taking the guess work out of planning a holiday, and may offer experiences that would otherwise be inaccessible to independent travellers making their own arrangements.

For example, planning and organizing your own expedition to go trekking in Western Croatia would involve months of research to identify routes, find local guides, arrange transport and pack animals, and considerable expense to transport equipment and gear or purchase it locally. A local company can organize all this for you at much less cost and in less time than it would take for you to do it yourself. Inbound operators usually specialize in package travel arrangements of this kind, and may have both group and independent travellers as clients. Inbound operators operate their own tours, although the services of many local companies may be packaged and resold as part of this tour. Inbound operator usually specialize in one country or region. They may offer tours catering to a broad range of interests if they are located in a country that is not well known to travellers, but if they are in a well known destination where it is easy for independent travellers to make their own arrangements they usually focus on specialty travel.

Ground Operators

ervices directly to overseas customers. These operations focus on providing travel services on the ground, including activities like horseback riding, boat trips or guided diving tours, cooking or wine tours, etc. that form part of a larger experience or packaged tour. Ground operators may sell their services directly to independent travellers that have already reached a foreign destination – this is common in more well known travel destinations. In lesser known destinations, where there are relatively fewer independent travellers, ground operators usually work mainly with tour operators (either inbound or outbound) to market their products or services.

Local Service Providers

This term is used frequently to refer to ground operators, but more commonly it is applied to operations that provide local services such as accommodations (hotels, guest houses, families offering homestays), meals, local guides, equipment rental, cultural performances, and other specific services. Local service providers may include museums, parks, ferry lines, or domestic airlines. Often, there is little distinction made between ground operators and local service providers, and the two terms may be used interchangeably.

Travel Resellers and Portals

Travel resellers and travel portals offer consumers the convenience of being able to review and compare many travel options in one catalog or on one Web site, and make it easy to find travel packages, to book them, and to pay for them. Most resellers and portals earn a commission from the operator whose package is sold via their catalog or Web site, and they may resell trips from both inbound and outbound operators. Travellers may purchase products directly from resellers and portals, but travel agents and travel agencies also look for products to sell from these sources, and most resellers and portals have a commission arrangement for agents. Resellers and portals commonly have well defined target markets, and the theme of the trips they sell will reflect this. They may focus on budget or low cost travel, or focus on other specialty travel interest such as eco-tours, adventure tours, the gap year market (young adults taking time off to travel between finishing high school or college and starting a career), women travellers, or travellers over 50. The following table presents an overview of the differences between the different types of travel operations in the leisure travel industry in terms of their markets and their main distribution channels:

	Target Markets	Main Products/Services or Clients	Distribution Channels
Travel Agencies	Mass market, general interest travel and package travel to more well known destinations	Flight and other travel arrangements, accommodation and event tickets, package tours for groups and individuals (for outbound). Products	Direct sales to consumers. Inbound agencies may sell to outbound agencies or place packages

		are mostly sourced from tour operators, ground operators, and local service providers, but also from travel resellers and portals. Examples: package cruise in the Mediterranean, all inclusive holiday in Turkey, beach holiday package in Spain with accommodation and flights.	with resellers and portals. Mass marketing done through advertisement via direct mail, media, and via agency offices.
Tour Operators	with more specific interests, usually a defined audience in the domestic market.	Package travel to a variety of destinations within a specific area of interest, for groups or independent travellers. Products are mostly sourced from inbound operators, or may be designed in house with inbound operators, ground operators, and local service providers in the destination country supplying many of the services. Examples: package tour to the Galapogos, 12 day trek in Bhutan, 9 day cultural tour of China, volunteer work holiday in India with 2 weeks of touring and one week of volunteer work. groups in the domestic market via specialty publications, membership	Outbound Travellers Direct sales to consumers. Some outbound operators may sell certain products through resellers or portals, or through specialized agencies. Targeted marketing through direct mail (of catalogs, brochures), via Web site and customer loyalty programmes, at travel fairs, and to special interest
Tour Operators	interest in a specific destination or activity, usually long haul travellers in other markets.	groups and clubs. Inbound Package travel for groups or independent travellers in one destination or a region, may cover several areas of interest or be more focused, for groups or independent travellers. Products are usually designed in house, with some services from ground operators and local service providers resold as part of the package. Examples: 12 day trek in Western Mongolia, package tour of the Gobi Desert, homestay holiday with a nomadic family in Mongolia. marketing via Web site.	Travellers with an Sales to outbound tour operators, some direct sales to consumers and through resellers or portals. Targeted marketing via direct contacts with outbound tour operators, travel fairs, and to special interest groups in foreign markets via direct mail, special interest publications, and some direct

Ground Operators	Target clients are inbound and outbound tour operators offering package services in the destination, as well as independent travellers that have already arrived incountry.	Services for tour operators or independent travellers in one destination or a region. Offer own products and services with some services from local service providers resold as part of the package. Examples: one day sightseeing excursion in Dubrovnik, 3 day diving boat excursion, one day wine cellar tour with wine tasting.	Direct contacts with tour operators, local advertising, on the street advertising in the tourist season, some marketing through Web sites.
Local Service Providers	Target clients are mainly inbound but sometimes outbound tour operators offering package services in the destination, as well as independent travellers that have already arrived incountry.	Services for tour operators or independent travellers in one locality. Offer own services, with very few resold services added to the package. Examples: hotels, restaurants, traditional musical performance, national park entrance, horse rental, car hire.	Direct contacts with tour operators, local advertising, on the street advertising in the tourist season, rarely any marketing through Web sites except in the case of
accommodations.		Travel	Long and sho
Resellers and Portals	haul travellers, usually with more specific interests but sometimes with general interests, may cover markets in more then one country.	Similar to package services sold by outbound tour operators, but collections may be grouped to appeal to a specific audience. Examples: 14 day eco-tour in Sri Lanka, walking tour of vineyards in France for 50+ travellers. promotions, and	Direct mailing, advertisement through mass media and special interest publications, internet marketing via Web site, special web advertising.

MARKETING

We all know that simply establishing a tourism company does not guarantee the arrival of tourists. We have to make the business work. But how do you do this? How much do you need to spend on publicity and how will you achieve it – through web promotion, word of mouth, advertising? How do you create awareness of your business other than communicating directly with tourists? How do you plan to grow your business over a period of time? A successful business will need to develop suitable products for the market, price them correctly, promote them effectively, distribute them to the final customer and evaluate the results of the total programme. Then the whole process starts again.

This is marketing. It is not solely attending travel fairs and making brochures. These are just a small part of the field of promotion, which is only a part of the marketing process.

A general definition for marketing could be as follows:

- "Marketing is the management function which organizes and directs all those business activities involved in assessing customer needs and converting customer purchasing power into effective demand for a specific product or service to the final consumer or user so as to achieve the profit target or other objective set by the company or organization."

This definition leads to some very important points to bear in mind. Firstly, marketing is a management function. Some tour operators employ staff specifically in a marketing role. Others will have the marketing function solely undertaken by the manager or director. In either situation, there must be clear goals for the company. A marketer can not simply come into a business and make it more profitable. They must understand the philosophy of the company, what the goals are, where the interests lie and so on. The second important point is assessing customer needs.

A company will only succeed if it can produce or supply what is demanded by consumers. There would be little point, for example, in running two week 'Pumpkin Picking' tours. The demand for this type of activity is likely to be very small, difficult to sustain and difficult to market. Tour operators must provide what tourists want.The next stage looks in detail on consumer needs, understanding clients and market research. I have personally seen many people establish a tourism company hoping that tourists will come, but without having ever given any consideration to what they are selling and to whom. The third point is converting customer purchasing power into effective demand. Take a look at the letter below,

Dear Sir,

I have just started a tourism company in Croatia. We are called Croatian Tours and Travel Agency Co. Ltd. We can do lots of different types of trips to all parts of the country, from sightseeing to adventure and specialty travel, and food and wine tasting. We can also organize sailing and beach apartment rentals.. We hope that you can cooperate with us and send us some tourists from your company.

Thanks.

Imagine that you had received a letter like this from a tour operator. You'd probably throw it straight in the rubbish bin. They have no idea of selling, packaging, planning – in fact no idea of the tourism industry or business at all. A letter like this would get you nowhere. Getting people interested in your company requires careful planning and thoughtful promotion. Achieving a profit target. For most of us, this is the reason why we have a company. We need to make money. There are of course other reasons why you may be involved in tourism such as the enjoyment of meeting new people or traveling to the countryside. However, what is important here is the fact that marketing is very closely linked to profit. For example, is it better to spend $1000 on brochures for an increase in profit of $100,000 or to attend a travel fair at a cost of $20,000 for an anticipated profit of $80,000? Obviously, you would choose the first option. You do specific marketing activities to get forecasted results, not simply because that's what every other tourism company does and because you think you ought to. Marketing a company, its products and services is no easy task. It's therefore essential to have in place a marketing plan. This plan can of course change and your document should never be set in stone. The plan should change at least once a year. Because tourism is subject to outside influences, (we have seen evidence of this with the Iraq war, 9/11, Bali bombings and SARS in Asia.), modifications may need to be made at short notice to accommodate these influences.

MARKETING PLAN

A marketing plan must be supported by extensive, research-based data on markets, consumers and the environment. The plan can only be written once this research has been undertaken. As I have said earlier, you cannot sell a product or service based on your own intuition that people will want it. This is especially true if you require funding from an external source to help you grow your business. Just because you think something will sell, doesn't mean that people will buy. This is no defined format for a marketing plan. There are big differences between organizations and these differences have to be reflected in the plan.

Firstly, the plan has three major areas that should be considered after gathering your research:

- *Objectives*: What are you trying to achieve?
- *Strategies*: How are you going to achieve it?
- *Tactics*: What are the actions you will undertake to do all this?

The contents of a typical marketing plan could include the following:

- Introduction and Background
  - Introduction
  - The current position
  - Objectives
  - Relationship of Marketing Plan to overall Business Plan
- The Marketing Strategy
  - Marketing for Croatia
  - Company Marketing
  - Research
  - Promotion and Communication
  - Pricing
  - Corporate Image
  - Market segments and Distribution Channels
  - Product development

- People
- Implementation Strategy
  - Trade Fairs
  - Web site and Digital Media
  - Printed Media
  - Direct Mail
  - Personal Communications
  - Advertising
  - Membership
- Budget
- Evaluation

The marketing plan serves several purposes:

- It is a managerial control document which aims to ensure that clear goals and targets have been established in order that the organization does not drift about.
- It provides a detailed inventory as to how the marketing budget is to be spent and why it has been allocated in the ways set out. Alll sales and revenue targets must be identified and justified.
- It provides and agreed basis of action that can be circulated to every individual involved in its implementation. As a result, it acts as a mechanism for ensuring that everyone is clearly identified with marketing aims.
- It provides a set of benchmarks against which marketing programmes can later be evaluated and refined for the future. Without explicit targets, evaluation of marketing efforts is impossible.

BEING COMPETITIVE

A tourist wanting a general tour of Croatia or an overseas tour operator wanting to partner with a Croatian operator has a number of choices. Within Croatia, there are over XX tourism companies and travel agencies offering tours throughout the season. Why should the Tourist Company or tourists choose you? All operators offer vehicles, guides, hotel bookings, visits to attractions, cultural events, or other activities. These factors are comparable, meaning we can easily identify and compare them. If you offer the same as the other companies, you are unlikely to be very successful in your business. And if you are, it's likely that you have had to reduce your prices significantly to do so.

Of course you need to assess other tourism companies in Croatia to see what they are doing. But additionally, you need to look further a field and understand why tourists or tourism companies are sending their tourists to other destinations in the region. You need to be competitive and compete against both other Croatian tour operators and those operators in neighbouring countries. So how do you compete? Competitive advantages are built up through competitive activities, orientated towards doing the same things that rivals do, but better, and also doing different things to other competing companies. Imagine that you are purchasing a new computer. There are lots of similar ones available, all offering the same specifications - size of disk space, speed of operation, availability of accessories, etc - the comparative advantages. So how do you choose which one to purchase?

You focus not only on price but length of guarantee, reliability of after-sales service, reliability of retailer and ability to upgrade the computer - the competitive advantages. In the same way with your company, you need to either do the same things better than other Croatian tour operators or provide better and different products and services. We're not talking about just going to different locations or doing different activities. Look at the whole operation of you company. What could you do better than anyone else or do that nobody else is doing? You could look at booking procedures, cancellation policies, return client incentives, gifts for guests, specialist language guides, lengths of trips, profits going to local charities or communities. These are competitive advantages in the tourism industry that may just make a tourist decide to go with you rather than another company.

$$\frac{\text{Value}}{\text{Effort}} = \frac{\text{Service Facilities}}{\text{Cost}} + \frac{\text{\& Experience Gained}}{\text{Effort Required}}$$

In the past, 'value for money' has often been a term used when purchasing a service - measuring the diversity of services or quality of services against the cost for those services. However, new theories suggest that this does not fully reflect a tourist's way of thinking. The tourism services offered have to be combined with the feelings and sensations obtained from undertaking travel with your company. These then are measured against not only the cost of the trip but also against the efforts the tourist had to go to arrange and undertake the trip and the obstacles or deterrents they faced. If the services were poor, the experience unrewarding, the price high or the trip difficult to organize or undertake then you will not be a competitive business - no matter how wonderful your trip was presented in a brochure. To compete successfully, your business has to offer to the market greater value than your rivals for the same effort on the part of the tourists - or the same value for less effort.

DESTINATION MARKETING

In almost all cases, a tourist will decide to come to Croatia before they decide to travel with your company. In the same way, an overseas tour operator will look for a partner in Croatia after they have decided to take clients to Croatia. Therefore, you are not only trying to sell the products and services your company offers but Croatia itself as a tourism destination. Imagine you are attending a travel fair in London. A stand display emblazoned by your company name and a list of the activities you do is unlikely to attract many people, unless your company name includes the words 'Croatia' or 'Croatian'. The decision making processes of tourists is discussed later in the stage, but at this stage, you need to be aware that marketing the country is likely to bring more success than marketing solely your company.

The main thing that any tourist is purchasing when they come here is a Croatian experience, not the services of your guide or the quality of hotels. This is a decision they make after they have decided to come here. For someone who has never been to Croatia before, whether they are a tourist or a foreign tour operator, they will firstly want to know why they should come here and what the attractions and benefits are over other destinations. This is where competitiveness comes in again. You need to highlight what Croatia has that is better than other neighbouring countries and what is does better or differently than the competing destinations. Never be complacent and believe that tourists will always want to come to Croatia. Never also believe that everyone knows where Croatia is. Some of you will know from experience that those attendees at travel fairs first ask questions about the country rather than about your company. How sunny is it there? Where is Croatia? Didn't you have a war?

MARKETING RESEARCH

Marketing research is the design of a plan for the collection of data, the purpose of which is to answer a given question. Such a question could be "Which country's outbound tourists offer the best opportunity for long term sustainable growth?" or "Who is my biggest competition?". Answers to these questions are vital for understanding the market within which your business operates.

Research can fall into two areas:

1. A descriptive role whereby the aim is to focus on what is happening by concentrating on the collection of factual data to provide a picture of the current situation, or
2. An analytical role by shifting the focus to why things are happening in an attempt to explain the situation by seeking out reasons.

In order to develop a marketing plan, it is imperative that information is gathered on the business's performance and the marketplace. Answers are needed for a business to be able to make decisions. Without such information, any decisions being made run the risk of being bad ones which could prove very costly both financially and otherwise to the long term health of the business. Marketing research needs to be undertaken on a regular basis. Changes within the marketplace, among consumers and within the business will all have an effect on the business. Although information gathered from marketing research will not be perfect, if the research is well planned and executed, it will mean that decisions taken will be more likely to prove successful. There are various steps in undertaking research. Identify and define the problem - Before beginning the task of gathering information, it is first necessary to identify the problem for which research is required. You do not want to start gathering information only to find later that the information does not answer the questions you have. Investigate available sources - You do not want to start collecting information if that information already exists. You should seek out information which is already available.

The Learning Tools, will get you started with places to look for information:

- *Determine research plan*: Once all available sources of data have been evaluated, a plan is formulated to identify what further information is required and how it should be collected. This will involve generating hypotheses to be tested and methodo-logies. Methods could be interviews, surveys and observation.
- *Data collection*: Data should be collected based on the methodology outlined in the research plan.
- *Data analysis*: Based on the information collected analysis techniques will differ according to whether the information is quantitative or qualitative.
- *Present research results*: The information should be tabulated and interpreted so that recommendations can be made regarding the appropriate course of action to take.

When looking for secondary data (data from sources other than your business), sources could include government agencies, trade associations, trade press and magazines, subscription sources, the press, internal company records, international organizations A tour operator's need to do marketing research will fall into several areas:

- *Consumer satisfaction*: If you regularly receive clients, you will need to get feedback on the satisfaction of the services and products you are selling. This form of research would normally be in the form of a questionnaire that would be distributed to clients prior to their departure. The results of this research should help you to make changes to the way you run your operations to improve satisfaction.
- *Overseas Operator*: To sustain and grow the partnerships you have with foreign operators, you will need to undertake research on their satisfaction with your products and services. It may be that tourists will give feedback to them rather than to you. In which case, again some adjustments may be needed to your operations to ensure that satisfaction levels are maintained. Undertaking research is in itself, a marketing tool. Showing that you actively encourage feedback will impress the clients.
- *Industry trends*: Whether you just subscribe to industry trade magazines or e-newsletters or purchase reports on trends within the international tourism industry, it is important that you have some

familiarity on what changes are taking place in the popularity of competing destinations, consumer preference for destinations and growing markets for specific activities.

Market Segments and Channels

The Market Segments and Market Channels Presentation of the Learning Tools will walk you through the steps of understanding market segments and channels. The Marketing and Distribution Channel Worksheet that follows it will guide you through the basics of developing a marketing plan.

MAIN MARKETING TOOLS

TRADE FAIRS

Travel fairs and exhibitions can be a highly-cost effective sales and marketing tool combining all the best characteristics of advertising, promotions, direct mail and selling, either through tour operators and travel agents or, in the case of public shows, directly to consumers. Benefits include direct sales, new product launches, lead generation, penetration of new markets, building and maintaining client/customer relations, market research, database building and networking.

Research suggests that more than 80per cent of visitors to trade fairs are decision makers. Taking part in a trade fair without first having a clear view of why you are there is an almost certain recipe for failure.

Setting objectives is, therefore, an important starting point for any exhibition, giving direction to all aspects of your participation. Setting your objectives will make it possible to measure objectively the result of the exhibition, instead of making such a Judgement merely subjective. At the same time, objectives will help you establish budgetary requirements, motivate your staff and justify your participation next time around.

The goals you set for yourself need to be formulated as concretely as possible. They must be realistic, open to evaluation and have a time limit in order to facilitate and provide a firm base for future work. Possible objectives could include; increase in sales, meeting new clients, obtain market intelligence, launch new products, penetrate a new market, change or enhance company image, carry out market testing and study the activities of competitors.

In order to ensure that your objectives are appropriate and attainable, you need to:

- Know what you want to sell or communicate
- Know your target market
- Quantify your objectives in order to set a goal
- Ensure your targets are achievable
- Prioritize your objectives
- Communicate your objectives to your staff

Once you have defined your main goals, the next step is to give careful consideration to which sector of the travel industry you want to direct your sales and marketing efforts towards. How can you best attract your chosen targets to visit your stand? You could specifically invite companies to the fair, make pre-booked appointments or hold a reception on your stand for selected guests. By staying focused on your target market at all times, you will stand a better-than-average chance of getting your messages across and building new business. For some, having a stand of their own is the most natural way to participate, while others may find it more desirable or cost-effective to share stand space with others. Sharing with a national airline, a tourism board, a hotel or other tour operator who is not a direct competitor may enhance your presence. Since most tour operators will wish to work directly with overseas operators, it makes sense that attending wholly public fair would not be in your best interests. Your decision on where to exhibit should be made only after careful consideration of the event, the audience it is likely to attract, its timing and location and the cost, not only of exhibiting but also of attending including meals, accomm-odation and flights.

In deciding which fair(s) to participate, you should identify all the possibilities, compile as much information as possible; from organizers (attendance figures, breakdown of visitors, etc), cost implications and comments from other exhibitors. The more information you collect, the easier it will be to cut out those exhibitions that do not match your marketing objectives or your budget.

Similarly, timing of the event, the size and importance of their venues and their geographical catchment area will help you reach a decision. Planning is essential to protect your investment in trade fairs, it is the key to getting the best possible return, to ensure smooth and stress free exhibiting, project a cohesive, positive and memorable message and improve your participation the next time around.

Planning for an exhibition should be thorough enough that no surprises crop up during the actual exhibition, the time when all your efforts should be directed towards sales work. One person in the business should be responsible for making all the arrangements. Most fairs will provide you with a manual which should be fully understood.

A timetable should be drawn up highlighting key tasks and deadline dates. You should draw up a budget for your participation based on the activities you plan to become involved in. The budget should also be linked to the forecasts for the benefits that you expect to achieve.

The budget could be broken down into some areas:

- Stand space
  - Space rental
  - Design and construction (for space only stands)

  - Displays
  - Furniture
  - Accessories and equipment
  - Electrical installations
  - Connections – water, telephone, fax
  - Plants and Flowers
  - Cleaning and Security Services
  - Audiovisual equipment
  - Insurance
  - Catering
  - Incidentals
- Transport of materials
  - Packing
  - Air Shipment
  - Insurance
  - Customs Fees
  - Storage
  - Handling charges
- Personnel Costs
  - Staff transportation
  - Accommodation
  - Local transportation
  - Meal allowances
  - Interpreters
  - Entertainment
- Promotional Costs
  - Telephone and Mail marketing
  - Brochures and Catalogues printing
  - Post fair distribution of materials
  - Promotional video
  - Press packs
  - Translation of material
  - Promotional give aways
  - Passes for customers
  - Advertising in official fair catalogue
  - National and international magazine advertising
  - Other advertising
  - Sponsorship of fair activities

Your stand at a travel fair should make a strong visual impact and convey at a glance who you are and what you have to offer. For most tour operators, the shell scheme option will provide the best option. It will make it easier to present your products and services, is more cost efficient and minimizes the amount of time you need to spend at the venue during buildup and break down of the exhibition. A shell scheme is a basic framework or shell erected by the organizers appointed contractor on your behalf. Take only the space you need at a fair. If you take too much, you will be left with the problem of having nothing to fill it with.

The location of your stand within the exhibition is important, though with many wellestablished fairs, you may not have much option. You have a stand of the right size, properly equipped, containing the right exhibits and staffed by knowledgeable and well-prepared personnel able to negotiate on behalf of your company. If you have the chance to choose the location for your stand, look for the busiest areas of the hall where traffic flow is likely to be high. Also, take into account the location of competitors' stands, location of service and access points (entrances, stairways, feature areas, restaurants).

The design of the stand should reflect the messages that you wish to give to your clients and potential clients. If you want to get your company better known to all visitors then an open eye-catching display is most appropriate. With graphics, they should visualize clearly what you do, have brief messages and promote benefits and not features. Ensure that the messages can be read clearly.

Remember that if you choose a shell scheme you will still need to decorate it. A shell scheme will normally include a signboard, basic furniture, carpet and electrical connections. It will not do anything to promote your company. If an exhibition organizer does its job properly, it will deliver thousands of potential clients to the exhibition halls. What it will not do and cannot do is persuade those buyers to visit your stand, rather than those of your competitors. That is your job and your organization is the only one that stands to lose out if you do not do it. It is important to inform your target audience that you are exhibiting and about your profile at the show. You will also invite them to the stand and set up specific appointments with them. The key to effective promotion is to match your promotional strategy to your exhibition objectives; to coordinate your activities carefully; to explore all available avenues for promotion before, during and after the event and to heed all deadlines.

In order to promote your attendance before and during the fair, you could consider:

- Advertising in trade magazines and newspapers
- Undertaking direct mail
- Sponsoring fair events or merchandise
- Incentives and small give always
- Advertising in fair catalogue

The number of staff required to man the stand depends upon the size of your stand, the number of leads anticipated and facilities and activities on the stand. As a rule, you should allow one staff member per 4-5 square metres of floor space, this being the space required to allow two people to conduct a conversation comfortably. On person should be in charge and in attendance at the show all the time. Make sure that the staff on your stand really are friendly, approachable and well informed in the company products and services.

Staff training and briefing are essential to exhibition success; training in encouraging visitors on to the stand, how to open and close a conversation, how to qualify visitors and the impact of body language. Also make sure that your staff know what they should be selling and how. The stand should be manned at all times and should be kept tidy. The essence of sales technique if firstly to arouse interest of the prospects and discover his/her needs or problems. Then steer the conversation towards the way your products or services can solve these. Every person with whom you come into contact then receives individual attention depending on need.

The following sales techniques are important:

- Concentrate on people in your target markets
- Present briefly yourself and your product
- Chart the customer's needs and desires
- Steer the conversation towards the customer's needs and how your product/service satisfies these
- In all cases, make a note of the person's name, company, addressm etc and follow up after the fair, giving additional information and/or making your offer

The visitor information you capture at exhibitions and the way it is recorded, will have a direct effect on the speed and efficiency with which you follow up your leads. Only collecting business cards is not an effective way to compile visitor information, even if you do scribble action points on the back.

There are four steps to an effective follow-up after the fair:

1. Prioritize leads according to urgency
2. Follow up leads immediately
3. Pursue leads on an ongoing basis
4. Track leads to provide some measure of return on investment

When measuring the effectiveness of exhibition participation, there are two areas you need to look at. Firstly, the extent to which you achieved your specific objectives and secondly the extent to which the exercise proved cost effective. Look at the value of sales achieved, the number of qualified leads, the number of new contacts made, the level of awareness before and after the show, the number of promotional materials distributed, the media coverage generated, the value of market research undertaken and other benefits. The following is a suggested timetable of activities that may need to be undertaken when planning participation at a fair.

- 10-12 Months before the fair:
  - Make an initial selection of the itineraries and services that you will be selling

  - Calculate how much space you will require
  - Go over documentation from previous editions of the fair, if you were present at them
  - Draw up an initial budget
  - Get in contact with the fair organizers to let them know that you are interested in participating and request your space pre-registration
  - Examine the fair's rules and regulations
  - Fill out and submit the pre-registration and request information on promotional activities
- 8-10 Months before the fair
  - Draw up a plan and budget for the promotional activities organized prior to the fair
  - Budget for post-fair promotional activities
  - Decide on which information and sales material you will need
  - Analyse your needs for other material and where appropriate, design and develop it
  - Make allowances for trips and book tickets
  - Provide for accommodation and make reservations
- 6-8 Months before the fair
  - Design a support advertising campaign, objectives and timeframe
  - Launch the information campaign aimed at customers and trade media
  - Coordinate promotional activities with the fair organizers
  - Order promotional articles that will be handed out during the fair
  - Anticipate and organize logistics and transport tasks
  - Define the decoration, atmosphere and identity of your stand
- 4-6 Months before the fair
  - Coordinate planned activities with programmes and fair regulations – stand build up, advertising material, promotional material, miscellaneous activities
  - Identify new prospective clients and send them information
  - Order fair organizational services, external services, insurance
  - Design incentives for attracting visitors to the stand
- 2-4 Months before the fair
  - Intensify marketing actions to attract visitors
  - Select and allocate functions to the personnel that will be present on the stand and decide if you need to train staff in sales, train staff in corporate image, conduct practice sessions with products and sales arguments, instruct external personnel,
  - Send information for the fair catalogue
  - Check if periodic payments have been settled with the fair organizers

- 0-2 Months before the fair
  - Check the materials that should be taken to the fair – office materials, sales material, give aways
  - Organize press activities
  - Distribute information on new products, etc to technical magazines and the fair's press office
  - Send out passes and invitations to customers
  - Collect information on the seminars and conferences that are being organized
  - Prepare a form for registering the details provided by visitors that come to your stand
- During stand build up and fair
  - Build up the stand as soon as possible
  - Checklist in hand, make sure that none of the elements, materials or services ordered for the stand are missing
  - Locate the fair organization's offices and services
  - On a daily basis, supervise stand cleaning, stocks of promotional materials
  - Exchange information with other staff on a regular basis
  - Gather competitor information, make notes and compare with equivalent aspects in your own company
- After the fair
  - Supervise stand break down and packing of material and equipment
  - Organize the transport of material, equipment and products
  - Arrange a meeting with all personnel involved in the project to analyse results
  - Launch actions for following-up leads generated at the fair

Brochures and Printed Materials

As we stated earlier, a tour operator's brochure is important because of the intangible nature of the product that is being sold. The brochure should invite people to buy the itineraries it advertises, provide the information necessary to persuade the client to purchase a holiday and create and reinforce the company's image with its clients. Most brochures are designed to an A4 format in Europe and Letter size in the US so the size of your brochure will be important according to the market you are targeting. Most brochures are printed on glossy colored paper.

The bigger the brochure, the flimsier the paper it is printed on tends to be, both to keep down production costs and to stop it becoming unmanageably heavy. Pull out price pages are normally printed on cheap colored paper. Some companies will also have slightly thicker front covers to protect the brochures in transit and on the shelves, and to create a better image. Although many operators will produce full colour brochures, it is cheaper to choose fewer colors. A full Colour brochure could include some pages that are one or two Colour (those pages used for terms and conditions, booking information, etc) to cut down costs. Colour is important. Bright colors usually signify cheaper tours. Pale and dark colors signify more expensive tours. Every brochure should contain clear, legible, comprehensive and accurate information to enable the client to exercise and informed Judgement in making his choice.

Content could include:

- A company's legal identity
- Means of travel
- Destinations or itineraries
- Dates of fixed departures (if you have them)
- Nature of accommodation and meal facilities
- Additional facilities
- Booking conditions
- Insurance details
- Price policy
- Health matters
- Arbitration
- Publication date
- Difficulty ratings
- Maps
- Pictures of attractions, accommodations or previous clients

Of course the content of your brochures may vary according to whether you are targeting the travel trade or consumers. If you are selling tours in Europe, you may like to familiarize yourself with the EC Package Travel Regulations that outlines how European tour operators must present their information and what brochures must include. The front cover of the brochure is particularly important since it is what the client will see first of all. The cover must therefore be designed to be eye-catching but must simultaneously convey certain crucial messages.

It should show the company name and a logo. The choice of picture can make it clear what sort of product is on offer and also for whom the product is aimed at. The more expensive and exotic the product on offer, the less likely it is to show clients on the cover at all, preferring to concentrate on what they will see at their chosen destination.

The main part of the brochure should be clearly structured so that clients can easily identify the information they require. A contents page may be appropriate for brochures with many pages. Colored borders for pages also help in this regard. General information is usually found at the rear of the brochure. This would include guidelines for making bookings; information on what is included in the price, insurance and cancellation policies, a booking form, and health and visa requirements. If there are suitable destination marketing materials available that provide much of the destination information, then a company's promotional materials can focus more on their own particular itineraries.

The text of a brochure needs careful consideration. Firstly, there should be no grammatical or spelling mistakes.

Secondly, the text should present your products in a way that will make them appealing to potential customers. For Croatian operators, the text should emphasize the the beauty of the nature and uniqueness of the culture, history, cuisine, architecture, etc. as well as the prospects for adventure, good sailing, or outdoor sports. Many brochures will also use "you", "we" and "our" to emphasize the central role of clients and their needs and how 'at home' they will feel even though they are abroad.

Photographs have the same purpose of the text, to portray the destination and products in a positive light. The photographs should complement the text and be relevant to it. Obviously the photos should be of a high quality in terms of resolution. Also, they need to be professional.

It would not be appropriate for example to have pictures of clients wearing raincoats standing on a cloudy beach. There should be a good use of Colour. Many brochures will use pictures of previous clients enjoying themselves, inviting would-be buyers to imagine themselves in their place. If you use pictures of previous clients be sure that the clients are typical of those you are trying to attract

Web sites

A Well designed Web site will contain much the same information as a well conceptualized brochure. The difference here is that you have much more room for photos, and your use of Colour is limited only to the web palette of colors likely to display well on most monitors. You can also make inquiries, bookings, and other interactive functions easy for customers by using web forms, online reservations and payment, etc. Hundreds of Web sites exist with excellent features. Search (Google) company Web sites in your line of business and see which features you think are best, and try to integrate these features into your site planning.

Have a professional web developer do your site, and insist that current standards be used in the coding of your Web site. Because most search engines give sites using frames poorer rankings, for example, most new websites are now laid out using CSS, which also makes them faster to load. Decide if you will use HTML or XHTML, make sure the site is viewable in the most popular browsers (IE, Firefox, Netscape, and Opera are just a few). Finally, make sure you do a good job of search engine optimization.

PRODUCT DEVELOPMENT

DEVELOPING A PRODUCT

In designing a tourism product, you want to put together all the information you have collected about your target market and clients. The Product Development and Planning Sheet will help you organize the information. Once you have the facts laid out using the worksheet, developing an itinerary is the next step. Use the template provided (Product Development Planning Part 2) to lay out an itinerary with all the details. A Sample Itinerary is included in the Learning Tools. Studying the itineraries of leading outbound tour operators will give you many ideas about how to improve your own, but this is largely a creative process, and this manual cannot lead you through it step by step. Rather, the feedback you get from clients and outbound tour operators should guide you in continually improving your itineraries. Pricing your product is a process unique to each company. The Pricing Spreadsheet thatis given as an example is only one way to go about pricing a product. You will have to develop your own spreadsheet or tool that is adapted to your products and services. Just make sure you review all the possible costs associated with each itinerary and ensure you have accounted for them.

OPERATIONS AND MANAGEMENT

Once you have your products designed, you should ensure that you are set up to operate your tours when they sell, and to manage your business so that your trips run smoothly, the service you give is of good quality, and you have sufficient resources to serve your clients. This manual is not intended to teach you the details of running a small business, but Operations Workflow and Management gives you an illustration of the basic workflow of an outbound tour operator, and some tips on how to organize your operations. If you have a background in small business, it will be easy to adapt this information to setting up a tour company operation. There are some key issues that new tour operators should pay attention to when starting operations. These are listed below.

Key Issues for New Companies:

- *Keeping Track*: Set up an efficient documentation and filing system before you get much business. It takes too much time to fix it later.
- *Safety*: Client safety should be your absolute first priority. Train all trip staff in first aid (accredited course like Red Cross).
- *Liability Insurance*: Products sold in the EU must be backed by Errors and Omissions insurance. You should carry liability insurance for this and for Product Liability. Consider whether you need Employers Liability and insurance on your equipment.
- *Terms and Conditions*: In some cases, clients should sign a document accepting the risks of travel and releasing the tour operator from liability in case of accident and other unplanned events (lost time

from delays, trip cancellation due to forces of nature, etc.) Spend a lot of time on your Terms and Conditions document.

- *Travellers Insurance*: In most cases, require your clients have valid travellers health and accident insurance that also covers emergency evacuation. You should collect at the start of the trip a copy of this and of their passport.
- *Service Providers*: If possible, have multiple service providers identified for each service that is offered as part of your published trips.
- *Hiring staff (esp. guides)*: An experienced guide from another company is not always the best solution.
- *Staff training*: Is Every Year no matter how long the employee has been in the business. Learning new skills is an ongoing process and you should have refresher courses prior to each season.
- *The Guide or Trip Leader*: Is the most important person to the client since they are in contact every day for several days. The client doesn't care about the company director, president, manager. Guides must be able to solve most problems ON THE SPOT, without help from you.
- *Focus on Your Business*: If you are a tour operator, don't try to run a hotel, ticketing agency, and restaurant as part of that business.
- *Ticketing Agent*: A good agent or agency handling your air tickets is worth their weight in gold. If the client can't get to Croatia they are not coming on your trip. Eventually you may need ticketing agents in your major markets.
- *Response Time*: The most important factor of getting good business is answering inquiries quickly – and answering the questions the client ASKED!!!!!! Excellent = same day, good = 24 to 48 hours. Over 48 hours = lost client in most cases.
- Service Providers often need to be educated about the tourism business (eg. hotels that ask for full advance payment)
- Make sure your contract with the service provider lays out rates and terms for the whole season – or you will not be able to respond quickly to requests.
- Some service providers are very difficult to work with. Often if they see you are taking clients t another service provider they will make an effort to change.
- Keep service providers informed about your operations and the markets you serve. Give them client feedback from your trips, so they can also work to improve their services.

WORKING WITH OUTBOUND OPERATORS

You are ready to begin contacting outbound operators and agents you have found as part of your marketing research. Don't forget to refer to the specialty travel indexes provided in Travel Research Links in the Tools. Here are some tips on working with outbound operators.

- *First Do Homework*:
  - Before approaching an operator, study their product well.
  - Make sure if you contact them your communication indicates that you understand in general their product type, travel style, and how their itineraries are set up.
  - Make sure you have something of interest to offer them (not already in their catalog), so they will be more disposed to answering your questions.
  - Do not be afraid of asking questions to clarify their requirements. The operator should understand you seek to improve your product offering to them. It is better to ask than to most tour operators expect a certain amount of back and forth before getting the right trip.
- *Getting in the Door*:
  - Sending interesting product descriptions with photos and prices is often effective. Save them time and effort.
  - A familiarization trip is the best way to attract AND repel clients. The outcome will depend on how well you have done your homework and prepared for the visit.
  - Travel fairs are NOT the best place to meet people… it's where people come find you. Try and schedule meetings with your targeted operators before or after the fair – or making a separate trip.
  - Using the right terms is an indication of how easy you will be to work with. Make an effort to learn the terminology of the business.
- *Establishing Relationships*:
  - Signing a contract for one or more trips a season is the first step in the relationship.
  - Offer reliable service
  - Be flexible when you can
  - Offer something new every year that helps them sell their trips.
  - Stick to the terms of the contract you have signed. If you must change something, wait until the contract is up for renewal and give good reasons for the change.
  - Take client feedback seriously, and respond in a positive and appropriate manner. No responses or argumentative ones, and business will go elsewhere.
- *Building Relationships*:
  - Take clients on your trips – especially if they do not use their

own trip leaders and do not get to experience the product first hand.
  - Visit clients in their offices when you have a chance, and get to know the staff there.
  - Pass on discounts or cost savings when appropriate.
  - If you sell an itinerary as an exclusive, ensure that you do not offer the same trip to another client.
  - Treat their traveller information as privileged. Never use it for direct marketing or to "steal clients". Word will get around faster than you can imagine.
  - Make it as easy as possible for them to book with you.
- *Building Relationships*:
  - Working well with their trip leaders is an excellent way to build your trip portfolio with any operator. Take trip leaders on mini fam trips if you can keep them in country a few extra days.
  - Always inform the client of any problems as they arise, and steps you are taking to resolve them. If you cannot reach the client, take detailed notes so you can give a good accounting of your actions in case of problems or emergencies.
  - Always take responsibility for any mistakes made by your office or your staff. If you are honest and bring up problems first, your client will see the incident in a far better light.
- *Tips*:
  - For every itinerary you send, detail what is included in the price and what is excluded.
  - Calculate price breaks according to pax breaks used by your client.
  - Usually, a trip leader position is offered FOC – this does not mean you pay for their trip leader to travel. It means the cost is already factored in to your pax breaks.
  - If there are changes, always send a new itinerary with a different reference number – in PDF form or by fax. The client should agree in writing and reference this number. This will help avoid any misunderstanding.
- *Unpleasant Surprises*:
  - Serious operators do not ask you to pay airfare.
  - Operators who put continuous downward pressure on prices may not be serious about quality. Selling trips with very low margins does not help your business.
  - Try and check out operators to ensure they are reputable before offering fam trips or giving away detailed information.
  - Be prepared to have any itinerary you publish get copied – and

purchased from another cheaper supplier. That's life in the business!
- Contact lists are gold – keep them secure.
- Before making big non-refundable deposits on a trip with a new customer, run a credit check.

CONTINUOUS IMPROVEMENT

Finally, as your business develops, you will want to continually improve your product and service. Remember the part on Being Competitive? Using what you know now about competitive products and the simple Gap Analysis Tool of the Learning Tools, you will be able to build a stronger business year by year.

7

Improving Tour Operator Performance

INTRODUCTION

Once there was just the financial bottom line. Now companies recognise they must be accountable for their social, environmental and economic impacts – the new triple bottom line. They recognise the need to preserve the environment, to look after their workforce and to give something back to communities. All this needs to be done while running a profitable business. This whole approach is corporate social responsibility or CSR. It is about customer satisfaction, environmental protection, and a positive contribution to development. It means developing quality products and offering customer choice.

It includes training staff, providing a healthy and supportive working environment and entering long-term partnerships with suppliers. CSR adds value through product differentiation and increased quality, as well as by preventing the degradation of the very base of the tourism experience, *i.e.* nature and cultural heritage. Customers have rewarded those companies that have adopted an ethical stance. Co-op's market research found that more than a quarter of current account holders cited ethics or the environment as the reason for opening their accounts. CSR makes sense for companies. It is not just the communities, customers and environment that gain. The business benefits of CSR enable it to be a successful model for all.

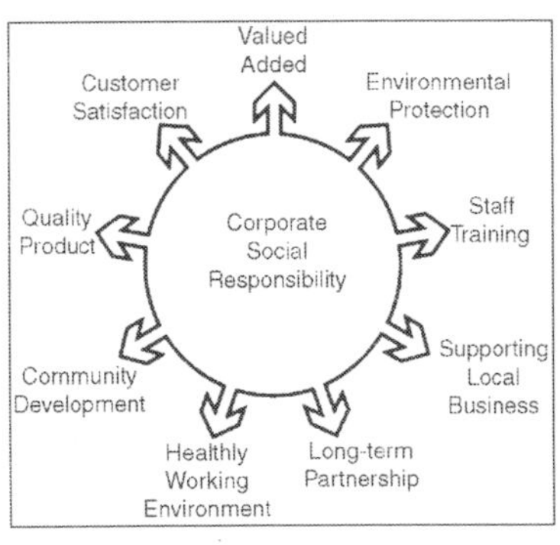

SUSTAINABLE TOURISM

Tourism has mixed impacts. On the positive side tourism provides jobs, brings foreign exchange and provides income to support local development. It can also directly support local industry and encourage communities to place greater emphasis on environmental protection. However, one of the main problems is that the benefits of tourism often bypass the local population, and tourism related activities can contribute to the degradation of the environment. They can put pressure on scarce local resources such as land and water, pollute the environment and reduce biodiversity. Money may not reach the local economy, and the jobs available may be poorly paid and provide insecure employment. Taking action to increase the positive impacts and reduce the negative impacts is vital to the future sustainability and profitability of tourism. A forwardlooking business will address these issues before it is too late, and CSR can provide a useful framework by which to do this.

WHAT IS ALREADY HAPPENING

Many tour operators are already undertaking CSR activities, such as giving money to charity, surveying suppliers on their sustainability practices, or providing information to their customers on local customs and how to protect the environment. However, these actions are often ad-hoc and may be limited to the manager or a few staff members in a company. To be successful, CSR actions need to be part of core business and integrated throughout the supply chain. This means a systematic application of business ethics to all operations.

REPORTING ON PERFORMANCE

To judge the success of any CSR action, companies need to measure their impacts. For others to understand, they need to communicate the results. This process of reporting on performance has become an important tool to demonstrate these impacts. Many companies are producing social and environmental reports. However, to be meaningful, these need reports to be comparable between companies, and provide information on all areas of business practice. Not everything can be done at once. The key is to start the process and do something.

CORPORATE SOCIAL RESPONSIBILITY

CSR IN MORE DEPTH

CSR calls for a consistent set of policies, programmes and practices that will integrate social, environmental and economic principles into existing business processes. This needs to be from head office throughout the supply chain, making it part of core business operations.

Business for Social Responsibility, a responsible company should be active in the following areas:

- *Mission/ vision/ values*: Reflecting CSR in the company's underlying principles.
- *Business ethics*: The integration of a company's core values into its policies, practices and decisionmaking *e.g.* policies on covering corruption and bribery.
- *Governance/ accountability*: How the board of directors operates, how the company engages stakeholders and how it measures, reports and verifies its impacts.
- *Community involvement*: The company's donated resources to the communities where it operates *e.g.* donations of goods and money, staff volunteering time.
- *Community economic development*: Increasing economic benefits to local communities *e.g.* favouring excluded businesses, supporting activities that stimulate wealth creation, and community participation in decision-making.
- *Human rights*: The basic standards of treatment to which all people are entitled *e.g.* avoiding forced and child labour, protecting indigenous rights.
- *Environment*: Increasing efficiency and minimising pollution and physical degradation *e.g.* energy efficiency, waste reduction and recycling, reducing resource use.
- *Workplace*: The human resource policies that directly affect employees *e.g.* paying fair wages, training and education, non-discrimination.
- *Marketplace/ consumers*: The activities involved in marketing, production and distribution *e.g.* accurate marketing, consumer privacy, product safety and disposal.

WHY CSR MAKES SENSE FOR TOUR OPERATORS

CSR makes sense for companies. It is not just the communities, customers and environment that benefit. It is the business benefits of CSR that enable it to be a successful model.3 The business benefits for tourism include:

- *Responding to consumer demand*: Market research by Tearfund in 20004 showed that half of those interviewed were more likely to book a holiday with a tour operator that has an ethical code, and the majority of those were willing to pay for that guarantee. ABTA research in 2002 found that 87per cent of holidaymakers said it is important that their holiday does not damage the environment, and 76per cent feel that tourism should benefit those in the destination, through jobs and business opportunities. The research showed that 59per cent wanted information about local issues in their resort before they booked.5 Those operators that lead the field and become more responsible are likely to be rewarded with increased sales.
- *Improved service*: Contributing to poverty reduction in a destination

and having a strong commitment to the workforce can create good morale and ensure a better welcome for customers. Investment in training will improve the quality of the product and customer service. Supporting local businesses will enhance the cultural experience.

- *Risk management*: Operating in a more sustainable way will greatly reduce the risks that a company faces. It will protect the company's image by dealing with problems before they get out of hand or are published in the media (as for health and safety considerations). Investment in staff can help to keep a high morale and therefore reduce staff turnover. Supporting community development will ensure good will and co-operation, and will ultimately safeguard the company's investment. Sound environmental management will ensure that the destination is desirable for visitors and the community in the long-term.
- *Cost savings*: Installing energy efficient systems at head office can save money as well as protecting the environment *e.g.* through reducing heat loss or reducing the quantity of waste disposed. Recycling and cutting paper use can also save money.
- *Pre-empting government regulation*: Governments are under increasing pressure by NGOs, unions and the general public to regulate the business sector. This pressure increases if bad practices are uncovered. Businesses that behave in a sustainable way that exceeds all existing legislation and builds on good practice can reduce the need for legislation. Those that develop their own codes of conduct and have independently verified reports will be in a strong situation to influence any proposed legislation. For the moment the UK and EU governments have favoured a voluntary approach to CSR, but this will be reviewed in the future. The onus is on companies to show that they are responsible, or face the threat of future legislation.
- *Growth of socially responsible investment (SRI)—*: A growing number of investors want a good return for their money in a socially responsible manner. In the last five years, investment in SRI and ethical funds quadrupled from £0.8 billion to £3.3 billion6 The Ethical Investment Research Service shows that 77per cent of pension fund members want their funds to develop an SRI policy, as long as it does not hurt their financial interests.7 Those tour operators that are listed and that are ethical will be the ones to gain from this increased ethical investment.

THE PROCESS OF CSR

For those starting to explore these issues, it can seem like a maze of terms and plethora of processes and tools to choose from. To provide some clarity we show below how a process of implementing CSR is likely to work for a tour operator, and some examples of what may be included under each step. Like any process, each step is not isolated and there is likely to be significant overlap. These steps give a route map for implementing CSR in your company. They highlight some of the main challenges facing tour operators and also point towards some of the performance indicators of good practice.

Step 1

Commitment to being a responsible tour operator. It will involve writing a basic policy, defining goals and objectives, appointing staff members and committing funds to carry out the commitments.

- Establish a clear policy and objectives for responsible tourism and ensure that it covers operations both in the UK and in overseas destinations, right through the supply chain. Ensure there is support for this at board level.
- Appoint a responsible tourism staff member who will oversee the development and integration of these issues throughout the organisation. Commit funds to becoming more responsible.

Step 2

- Planning in more detail what it means to be responsible. It will involve consultation with all relevant stakeholders, developing management systems to cover environmental and social issues, and awareness raising and training of staff. It will also mean setting measurable targets, and developing guidelines and procedures.
- Take time to research destinations and speak to local development and environment groups and tourism associations, not just to the hotels. Find out which local businesses you could use, and with whom you may be able to develop a partnership. Also research attitudes and expectations of tourists.
- Train staff at head office and in the destinations so that they understand the policies and are able to implement them.

Step 3

Implementation of the policies and plans. Implementation should produce the desired improvements in product design, community development and co-operation, staff morale and performance, environmental preservation and customer satisfaction.

- Work throughout your supply chain to develop and implement purchasing policies that will focus on local ownership, use local labour, foods and crafts. Work with your suppliers to encourage good environmental management and build this up to include social areas such as employment standards and minimum wage levels.

- Brief local agents and representatives on your policies and objectives.
- Produce and disseminate a code for tourists to help them travel in a more informed and responsible way. Include advice on how they can support local development projects.

Step 4

Monitoring and Reporting performance is vital to understanding what differences are being made, and to communicate this with all stakeholders.

A report addressing the company's sustainability performance and the effectiveness of its CSR policies is the most effective way to communicate the achievements made. The report should ideally be independently verified so that a company's claims are substantiated and therefore seen as credible.

- Monitor your activities regularly so that you can learn from them and plan how to increase the impact each year.
- Publicise your performance to clients and share it with others *e.g.* on the internet, in brochures and in advertising.
- Use your annual report to report on your performance and to gain support among your key stakeholders.

Step 5

Improving Your Performance

The reason for getting involved in CSR is to increase the benefits for everyone. Regular review of the results achieved is essential for learning and making improvements. The sustainability reports also help companies to understand in which areas the company is not performing in a sustainable manner *e.g.* environmental degradation, low staff morale, threatened consumer action, few benefits to local communities.

- Set clear targets for year-on-year improvement in terms of building partnerships, using local suppliers and encouraging social and environmental improvements in hotels.
- Make changes to your business practices based on the information gathered.

REPORTING ON THE SUSTAINABILITY OF YOUR COMPANY

Reporting is the fourth stage in a process of CSR. It is absolutely essential to measure impact, be accountable to stakeholders and improve the performance of the business. It involves publicising the positive impacts you are having and developing strategies for improvements in the weaker areas.

BENEFITS OF REPORTING

- *Improved public image*: Companies with a credible report show that they are concerned about their impact and take their social and environmental responsibility seriously.

- *Improved sales*: For companies that demonstrate to customers that their holidays will bring benefits to those living in destinations, protect the environment and provide a good quality holiday.
- *Long-term sustainability*: Reporting can act as a check on whether the activities of a company are sustainable, or whether they will need to change in order to guarantee their long-term survival. It can act as an early warning system and indicate priority areas for action.
- *Better communication and co-operation*: Through regular consultation and feedback with staff and those in destinations. Consultation is necessary for gathering the information needed for a report.
- *Responding to demand for increased accountability*: The Prime Minister has recently called for the top 350 companies in the UK to produce environmental reports. An independent report into the UK Company Law Review (2001) recommended that all directors report annually on social and environmental issues. The Enron and World.com situation has placed pressure for increased financial accountability. However, NGOs and customers are increasingly wary of well-written policies that are not backed up with practical evidence.
- *Monitoring and benchmarking your performance*: Reporting requires regular monitoring of a company's performance. Companies can compare their own performance year on year, and can also compare their performance in relation to other companies.

REPORTING USING THE GLOBAL REPORTING INITIATIVE (GRI) GUIDELINES

There are a number of different guidelines available to use for reporting. They focus on different areas of company operation *e.g.* AccountAbility 1000 looks at accounting practices and management procedures, SA8000 focuses on labour issues and the ISO14000 series looks at environmental management. The Global Reporting Initiative (GRI) has combined and built on these major guidelines to produce one overall framework.

The GRI supports an incremental approach to reporting and companies are encouraged to start reporting on a few issues and to increase the depth and scope of their reporting each year.

In addition to the GRI core guidelines, a Tour Operators' Sector Supplement has been developed under the co-ordination of the Tour Operators' Initiative (TOI). Those involved include members of the TOI, representatives of tour operators' suppliers (accommodation, cruise liners, airlines, ground transport), local authorities, tourism boards, environment and development groups and labour unions. *e.g.* year 3: give advice at the destination briefing session on using the local markets and eating in locally-run restaurants *i.e.* how to ensure tourism money benefits the local economy.

JOIN THE TOI PILOT PROJECT

For tour operators to start reporting, it can seem like a daunting task. The TOI has developed significant expertise in this area over the past two years through its members, the secretariat and other involved groups such as development and environment experts, labour groups, local authorities and tourism boards. Members of the TOI will get support from their fellow members as well as the secretariat and a network of experts that have also contributed to the development of the indicators. Any tour operator committed to sustainable development can join the TOI. All members have signed a Statement of Commitment and pay an annual membership fee to support joint activities. During 2003 the pilot will develop a manual of detailed advice and guidance to enable operators to understand what the performance indicators mean, what information to gather and how to gather it. In 2004 participating tour operators will collect the information for their own reports, ready to make their first social and environmental report in 2005. Currently UK members of the TOI are British Airways Holidays, First Choice, Exodus, Discovery Initiatives, TUI Northern Europe.

JOIN THE SUSTAINABLE TOURISM INITIATIVE

The UK Sustainable Tourism Initiative (STI) is a body consisting of tour operators, government and NGOs. The aim is to 'work together to create a step-change in the implementation of sustainable tourism practices by the UK outbound tourism industry.' It has been in its development phase for 18 months and is due to be launched early in 2003. Part of its remit is to enable companies to implement changes in their own organisation to become more responsible.

Operators who are not members should join and gain from the expertise and tools that are being developed. Each member company is asked to feedback annually on their activities. The STI will therefore need to provide guidance on what tour operators should report on annually. This should be based on the GRI/ TOI guidelines and indicators. The STI should consider doing this at the earliest possible opportunity and holding a seminar to train the tour operators' staff who will be responsible for reporting.

8

Industry Trade Groups

ASSOCIATION OF EUROPEAN AIRLINES

The Association of European Airlines is a non-profit industry organisation, bringing together 35 major European Airlines as the voice of the European Airline Industry for more than 50 years. Based on its extensive knowledge of the industry, AEA is an essential industry platform, and is relied upon by policy-makers as a trustworthy contributor to the debates around the decision-making process. AEA works in partnership with the institutions of the European Union and other stakeholders in the value chain, to ensure the sustainable growth of the European airline industry in a global marketplace.

AEA Member Airlines carried 326 million passengers and 5.5 million tonnes of cargo in 2009 and provide direct employment to 383,000 people in 2009. They operate 11,200 flights a day, serving 630 destinations in 160 countries, with a global turnover of □ 70 billion. The AEA had its beginnings in 1952 when the presidents of Air France, British Airways, KLM, Lufthansa, Sabena Airlines and Swissair formed a joint study group. It now includes many major European airlines. The offices of AEA are located on Avenue Louise in central Brussels, Belgium.

AFRICAN AIRLINES ASSOCIATION

The African Airlines Association, also known by its abbreviation AFRAA, is a trade association of airlines which hail from the nations of the African Union. Founded in Accra, Ghana in 1968, and today headquartered in Nairobi, Kenya, the primary purpose of AFRAA is to establish and facilitate co-operation between African airlines.

AIR TRANSPORT ASSOCIATION

The Air Transport Association of America, Inc. is America's oldest and largest airline trade association. ATA's member airlines and their affiliates transport more than 90 Per cent of U.S. airline passenger and cargo traffic. U.S. airlines founded the association in 1936 and it is based in Washington,

D.C.. It is the only trade organization that represents the principal U.S. airline and is the airlines' key voice before Congress. ATA advocates on behalf of the airline industry to the U.S. Congress, state legislatures, the Department of Transportation and the Federal Aviation Administration. ATA has played a major role in all government decisions concerning aviation since its founding, including the creation of the Civil Aeronautics Board, the creation of the air traffic control system and airline deregulation.

ATA's stated purpose is to "foster a business and regulatory environment that ensures safe and secure air transportation and enables U.S. airlines to flourish, stimulating economic growth locally, nationally and internationally." ATA's senior staff members have testified before Congress on numerous legislative and regulatory matters including aviation safety, airline consumer issues, aviation security, airspace congestion, and aviation and the environment. ATA works with its members on legal and technical issues affecting the U.S. airline industry. ATA operates member committees related to fuel; airports; engineering and maintenance; the environment; training; security; ground safety; medical issues; and international affairs.

ATA advocates common industry positions before state and local governments to assure governmental and public understanding of all aspects of air transport. ATA's stated priorities include maintaining airline safety; reforming energy-commodity markets; creating an international framework for reducing industry emissions; accelerating modernization of the air traffic control system; and reducing government taxes on airlines. The Air Transport Association also has been very involved in promoting fuel efficiency and alternative fuel development. The Air Transport Association supports NextGen modernization of the air traffic control system. This system will update the current 1950's radar based technology with a modern, satellite-based navigation system. Aviation experts predict that a modern air traffic management system will save jet fuel and reduce delays by allowing planes to fly shorter routers and by allowing more aircraft to fly safely at any given time.

Modernizing the air traffic control system would also reduce the amount of time that airplanes spend waiting on runways and in holding patterns. Since 1937, ATA annually has released an economic report on the U.S. airline industry that includes statistics on operational and financial results for passenger and cargo operations. This report includes data on industry revenue, expenses, traffic, fuel use, safety, economic impact and employment. ATA also publishes a handbook on the airline industry that provides background information on airline economics, operations, safety, security and history. The Air Transport Association released the newest version of ATA Spec 100 in 1999. The ATA Web site, this information will not be revised, and has been combined with ATA Spec 2100 to produce the ATA iSpec 2200: Information Standards for Aviation Maintenance manual.

This specification defines a widely-used numbering scheme for aircraft parts and the appearance of printed aircraft maintenance information. The Federal Aviation Administration's JASC (Joint Aircraft System/Component) code table provides a modified version of ATA Spec 100. ATA Spec 100 contains format and content guidelines for technical manuals written by aviation manufacturers and suppliers, and is used by airlines and other segments of the industry in the maintenance of their respective products. This document provides the industry wide standard for aircraft systems numbering, often referred to as the ATA system or ATA chapter numbers. The format and content guidelines define the data prepared as conventional printed documentation. In 2000, ATA Spec 100 and ATA Spec 2100 were incorporated into ATA iSpec 2200: Information Standards for Aviation Maintenance. ATA Spec 100 and Spec 2100 will not be updated beyond the 1999 revision level.

EUROPEAN LOW FARES AIRLINE ASSOCIATION

BACKGROUND

The European Low Fares Airline Association (ELFAA) represents 10 airline members from 9 European Countries carrying over 60 million passengers or roughly 15per cent of intra-European passengers in 2004. Our members currently are:

- Air Berlin (Germany),
- Flybe (UK),
- Hapag-Lloyd Express (Germany),
- Norwegian (Norway, Ryanair (Ireland),
- Sky Europe (Slovakia),
- Sterling (Denmark),
- Sverige Flyg (Sweden),
- Transavia (Netherlands), and
- WIZZ Air (Hungary).

None of ELFAA's members belong to the Airline Group. Low Fares Airlines have been responsible for the huge growth in air transportation since the liberalization of air travel within Europe and to continue their success, low fares airlines must continually seek efficiency gains not only within their own organization but also throughout the supply chain. The supply of air traffic services accounts for some 12per cent+ of a European low fares airline's cost base and this percentage will continue to increase as a percentage of the whole as other costs continue to decrease. Air traffic services are a notable part of the supply chain which remains highly inefficient and where costs are unacceptably high and continuously increasing. It is also an area over which airlines have little or no influence. It is hoped that the Charging Directive still being considered by the European Commission in connection with the Single

European Sky will be more biting than has been experienced before and that this will begin to be a driver of efficiency gains by air traffic service providers across Europe. The CAA will therefore need to ensure that provision is made within the Price Control to allow for a mid-term review to take any significant requirements into account at the earliest opportunity rather than wait for the subsequent regulatory period.

GENERAL COMMENTS

ELFAA welcomes the CAA's view that although NATS Holdings Ltd is 41.9per cent owned by a consortium of some UK airlines, the role of the Airline Group in itself is insufficient to permit a less intrusive form of regulation and that regulatory incentives remain essential. Although non-Airline Group members are supposed to be represented on the Board, there is no clear line of communication through which these airlines can make their views known and it is therefore difficult for our airlines to accept that this is the case. We therefore rely on the CAA as an independent regulator to ensure that non-Airline Group members are not disadvantaged in any way and that their views are in fact taken into account on an equal basis. We remain genuinely concerned that trends in the UK unit rate continue to show no real positive benefit as a result of NATS having been privatized and the UK remains one of the highest rates in Europe.

This is not the outcome which was reasonably expected as a result of the privatization of NATS. In addition to this, non-Airline Group airlines have been forced to share in a risk element which would normally be shouldered by shareholders themselves. We would again point out NATS' agreement that achieving the European average rate by 2008 was a realistic objective and the Regulator should therefore be firm in ensuring that this happens as well as securing a high level of service. In fact, NATS, being the only privatized air traffic service provider in Europe, should be leading the way and be a model of efficiency for other providers in Europe. There is no real evidence that this has been the case. Work carried out by Euro control's Performance Review Committee has highlighted areas for efficiency gains and the Regulator should therefore secure a challenging target to ensure that all possible areas are considered. The Price Control should take into account not only the fact that NATS is a monopoly provider of services in UK airspace but also that an element of risk-sharing was forced onto users as part of the Composite Solution and prices were increased. This lower risk element should be adequately reflected in the level of return allowed. Although NERL's gearing is high, this issue has already been addressed through the application of the Composite Solution and therefore should not be taken into account again in determining the Price Control. We are also concerned that the element of risk bearing by NERL is being reduced through the back door and would appreciate a full listing of those elements being proposed which effect the level of risk so that the overall impact is fully transparent. The CAA should also ensure that changes to charging principles or cost allocation as a result of SES requirements are not used as a smokescreen and that real reductions to charges overall are achieved. Although the Single European Sky initiative is moving towards more competition, this will take time to achieve and meanwhile moves need to be made across Europe to ensure that greater efficiencies and higher performance levels are achieved in the immediate future. ELFAA has already commented to Euro control States that stricter disciplines need to be introduced into Air Navigation Service Providers to simulate the level of competition which exists in a truly competitive environment.

Several excesses exist within ANSPs that simply would not exist in a competitive environment and users should not be expected to pay for them. In considering the Price Control for CP2, the implications of new EC legislation need to be fully taken into account. The Passenger Compensation Legislation whereby airlines must provide assistance to passengers in respect of long delays as a result of, *i.e.*, ATC problems and also the SES package of legislation which is intended to improve both the performance and also efficiency of air traffic services provider are both relevant although little mention has been made of them.

CAA PROPOSALS - THE FRAMEWORK

Regulatory Period

This should be for a further 5 year period as normal. However allowance should be made for a mid-term review to be carried out if necessary to allow for any appropriate adjustments resulting from the SES Mandates to be implemented so that benefits resulting from these flows through to airlines at the earliest opportunity in line with the objective of the SES initiative those European airlines should benefit from this initiative.

Setting the Control on the Basis of an Established Regulatory Asset Base

This approach should be maintained. However, no new capital expenditure should be allowed unless cooperation with other providers has been considered first as a way of avoiding or significantly reducing the need for this capital expenditure.

Scope of the Price Control

We welcome the extension of the price control to include NERL's Terminal Approach business and would argue that the price control should also include the Approach and Aerodrome business, especially in areas which are not really and easily open to competition such as London. This should not, however, automatically give NERL the right to make changes in the way that current charges are levied, merely that the appropriate level of revenue and costs should be taken into account in arriving at the final decision on the Price Control. Emphasis should be made here that any change to the way in which charges are levied should be subject to full and proper user consultation and not be unduly influenced by the Board to which non-Airline Group airlines have no direct input.

Single Till vs. Cost Allocation

We completely support the single till approach. The SES initiative will present NERL with various opportunities for making additional revenues. The cost of providing these services may be difficult to allocate and could result in a high degree of conflict between users and NERL. To avoid this situation the single till approach should be adopted.

Level of Fixed and Variable Elements

It was our understanding that the 50/50 sharing of risk was a one-off exceptional risk for airlines for CP1 only. It should not therefore be carried through into CP2 thereby making it a permanent feature. The recovery of revenues should therefore revert to a flexible only allowance for CP2 in accordance with the terms of the Composite Solution.

Measure to be Used for Traffic Volumes

The use of CSUs as the measure of traffic volumes should be continued. This not only matches the Euro control charging structure and is therefore more easily understood but also any change would be complicated for little or no value added.

Smoothing of Correction Factor

Any corrections should be made as soon as possible so that the adjustments relate as closely as possible the users concerned. Smoothing should not therefore be over a 2-year period.

CAA'S INITIAL PROPOSALS-SERVICE QUALITY INCENTIVE

ELFAA agrees that stronger measures should be in place to incentives NERL to improve its service quality. In view of the Passenger Compensation Regulation now in place which requires airlines to provide assistance to passengers in the event of long delays attributable to air traffic service problems, there should be a greater emphasis on the penalties to be paid for delays with periods introduced which are in line with those in the Regulation. Because assistance must be given to passengers irrespective of the time of day, the penalties should be at the same level throughout the day and not especially loaded for peak times. Low fares airlines operate with high load factors throughout the day and the financial cost of ATC delays will be high and could even be greater than the total revenue from the flight delayed. The level of penalties payable for long delays should be commensurate with the level of additional cost incurred by the delayed flight and a mechanism put in place to ensure that any payments are made to airlines on a regular basis.

Penalty payments in respect of delays should also recognise that often intra-European flights are delayed, especially early morning, as transatlantic flights are given priority. In addition, delay payments should be calculated not on an average "London' basis as this could disadvantage a particular airline or group of airlines as a result of the averaging out of the times involved, *e.g.*, Stansted could be the limit whereas Heathrow could be under the limit. The mechanism adopted should therefore ensure fair and equitable treatment between users/ classes of users.

CAA'S INITIAL PROPOSALS-SETTING THE LEVEL

Operating Expenditure

In view of the fact that NATS is amongst the highest unit rates in Europe, it is essential that they are given challenging targets so that more realistic cost reductions can be achieved. It is noted that NATS has been involved jointly with the CAA in a benchmarking study on operating costs and it is therefore impossible to accept this work as being independent and impartial. The CAA has recognized that NATS' salary levels are often substantially higher than in other businesses even before pension benefits are taken into account and also that NATS is proposing to increase average real wages beyond the 1.4per cent average drift predicted over the period.

In addition NERL's operating expenditure is broadly comparable to the average among European ANSPs although this does not take into account the fact that salary levels in some countries are higher due to higher social costs etc. Although the fact that non-ATCO costs at some 2per cent - 8per cent higher can be explained in part by NERL'S use of ATSAs, this is not acceptable. The CAA's proposals to apply a 2per cent real cost reduction in underlying costs for the first 2 years from April 2005 and 3per cent thereafter is not considered to be sufficiently challenging. NERL should be incentives to make greater cost reductions by changing working methods and users should not be charged with certain staff costs which are unreasonable compared with the industry in general.

Absenteeism levels of 2per cent are achieved in the low cost sector and this more efficient target should also be applied to NERL. In addition, users should not be charged with the cost of holiday entitlements which are those prescribed in the European Working Time Directive. These excesses would not exist in a truly competitive environment and should not, therefore, be allowed for in the Price Regulation which is intended to act as a proxy for competition.

Historical and Future Capital Expenditure

Now that SES regulations are in place, it is essential to ensure that the asset base only includes elements that continue to be necessary and do not allow for duplicated facilities that are not required. Consideration of the possibility of cooperation with other States should first be undertaken. An example of this is the New Scottish Centre. Now that the sharing of service provision between States is being encouraged we are not aware that any review has taken place to ensure there is still a requirement for this facility or whether, in fact, sufficient contingency could in fact be provided by Ireland's Service Provider. We therefore need to be assured that the CAA has considered how new approaches to the provision of ATS have been taken into account and the view arrived at that the proposed asset base remains appropriate.

Cost of Capital

The cost of capital should take into account the fact that NERL is a relatively low risk monopoly business. It is difficult to gauge how much risk sharing is being passed onto users through the back door under this set of proposals hence the former request for a summary. The CAA is proposing a cost of capital allowance of 6.5per cent but this is considered to be high, especially in view of the fact that overall the proposals are not sufficiently challenging. PwC have proposed a mid-point estimate of 6.1per cent pre-tax real. If other elements of the Price Control are tightened up then it might be reasonable for NERL to be allowed a cost of capital not exceeding of 6per cent. If the other elements are not made more challenging then the cost of capital should be significantly reduced.

EUROPEAN REGIONS AIRLINE ASSOCIATION

Founded in 1980, European Regions Airline Association, ERA, is a non-profit trade association representing almost 200 companies involved in European air transport, including airlines, airframe and engine manufacturers, airports, suppliers and service providers from all over Europe. The Association promotes the interests of intra-European airlines by lobbying the European Commission and other European regulatory bodies on policy matters, promoting the social and economic importance of air transport and its environmental commitments, holding an annual conference and other networking events, publishing a monthly journal and providing expert advice and guidance on all air transport regulatory matters.

- ERA was founded in Switzerland in 1980 with 5 airline members.
- In 1987 ERA moved to its current location Fairoaks Airport near Chobham, Surrey, United Kingdom.
- Today, ERA is the largest body representing the interests of regional airlines in Europe.

ERA is governed by a Board, which is elected from and by the membership each year. The Board is responsible for overseeing the activities and strategy of the Association. The ERA Directorate works on behalf of its members and the Board. The Directorate comprises five different departments. Business development incorporates membership recruitment and retention and ERA conferences and events, including the annual General Assembly and the Regional Airline Conference.

Corporate Communications covers all electronic communications, including the ERA Web site and weekly News Updates; media relations; the ERA Awards Programme; Crisis communications and all other press and PR activities. Industry Affairs handles all issues concerning air transport policy; airports and ground operations; environmental issues; airspace issues; user charges and traffic statistics.

Technical Services incorporates air safety and security, flight operations and maintenance. ERA Communications Ltd is a separate arm of the Directorate which is responsible for producing ERA's monthly journal, Regional International, and the annual Yearbook membership directory.

INTERNATIONAL AIR TRANSPORT ASSOCIATION

THE FOUNDING OF IATA

IATA (International Air Transport Association) was founded in Havana, Cuba, in April 1945. It is the prime vehicle for inter-airline cooperation in promoting safe, reliable, secure and economical air services - for the benefit of the world's consumers.

The international scheduled air transport industry is now more than 100 times larger than it was in 1945. Few industries can match the dynamism of that growth, which would have been much less spectacular without the standards, practices and procedures developed within IATA.

At its founding, IATA had 57 members from 31 nations, mostly in Europe and North America. Today it has some 230 members from 126 nations in every part of the globe. The modern IATA is the successor to the International Air Traffic Association founded in the Hague in 1919 - the year of the world's first international scheduled services.

EARLY DAYS

The old IATA was able to start small and grow gradually. It was also limited to a European dimension until 1939 when Pan American joined.

The post-1945 IATA immediately had to handle worldwide responsibilities with a more systematic organization and a larger infrastructure. This was reflected in the 1945 Articles of Association and a much more precise definition of IATA's aims than had existed before 1939.

- To promote safe, regular and economical air transport for the benefit of the peoples of the world, to foster air commerce, and to study the problems connected therewith;
- To provide means for collaboration among the air transport enterprises engaged directly or indirectly in international air transport service;
- To cooperate with the newly created International Civil Aviation Organization (ICAO - the specialized United Nations agency for civil aviation) and other international organizations.

The most important tasks of IATA during its earliest days were technical, because safety and reliability are fundamental to airline operations. These require the highest standards in air navigation, airport infrastructure and flight operations. The IATA airlines provided vital input to the work of ICAO, as that organization drafted its Standards and commended Practices. By 1949, the drafting process was largely complete and reflected to the Chicago convention, the treaty which still governs the conduct of international civil aviation. In those early days, ICAO coordinated regional air navigation and support for airports and operational aids in countries which could not themselves afford such services. IATA provided airline input to ICAO and to sessions of the International Telecommunications Union on wavelength allocation. The standardization of documentation and procedures for the smooth functioning of the world air transport network also required a sound legal basis. IATA helped to mesh international conventions, developed through ICAO, with US air transport law which had developed in isolation prior to World War Two.

The Association made a vital input to the development of Conditions of Carriage the contract between the customer and the transporting airline. One early item on the legal agenda was revision and modernization of the Warsaw Convention - originally signed in 1929 - on airline liability for passenger injury or death and cargo damage or loss. This work continues. Once they were operating within a sound technical and legal framework, airlines' next requirements were for answers to questions such as: who can fly where? What prices are to be charged? How is the money from multi-airline journeys - that is, interlining - to be divided up, and how do airlines settle their accounts? The Chicago Conference of 1944 which gave birth to the Chicago Convention tried to achieve a multilateral answer to the first two questions, but failed to do so.

The questions of who flies, and where, were resolved on a bilateral basis. The benchmark Bermuda Agreement of 1946 between the US and the UK was the first of almost 4,000 bilateral air transport agreements so far signed and registered with ICAO. In the early days, governments insisted on the right to oversee the prices charged by international airlines but could not, in practical terms, develop those prices for themselves. IATA was delegated to hold Traffic Conferences for this purpose, with all fares and rates subject to final government approval. The aim was twofold: ensuring that fares and rates would not involve cut-throat competition, while ensuring that they could be set as low as possible, in the interests of consumers. A coherent pattern of fares and rates pattern was established, avoiding inconsistencies between tariffs affecting neighbouring countries - and thereby avoiding traffic diversion.

The predictability of fares and rates in this pattern also enabled airlines to accept each others' tickets on multi-sector journeys and thus gave birth to interlining. Today, 50 million international air passengers a year pay for their ticket in one place, in one currency, but complete their journey using at least two, and sometimes five or more, airlines from different countries using different currencies. The first worldwide Traffic Conference was held in Rio de Janeiro in 1947. It reached unanimous agreement on nearly 400 resolutions covering all aspects of air travel. Fare construction rules for multi-sector trips, revenue allocation - pro-rating - rules, baggage allowances, ticket and air waybill design and agency appointment procedures were typical details agreed at this pioneering meeting. Today, that pioneering work is reflected in the currently applicable IATA Resolutions dealing with these and many other subjects.

Notable examples are:

- *The Multilateral Interline Traffic Agreement*s: These are the basis for the airlines' interline network. Close to 300 airlines have signed them, accepting each others' tickets and air waybills - and thus their passenger and cargo traffic - on a reciprocal basis.
- *Passenger and Cargo Services Conference Resolutions*: These prescribe a variety of standard formats and technical specifications for tickets and air paybills.
- *Passenger and Cargo Agency Agreements and Sales Agency Rules*: These govern the relationships between IATA Member airlines and their accredited agents with regard to passenger and cargo.

Debt Settlement between airlines, largely arising from interlining, takes place through the Clearing House, which began operations in January 1947. During its first year, 17 airlines cleared (US) $26 million. The IATA Clearing House today.

GROWTH AND DEVELOPMENT

International air transport grew at double-digit rates from its earliest post-1945 days until the first oil crisis in 1973. Much of the impetus for this growth came from technical innovation. The introduction of turbo-propeller aircraft in the early 1950s, transatlantic jets in 1958, wide-bodied aircraft and high by-pass engines in 1970 and later, advanced avionics were the main innovations. They brought higher speeds, greater size, and better unit cost control and, as a result, lower real fares and rates. Combined with increased real incomes and more leisure time, the effect was an explosion in demand for air travel.

Increased Demand for Air Travel Led to Increased Activity for IATA

Technical work evolved into seven broad areas. Avionics and Telecommunications included the vital air navigation function; Engineering and Environment developed IATA policy on aircraft noise and other emissions; Airports defined airline requirements for airport terminals; Flight Operations worked on safety factors such as minimum aircraft separation standards and air routings; Medical monitored health standards for flight crews and facilitated air travel for disabled passengers; Facilitation attempted to speed the flow of people and goods through airports - particularly, customs and immigration; Security worked on measures to safeguard passengers and cargo by preventing hijacking and sabotage and on minimizing fraud and theft of tickets.

IATA's legal efforts anticipated the effects of new technology associated with the period of rapid growth. It was able to advise the industry on new aircraft and systems, electronic data processing and advances in sales and marketing techniques. Since acts of hijacking and sabotage became more frequent during this period, IATA assisted in the development of the Tokyo, Hague and Montreal Conventions, the first international legal counter-measures. Automation became commonplace in airline operations during the 1960s. Standardization in its use was less commonplace and IATA began its involvement in perfecting standard message formats for inter-company data exchange, which continues to this day. The goal has been to save money for the airlines, while enhancing airline service.

This philosophy was carried over to many activities during the 1950s and 1960s. Development of the Clearing House was followed by the establishment of Billing and Settlement Plans and Cargo Accounts Settlement Systems—in effect, one-way clearing houses to speed the flow of revenue from agents to airlines. Sales Agents were given the opportunity to prove their professional status under an accreditation process, and training—in conjunction with the Universal Federation of Travel Agents' Associations and the Federation of Freight Forwarders' Associations—was introduced. The pattern for airline-agent relations was set with the introduction of the Standard Agency Agreement in 1952. There are now nearly 81,000 IATA agents worldwide and 135,000 students have enrolled for IATA-sponsored agency training courses since they were introduced. International air transport creates special problems of taxation. This was a concern even before World War Two. IATA makes specific challenges to the legality of certain taxes and points out to governments the counter-productive effect of excessive aviation taxation in general. User Charges - payment for using airports and air navigation services - mushroomed during the 1960s and 70s.

IATA's task is to minimise their impact by ensuring that the charges are for facilities actually required, that charges are cost-related and that productivity improvements are built into cost projections. Currency earned by airlines abroad is sometimes blocked by the central bank of the country in which it is earned. IATA works to free it, for transfer back to the airline that earned it. Unit Load Devices, or ULDs - principally, containers - allow rapid, economical cargo handling. IATA Members developed the technical specifications for containers and created a ULD control centre, to keep track of their movements. Until 1955, there was a complete embargo on the air transport of toxic, flammable or corrosive materials. Then IATA developed Dangerous Goods Regulations for their safe carriage. A decade later, Live Animals Regulations provided for suitable standards for the in-flight welfare of animals.

A TWO TIER IATA

Between the late 1940s and the early 1970s, it could be said that flight was transformed from "a scientific phenomenon to a public utility at the disposal of the entire world." At the same time, the popularisation of civil aviation led to growing demands that the "public utility" view of the industry on the part of governments be modified to encompass greater competition and wider access to markets.

These demands were fuelled by competition for leisure travellers provided by charter companies and the challenge of stimulating demand to fill the new wide-bodied aircraft. Potential demand for air travel had extended well beyond the original client base of bureaucrats, businessmen and the well-to-do. New travel products and greatly increased price flexibility were needed. As a result, the old basis for conducting IATA Traffic Conferences needed modification. At the same time the US Government, which had first given IATA Traffic Conferences immunity from national anti-trust law in 1946, began its own review of air transport regulation which, although domestic in scope, was bound to have international repercussions.

The international dimension of the US review resulted in a "Show Cause Order". Hearings took place in 1979, at which IATA was called upon to show cause why anti-trust immunity should not be removed from its Tariff Coordination activities. The outcome mainly affected North Atlantic passenger fares which, for some years, were subject to special rules under an inter-governmental Memorandum of Understanding (MoU) between the US and ECAC states. The present position is that all Tariff Coordination activities continue to be protected. Eventually, IATA was re-organised on a two-tier basis in October 1979.

The tiers comprised:

- Trade Association (technical, legal, financial, traffic services and most agency matters)
- Tariff Coordination (passenger fares, cargo rates, and related conditions and charges) At present, some 100 Members, including the world's largest airlines, continue to participate in Tariff Coordination.

FROM A NEW TRADE ASSOCIATION TO A NEW STRATEGIC THRUST

The IATA that emerged since 1979 has put an increasing share of its resources into trade association activities. IATA also changed the basis of its funding. Much of the association's funding is now done through the marketing of its products and services to Member airlines, other airlines and others in the travel, transport and tourism industry. As a result airlines can access a broader array of professional services, tapping into IATAs expertise. And IATA has greater flexibility in the way it approaches its tasks, while remaining devoted to its non-for profit operations principles. In many ways, those tasks remained the same as in 1945, or even in 1919.

But IATA gave them new relevance and focus by redefining its mission and goals in 1994:

- *Safety and security*: tTo promote safe, reliable and secure air services.
- *Industry recognition*: To achieve recognition of the importance of air transport worldwide social and economic development.
- *Financial viability*: To assist the industry to achieve adequate levels of profitability, by optimising revenues (yield management) while minimising costs (fuel, charges and taxation).
- *Products and services*: Provide high-quality, value for money, industry required products and services that assist the airlines in meeting the needs of the consumer.
- *Standards and procedures*: To develop const-effective, environmentally-friendly, standards to facilitate the operations of international air transport.
- *Industry support*: To identify and articulate common industry positions and support the resolutions of key industry issues (congestion, infrastructure).

These objectives proved to be relevant and most were carried over to the new millennium, where they still form most of IATAs current mission.

ENSURING THE VIABILITY OF AIR TRANSPORT

While the 20th century saw the creation and rapid growth of the air transport industry, the beginning of the 21st century was marked by great challenges met with major transformations. Over the last decade, the industry has been rocked by a series of successive crises and shocks. These include terrorism, pandemic threats, volcanic eruptions, global economic upheavals and an unprecedented rise in the cost price of fuel. Between 2000 and 2009, airlines posted a net loss of $50 billion. All this has made IATA's leadership more crucial than ever. In 2002 IATA's newly appointed Director General and CEO Giovanni Bisignani began a complete restructuring of the association to increase IATA's relevance and speed in driving major industry changes.

Initiatives spearheaded by IATA under Bisignani include:

- *The IATA Operational Safety Audit (IOSA)*: IOSA is the global standard for airline safety management and by 2009 airlines were required to achieve IOSA registration as a condition of IATA membership. This is the flagship component of a comprehensive 6 point safety strategy that includes audits, cargo, flight operations, infrastructure, training and data collection.
- *Environment*: IATA led the alignment of the whole aviation industry—airlines, airports, manufacturers and air navigation service providers—in a long term strategy to achieve carbon-neutral growth by 2020 and to cut aviation's carbon emissions by half by 2050.
- *Simplifying the Business (StB)*: In 2004 IATA launched this initiative to use technology to improve customer convenience and reduce costs. Four years later, achievement of 100per cent e-ticketing marked a major milestone for the industry. StB is now targeting industry savings of nearly $17 billion with initiatives ranging from bar coded boarding passes (BCBP) to Fast Travel, Baggage Improvement Programme (BIP) and e-freight.
- *Savings*: IATA embarked on a major initiative to reduce costs across the air transport value chain, particularly with monopoly suppliers. By 2010 this ongoing campaign has claimed industry savings exceeding $17 billion.
- *Financial*: IATA operates industry financial systems which now settle in excess of $300 billion a year with a success rate of over 99.9per cent. Unit costs for this system have been decreased by over 80per cent since 2000.

Bisignani has also strengthened IATA's position as the voice of the industry, with firm advocacy and lobbying to focus governments on the long term issues for viability of aviation, such as liberalization, environment and taxation.

IATA continues to help airlines respond to the requirements of the 21st century air transport system. Airlines have created a modern, interdependent world over the past 60 years: IATA is working to ensure that the world's most exciting industry meets its greatest possible potential for the years ahead with Vision 2050, outlined by Bisignani at the June 2010 IATA Annual General Meeting.

MISSION

Air transport is one of the most dynamic industries in the world. The International Air Transport Association (IATA) is its global trade organization. Over 60 years, IATA has developed the commercial standards that built a global industry. Today, IATA's mission is to represent, lead and serve the airline industry. Its members comprise some 230 airlines - the world's leading passenger and cargo airlines among them - representing 93 Per cent of scheduled international air traffic.

Representing

ATA seeks to improve understanding of the industry among decision makers and increase awareness of the benefits that aviation brings to national and global economies. It fights for the interests of airlines across the globe, challenging unreasonable rules and charges, holding regulators and governments to account, and striving for sensible regulation.

Leading

IATA's aim is to help airlines help themselves by simplifying processes and increasing passenger convenience while reducing costs and improving efficiency. The groundbreaking Simplifying the Business initiative is crucial in this area. Moreover, safety is IATA's number one priority, and IATA's goal is to continually improve safety standards, notably through IATAs Operational Safety Audit (IOSA). Another main concern is to minimize the impact of air transport on the environment.

Serving

IATA ensures that people and goods can move around the global airline network as easily as if they were on a single airline in a single country. In addition, it provides essential professional support to all industry stakeholders with a wide range of products and expert services, such as publications, training and consulting. IATA's financial systems also help carriers and the travel industry maximize revenues.

For the benefit for all parties involved:

- For consumers, IATA simplifies the travel and shipping processes, while keeping costs down. Passengers can make one telephone call to reserve a ticket, pay in one currency and then use the ticket on several airlines in several countries.
- IATA allows airlines to operate safely, securely, efficiently and economically under clearly defined rules.
- IATA serves as an intermediary between airlines and passenger as well as cargo agents via neutrally applied agency service standards and centralized financial systems.
- A large network of industry suppliers and service providers gathered by IATA provides solid expertise to airlines in a variety of industry solutions.
- For governments, IATA seeks to ensure they are well informed about the complexities of the aviation industry to ensure better, long-term decisions.

PRIORITIES

Safety and Security:

- Implement a data sharing agreement with ICAO, the US and the EU and deliver a joint safety report.
- Design a prototype "Checkpoint of the Future".
- Implement Secure Freight in two new countries.

Environment:

- Continue promoting major air traffic infrastructure projects (*e.g.* SESAR in Europe and NextGen in the US).
- Fight a global climate-related tax on passengers, carbon or fuel.
- Secure fuel and carbon reporting for at least 70per cent of IATA members operations.

Simplifying the Business:

- *Fast Travel*: Implement all five Fast Travel initiatives (Document check, Bags ready-to-go, Flight re-booking, Self-boarding, Bag recovery) at five major airports.
- e-services: Ensure that 40 airlines and all six major global distribution systems start issuing Electronic Miscellaneous Documents.
- Baggage Improvement Programme: perform 60 diagnosis visits and implement 70 self-help airports.
- e-freight: Ensure 10per cent market penetration on trade lanes where e-freight was available in 2010.

Financial:

- Achieve savings/cost avoidance of US$3 billion in industry taxes, charges and fuel fees, including at least US$1.5 billion in real cost reductions.
- Strengthen IATA Settlement Systems controls through consolidation of the remittance and settlement function into regional hubs by mid 2011.

Regulatory:

- Gain European Aviation Safety Agency recognition for the IATA Operational Safety Audit (IOSA).
- Obtain one regulator's acceptance of a pilot training initiative that includes multi-crew pilot licensing and evidence based training.
- Prevent regulatory action on slots that would adversely affect the four cornerstones of the World Scheduling Guidelines.

INTERNATIONAL CIVIL AVIATION ORGANIZATION

The International Civil Aviation Organization (ICAO), a specialized agency of the United Nations, codifies the principles and techniques of international air navigation and fosters the planning and development of international air transport to ensure safe and orderly growth. Its headquarters are located in the Quartier International of Montreal, Quebec, Canada. The ICAO Council adopts standards and recommended practices concerning air navigation, its infrastructure, Flight inspection, prevention of unlawful interference, and facilitation of border-crossing procedures for international civil aviation.

In addition, the ICAO defines the protocols for air accident investigation followed by transport safety authorities in countries signatory to the Convention on International Civil Aviation, commonly known as the Chicago Convention. The ICAO should not be confused with the International Air Transport Association (IATA), a trade organization for airlines also headquartered in Montreal, or with the Civil Air Navigation Services Organisation (CANSO), an organization for Air Navigation Service Providers (ANSP's) with its headquarters at Amsterdam Airport Schiphol in the Netherlands.

HOW IT WORKS

The constitution of ICAO is the Convention on International Civil Aviation, drawn up by a conference in Chicago in November and December 1944, and to which each ICAO Contracting State is a party. The Organization is made up of an Assembly, a Council of limited membership with various subordinate bodies and a Secretariat. The chief officers are the President of the Council and the Secretary General.

The Assembly

The Assembly, composed of representatives from all Contracting States, is the sovereign body of ICAO. It meets every three years, reviewing in detail the work of the Organization and setting policy for the coming years. It also votes a triennial budget.

The Council

The Council, the governing body which is elected by the Assembly for a three-year term, is composed of 36 States. The Assembly chooses the Council Member States under three headings: States of chief importance in air transport, States which make the largest contribution to the provision of facilities for air navigation, and States whose designation will ensure that all major areas of the world are represented. As the governing body, the Council gives continuing direction to the work of ICAO. It is in the Council that Standards and Recommended Practices are adopted and incorporated as the Convention on International Civil Aviation. The Council is assisted by the Air Navigation Commission (technical matters), the Air Transport Committee (economic matters), the Committee on Joint Support of Air Navigation Services and the Finance Committee.

The Secretariat

The Secretariat, headed by a Secretary General, is divided into five main divisions: the Air Navigation Bureau, the Air Transport Bureau, the Technical Co-operation Bureau, the Legal Bureau, and the Bureau of Administration and Services. In order that the work of the Secretariat shall reflect a truly international approach, professional personnel are recruited on a broad geographical basis.

ICAO works in close co-operation with other members of the United Nations family such as the World Meteorological Organization, the International Telecommunication Union, the Universal Postal Union, the World Health Organization and the International Maritime Organization. Non-governmental organizations which also participate in ICAO's work include the International Air Transport Association, the Airports Council International, the International Federation of Air Line Pilots' Associations, and the International Council of Aircraft Owner and Pilot Associations.

STANDARDS

The ICAO also standardizes certain functions for use in the airline industry, such as the Aeronautical Message Handling System AMHS; this probably makes it a standards organization. The ICAO defines an International Standard Atmosphere (also known as ICAO Standard Atmosphere), a model of the standard variation of pressure, temperature, density, and viscosity with altitude in the Earth's atmosphere.

This is useful in calibrating instruments and designing aircraft. The ICAO standardizes machine-readable passports worldwide. Such passports have an area where some of the information otherwise written in textual form is written as strings of alphanumeric characters, printed in a manner suitable for optical character recognition.

This enables border controllers and other law enforcement agents to process such passports quickly, without having to input the information manually into a computer. ICAO publishes Doc 9303, Machine Readable Travel Documents, the technical standard for machine-readable passports. A more recent standard is for biometric passports. These contain biometrics to authenticate the identity of travellers. The passport's critical information is stored on a tiny RFID computer chip, much like information stored on smartcards.

Like some smartcards, the passport book design calls for an embedded contactless chip that is able to hold digital signature data to ensure the integrity of the passport and the biometric data.

Communication, Navigation, Surveillance/ Air Traffic Management (CNS/ ATM) systems are communications, navigation, and surveillance systems, employing digital technologies, including satellite systems together with various levels of automation, applied in support of a seamless global air traffic management system.

CODES REGISTERED WITH ICAO

Both ICAO and IATA have their own airport and airline code systems. ICAO uses 4-letter airport codes and 3-letter airline codes. In the continental United States, the ICAO codes are usually the same as the IATA code, with a prefix of "K" — LAX is KLAX. Canada follows a similar pattern, where a prefix of "C" is usually added to an IATA code to find the ICAO code — YEG is CYEG. In the rest of the world, the codes are unrelated, as the IATA code is phonic and the ICAO code is location-based; for example, Charles de Gaulle Airport has an ICAO code of LFPG, and an IATA code of CDG.

ICAO is also responsible for issuing alphanumeric aircraft type codes that contain 2–4 characters. These codes provide the identification that is typically used in flight plans. An example of this is the Boeing 747 that would use (depending on the variant) B741, B742, B743, etc. ICAO provides telephony designators to aircraft operators worldwide.

These consist of the three-letter airline identifier and a one- or two-word designator. They are usually, but not always, similar to the aircraft operator name. For example, the identifier for Aer Lingus is EIN and the designator is Shamrock, while Japan Airlines International is JAL and Japan Air. Thus, a flight by Aer Lingus numbered 111 would be written as "EIN111" and pronounced "Shamrock One Eleven" on the radio, while a similarly numbered Japan Airlines flight would be written as "JAL111" and pronounced "Japan Air One Eleven". ICAO maintains the standards for aircraft registration ("tail numbers"), including the alphanumeric codes that identify the country of registration.

REGIONS AND REGIONAL OFFICES

The ICAO has seven regional offices serving seven regions:

1. Asia and Pacific, Bangkok, Thailand
2. Middle East, Cairo, Egypt
3. Western and Central Africa, Dakar, Senegal
4. South America, Lima, Peru
5. North America, Central America and Caribbean, Mexico City, Mexico
6. Eastern and Southern Africa, Nairobi, Kenya
7. Europe and North Atlantic, Paris, France

ICAO AND CLIMATE CHANGE

Emissions from international aviation are specifically excluded from the targets agreed under the Kyoto Protocol. Instead, the Protocol invites developed countries to pursue the limitation or reduction of emissions through the International Civil Aviation Organisation (ICAO). ICAO's environmental committee continues to consider the potential for using market-based measures such as trading and charging, but this work is unlikely to lead to global action. It is currently developing guidance for states who wish to include aviation in an emissions trading scheme (ETS) to meet their Kyoto commitments, and for airlines who wish to participate voluntarily in a trading scheme. Emissions from domestic aviation are included within the Kyoto targets agreed by countries. This has led to some national policies such as fuel and emission taxes for domestic air travel in the Netherlands and Norway respectively. Although some countries tax the fuel used by domestic aviation, there is no duty on kerosene used on international flights.

(Aviation Environment Federation) ICAO is currently against the inclusion of aviation in the European Union Emissions Trading Scheme (EU ETS). However, the EU is pressing ahead with its plans to include aviation from 2011.

INVESTIGATIONS OF AIR DISASTERS

Most air accident investigations are carried out by an agency of a country that is associated in some way with the accident - for example the Air Accidents Investigation Branch carried out accident investigations on behalf of the British Government. ICAO has however conducted two investigations involving air disasters, both incidents involving passenger airliners shot down while in international flight over hostile territory.

The first incident occurred on 21 February 1973, during a period of tension which would lead to the Israeli-Arab "October war", when a Libyan Arab Airlines Flight 114 was shot down by Israeli F-4 jets over the Sinai Peninsula. The second incident occurred on 1 September 1983, during a period of heightened Cold War tension, when a Soviet Su-15 interceptor shot down a straying Korean Air Lines Flight 007 near Moneron Island just west of Sakhalin Island.

KAL 007 was carrying 269 people, including 22 children under the age of 12, and a sitting U.S. congressman, Larry McDonald.

INTERNATIONAL SOCIETY OF TRANSPORT AIRCRAFT TRADING

The International Society of Transport Aircraft Trading (abbreviated ISTAT) is a non-profit aviation industry association. Founded in 1983, ISTAT is dedicated to fostering and promoting interest and educational opportunities in commercial aviation, while also providing a forum for networking among those involved in the industry.

ISTAT MEMBERSHIP

ISTAT currently has more than 1700 members worldwide involved in operating, manufacturing, maintaining, selling, purchasing, financing, leasing, appraising, insuring or otherwise engaging in activities related to commercial transport category aircraft. ISTAT is governed by its bylaws and the volunteer ISTAT Board of Directors, which is composed of and elected by the members.

ISTAT FOUNDATION

The ISTAT Foundation fosters interest in, creates opportunities for, and provides assistance through the global aviation community by offering scholarships, grants, internships and humanitarian aid worldwide. The Foundation awards more than $250,000 in scholarships, grants and humanitarian efforts annually to worthy recipients around the world. Grants are awarded to institutions involved in both elementary and higher education as well as to humanitarian organizations. Scholarships have been presented to students on an international stage with recipients from the U.S., U.K., Turkey, The Netherlands, China, Germany, Australia, and Kenya. The Foundation's most recently established internship programme matches aviation-focused college students to internship positions open at ISTAT member companies.

ISTAT CERTIFIED APPRAISERS' PROGRAMME

ISTAT has established rigorous testing and qualification standards for members who are engaged in appraising aircraft and support equipment.

Within ISTAT is a core group of professional aircraft appraisers who work cooperatively for the elevation of the appraisal profession within the world aviation community.

Each ISTAT member, who has satisfactorily demonstrated that he or she is qualified to appraise airline transport aircraft, has been granted the right to use one of the ISTAT professional designations, established by ISTAT and predicated upon a set group of criteria.

ISTAT EVENTS

Annual U.S. Conference

Each spring, the aviation industry comes together at the ISTAT Annual U.S. Conference, where delegates gain access to key insights from the leaders and influential members of the aviation industry. The 2010 Annual Conference will be held March 14–16 in Orlando, Florida.

Annual European Conference

The ISTAT European Conference provides a more intimate gathering of aviation professionals each autumn, set at different European locations. The 2009 European Conference will be held October 11–13 in Dubrovnik, Croatia.

Air Show Receptions

Annually, ISTAT hosts receptions at selected air shows, which take place at distinctive venues around the globe, including Dubai, Singapore, Farnborough, and Paris.

REGIONAL AVIATION ASSOCIATION OF AUSTRALIA

The Regional Aviation Association of Australia (RAAA) is an organisation representing the interests of regional aviation in Australia. It was formed in 1980 as the Regional Airline Association of Australia and amended its name in 2001 when its charter was widened to include "aerial work operators" as well as regional airlines and air charter companies "and the businesses that support them". Its stated aim is "to promote the maintenance of a viable regional aviation industry".

9

The Demand for Recreation and Group Travel

Understanding why human beings engage in recreational and tourism activities is an increasingly important and complex area of research for social scientists. Historically, geographers have played only a limited part in developing the literature on the behavioural aspects of recreational and tourists' use of free time, tending to have a predisposition towards the analysis of aggregate patterns of demands using quantitative measures and statistical sources. This almost rigid demarcation of research activity has, with a few exceptions, meant that behavioural research in recreation and tourism has only recently made any impact on the wider research community, with notable studies applying spatial principles to the analysis of recreational and tourism behaviour.

Within the recreational literature, the geographers' contributions have often been subsumed into social science perspectives, such as sociology, psychology and planning, so that the spatiality and placefulness of their contribution has been implicit rather than explicit. For this reason, this chapter discusses some of the key behavioural issues associated with recreation and tourism demand followed by an analysis of the major data sources which researchers use, emphasising how the geographer has used and manipulated them to identify the patterns, processes and implications of such activity.

Within the literature on recreation and tourism, there is a growing unease over the physical separation of the theoretical and conceptual research that isolates behavioural processes and spatial outcomes, and fails to derive generalisations applicable to understanding tourism in totality. According to Moore *et al.* (1995:74) there are common strands in the 'relationships between the various motivating factors applicable to both leisure and tourism'; and as Leiper (1990) argued, tourism represents a valued category of leisure, where there is a degree of commonality between the factors motivating both tourist and recreational activities and many of the needs, such as relaxation or being with friends, can equally be fulfilled in a recreational or tourism context. Although there is some merit in Leiper's (1990) approach, grouping leisure into one amorphous category assumes that there are no undifferentiated attributes which distinguish tourism from leisure. As Pigram and Jenkins (1999:19) confirm, 'the term recreation demand is generally equated with an individual(s) preferences or desires, whether or not the individual has the economic and other resources necessary for their satisfaction'.

In this respect, it is the preference-aspiratio-desire level, reflected in behaviour or participation in activities. It is interesting to note that Leiper's (1990) approach has a great deal of validity if one recognises that some tourism motivations may in fact differentiate tourism from leisure experiences, just as the reverse may be true, and that ultimately the particular range of motives associated with a tourism or recreational activity will be unique in each case despite a range of similarities.

For this reason, the following discussion examines recreational demand, emphasising many of the explanations commonly advanced in the recreational literature followed by a discussion of the tourism context and the issues raised, bearing in mind the need to compare and contrast each literature base in the light of the arguments advanced by Moore *et al.* (1995) and Leiper (1990).

RECREATIONAL DEMAND

Human activity related to recreation and tourism is a function of an individual's or group's willingness or desire to engage in such pursuits. Yet understanding this dimension in recreation and tourism requires a conceptual approach which can rationalise the complex interaction between the desire to undertake leisure activities, however defined, and the opportunities to partake of them. As Coppock and Duffield (1975:2) argued: 'the success of any study of outdoor recreation depends on the synthesis of two contrasting elements: the sociological phenomenon of leisure or ... that part of leisure time which an individual spends on outdoor recreation [and tourism] and ... the physical resources that are necessary for the particular recreational activities.'

In other words, Coppock and Duffield (1975) ackno-wledged the need to recognise the interrelationship between human demand as participation or a desire to engage in recreation and tourism, and the supply of resources, facilities and opportunities which enable such demand to be fulfilled. The concepts of demand and supply have largely been developed and applied to conventional market economies, where the individual has a choice related to the consumption of recreation and tourism. According to Smith (1989:45):

Recreation geographers use the work [demand] in at least four different ways. The most traditional sense is a neoclassical definition: demand is a schedule of the quantities of some commodity that will be consumed at various prices.... A second definition of demand is that of current consumption ... [which] is of limited utility to recreation planners because it tells nothing about trends in participation or about current levels of unmet need. Demand is also used to refer to unmet need. This is sometimes referred to as latent demand. ... Finally, demand is used to describe the desire for a psychological experience. In contrast, Patmore (1983:54) acknowledges, 'leisure is far more easily recognised than objectively analysed ... the difficulties are only in part conceptual: equally important are the nature and limitations of available data', which this section will seek to explain in a recreation context.

According to Pigram (1983) there is a general lack of clarity in the use of the term *demand* in the recreational literature. One can distinguish between demand at a generic level, where it refers to an 'individual's preferences or desires, whether or not the individual has the economic or other resources necessary for their satisfaction' reflecting behavioural traits and preference for certain activities. At another level, there are the specific activities or participation in activities often expressed as visitation rates and measured to reflect the actual observed behaviour.

One factor that prevents observed demand equating with participation is the concept of latent demand (the element which is unsatisfied due to a lack of recreational opportunities). Knetsch (1969) identified the mismatch and confusion between participation and demand, arguing that one cannot simply look at what people do and associate it with what people want to do, so ideally any analysis of demand should also consider why people do not participate, and examine ways of overcoming such obstacles by the provision of new resources as well as understanding social and cultural barriers. As Pigram and Jenkins (1999:20) argued, 'In the real world, recreation demand rarely equals participation.

The difference between aggregate demand and actual participation (or expressed, effective, observed, revealed demand) is referred to as latent demand or latent participation-the unsatisfied component of demand that would be converted to participation if conditions of supply of recreation opportunities were brought to ideal levels'. Attempting to summarise the factors which influence the decision to participate in recreation led Pigram (1983) which highlights the complex range of variables that affect the process.

Most research has examined effective demand which is actual participation rather than latent demand, and the geographers' contribution has largely been related to the spatial and temporal expression of demand in relation to supply (*i.e.* demand at specific sites). This is very much resource specific, and dates back to the geographical tradition of resource identification, use and analysis which can be traced to at least the 1930s. However, Coppock and Duffield (1975) also distinguish between passive recreation and active recreation, thereby beginning to differentiate between different forms of demand. While passive recreation is by far the most important type numerically, it is difficult to study due to its diffuse and often unorganised nature. Coppock and Duffield (1975:40) argued that Active recreation in the countryside differs from passive recreation in a number of ways. Not only are participants a minority of those visiting the countryside for outdoor recreation, but they are generally younger and differ in respect of a number of socio-economic characteristics: they often depend on particular (and sometimes scarce) recreational resources in the countryside ... yet as with passive recreation, information about such activities is scanty. This illustrates the necessity of trying to measure recreational demand together with gauging the types of factors which can facilitate and constrain recreational demand. But what motivates people to engage in recreational activities?

Crandall's list of motivations:

- Enjoying nature, escaping from civilisation
  - To get away from civilisation for a while
  - To be close to nature
- Escape from routine and responsibility
  - Change from my daily routine
  - To get away from the responsibilities of my everyday life
- Physical exercise
  - For the exercise
  - To keep in shape
- Creativity
  - To be creative
- Relaxation
  - To relax physically
  - So my mind can slow down for a while
- Social contact
  - So I could do things with my companions
  - To get away from other people
- Meeting new people
  - To talk to new and varied people
  - To build friendships with new people
- Heterosexual contact
  - To be with people of the opposite sex
  - To meet people of the opposite sex
- Family contact
  - To be away from the family for a while
  - To help bring the family together more
- Recognition, status
  - To show others I could do it
  - So others would think highly of me for doing it
- Social power
  - To have control over others
  - To be in a position of authority

- Altruism
  - To help others
- Stimulus seeking
  - For the excitement
  - Because of the risks involved
- Self-actualisation (feedback, self-improvement, ability utilisation)
  - Seeing the results of your efforts
  - Using a variety of skills and talents
- Achievement, challenge, competition
  - To develop my skills and ability
  - Because of the competition
  - To learn what I am capable of
- Killing time, avoiding boredom
  - To keep busy
  - To avoid boredom
- Intellectual aestheticism
  - To use my mind
  - To think about my personal values

Table. Kabanoff's List of Leisure Needs.

Leisure needs scale	Items comprising scales	Item means	
1	Autonomy	Organise own projects and activities	2.78
		Do things you find personally meaningful	3.39
2	Relaxation	Relax and take it easy	3.20
		Give mind and body a rest	2.94
3	Family activity	Bring family closer together	2.81
		Enjoy family life	3.30
4	Escape from routine	Get away from responsibilities of everyday life	2.85
		Have a change from daily routine	3.12
5	Interaction	Make new friends	2.35
		Enjoy people's company	2.55
6	Stimulation	To have new and different experiences	2.66
		For excitement and stimulation	2.89
7	Skill utilisation	Use skills and abilities	2.89
		Develop new skills and abilities	2.61
8	Health	Keep physically fit	2.47
		For health reasons	2.46
9	Esteem	Gain respect or admiration of others	2.11
		Show others what you're capable of	2.15
10	Challenge/competition	Be involved in a competition	1.87
		Test yourself in difficult or demanding situations	2.31
11	Leadership/social power	Organise activities of teams, groups, organisations	1.79
		To gain positions of leadership	1.48

Argyle (1996) argues that part of the reason why people undertake leisure and recreational activities can be found in the process of socialisation and personality traits, where childhood influences such as parents and peers are forms of social influence and learning that affect future activity choice. In fact, nearly half of adult leisure interests are acquired after childhood, and personality factors influence preferences towards specific forms of recreation. However, understanding the broader psychological factors which motivate individuals to undertake forms of recreation is largely the remit of psychologists, being an intrinsic form of motivation (*i.e.* something one is not paid to undertake).

A simplistic approach to recreational motivation is to ask recreationalists what actually motivates them. Crandall (1980) outlined 17 factors from leisure motivation research, derived from a synthesis of previous studies in this field, while Kabanoff (1982) identified a similar list of factors. It is apparent that relaxation, the need for excitement and self-satisfaction are apparent, though Argyle (1996) argues that specific motivations are evident in particular forms of recreation. Torkildsen (1992:79), however, posits that homeostasis is a fundamental concept associated with human motivation where people have an underlying desire to maintain a state of internal stability. Human needs, which are 'any lack or deficit within the individual either acquired or physiological', disturb the state of homeostasis. At a basic level, human needs have to be met where physiological theory maintained that all human behaviour is motivated. This leads to one of the most commonly cited studies in relation to recreation and tourism motivation-Maslow's hierarchy of human needs.

MASLOW'S HIERARCHY MODEL OF HUMAN NEEDS

Within the social psychology literature on recreation and tourism, Maslow's (1954) needs hierarchy remains one of the most commonly cited theories of motivation. It follows the principle of a ranking or hierarchy of individual needs, based on the premise that self-actualisation is a level to which people should aspire. Maslow argued that if the lower needs in the hierarchy were not fulfilled then these would dominate human behaviour. Once these were satisfied, the individual would be motivated by the needs of the next level of the hierarchy. In the motivation sequence, Maslow identified 'deficiency or tension-reducing motives' and 'inductive or arousal-seeking motives', arguing that the model could be applied to work and non-work contexts.

Despite Maslow's research shaping much of the recreation and tourism demand work, how and why he selected five basic needs remains unclear, though its universal application in recreation and tourism appears to have a relevance with regard to understanding how human action is related to understandable and predictable aspects of action compared to research which argues that human behaviour is essentially irrational and unpredictable.

While Maslow's model is not necessarily ideal, since needs are not hierarchical in reality because some needs may occur simultaneously, it does emphasise the development needs of humans, with individuals striving towards personal growth. Therefore, Maslow assists in a recreational (and tourism context) in identifying and classifying the types of needs people have. Tillman (1974) summarised some of the broader leisure needs of individuals within which recreational needs occur, and these may include the pursuit of:

- New experiences (*i.e.* adventure);
- Relaxation, escape and fantasy;
- Recognition and identity;
- Security (freedom from thirst, hunger or pain);
- Dominance (to control one's environment);
- Response and social interaction (relating and interacting with others);
- Mental activity (to perceive and understand);
- Creativity;
- A need to be needed;
- Physical activity and fitness.

A different perspective is offered by Bradshaw (1972), who argued that social need is a powerful force, explaining need by classifying it as normative, felt, expressed and comparative need. Mercer (1973), Godbey (1976) and McAlvoy (1977) extended Bradshaw's argument within a recreational context, modifying the four categories of need by adding created, changing and false needs. Normative needs are based on value judgements, often made by professionals who establish that what they feel is appropriate to the wider population. Felt needs, which individuals may have but not necessarily express, are based on what someone wants to do and is a perceived need.

Expressed needs relate to those needs and preferences for existing recreational activities which are often measured but can only be a partial view of demand, since new recreational opportunities may release latest demand. Comparative needs are apparent where existing provision for the general population is compared with special groups (*e.g.* the elderly, ethnic minorities or disabled) to establish if existing provision is not fulfilling the needs of the special group. Created needs may result from policy-makers and planners introducing new services or activities which are then taken up by the population.

A false need is one that may be created by individuals or society, and which is not essential and may be marginal to wider recreational needs. Changing needs, however, are a recognition of the dynamic nature of human needs which change through time as individuals develop and their position in the life cycle changes. Thus what is important at one point in the life cycle may change through time as an individual passes through four key stages (Ken and Rapoport 1975):

- Youth (school years);
- Young adulthood;
- Establishment (extended middle-age);

- Final phase (between the end of work and of life).

Other researchers (*e.g.* Iso-Ahola 1980; Neulinger 1981) prefer to emphasise the importance of perceived freedom from constraints as a major source of motivation. Argyle (1996) synthesises such studies to argue that intrinsic motivation in leisure relates to three underlying principles:

- Social motivation;
- Basic bodily pleasures (*e.g.* eating, drinking, sex and sport);
- Social learning (how past learning explains a predisposition towards certain activities).

One useful concept which Csikszentmihalyi (1975) introduced to the explanation of motivation was that of flow. Individuals tend to find a sense of intense absorption in recreational activities, when self-awareness declines, and it is their peak experience - a sense of flow - which is the main internal motivation. The flow is explained as a balance resulting from being challenged and skill which can occur in four combinations:

- Where challenge and skill are high and flow results;
- Where the challenge is too great, anxiety results;
- If the challenge is too easy, boredom may occur;
- Where the challenge and skill level is too low, apathy may result.

But this does not mean that everyone always seeks recreational activities which provide forms of high arousal. Some recreational activities may just fulfil a need to relax, being undemanding and of low arousal. As Ewert and Hollenhurst (1989) reported, those who engaged in outdoor recreational sports with a high-risk factor (*i.e.* whitewater rafting) viewed the sport as providing a flow experience, and the study predicted that as their skill level improved they would increase the level of participation and risk. Yet even though this occurred the internal motivation of the group remained unchanged, where low and high arousal seem to be juxtaposed. Thus levels of arousal vary from time to time, a factor which can be used by adventure tourism operators to manage the adventure experience and increase the level of satisfaction of participants.

Recreation may also lead to an enhanced self-image, where the identity becomes a basis for motivation because recreational activities can lead to a sense of belonging to a particular and identifiable group. Some activities may also require the development of special skills and enhanced self-esteem. Where recreational activities require a degree of competency, Bandura (1977) proposed that perception of one's ability to perform the skill is a motivator and may result in self-efficacy, a form of self-confidence and judgement of one's ability.

In spite of the significance of motivation, it is apparent that no single theory or even a clear consensus exists in relation to recreation. Instead, 'in theories of motivation need is seen as a force within the individual to gain satisfactions and completeness. There appear to be many levels and types of need, including the important needs of self-actualisation and psychological growth'.

An understanding of needs and intrinsic motivation and some of the ideas implicit in studies of recreational motivation may offer a range of insights into why people engage in recreational activities. But not only is it necessary to understand why people engage in recreation, but also what factors or barriers may inhibit them from participating. Torkildsen (1992) outlines the influences on leisure participation in terms of three categories: personal, social and circumstantial, and opportunity factors. These influences are also of value in understanding some of the constraints on recreation.

BARRIERS TO RECREATION

Within the wider literature on recreation and leisure, a specialist research area has developed, focused on constraints, namely those factors, elements or processes which inhibit people from participating in leisure activities. From the diverse range of studies published, two forms of constraint have been identified: intervening constraints, namely those which intervene between a preference and participation, and antecedent constraints, which influence a person's decision not to undertake an activity.

Table. Influences on Leisure Participation.

Personal	Social and circumstantial	Opportunity factors
Age	Occupation	Resources available
Stage in life cycle	Income	Facilities - type and quality
Gender	Disposable income	Awareness
Marital status	Material wealth and goods	Perception of opportunities
Dependants and ages	Car ownership and mobility	Recreation services
Will and purpose in life	Time available	Distribution of facilities
Personal obligations	Duties and obligations	Access and location
Resourcefulness	Home and social environment	Choice of activities
Leisure perceptions	Friends and peer groups	Transport
Attitudes and motivation	Social roles and contacts	Costs: before, during, after
Interests and preoccupations	Environment factors	Management: policy and support
Skill and ability - physical, social and intellectual	Mass leisure factors	Marketing
Personality and confidence	Education and attainment	Programming
Culture born into	Population factors	Organisation and leadership
Upbringing and background	Cultural factors	Social accessibility
		Political policies

Although the constraints on recreation and leisure literature can be dated to the 1960s, the 1980s saw a range of studies published, a number of which have set the research agenda in recent years. In the initial formulation, Crawford and Godbey (1987) proposed that constraints were associated with intrapersonal, interpersonal and structural constraints. In the subsequent reformulation of their thinking, Crawford *et al.* (1991) proposed a hierarchical process model, with their three types of constraint integrated. As a consequence of their model, they proposed, which indicates that:

- Participation in leisure is a negotiation process, where a series of factors became aligned in a sequence;
- The order in which constraints occur leads to a 'hierarchy of importance', where intrapersonal constraints are the most powerful in sequence ending with no structural constraints;
- That social class has a strong influence on participation and non-participation leading to a hierarchy of social privilege, *i.e.* social stratification is a powerful conditioning factor and may act as a constraint.

This research has provided a framework for further evaluations of constraints (*e.g.* Samdahl and Jekubovich 1997, and subsequent criticisms by Henderson 1997). In fact, subsequent research by Jackson *et al.* (1993) suggested that the real key to understanding leisure constraints was embedded in the negotiation process: namely how an individual will proceed with experiencing an activity even when constraints are apparent. Ultimately, Pigram's (1983) model helped to frame the context in which participation may occur, and the way that process may be affected by underlying constraints on one's participation.

It is against this background that one can appreciate the use of leisure time and leisure space in different cultures and among groups where leisure time in a western conception is inappropriate. For example, in a fascinating review of poor rural women's leisure experiences in Bangladesh by Khan (1997), it is evident that 'the conventional approach to leisure studies which has a myopic view of leisure as free or non-obligatory time' is meaningless due to blurring of boundaries between free or non-work time and obligatory activities which are often cumbersome and all-encompassing in everyday life. At an empirical level, a range of notable studies have highlighted the prevailing constraints to recreation. For example, Kay and Jackson's (1991) notable study of 366 British adults' recreational constraints identified:

- 53 per cent who cited money as the main constraint;
- 36 per cent who felt lack of time was the main limitation;
- Conflicts with family or work, transportation problems and health concerns as other contributory factors.

A study in Alberta which surveyed 1,891 people asked respondents to rate 15 possible barriers to a desired activity, and the results highlighted social isolation, accessibility, personal reasons (lack of confidence or skill), costs, time and facilities as the main constraints. It has been proposed that such constraints have a specific ordering in terms of importance, with the most significant constraints being interpersonal ones, followed by structural ones (*e.g.* lack of time or money). Yet such arguments have been queried by Shaw *et al.* (1991), who found that in a survey of 14,674 Canadians, of 11 constraints, only lack of energy and ill-health were associated with a lower rate of participation. Therefore, barriers may be negotiable or solvable, as Kay and Jackson (1991) suggest. Patmore (1983) summarises the main physical barriers to recreation in terms of:

- Seasonality;
- Biological and social constraints;
- Money and mobility;
- Resources and fashions;

with the availability of time also being a major constraint.

Coppock and Duffield (1975:8) recognised the principal variations which exist in terms of demand due to variable uses of leisure time budgets by individuals and groups in relation to the day, week and year.

Both Coppock and Duffield (1975) and Patmore (1983) use similar data sources (*e.g.* the UK's Pilot National Recreation Survey (British Travel Association and Univeristy of Keele 1967 and 1969) and sociological studies of family behaviour in the pioneering study by Young and Wilmott (1973)) to examine time budgets, variations in demand and constraining factors. One of the most important distinctions to make is that 'the weekend thus represents a large increase in the time that can be committed to leisure pursuits, which in turn affects the weekend time budget'. Yet when one looks beyond the day and week to the individuals and groups concerned, a wider range of influences emerge which are important in explaining recreation patterns. Argyle (1996) highlights the fact that one of the main reasons for examining constraining and facilitating factors is to understand 'how many people engage in different kinds of leisure, how much time they spend on it, and how this varies between men and women, young and old, and other groups'. This is because some groups such as 'women, the elderly and unemployed face particular constraints which may affect their ability to engage in leisure and recreational activities which people do because they want to, for their own sake, for fun, entertainment or self-improvement, or for goals of their own choosing, but not for material gain'.

SEASONALITY

Patmore (1983:70) argued that 'one of the most unyielding of constraints is that imposed by climate, most obviously where outdoor activities are concerned. The rhythms of the seasons affect both the hours of daylight available and the extent to which temperatures are conducive to participant comport outdoors.' This is reflected in the seasonality of recreational activity which inevitably leads to peaks in popular seasons and a lull in less favourable conditions. Patmore (1983) identified a continuum in recreational activities from those which exhibit a high degree of seasonality to those with a limited degree of variation in participation by season. The first type, which is the most seasonal, include outdoor activities often of an informal nature which are weather dependent. The second, an intermediate group, is transitional in the sense that temperature is not necessarily a deterrent since a degree of discomfort may be experienced by the more hardened participants (*e.g.* when walking and playing sport). The final group is indoor activities which can be formal or informal, and have virtually no seasonality. In addition, the physical constraints of season, climate and weather inhibit demand by curtailing the periods of time over which a particular resource can be used for the activity concerned, although resource substitution (*e.g.* using a man-made ski slope instead of a snow-clad one) may assist in some contexts, but often the man-made resource cannot offer the same degree of excitement or enjoyment.

ACCESS TO RECREATIONAL OPPORTUNITY

Argyle (1996) observed that while many studies emphasised lack of money as a barrier to engaging in recreational activities, Coalter (1993) found that it had little impact on participation in sports. In fact, Kay and Jackson (1991) also acknowledged that money or disposable income was a barrier to undertaking activities which were major consumers of money (drinking and eating socially) whereas it had little impact on sport which was comparatively cheap.

Income, occupation and access to a car combined have a significant impact on participation, and as Patmore (1983:78) succinctly summarised, 'those with more skilled and responsive occupations, with higher incomes, with ready access to private transport and with a longer period spent in full-time education tend to lead a more active and varied leisure life, with less emphasis on passive recreations both within and beyond the home'.

It is the car which has provided the greatest degree of personal mobility and access to a wider range of recreational opportunities in time and space since the 1960s in many developed countries (and earlier in some cases such as the USA and Canada).

For example, most car-owning households in UK studies have twice the propensity to participate in sport and recreation than non-car-owning households. Even so, Martin and Mason (1979:62) observe that 'one of the paradoxes of leisure is that while time and money are complementary in the production of leisure activities, they are competitive in terms of the resources available to the individual. Some leisure time and some money to buy leisure goods and services are both needed before most leisure activities can be pursued.'

GENDER AND SOCIAL CONSTRAINTS

The influence of gender on recreation remains a powerful factor influencing participation, a feature consistently emphasised in national surveys of recreational demand. As Argyle (1996:44) argues, 'there is an influential theory about this topic, due to a number of feminist writers, that women have very little or no leisure, because of the demands of domestic work and the barriers due to husbands who want them at home ... [and] that leisure is a concept which applies to men, if it is regarded as a reaction to or contrast with paid work'. Thus women with children appear to have less time for recreation, while those in full- and part-time employment have less time available than their male counterparts.

These general statements find a high degree of support within the recreational literature, with gender differences in part explained by the male free time occurring in larger blocks and in prime time.

Even so, studies by Talbot (1979) explore this theme in more detail. Rodgers (1977) documents the wide discrepancy in male:female participation in sport as a form of recreation within a European context where for every 100 females engaging in sport, there were 188 male participants in Britain, 176 in Spain, 159 in France, 127 in Belgian Flanders, 127 in Norway, 116 in the Netherlands and 111 in former West Germany.

While definitions and the variations in data sources may in part explain the variability, the presence of a gender gap is prominent. Age also exerts a strong influence on participation in recreation, with Hendry *et al.* (1993) describing adolescence as the peak time of leisure needs.

Therein lie two key explanations of participation and constraints. Stages in the life cycle present a useful concept to explain why women with young children appear to have fewer opportunities for recreation than adolescents. Likewise, physical vigour and social energy are traditionally explained in terms of a decline in the later stages of adulthood resulting in a decline in active recreation throughout later life.

The Greater London Recreation Survey of 1972 (Greater London Council 1976) identified some of these traits in that:

- Activities exist where participation markedly declined by age (*e.g.* energetic sports like football);
- Activities occur with sustained participation through the life cycle (*e.g.* tennis and indoor swimming);
- Some activities exist where participation increased as a person got older (*e.g.* golf and walking).

In fact these results not only illustrate the importance of age (and to a degree gender), but also the need to consider the significance of the life cycle in relation to changes or 'triggers' (Patmore 1983). One such trigger is retirement, and while it is sometimes interpreted as a stressful life event, Long (1987) found that for 58 per cent of male retirees there was no change in their leisure activities, while 8 per cent undertook education, 3 per cent developed an interest in photography and 3 per cent partook of sport. What Argyle

(1996:63) emphasises from studies of retirement are that 'people carry on with the same leisure as before, though they are more passive and more house-bound, and do not take up much new leisure'.

CASE STUDY: THE GEOGRAPHY OF FEAR IN RECREATION AND LEISURE SPACES: GENDER-BASED BARRIERS TO PARTICIPATION

Since the 1980s there has been a growing interest in the role of fear, personal safety and the spatial implications in the urban environment. There has also been an accompanying interest in the gender dimensions of personal safety, which has important implications within an urban environment in relation to the use of public leisure resources such as open space and urban parks. In fact, the concern with such issues may be traced to the changes in the discipline of geography 'and transformative developments both resulting from, and contributing to, a number of new and competing philosophies with the social sciences'. In relation to leisure and recreation geography, this transformation effect can be related to the concern with gender relations and theoretical perspectives associated with the new cultural geography as a mechanism to conceptualise and theorise leisure space.

One of the central tenets of this approach is embodied in Green *et al.*'s (1990:311) comment where 'A significant aspect of the social control of women's leisure is the regulation of their access to public places, and their behaviour in such places'. These critical perspectives have only recently begun to emerge in tourism geography, where empirical, logical-positivist approaches to personal safety have paid little attention to gender and public places.

In conceptual terms, the analysis of the geography of fear, particularly the implications for gender, is a good illustration of the participation issues for particular groups of women. The application of this perspective to recreational and leisure spaces in the city reveals the male domination of public leisure space. The new cultural geographies have seen leisure and recreational geographers move away, albeit slowly, from a positivist paradigm and the model-building era as new perspectives were conceptualised and theorised. The rise of feminist perspectives in leisure studies by geographers is a notable development, with the impetus provided by landmark studies by feminist leisure studies.

One of the principal problems with the emergence of a new cultural geography is epitomised in Sharmar-Smith and Hannam's (1994:13) comments: 'Place is a deceptively simple concept in geographical thought. We want to make it difficult, uneasy.' Herein lie many of the criticisms of the new cultural geography: one must have a sound grounding in social theory, cultural studies and a knowledge of the new tenets underpinning the debates. One consequence is that 'the new cultural geography as it has been referred to since the early

1990s demonstrates that space, place and landscape - including landscapes of leisure and tourism - are not fixed but are in a constant state of transition as a result of continuous, dialectical struggles of power and resistance among and between the diversity of landscape providers, users and mediators'. This means that the focus is on agency rather than structure, criticising earlier geographical studies of leisure and recreation which did not problematise space or recognise the human element in the landscape.

This perspective - and one has to recognise it is only one perspective in geographical research - emphasises the diversity, differences and nuances in cultural phenomena which is the antithesis of logical positivist geographical thought that searches for certainty, coherence and generalisations in relation to patterns, forms and processes of spatial phenomena. As a consequence the new interest in leisure and tourism as cultural phenomena in the 'post-positivist geography [is such] that the new cultural geography has emerged and become merged with sociological and cultural studies analyses which are now combining to investigate the multiplicity of behaviours, meanings, consumption trends and identities constructed in and through leisure and tourism', and this case study focuses on the sexuality dimension.

Given the growing interest in feminism within the leisure constraints literature, and the concern with constraints to participation, it is timely to focus on the issue of fear, derived from Madge's survey of Leicester's urban park system.

IMPLICATIONS FOR SOCIAL EXCLUSION

Urban parks are estimated to be used by 40 per cent of the British population on a regular basis, but critics argue that urban parks as a recreational resource are being avoided by the general public. This is particularly acute for certain groups of the population (*e.g.* women, children and ethnic groups), where fear acts as a constraint on use. This adds a new dimension to the recreational constraints literature. Explanations of the growing neglect of urban parks within the UK have been related to a decline in public spending, from 54 per cent of leisure budgets in 1981 to 1982 to 44 per cent in 1991 to 1992, although these statistics need to recognise greater financial efficiencies derived from contracting out park services.

In the 1990s there was growing evidence that urban parks were not perceived as peaceful sanctuaries for recreational and leisure pursuits among the wider population. Burgess *et al.*'s (1988a) innovative Greenwich Open Space Project documented the dimensions of fear. Dimensions included antisocial behaviour among teenagers and vandalism that reduced local enjoyment and participation. Similar concerns of insecurity, fear and use of parks and open spaces have also been recorded in Australia, and North America. Additional research shows how women, black people, the elderly and the gay community may be excluded from using urban space as freely as other subgroups of the population. As Burgess *et al.* (1988a: 472) remarked in the Greenwich context: 'many people expressed feelings of insecurity and vulnerability in open spaces, reflecting fears of personal attack and injury.

Among the Asian community, these feelings are exacerbated by the growth in incidence of racially motivated attacks in public open spaces.' The outcome, as Madge (1997:238) recognised, was that 'This fear, which reflects structural inequalities in society, is translated into spatial behaviour which usually involves a reluctance to occupy certain public spaces at certain times of the day'. For the geographer, it is the spatial manifestation of that fear and its implications for recreational resource use. Although the evolution and development of Leicester's urban parks are reviewed later, it is worth observing the socio-demographic context of Madge's study prior to outlining the principal findings.

Leicester, located in the East Midlands in the UK, is a medium-sized city with a population of 272,000 people. What is notable is its diverse ethnic mix: 72 per cent of the population are white, 24 per cent are Asian, 2 per cent Afro-Caribbean, 2 per cent Chinese and other 'ethnic groups'. Despite the city's urban-industrial development, it is widely acknowledged that the city has an enviable distribution of open space. By 1994, Leicester City Council was responsible for over 1200 ha of open space, which comprised 20 per cent of the total city area. This is a significant level of provision within an international context, and certainly enhances the city's green and open feel as a British city. In this context, Madge's (1997) analysis of the geography of fear was timely. The sampling framework, namely face-to-face interviews with Leicester residents at on-street locations sought to derive a sample of city-wide park and open space use, with some 535 respondents interviewed. From the survey, ten main constraints emerged which influenced park use. In order of importance these were:

- Fear
- Weather
- Lack of time due to work
- Family constraints
- Lack of transport
- Lack of interest
- Limited awareness of facilities available
- Housework
- Distance of parks/too far away
- Physically unable to get to the parks.

Some 43 per cent of respondents attributed fear as a 'very important' factor constraining their use of parks. The gender difference was striking with 75 per cent of women compared to 50 per cent of men stating fear was a major constraint on park use. This is in line with Westover's (1985) finding in North

America, where 90 per cent of female respondents felt unsafe if alone in parks. Studies of victimisation in Leicester (*e.g.* Willis 1992) recognise that women have a greater sense of insecurity due to their vulnerability to crime.

When ethnicity was examined, Asian groups expressed higher levels of fear compared with white and Afro-Caribbean groups reflecting victimisation statistics, racial abuse and attacks in the urban environment. In terms of age, those over 45 expressed the greatest levels of fear. As Madge (1997:241) rightly acknowledged: 'The result of fear of crime is, however, concrete: the elderly are less likely to use public parks for recreation.'

In terms of causes of fear, Madge (1997) observed that the main causes of fear of park use were: anxieties related to actual or potential bodily harm (*e.g.* mugging, sexual attack, loitering people, gangs of youths, dogs and racial attack). Women's fears were greatest in relation to fear of sexual attack by men. These findings reflected the prevailing levels of fear of sexual violence which women in Leicester harbour, particularly the high level of sexual harassment which was rarely reported (Women's Equality Unit 1993). In fact 77 per cent of female respondents were fearful of sexual attacks in parks, a much higher figure than in similar surveys in Edinburgh and Seattle. Fear of racial attack was also much higher for Afro-Caribbean and Asian groups than for white groups.

The implications of these findings are reflected in the behaviour and use of parks. Women tended to avoid large open spaces, unlit areas and those areas with dense undergrowth and trees. The onset of nightfall also elevated fear of using such places, especially if they were alone. As Madge suggested, 'Fear is a significant factor structuring the use of public parks in Leicester. The intensity and cause of fear varied with social traits of gender, ethnicity and age and affected spatial behaviour regarding use of parks. The geography of fear is mediated through a set of overlapping social, ideological and structural power relations which become translated into spatial behaviour.'

The findings of Madge's study highlight how a new constraint on leisure behaviour has specific gender, ethnic and social ramifications for recreational resource use. Although Madge (1997) criticises the existing recreational literature for neglecting this issue, fear is a more profound issue in urban environments than has hitherto been the case in recreational research. While Hoyles (1994) argued for a greater feminisation of public space, and Madge (1997) argued for increased informal surveillance to encourage public participation and use of parks and open spaces, creating safer parks is deeply embedded in more complex notions of creating safe cities. Koskela and Pain (2000) point to the problems and failures of designing out fear from the urban environment, given the extent to which fear of crime pervades city spaces.

In a review of urban public space in Tokyo and New York, Cybriwsky (1999) recognised the growth in the surveillance of public spaces to improve security which could lead to a return to private spaces and attempts to modify social behaviour in recreational spaces. This is a feature which Giddens (1990:20) recognised whereby 'surveillance is a means of levering the modern social world away from traditional modes of social activity'. Indeed, Koskela and Pain (2000:279) argued that 'Geographers and planners should take greater account of the complexity of fear. ... Places have some influence on fear, but perhaps of equal or greater significance is the ways in which fear shapes our understanding, perception and use of space and place.'

This is certainly a truism in the case of recreational use of urban parks in Madge's (1997) findings which have a wider application to urban recreational resource use in the developed world. A great deal of progress will need to be made in addressing fear of crime and recreational and leisure spaces in urbanised societies until Koskela and Pain's (2000:274) analysis that 'Green urban spaces and woodlands are commonly perceived as dangerous places and feelings of insecurity often have a deterrent effect on women's use of them' is no longer a valid assessment.

- The geography of fear is an important factor shaping participation by certain social groups in recreational activities.
- The problem of fear affects certain groups' participation patterns (*e.g.* the elderly and women) more than others.
- The creation of safer recreational open spaces is more problematic since it will involve greater surveillance, monitoring and control of informal leisure spaces.
- The new cultural geography, particularly the geography of gender, provides invaluable insights to explain how women's leisure space is embedded in notions of fear, constraints on the use of urban space and the resultant inequalities.

RESOURCES AND FASHIONS

While models of participation and obstacles to recreation have attempted to predict the probability of people participating in activities, using variables such as age, sex, marital status and social variables (*e.g.* housing tenure, income and car ownership), predictions decline in accuracy when attempting to identify individual activities (*e.g.* golf). What such recreational models often fail to acknowledge is the role of choice and preference given a range of options. In this respect, geographical proximity to recreational resources and access to them is a major determinant. This is demonstrated by Burton (1971), who found that in Britain, people were three times as likely to use a recreational resource if they lived between half and three-quarters of a mile away, a feature emphasised by Patmore (1983) and Page *et al.* (1994) in research on urban parks.

This shows that the proximity to a recreational resource increased the propensity for use at a swimming pool, yet for leisure centres where attendees used cars to visit them, the distance-decay function had a less rapid decline in attendance in relation to distance. Outside urban areas, the occurrence of recreational resources are more varied in their spatial distribution, and recreational opportunities need to be closely examined in relation to demand and supply. To provide a number of detailed insights into the patterns of recreation in different countries, and how demand is influenced and constrained, a number of national recreational patterns are examined followed by a case study of regional demand.

MEASURING RECREATIONAL DEMAND

Most geographers acknowledge the continued lack of suitable data on recreational demand, as Patmore (1983:55) explains:

Prior to the 1960s sources were scattered and fragmentary, and lacked any coherent basis. The studies undertaken for the American Outdoor Recreation Resources Review Commission and published in 1962 gave the impetus for work in Britain. Two wide-ranging national surveys were carried out later in the latter part of that decade: the Pilot National Recreation Survey ... and the Government social survey's Planning for Leisure.... These surveys remain unique at national level.

Although such surveys also have a number of limitations - they were 'one-off' studies, the methods of data collection did not allow comparability of the data for each survey, and the results are often dated on publication due to the time required to analyse the results - they were a starting point for analysing demand. Yet since 1972 no major survey specifically focusing on leisure has been undertaken in the UK, although the General Household Survey (GHS), which normally occurs every four years, has included a number of questions on leisure.

PROBLEMS AND METHODS OF MEASURING RECREATIONAL DEMAND

When seeking to understand their recreational habits, asking individuals questions about their recreational habits using social survey techniques remains the most widely used approach. A landmark study by Rowntree and Lavers (1951) of *English Life and Leisure* provides a good illustration of the early use of a diverse range of research methods and sources to construct patterns of participation in leisure and recreation in post-war Britain. Even so, researchers recognise that precision is needed to identify participation, non-participation and the frequency of each.

For this reason, questions on surveys need to follow the type of format used on the GHS, to provide both a temporal and quantitative measure of demand.

Patmore (1983:57) cites the GHS, which begins by asking respondents: 'What ... things have you done in your leisure time ... in the four weeks ending last Sunday?' Survey data rarely record all the information a researcher seeks (*e.g.* respondents' recall ability may not accurately record the full pattern), or respondents have a different understanding of a term to that intended by the researcher. As a result, a variety of survey techniques are necessary to derive a range of complementary and yet unique insights into recreation demand.

Within the recreation literature, three techniques have primarily been used:

- A continuous record of recreation activities of a sample population for a given time period which involves respondents keeping a diary of activities (the time budget approach) (Zuzanek *et al.*'s (1998) cross-national survey of Dutch and Canadian use of time is a good source to consult).
- Questionnaire surveys which require respondents to recall activities either in the form of an individual case study, which are detailed and sometimes contain both qualitative and quantitative questions and which are inevitably small-scale due to the time involved in in-depth qualitative interviews.
- Questionnaire surveys which are large scale, enabling subsamples to be drawn which are statistically significant. Such surveys may be derived using simple and unambiguous questions which focus on a specific recreation activity or one that covers the entire spectrum of leisure activities (*e.g.* the GHS which surveyed 17,574 people in 1993 in Great Britain aged 16 and over). To illustrate how these techniques have been used and the way such data have been analysed, the time budget approach and national surveys of recreational activities are now examined.

According to Coppock and Duffield (1975:5), 'recreation takes place in that portion of people's lives in which they are free (within constraints) to choose their activities, that is, their leisure time, [and] how they spend their time (time-budgets) is of paramount importance in any attempt to establish recreational demand, since it determines where recreational activities are possible'.

Therefore, time budget analysis is a vital tool in analysing demand. Time budgets provide a systematic record of a person's use of time. They describe the duration, sequence and timing of a person's activities for a given period, usually of between a day and a week. When combined with the recording of the location at which activities occur, the record is referred to as a space time budget.

Time budget studies provide for the understanding of spatial and temporal behaviour patterns which may not be directly observable by other research techniques either because of their practicality or their intrusion into individual privacy. Such studies are often undertaken through the use of detailed diaries which are filled in by participants. However, this method has not been widely used in comparison with more traditional survey techniques due to the difficulty for individuals of accurately keeping records. For example, in 1966 and 1974 to 1975 the British Broadcasting Corporation used its Audience Research Department to recruit people to keep a diary for a full week with half-hour entries. Yet even in such a short time span, diarists' willingness to record information accurately declined towards the end of the week.

However, pioneering research by Glyptis (1981a) used a diary technique which examined a sample of 595 visitors to the countryside. Respondents kept a diary record spanning three days and five evenings, recording the dominant pursuit in half-hour periods.

While respondents identified up to 129 different leisure activities, each cited an average of 11. The value of the study was that through the use of cluster analysis to statistically analyse the sample and to group the population for more detail of this technique), it identified the leisure lifestyles of respondents with distinct groupings, where people of different social classes engaged in similar activities. The value of such research is in the identification of factors beyond simplistic analogies of demand determined by biological, social and economic factors.

INTERNATIONAL PERSPECTIVES

The most useful survey of national surveys of leisure time and the recreational activities undertaken may be found in Cushman *et al*. (1996a) which reviews international data on leisure and the existence of cross-national comparative research. It is also useful since the origins and role of participation surveys are reviewed, a feature subsequently updated by Parker (1999) in the UK context.

THE UNITED KINGDOM

Since the publication of Patmore's (1983) detailed review of data sources for analysing leisure and recreation patterns in the UK, Veal (1992) updated the situation pointing to the GHS and the role of the Australian Commonwealth government in commissioning the first National Recreation Participation Survey in Australia in 1985 to 1986.

This section examines demand at the national level in a number of countries to provide comparisons. However the most up-to-date and accessible source which documents these issues in the UK is the Office of Population and Censuses (OPCS) Social Trends. The 1999 edition compiles data from a wide variety of sources and examines:

- Use of time for leisure and other activities showing that men in full-time employment had around two more hours of free time than women in full-time employment.
- Participation in home-based leisure activities in the period 1977 to 1997 indicated that watching television remained the most important

pastime, while other activities vary by age and sex (*i.e.* gardening is more popular among men aged 25 years or more).

Table. Participation in Home-based Leisure Activities: by Gender, in Great Britain 1977-97.

	1977	**1987**	**1996-97**
Males			
Watching TV	97	99	99
Visiting/entertaining friends or relations	89	94	95
Listening to radio	87	89	90
Listening to records/tapes/ CDs	64	76	79
Reading books	52	54	58
DIY	51	58	58
Gardening	49	49	52
Dressmaking/needlework/ knitting	2	3	3
Females			
Watching TV	97	99	99
Visiting/entertaining friends or relations	93	96	97
Listening to radio	87	86	87
Listening to records/tapes/ CDs	60	71	77
Reading books	57	65	71
DIY	22	30	30
Gardening	35	43	45
Dressmaking/needlework/ knitting	51	47	37

Note: Percentage in each age group participating in each activity in the four weeks before interview.

- Day visits form a popular activity in terms of leisure time and derived from the 1998 UK Day Visits Survey examined round trips from home to locations in the UK. Between 1994 and 1998, leisure day visits increased by 15 per cent, rising to 5.9 billion in 1998. The two most commonly cited reasons for day visits were to drive out for a drink to a restaurant or public house, or to visit friends and relatives. In terms of gender, males were more likely to go out for a drink than females while females would tend to visit friends and relatives more than males.
- In terms of tourism, Blackpool Pleasure Beach was the UK's most popular tourist attraction (7.1 million visits in 1998), with the British Museum the second most popular (5.6 million visits in 1998).

- In 1998, 56 million holidays of four nights or more were taken by British residents, a rise of 36 per cent on 1971. The number of domestic holidays taken fell slightly in the of consumption of high forms of culture (*e.g.* visiting museums, exhibitions and concert halls).

Table. Participation in the Most Popular Sports, Games and Physical Activities: by Gender and Age, in the UK 1996-97

	16-19	20-24	25-34	35-44	45-54	55-64	65 and over	All aged 16 and over
Males								
Walking	57	57	50	53	51	50	37	49
Snooker/pool/ billiards	54	45	29	19	13	9	5	19
Cycling	36	24	19	18	12	8	5	15
Swimming	18	17	17	20	10	7	5	13
Soccer	47	28	17	10	2	1	-	10
Females								
Walking	45	43	44	45	49	43	25	41
Keep fit/yoga	29	28	24	20	14	12	6	17
Swimming	23	21	26	22	14	12	5	16
Cycling	14	11	10	12	7	4	2	8
Snooker/pool/ billiards	24	17	6	3	1	-	-	4

Table. Day Visits from Home: by Gender and Main Activity, 1998.

Great britain	Percentages		
	Males	**Females**	**All**
Eat/drink	21	15	18
Visit friends	14	19	17
Walk/hill-walk/ramble	16	14	15
Shop	9	15	12
Entertainment	5	7	6
Indoor sport	7	4	5
Outdoor sport	8	3	5
Hobby/special interest	4	5	5
Drive/sightsee	3	3	3
Swimming	2	3	3
Leisure attraction	2	2	2
Watching sport	2	1	2
Cycling/mountain biking	3	1	2
Informal sport/games	2	2	2
Other	2	5	3
All visits	100	100	100

Table. Holidays Abroad: by Destination.

	1971	1981	1991	1998
Spain	34.3	21.7	21.3	27.5
France	15.9	27.2	25.8	20.2
United states	1.0	5.5	6.8	7.0
Greece	4.5	6.7	7.6	5.3
Italy	9.2	5.8	3.5	4.0
Portugal	2.6	2.8	4.8	3.6
Irish republic	-	3.6	3.0	3.5
Turkey	-	0.1	0.7	3.0
Netherlands	3.6	2.4	3.5	2.7
Cyprus	1.0	0.7	2.4	2.6
Belgium	-	2.1	2.1	2.3
Germany	3.4	2.6	2.7	1.8
Malta	-	2.6	1.7	1.3
Austria	5.5	2.5	2.4	1.3
Other countries	19.0	13.7	11.8	13.9
All destinations (=100per cent)				
(thousands)	4,201	13,131	20,788	32,306

1990s, compensated by overseas trips. The most popular destination remained Spain in 1998, with Europe the dominant destination for British holidaymakers. The USA remains the most popular non-European destination.

- In 1998, people aged 65 or more were the least likely to go on holiday, with those aged 45 to 54 years of age the most likely to take a holiday overseas.
- In terms of sporting activities, men are consistently more likely than women to participate in sport. In 1996 to 1999, 71 per cent of men and 57 per cent of women participated in at least one sporting activity in the four weeks prior to being interviewed for the GHS.

POLAND

Poland is an interesting example, given the new roles for recreation in the post-communist state, since market reforms and ideological change has led to new roles for leisure post-1989. Although one consequence of austerity programmes to deal with budget deficits, a number of pre- and post-communist data sources exist to reconstruct leisure participation. The government Central Statistical Office (GUS) collects the majority of data. Jung (1996) noted that over the period between 1972 and 1990, participation trends showed:

- Listening to the radio and watching television remained the dominant activities in terms of participation.
- Former communist culture activities, such as going to the cinema, theatre and opera declined in importance from over half of the population in 1972 to under one-third by 1990.
- Economic and political reforms in the 1980s may account for a sharp decline in participation

More detailed time budget studies have been examined by Olszewska (1989), and Jung (1996) highlighted a number of key global influences upon leisure participation: a growing media influence on mass culture, outbound travel by the Polish population (and inbound tourism), despite the withdrawal of state social subsidies for holiday travel. The electronic mass media also had an impact on leisure consumption. In the post-communist era, problems associated with the commercialisation of leisure and a growing polarisation of wealth, less economic security, rising unemployment and increasing rates of crime provide a new context for leisure participation.

HUNGARY

Fukaz (1989) examined the Csepel project undertaken in Hungary, which in 1969 sampled 400 blue-collar workers in one of the country's largest metal factories. Further in-depth interviews were undertaken in the period 1969 to 1972, 1975 to 1979 and 1979 to 1982, to collect time budget data as well as in-depth case studies. The longitudinal nature of the survey up to 1982 allows changes to be charted through time, and a simulation sample in 1985 (not using the original 1969 workers) provided a further in-depth case study. While the Csepel project is not representative of the Hungarian population, macro-economic changes in Hungarian society are reflected in the lifestyles of the population and these are reflected in the Csepel sample.

Over the period 1969 to 1985, hours of work in Hungary were reduced from 48 to 40 hours a week, which is often argued by researchers as a pre-condition for the expansion of leisure. But in Hungary the reduction in official hours of work was accompanied by increases in overtime working and the growth of second jobs. Fukaz (1989:41) argued that 'as Hungary's economy developed, the prestige of leisure appears to have grown.... Only 6.4 per cent in 1976 and 3.9 per cent in 1979 preferred work to leisure on Saturdays'. Yet the evidence from the Csepel study indicates that 'the main obstacles to a growth and enrichment of leisure in Hungary are not rooted in inadequate leisure education, or in a weakening or absence of leisure values. Rather, the barriers have been erected by objective material and financial conditions. The latter have discouraged individuals from using reductions in official work time to enhance their leisure' preferring to use the time in some cases for pecuniary reward.

In terms of leisure activities undertaken by the Csepel workers, these were largely related to passive forms of recreation. The most popular activities were watching television and just relaxing, though seasonal variations exist, with winter leisure being home-based but urban work patterns tend to dominate leisure in present-day Hungary. The growth of second home ownership has also characterised weekend and vacation leisure time for those families with access to such resources.

These three examples of recreational demand show that the patterns of leisure activities for each population exhibit a common range of characteristics, in terms of the predominance of passive activities, and the constraints of urban living which largely structure the time budgets of those in employment due to weekday work commitments. In other words, the patterns of demand highlighted in the three national surveys point to the existence of factors which facilitate and constrain recreational activities in each particular context.

Even so, it is important to recognise the current criticisms and concerns with national participation surveys observed by Cushman *et al*. (1996b: 12) as 'Recently surveys have had a "bad press" from academics, particularly in light of the growing popularity - and indeed orthodoxy - of qualitative research methods in the field'. As a result, qualitative researchers point to the shortcomings, limitations and somewhat outmoded approach of quantitative 'positivist' research methods. However, so far the discussion of demand has focused on national patterns, and therefore attention now turns to the regional level to examine the contribution the geographer can make to the analysis of demand within a regional geographic framework.

THE REGIONAL DEMAND FOR LEISURE AND RECREATION

Within the studies of national recreational demand reviewed in the previous section, it is clear that the analyses of geographical patterns of demand were relatively scant, given the tendency for national studies to lack a regional dimension. It is the spatial variations in demand which are of interest to the geographer, and a number of studies have been undertaken which utilise the geographer's spatial analytical approach to examine demand patterns. North-West England is one such area which has seen a significant contribution made to understanding the scale and nature of regional recreational demand including evidence in Rodgers' (1969) insights from the *Pilot National Recreation Survey*, Rodgers' (1977) contribution to leisure in the North-West and Rodgers and Patmore's (1972) *Leisure in the North-West*.

The North-West of England is an interesting region with a variety of socioeconomic contrasts ranging from the urban decline apparent in inner-city areas through to a range of country districts with high levels of prosperity akin to South-East England. What Rodgers (1993) explored was the changing political climate for leisure provision at national level, namely the rolling back of the frontiers of the state and changing social philosophy that active and creative leisure pursuits deserved to 'be promoted as widely as possible, with the support of public funding and subsidy, to an increasing emphasis on the concept that the provision of recreation is simply another service industry best left to the operation of the market for most efficient delivery at least cost'.

This marks a shift in political ideology: that leisure is no longer a significant welfare service to be delivered to all sectors of the population at free or subsidised prices due to the contribution it makes to enhanced quality of life. Thus the move to a market-driven approach requires local authorities as the principal planners of community-based leisure provision to recognise the existence of leisure markets which comprise different forms of recreational demand in time and space. Local leisure markets are diverse, where a multitude of factors may affect their composition.

For example, those where unemployment, social stress due to environmental factors and low rates of population growth exist may offer little commercial opportunity for the private sector despite real leisure needs. Yet if left to the market, such needs may not be served adequately due to the apparent lack of prosperity or ability of individuals to pay for a resource that poor people view as a luxury item when they cannot always command the financial resources to meet basic needs. Thus, at a regional level, a detailed district-by-district assessment of the market is necessary to show which areas and markets may still require local authority support to avoid gross inequalities in access and provision from developing any further.

Rodgers (1993) used two principles to underpin an analysis of leisure markets:

- A significant proportion of demand is age-related, and changes through time will affect future needs;
- Aocio-economic well-being is a powerful determinant of the volume and pattern of demand in the present and the future.

By combining these factors in an overall assessment, Rodgers (1993) was able to develop a typology of districts and their ability to support a market-based approach to leisure provision. In terms of age-related markets, Rodgers (1993:119-20) identified four groups:

- The teenage-young adult, who is active and a major generator of recreational demand, especially active pursuits. Within the North-West, this group exhibits an almost universal decline;
- The family phase (aged 25 to 44 years), with a distinctive set of leisure interests;
- A post-family phase (aged 45 to 60 years), where active recreational interests are in decline but an interest in general leisure activities is strong;
- The elderly, with a significant range of passive leisure interests.

By analysing forecast population growth in each of these groups, Rodgers (1993:125) concluded that for planning future leisure provision the following characteristics needed to be incorporated into any geographical assessment of demand:

- A common feature of districts in the region is the absence of growth, except in the family phase. Rates of growth of 4 per cent above the national average are apparent in the age group 25 to 44 years for

1981 to 1991. The opportunities for market-driven provision include fitness training, outdoor pursuits in the countryside, water-sports and ten-pin bowling.

- In the post-family phase, growth rates are less than the national average, with a degree of localised growth in the industrial towns of Greater Manchester, West Lancashire and districts of North Cheshire though not in Merseyside. The most prominent activities are bowls, fishing, dance, keep fit and walking which are likely to have little appeal for private sector operators.
- The youth market exhibits a clear decline, except for areas where planned growth exists (*e.g.* new towns), with rates above the national average for Merseyside and parts of inner Manchester. In the period 1981 to 1991 a decline of 13 to 17 per cent exists in most districts, with the exception of Cheshire and West Lancashire.
- Among the elderly, trends are complex, but no patterns of growth are evident in traditional retirement areas.
- A number of extremes exist in subregional patterns of demand, with weaknesses in Merseyside which stretches beyond the inner-city districts. In East Cheshire (*e.g.* Congleton, Crewe and Nantwich) a profile of demand akin to the affluent South-East of England exists with different subgroupings of demand in other areas.

One of the most significant contributory factors to the size and nature of demand is clearly related to socio-economic contrasts. Social well-being is, according to Rodgers (1993:126), 'a strong influence on both the volume and structure of leisure demand and on the relative roles of public and commercial provision in meeting it'.

Using the Department of the Environment (DoE) Social Deprivation Index, which derives negative indices based on unemployment, overcrowding, single-parent and pension households, housing quality and ethnic origin, Rodgers (1993) ranked the districts in the North-West on this composite measure of social stress and also included levels of car ownership. The results were used to identify a range of geographically based leisure markets which were strong or weak in terms of demand, particularly in relation to their capacity to pay for recreational activities in a market-driven local leisure economy.

- Approximately 12 districts are in the top left quadrant, which represent areas of prosperity with comparatively little unemployment, high levels of car ownership and income generation and low levels of social stress. These districts exhibit some strength in demand despite a drop in numbers of people aged 13 to 24 years, while growth in the family and post-family sectors exists. These districts have the most appeal to commercial providers. Rodgers (1993:127) suggests that 'for large sections of the community and for many recreations a blend of private-sector and voluntary body provision, with local authorities acting largely with a market philosophy, might offer an effective formula. The case for massive direct subsidy is relatively weak, against the stronger conflicting claims of less fortunate areas' in the allocation of scarce public sector resources for recreation. Even so, pockets of target groups exist (*e.g.* housewives, the young and active elderly) who would benefit from some subsidy of their activities. In the north-west of the region, problems of access to recreational resources also exist in largely rural districts.

- A grouping which occupies the bottom right corner scores low on prosperity while the age-related markets show a major decline. This reflects the limited growth in a single age category and districts of population loss (*e.g.* Merseyside and some of the textile towns). Both the absolute numbers and spending power of the population are declining, where the case of recreational provision for social reasons is essential due to the concentration of disadvantaged groups (*e.g.* the unemployed, the poor, single-parent families, the elderly and ethnic minorities). Dependence upon state benefits underpins the case for public subsidy for provision due to the multiple deprivation existing in such areas.
- A further six districts such as Hyndburn and Rochdale score high on low prosperity indices, with selective growth in family and post-family groups with a strong ethnic dimension. The welfare case for provision is also apparent in this category.
- The remaining districts exhibit relatively prosperous populations with limited growth potential, with limited justification for public funding of their recreational services.

While Rodgers (1993) admits the allocation of scarce public resources raises controversial decision-making choices, it does illustrate the value of a spatial analytical approach to recreation, if a wide range of data and factors are taken into account. In other words, this case study illustrates the geographer's ability to synthesise a wide range of complex data sources and concepts to derive a series of spatially contingent generalisations and groupings of the population for a region as diverse as North-West England.Using concepts from social geography (*e.g.* social well-being and deprivation) and combining demographic data from districts across the region, the geographer is able to highlight the challenge for regional and local planners in the allocation of declining absolute public sector resources for recreational provision. Regional analysis epitomises the geographer's interest in places, and differences and similarities in both time and space. The greatest contribution geographical research has made is to the site-specific studies of demand, most notably site surveys. For this reason, the remaining focus of this section on recreation examines recreation site surveys.

THE SPATIAL ANALYSIS OF DEMAND AT THE MICRO LEVEL

Within the growing literature on geographical studies of recreation in the 1960s and 1970s, site surveys have become the most documented. As Glyptis (1981b: 277) indicated, 'numerous site surveys - mostly set in the format devised by Burton (1966) ... established the characteristics of visitors and their trips.

Social profiles, trip distances, modes of transport and the duration, purpose and frequency of visits are well documented.' Glyptis (1981b) also noted that the 1980s were ripe for behavioural analysis which had been neglected in relation to site surveys. While reviews of site surveys are too numerous to list, novel research methods which examine the behaviour rather than the socio-economic characteristics of recreationalists have remained less common in the published literature, although some reports have probed this area. Glyptis' (1981b) analysis of one 242 ha site - Westwood Common, Beverley near Hull (UK) - is one such example.

By employing participant observation methods to examine an undulating grassland area of common pasture land 13 km from the urban area of Hull, the spatial distribution of site use by recreationalists was observed and analysed. The main recreational activities observed at the site were sitting, sun-bathing, walking, picnicking, informal games and staying inside one's car. On a busy Sunday in summer, up to 2,000 visitors came to the site. Using dispersion maps, observational mapping permitted the visitor distributions to be located in time and space while length of stay (using car registration data) and maps of use for different days and times complemented traditional social survey methods to analyse visitor behaviour.

The site features, access points, availability of parking and location of landscape features and facilities permit a more detailed understanding of site use. Glyptis (1981b) used observations on five days in August and September between 11 a.m. and 6 p.m. to collate data. Visitor arrivals at the site during the weekend occurred between 12 noon and 2 p.m., and peak use occurred at 4.30 p.m., with the majority of visitors spending one to two hours on site.

The gradual increase in intensity of use by time of day varied by activity, with informal games and picnicking declining after Sunday lunch and walking increasing throughout the afternoon. Local users also displayed a preference to use the site at off-peak times, with increased patterns of dispersion and clumping through time. This reflects access roads, with visitors parking close to (within 15 yards) the site they visited. Visitors were also recorded going to landmarks and facilities (*e.g.* viewpoints) as well as buying refreshments (*e.g.* from mobile vans), with the density of use increasing through the day rather than the distribution.

Glyptis (1981c) devised a simple model to explain the dynamics of visitor dispersion. Thereafter, as the pace of arrivals slows, a degree of infilling and consolidation occurs. Then as people depart, dispersion occurs, with a more irregular pattern of distribution arising, although it may be affected by new arrivals in the afternoon who intensify the pattern. What Glyptis (1991:119) recognised was that even though 'sites clearly experience an increase in visitor density, visitor dispersion in a spatial sense remains fairly constant, even with space to spare and no restrictions on public access'.

Using nearest neighbour analysis, Glyptis (1981c) was able to measure the distances between groups of visitors, and that comfortable levels of tolerance exist for visitors in terms of proximity to other people, although the amount of personal space which recreationalists require may vary between different cultures. In fact, Glyptis (1991:119) remarked that 'as levels of use increase on a given day, the percentage occupancy of space actually decreases: visitors only ever use about a fifth of the space available to them, and at times of heaviest use they choose to occupy even less. In other words, site carrying capacity changes continually.'

This study also highlighted the significance of recreation sites with multiple uses, where a variety of recreational needs are capable of being met and, as Burton's (1974) survey of Cannock Chase, Staffordshire (UK) found, individual sites cannot be viewed in isolation: there are relationships between them and understanding them is vital to site management. Glyptis (1981c) highlighted a certain degree of consistency in visitor use of a site, explaining the patterns as a function of the resource base, visitor use and behavioural factors. It may be possible to accommodate or reduce capacity through simple modifications as 'the geographer is well placed to examine fundamental aspects of ... recreation, to diagnose issues in site management, and to propose solutions' (Glyptis 1981b: 285). Therefore, having outlined many of the factors and dimensions of recreational demand at a variety of spatial scales from the national, regional and local level, the discussion now turns to tourism demand.

TOURISM DEMAND

One of the fundamental questions tourism researchers consistently seek to answer is: Why do tourists travel? This seemingly simple proposition remains one of the principal challenges for tourism research. D.G. Pearce (1995a: 18) expands this proposition by asking 'What induces them to leave their home area to visit other areas? What factors condition their travel behaviour, influencing their choice of destination, itineraries followed and activities undertaken?' Such questions underpin not only issues of spatial interaction, but also lead the geographer to question:

- Why tourists seek to travel;
- Where they go;
- When they go and how they get there.

These basic issues have spatial implications in terms of the patterns of tourism, where tourism impacts will occur and the nature of management challenges for destinations which may attract a 'mass market' or be seeking to develop tourism from a low base. In other words, an understanding of tourism demand is a starting point for the analysis of why tourism develops, who patronises specific destinations and what appeals to the client market.

However, geographers are at a comparative disadvantage in answering some of the principal questions associated with tourism demand since 'geographers have not been at the forefront of this research which has been led by psychologists, sociologists, marketers and economists. Some of these researchers have touched on such issues as the potential significance of variations in motivation on destination choice'. However, tourist behaviour and the analysis of motivation has not traditionally been the logical positivist and empirical approach of traditional forms of spatial analysis on tourism with some exceptions. The area of tourist behaviour has a more developed literature within the field of social psychology than geography, and the emphasis in this section is on the way such approaches assist in understanding how tourist behaviour may result in the spatial implications for tourism.

The precise approach one adopts to the analysis of tourism demand is largely dependent upon the disciplinary perspective of the researcher. Geographers view demand in a uniquely spatial manner as 'the total number of persons who travel, or wish to travel, to use tourist facilities and services at places away from their places of work and residence', whereas in this context demand 'is seen in terms of the relationship between individuals' motivation [to travel] and their ability to do so' with an attendant emphasis on the implications for the spatial impact on the development of domestic and international tourism.

In comparison, the economist emphasises 'the schedule of the amount of any product or service which people are willing and able to buy at each specific price in a set of possible prices during a specified period of time. Psychologists view demand from the perspective of motivation and behaviour', while Uysal (1998) reviewed the wider context of tourism demand. In conceptual terms, there are three principal elements to tourism demand:

- *Effective or actual demand* comprises the number of people participating in tourism, commonly expressed as the number of travellers. This is most commonly measured by tourism statistics which means that most official sources of data are measures of effective demand.
- *Suppressed demand* is the population who are unable to travel because of circumstances (*e.g.* lack of purchasing power or limited holiday entitlement) which is called potential demand. Potential demand can be converted to effective demand if the circumstances change. There is also deferred demand where constraints (*e.g.* lack of tourism supply such as a shortage of bedspaces) can also be converted to effective demand if a destination or locality can accommodate the demand.

- *No demand* is a distinct category for the population who have no desire to travel.

According to Cooper *et al.* (1993:16) the demand for tourism may be viewed in other ways using a number of other concepts:

- *Substitution of demand* where the demand for a specific activity is substituted by another activity;
- *Redirection of demand* where the geographical distribution of tourism is altered due to pricing policies of competing destinations, special events or changing trends and tastes.

Therefore, it is apparent that the analysis of tourism demand as an abstract concept remains firmly within the remit of tourism economics.

However, the factors which shape the tourist decision-making process to select and participate in specific forms of tourism is largely within the field of consumer behaviour and motivation.

TOURIST MOTIVATION

According to Moutinho (1987:16), motivation is 'a state of need, a condition that exerts a push on the individual towards certain types of action that are seen as likely to bring satisfaction'. In this respect Cooper *et al.* (1993:20) rightly acknowledge that 'demand for tourists at the individual level can be treated as a consumption process which is influenced by a number of factors. These may be a combination of needs and desires, availability of time and money, or images, perceptions and attitudes'.

Not surprisingly, this is an incredibly complex area of research and it is impossible within a chapter such as this to overview the area in depth. Nevertheless, P. Pearce's (1993) influential work in this field outlined a 'blueprint for tourist motivation', arguing that in an attempt to theorise tourist motivation one must consider the following issues:

- The conceptual place of tourism motivation;
- Its task in the specialism of tourism;
- Its ownership and users;
- Its ease of communication;
- Pragmatic measurement concerns;
- Adopting a dynamic approach;
- The development of multi-motive perspectives;
- Resolving and clarifying intrinsic and extrinsic motivation approaches.

To date no all-embracing theory of tourist motivation has been developed which has been adapted and legitimised by researchers in other contexts. This is largely due to the multidisciplinary nature of the research issues identified above and the problem of simplifying complex psychological factors and behaviour into a set of constructs and ultimately a universally acceptable theory that can be tested and proved in various tourism contexts. As a result, Cooper *et al.* (1993:20) prefer to view the individual as a central component of tourism demand to understand what motivates the tourist to travel. Their research rightly acknowledges that:

No two individuals are alike, and differences in attitudes, perceptions and motivation have an important influence on travel decisions [where] attitudes depend on an individual's perception of the world. Perceptions are mental impressions of ... a place or travel company and are determined by many factors which include childhood, family and work experiences. However, attitudes and perceptions in themselves do not explain why people want to travel. The inner urges which initiate travel demand are called travel motivators.

If one views the tourist as a consumer, then tourism demand is formulated through a consumer decision-making process, and therefore one can discern four elements which initiate demand:

- *Energisers of demand*: Factors that promote an individual to decide on a holiday;
- *Filterers of demand*: Which means that even though motivation may prevail, constraints on demand may exist in economic, sociological or psychological terms;
- *Affecters*: Which are factors that may heighten or suppress the energisers that promote consumer interest or choice in tourism;
- *Roles*: Where the family member involved in the purchase of holiday products and the arbiter of group decision-making on choice of destination, product, and the where, when and how of consumption.

These factors underpin the tourist's process of travel decision-making although it does not explain why people choose to travel.

HIERARCHY MODEL AND TOURIST MOTIVATION

Within the social psychology of tourism there is a growing literature which has built upon Maslow's work (discussed earlier in relation to recreation) to identify specific motivations beyond the concept of needing 'to get away from it all' pioneered by Grinstein (1955), while push factors motivating individuals to seek a holiday exist, and pull factors (*e.g.* promotion by tourist resorts and tour operators) encourage as attractors.

Ryan's (1991:25-9) analysis of tourist travel motivators (excluding business travel) identifies the following reasons commonly cited to explain why people travel to tourist destinations for holidays, which include:

- A desire to escape from a mundane environment;
- The pursuit of relaxation and recuperation functions;
- An opportunity for play;
- The strengthening of family bonds;
- Prestige, since different destinations can enable one to gain social enhancement among peers;

- Social interaction;
- Educational opportunities;
- Wish fulfilment;
- Shopping.

From this list, it is evident that while all leisure involves a temporary escape of some kind, 'tourism is unique in that it involves real physical escape reflected in travelling to one or more destination regions where the leisure experience transpires ... [thus] a holiday trip allows changes that are multi-dimensional: place, pace, faces, lifestyle, behaviour, attitude.

It allows a person temporary withdrawal from many of the environments affecting day to day existence' (Leiper (1984) cited in D.G. Pearce (1995:19). Within most studies of tourist motivations these factors emerge in one form or another, while researchers such as Crompton (1979) emphasise that socio-psychological motives can be located along a continuum, Iso-Ahola (1980) theorised tourist motivation in terms of an escape element complemented by a search component, where the tourist is seeking something.

However, Dann's (1981) conceptualisation is probably one of the most useful attempts to simplify the principal elements of tourist motivation into:

- Travel as a response to what is lacking yet desired;
- Destination pull in response to motivational push;
- Motivation as fancy;
- Motivation as classified purpose;
- Motivation typologies;
- Motivation and tourist experiences;
- Motivation as definition and meaning.

This was simplified a stage further by McIntosh and Goeldner (1990) into:

- Physical motivators;
- Cultural motivators;
- Interpersonal motivators;
- Status and prestige motivators.

On the basis of motivation and using the type of experiences tourists seek, Cohen (1972) distinguished between four types of travellers:

- The organised mass tourist, on a package holiday, who is highly organised. Their contact with the host community in a destination is minimal.
- The individual mass tourist, who uses similar facilities to the organised mass tourist but also desires to visit other sights not covered on organised tours in the destination.
- The explorers, who arrange their travel independently and who wish to experience the social and cultural lifestyle of the destination.
- The drifter, who does not seek any contact with other tourists or their accommodation, preferring to live with the host community.

Clearly, such a classification is fraught with problems, since it does not take into account the increasing diversity of holidays undertaken and inconsistencies in tourist behaviour. Other researchers suggest that one way of overcoming this difficulty is to consider the different destinations tourists choose to visit, and then establish a sliding scale similar to Cohen's (1972) typology, but which does not have such an absolute classification.

In contrast, Plog (1974) devised a classification of the US population into psychographic types, with travellers distributed along a continuum from psychocentrism to allocentrism. The psychocentrics are the anxious, inhibited and less adventurous travellers while at the other extreme the allocentrics are adventurous, outgoing, seeking new experiences due to their inquisitive personalities and interest in travel and adventure.

D.G. Pearce (1995) highlights the spatial implications of such conceptualisations, that each tourist type will seek different destinations which will change through time. However, criticisms by P. Pearce (1993) indicate that Plog's model is difficult to use because it fails to distinguish between extrinsic and intrinsic motivations without incorporating a dynamic element to encompass the changing nature of individual tourists. P. Pearce discounts such models, suggesting that individuals have a 'career' in their travel behaviour where people 'start at different levels, they are likely to change levels during their life-cycle and they can be prevented from moving by money, health and other people. They may also retire from their travel career or not take holidays at all and therefore not be part of the system'.

These are:

- A concern with biological needs;
- Aafety and security needs;
- Relationship development and extension needs;
- Special interest and self-development needs;
- Fulfilment or self-actualisation needs.

Cooper *et al.* (1993:23) argue that 'the literature on tourism motivation is still in an immature phase of development, it has been shown that motivation is an essential concept behind the different patterns of tourism demand'. From the existing literature on tourist motivation, the problems of determining tourist motivation may be summarised as follows:

- Tourism is not one specific product, it is a combination of products and experiences which meet a diverse range of needs.
- Tourists are not always conscious of their deep psychological needs and ideas. Even when they do know what they are, they may not reveal them.
- Tourism motives may be multiple and contradictory (push and pull factors).
- Motives may change over time and be inextricably linked together

(*e.g.* perception, learning, personality and culture are often separated out but they are all bound up together) and dynamic conceptualisations such as P. Pearce's (1993) leisure ladder are crucial to advancing knowledge and understanding in this area.

Having examined some of the issues associated with what motivates tourists to travel, attention now turns to the process of measurement and recording tourist demand using statistical measures.

TOURISM STATISTICS

Ritchie argued that 'an important part of the maturing process for any science is the development or adaptation of consistent and well-tested measurement techniques and methodologies which are well-suited to the types of problems encountered in practice'. In this context, the measurement of tourists, tourism activity and the effects on the economy and society in different environments is crucial to the development of tourism as an established area of study within the confines of social science.

Burkart and Medlik (1981) provide a useful insight into the development of measurements of tourism phenomena by governments during the 1960s and their subsequent development through to the late 1970s. While it is readily acknowledged by most tourism researchers that statistics are a necessary feature to provide data to enable researchers, managers, planners, decision-makers and public and private sector bodies to gauge the significance and impact of tourism on destination areas, Burkart and Medlik (1981:74) identify four principal reasons for statistical measurement in tourism:

- To evaluate the magnitude and significance of tourism to a destination area or region;
- To quantify the contribution to the economy or society, especially the effect on the balance of payments;
- To assist in the planning and development of tourism infrastructure and the effect of different volumes of tourists with specific needs;
- To assist in the evaluation and implementation of marketing and promotion activities where the tourism marketer requires information on the actual and potential markets and their characteristics.

Consequently, tourism statistics are essential to the measurement of the volume, scale, impact and value of tourism at different geographical scales from the global to the country level down to the individual destination. Yet an information gap exists between the types of statistics provided by organisations for and the needs of users. The compilation of tourism statistics provided by organisations associated with the measurement of tourism has established methods and processes to collect, collate and analyse tourism statistics (World Tourism Organisation (WTO) 1996), yet these have been understood by only a small number of researchers and practitioners. Thus this section attempts to demystify the apparent sophistication and complexity associated with the presentation of statistical indicators of tourism and their value to spatial analysis, since geographers have a strong quantified methods tradition, which is reflected in the use and reliance upon such indicators to understand spatial variations and patterns of tourism activity.

All too often, undergraduate and many postgraduate texts assume a prior knowledge of tourism statistics and they are only dealt with in a limited way by most tourism texts, and where such issues are raised they are usually discussed in over-technical texts aimed at a limited audience (*e.g.* Frechtling 1996). A commonly misunderstood feature which is associated with tourism statistics is that they are a complete and authoritative source of information (*i.e.* they answer all the questions posed by the researcher).

Other associated problems are that statistics are recent and relate to the previous year or season, implying that there is no time lag in their generation, analysis, presentation and dissemination to interested parties. In fact, most tourism statistics are 'typically measurements of arrivals, trips, tourist nights and expenditure, and these often appear in total or split into categories such as business or leisure travel'. Furthermore, the majority of published tourism statistics are derived from sample surveys, with the results being weighted or statistically manipulated to derive a measure which is supposedly representative of the real-world situation. In reality, this often means that tourism statistics are subject to significant errors depending on the size of the sample. The statistical measurement of tourists is far from straightforward, and Latham (1989) identifies a number of distinctive and peculiar problems associated with the tourist population:

- Tourists are a transient and highly mobile population, making statistical sampling procedures difficult when trying to ensure statistical accuracy and rigour in methodological terms.
- Interviewing mobile populations such as tourists is often undertaken in a strange environment, typically at ports or points of departure or arrival where there is background noise which may influence responses.
- Other variables, such as the weather, may affect the responses.

Even where sampling and survey-related problems can be minimised, one has to treat tourism statistics with a degree of caution because of additional methodological issues that can affect the results. For example, tourism research typically comprises:

- Pre-travel studies of tourists' intended travel habits and likely choice of destination (intentional studies);
- Studies of tourists in transit to provide information on their actual behaviour and plans for the remainder of their holiday or journey (actual and intended studies);

- Studies of tourists at the destination or at specific tourist attractions and sites, to provide information on their actual behaviour, levels of satisfaction, impacts and future intentions (actual and intended studies);
- Post-travel studies of tourists on their return journey from their destination or on-site experience or once they have returned to their place of residence (post-travel measures).

In an ideal world, where resource constraints are not a limiting factor on the generation of statistics, each of the aforementioned approaches should be used to provide a broad spectrum of research information on tourism and tourist behaviour. In reality, organisations and government agencies select a form of research which meets their own particular needs. In practice, most tourism statistics are generated with practical uses in mind and they may usually, though not exclusively, be categorised as follows:

- Measurement of tourist volume, enumerating arrivals, departures and the number of visits and stays;
- Expenditure-based surveys which quantify the value of tourist spending at the destination and during the journey;
- The characteristics and features of tourists to construct a profile of the different markets and segments visiting a destination.

However, before any tourism statistics can be derived, it is important to deal with the complex and thorny issue of defining the population - the tourist. Therefore, how does one define and differentiate between the terms *tourism* and *tourist*?

The terms *travel* and *tourism* are often interchanged within the published literature on tourism, though they are normally meant to encompass 'the field of research on human and business activities associated with one or more aspects of the temporary movement of persons away from their immediate home communities and daily work environments for business, pleasure and personal reasons'. These two terms tend to be used in differing contexts to mean similar things, although there is a tendency for the United States to continue to use the term 'travel' when in fact they mean tourism. Despite this inherent problem which may be little more than an exercise in semantics, it is widely acknowledged that the two terms are used in isolation or in unison to 'describe' three concepts:

- The movement of people;
- A sector of the economy or an industry;
- A broad system of interacting relationships of people (including their need to travel outside their communities and services that attempt to respond to these needs by supplying products).

From this initial starting point, one can begin to explore some of the complex issues in arriving at a working definition of the terms *tourism* and *tourist*. In a historical context, Burkart and Medlik (1981:41) identify the historical development of the term *tourism*, noting the distinction between the endeavours of researchers to differentiate between the concept and technical definitions of tourism. The concept of tourism refers to the 'broad notional framework, which identifies the essential characteristics, and which distinguishes tourism from the similar, often related, but different phenomena'.

In contrast, technical definitions have evolved through time as researchers modify and develop appropriate measures for statistical, legislative and operational reasons implying that there may be various technical definitions to meet particular purposes.

However, the concept of tourism, and its identification for research purposes, is an important consideration in this instance for tourism statistics so that users are familiar with the context of their derivation. While most tourism books, articles and monographs now assume either a standard definition or interpretation of the concept of tourism, which is usually influenced by the social scientists' perspective (*i.e.* a geographical, economic, political, sociological approach or other disciplines), Burkart and Medlik's (1981) approach to the concept of tourism continues to offer a valid assessment of the situation where five main characteristics are associated with the concept.

- Tourism arises from the movement of people to, and their stay in, various destinations.
- There are two elements in all tourism: the journey to the destination and the stay including activities at the destination.
- The journey and the stay take place outside the normal place of residence and work, so that tourism gives rise to activities which are distinct from those of the resident and working populations of the places, through which tourists travel and in which they stay.
- The movement to tourist destinations is of a temporary, short-term character, with the intention of returning home within a few days, weeks or months.
- Destinations are visited for purposes other than taking up permanent residence or employment remunerated from within the places visited (Burkart and Medlik 1981:42).

Furthermore, Burkart and Medlik's (1981) definition of tourism as a concept is invaluable because it rightly recognises that much tourism is a leisure activity which involves a discretionary use of time and money, and recreation is often the main purpose for participation in tourism. But this is no reason for restricting the total concept in this way and the essential characteristics of tourism can best be interpreted to embrace a wider concept. All tourism includes some travel but not all travel is tourism, while the temporary and short-term nature of most tourist trips distinguishes it from migration. Therefore, from the broad interpretation of tourism, it is possible to consider the technical definitions of tourism.

TECHNICAL DEFINITIONS OF TOURISM

Technical definitions of tourism are commonly used by organisations seeking to define the population to be measured, and there are three principal features which normally have to be defined:

- Purpose of travel (*e.g.* the type of traveller, be it business travel, holiday-makers, visits to friends and relatives or for other reasons).
- The time dimension involved in the tourism visit, which requires a minimum and a maximum period of time spent away from the home area and the time spent at the destination. In most cases, this would involve a minimum stay of more than 24 hours away from home and less than a year as a maximum.
- Those situations where tourists may or may not be included as tourists, such as cruise passengers, those tourists in transit at a particular point of embarkation/departure and excursionists who stay less than 24 hours at a destination (*e.g.* the European duty-free cross-channel day-trip market).

Among the most recent attempts to recommend appropriate definitions of tourism was the World Tourism Organisation (hereafter WTO) International Conference of Travel and Tourism in Ottawa in 1991 which reviewed, expanded and developed technical definitions, where tourism comprises 'the activities of a person travelling outside his or her usual environment for less than a specified period of time and whose main purpose of travel is other than exercise of an activity remunerated from the place visited', where 'usual environment' is intended to exclude trips within the areas of usual residence and also frequent and regular trips between the domicile and the workplace and other community trips of a routine character, where 'less than a specified period of time' is intended to exclude long-term migration, and 'exercise of an activity remunerated from the place visited' is intended to exclude only migration for temporary work. The following definitions were developed by the WTO:

- International tourism: consists of inbound tourism.
- Visits to a country by non-residents and outbound tourism residents of a country visiting another country.
- Internal tourism: residents of a country visiting their own country.
- Domestic tourism: internal tourism plus inbound tourism (the tourism market of accommodation facilities and attractions within a country).
- National tourism: internal tourism plus outbound tourism (the resident tourism market for travel agents and airlines) (WTO, cited in Chadwick 1994:66).

In order to improve statistical collection and improve understanding of tourism, the United Nations (UN) (1994) and the WTO (1991a) also recommended differentiating between visitors, tourists and excursionists (day trippers). The WTO (1991a) recommended that an international tourist be defined as: 'a visitor who travels to a country other than that in which he/she has his/her usual residence for at least one night but not more than one year, and whose main purpose of visit is other than the exercise of an activity remunerated from within the country visited'; and that an international excursionist (*e.g.* cruise ship visitors) be defined as 'a visitor residing in a country who travels the same day to a country other than which he/she has his/her usual environment for less than 24 hours without spending the night in the country visited and whose main purpose of visit is other than the exercise of an activity remunerated from within the country visited'.

Similar definitions were also developed for domestic tourists, with domestic tourists having a time limit of 'not more than six months' (WTO 1991a; UN 1994). Interestingly, the inclusion of a same-day travel, 'excursionist' category in UN/WTO technical definitions of tourism makes the division between recreation and tourism even more arbitrary, and there is increasing international agreement that 'tourism' refers to all activities of visitors, including both overnight and same-day visitors (UN 1994:5). Given improvements in transport technology, same-day travel is becoming increasingly important to some countries, with the UN (1994:9) observing, 'day visits are important to consumers and to many providers, especially tourist attractions, transport operators and caterers'. Chadwick (1994) moves the definition of tourists a stage further by offering a typology of travellers (tourists) which highlights the distinction between tourists (travellers) and non-travellers (non-tourists) which is summarised.

It is also useful because it illustrates where technical problems may occur in deciding which groups to include in tourism and which to exclude. From this classification of travellers, the distinction between international and domestic tourism needs to be made. Domestic tourism normally refers to tourists who travel from their normal domicile to other areas within a country. In contrast, international tourism normally involves a tourist leaving their country of origin to cross into another country which involves documentation, administrative formalities and movement to a foreign environment.

DOMESTIC TOURISM STATISTICS

D.G. Pearce (1995a) acknowledges that the scale and volume of domestic tourism worldwide exceeds that of international tourism, though it is often viewed as the poorer partner in the compilation of statistics. For example, most domestic tourism statistics tend to underestimate the scale and volume of flows since certain aspects of domestic tourist movements are sometimes ignored in official sources. The 'visits to friends and relatives, the use of forms of accommodation other than hotels (for example, second homes, camp and caravan sites) and travel by large segments of a population from towns to the countryside are not for the most part included'. This is supported by the WTO, who argue that 'there are relatively few countries that collect domestic travel and tourism statistics. Moreover some countries rely exclusively on the traditional hotel sector, thereby leaving out of account the many travellers staying in supplementary accommodation establishments or with friends and relatives'. Therefore, the collection of domestic tourism statistics requires the use of different data sources aside from the more traditional sources such as hotel records which identify the origin and duration of a visitor's stay.

To assist in the identification of who to include as a domestic tourist, the WTO (1983) suggests the following working definition: 'any person, regardless of nationality, resident in a country and who travels to a place in the same country for not more than one year and whose main purpose of visit is other than following an occupation remunerated from within the place visited.'

Such a definition includes domestic tourists where an overnight stay is involved and domestic excursionists who visit an area for less than 24 hours and do not stay overnight. In fact, Latham (1989:66) points to the variety of definitions which exist aside from those formulated by WTO and the following issues complicate matters further:

- *Purpose of visit*: All countries using this concept define a domestic tourist as one who travels for a purpose other than to perform a remunerated activity.
- *The length of trip and/or distance travelled*: Certain definitions state that travellers should, for example, be involved in an overnight stay and/or travel a prescribed minimum distance.
- *Type of accommodation*: For practical reasons, some countries restrict the concept of domestic tourism to cover only those persons using commercial accommodation facilities (after Latham 1989:66).

Problems in applying WTO definitions may also reflect an individual country's reasons for generating such statistics, which may not necessarily be to contribute to a better understanding of statistics *per se*. For example, WTO (1981) identified four uses of domestic tourism statistics:

- To calculate the contribution of tourism to the country's economy, whereby estimates of tourism's value to the Gross Domestic Product is estimated due to the complexity of identifying the scope of tourism's contribution.
- To assist in the marketing and promotion of tourism, where government-sponsored tourism organisations seek to encourage its population to take domestic holidays rather than to travel overseas for a discussion of this activity among Pacific Rim countries).
- To aid the regional development policies of governments which harness tourism as a tool for area development where domestic tourists in congested environments are encouraged to travel to less developed areas and to improve the quality of tourism in different environments.

- To achieve social objectives, where socially oriented tourism policies may be developed for the underprivileged which requires a detailed understanding of the holiday-taking habits of a country's nationals.

Regional and local tourist organisations also make use of such data to develop and market destinations and different businesses within the tourism sector. But how is domestic tourism measured? Burkart and Medlik (1981) argue that two principal features need to be measured: first, the volume, value and characteristics of tourism among the population of the country; second, the same data relating to individual destinations within the country.

The WTO (1981, cited in Latham 1989) considers the minimum data requirements for the collection of domestic tourism statistics in terms of arrivals and tourist nights in accommodation classified by:

- Month;
- Type of grade of accommodation establishment;
- Location of the accommodation establishment and overall expenditure on domestic tourism.

Latham (1989) argues that it is possible to generate additional data from such variables including length of stay, occupancy rate and average expenditure. Many countries also collate supplementary information beyond the minimum standards identified by WTO, where the socioeconomic characteristics of tourists are identified, together with their use of tourist transport and purpose of visit, though the cost of such data collection does mean that the statistical basis of domestic tourism in many less developed countries remains poor.

The methods used to generate domestic tourism statistics are normally based on the estimates of volume, value and scale derived from sample surveys due to the cost of undertaking large-scale surveys of tourist activities.

The immediate problem facing the user of such material is the type of errors and degree of accuracy which can be attached to such data. For example, Latham (1989) identifies the following sample surveys which are now used to supplement data derived from hotel records:

- *Household surveys*, where the residents of a country are interviewed in their own home to ascertain information of tourist trips for the purpose of pleasure. A useful example of a pan-European study is the EC Omnibus study. Even so, little progress has been made internationally to collate common data on household surveys since the OECD's attempt in 1967 to outline the types of data which national travel surveys should collect.
- *Destination surveys*, where high levels of tourist activity occur in a region or resort. Such studies frequently compile statistics on accommodation usage, sample surveys of visitors and may be linked to existing knowledge derived from household surveys.
- *En route surveys*, where tourists are surveyed en route to examine

the characteristics and features of tourists. Although it is a convenient way to interview a captive audience depending upon the mode of transport used, the results may not necessarily be as representative without a complete knowledge of the transport flows for the mode of tourist transport being surveyed.

The problem of incomplete questionnaires or non-response may occur where such surveys require a respondent to post the form back to the surveyor.

INTERNATIONAL TOURISM STATISTICS

The two principal organisations which collate data on international tourism are the World Tourism Organisation (WTO) and the Organisation for Economic Cooperation and Development (OECD). In addition, international regional tourism organisations such as the Pacific Asia Travel Association and the ASEAN Tourism Working Group also collect international tourism statistics. Page (1994b) reviews the major publications of the first two organisations in relation to international tourism, noting the detailed contents of each.

In the case of the WTO, the main source is the *Yearbook of Tourism Statistics*, which contains a summary of the most salient tourism statistics for almost 150 countries and territories. In the case of the OECD, their *Tourism Policy and International Tourism* (referred to as the 'Blue Book') is less comprehensive, covering only 25 countries, but it does contain most of the main generating and receiving areas. While the main thrust of the publication is government policy and the obstacles to international tourism, it does expand on certain areas not covered in the WTO publication.

In contrast to domestic tourism, statistics on international tourism are normally collected to assess the impact of tourism on a country's balance of payments, though as Withyman (1985:69) argued:

Outward visitors seem to attract less attention from the pollsters and the enumerators. Of course, one country's outward visitor is another country's (perhaps several countries) inward visitor, and a much more welcome sort of visitor, too, being both a source of revenue and an emblem of the destination country's appeal in the international market. This has meant that governments have tended to be generally more keen to measure inward than outward tourism, or at any rate, having done so, to publish the results.

This statement indicates that governments are more concerned with the direct effect of tourism on their balance of payments. Yet such statistics are also utilised by marketing arms of national tourism organisations to base their decisions on who to target in international campaigns. The wider tourism industry also makes use of such data as part of their strategic planning and for more immediate purposes where niche markets exist. Even so, Shackleford (1980) argued that the collection of tourism statistics should be a responsibility of the state to meet international standards for data collection (WTO 1996).

However, it is increasingly the case that only when the economic benefits of data collection can be justified will national governments continues to compile tourism statistics.

Where resource constraints exist, the collection and compilation of tourism statistics may be impeded. This also raises important methodological issues related to what exactly is being measured. As Withyman (1985:61) argued: 'In the jungle of international travel and tourism statistics, it behoves the explorer to step warily; on all sides there is luxuriant growth. Not all data sources are what they appear to be - after close scrutiny some show themselves to be inconsistent and often unsuitable for the industry researcher and planner.' The key point Withyman (1985) recognises is the lack of comparability in tourism data in relation to what is measured (*e.g.* is it visitor days or visitor nights?) and the procedures and methodology used to measure international tourism. Frechtling (1976) concluded that the approaches taken by national and international agencies associated with international tourism statistics were converging towards common definitions of trip, travel and traveller.

Yet the principal difficulty which continues to be associated with this is whether business travel should be considered as a discrete activity in relation to tourism. Chadwick (1994:75) notes that 'the consensus of North American opinion seems to be that, despite certain arguments to the contrary ... business travel should be considered part of travel and tourism'. While BarOn (1984) examines the standard definitions and terminology of international tourism as used by the UN and WTO, research by Ngoh (1985) is useful in that it considers the practical problems posed by such definitions when attempting to measure international tourism and find solutions to the difficulties. Latham (1989) suggests that the main types of international tourism statistics collated relate to:

- Volume of tourists;
- Expenditure by tourists;
- The profile of the tourist and their trip characteristics.

As is true of domestic tourism, estimates form the basis for most statistics on international tourism since the method of data collection does not generate exact data. For example, volume statistics are often generated from counts of tourists at entry/exit points (*i.e.* gateways such as airports and ports) or at accommodation. But such data relate to numbers of trips rather than individual tourists since one tourist may make more than one trip a year and each trip is counted separately. In the case of expenditure statistics, tourist expenditure normally refers to tourist spending within a country and excludes payments to tourist-transport operators.

Yet deriving such statistics is often an indirect measure based on foreign currency estimates derived from bank records, from data provided by tourism service providers or more commonly from social surveys undertaken directly with tourists. Research by White and Walker (1982) and Baretje (1982) directly questions the validity and accuracy of such methods of data collection, examining the main causes of bias and error in such studies. According to Edwards (1991:68-9), 'expenditure and receipts data apart, tourist statistics are usually collected in one of the five following ways':

- Counts of all individuals entering or leaving the country at all recognised frontier crossings, often using arrival/departure cards where high-volume arrivals/departures are the norm. Where particularly large volumes of tourist traffic exist, a 10 per cent sampling framework is normally used (*i.e.* every tenth arrival/ departure card). Countries such as New Zealand actually match the arrival/departure cards, or a sample, to examine the length of stay.
- Interviews carried out at frontiers with a sample of arriving and/or departing passengers to obtain a more detailed profile of visitors and their activities within the country. This will often require a careful sample design to gain a sufficiently large enough sample with the detail required from visitors on a wide range of tourism data including places visited, expenditure, accommodation usage and related items.
- Selecting a sample of arrivals and providing them with a self-completion questionnaire to be handed in or posted. This method is used in Canada but it fails to incorporate those visitors travelling via the United States by road.
- Sample surveys of the entire population of a country including travellers and non-travellers, though the cost of obtaining a representative sample is often prohibitive.
- Accommodation arrivals and nights spent are recorded by hoteliers and owners of the accommodation types covered. The difficulty with this type of data collection is that accommodation

As a government-sponsored survey which began in 1961, the International Passenger Survey now covers all ports of entry/exit to the UK. It is based on a stratified random sample of tourists arriving and departing from the UK by air and sea. According to Latham (1989:64), IPS' four principal aims are:

- To collect data for the travel account (which acts to compare expenditure by overseas visitors to the UK with expenditure overseas by visitors from the UK) of the balance of payments;
- To provide detailed information on foreign visitors to the UK, and on outgoing visitors travelling overseas.
- To provide data on international migration.
- To provide information on routes used by passengers as an aid to aviation and shipping authorities. owners have no incentive to record accurate details, particularly where the tax regime is based on the turnover of bed-nights.

The final area of data collection is profile statistics, which examine the characteristics and travel habits of visitors. For example, the UK's International Passenger Survey (IPS) is one survey that incorporates volume, expenditure and profile data on international tourism.

METHODOLOGICAL ISSUES

Latham (1989) reviews the major types of questionnaire/social survey type of data collection used for tourism statistics. He reports that among state-sponsored tourism research in the United States, conversion studies are a popular method to examine and evaluate advertising campaigns and visitor surveys, to assess a sample of visitors to individual states. The use of other methods of data collection are also discussed (*e.g.* diary questionnaires, participant observation and personal interviews). Yet few studies consider the issue of sampling, sample design and the sources of error which may arise from such surveys.

In fact the lack of research on the reliability of the estimate from a sample survey (the standard error) is rarely discussed in most tourism surveys. In many cases, large tourism surveys focus on the logistics of drawing the sample and the bias which may be reflected in the results. Therefore, any tourism survey will need to pay careful attention to the statistical and mathematical accuracy of the survey, especially the survey design and the effect it may have on the results, a feature which is discussed in great detail by Ryan (1995).

Ryan (1995) provides an excellent review of survey design, questionnaire design, sampling and also an insight into the statistical techniques to use for different forms of tourism data. As a result it serves as an important reference point for issues of methodology and the technical issues associated with the statistical analysis of tourism data. Without reiterating the excellent features of Ryan's findings, it is appropriate to consider some of the main accuracy problems associated with the collection of domestic and international tourism statistics.

PROBLEMS OF ACCURACY

Ryan (1995) argues that errors in data collection can lead to errors in data analysis. Among the most frequently cited problems associated with domestic and international tourism statistics are:

- The methods by which the data are collected, which are influenced by administrative, bureaucratic and legislative factors in each country;
- Sample sizes which are too small and lead to unacceptable sampling errors and in some instances where the sample design is flawed;
- The procedures for collecting tourism statistics are not adhered to by the agency collecting the data.

In addition, Edwards (1991:68) argues that a 'fourth potential reason - arithmetic mistakes and data processing errors - only occasionally produce significant errors'. In fact, Edwards (1991:68) supports the cause of 'tourist statisticians [who] are both knowledgeable and conscientious, but are having to work with tools which they know could produce inaccurate or misleading data', concluding that for any set of tourist data, potential sources of error obviously depend on the method of collection employed. This, in turn, tends to be largely determined by the legislative and administrative framework and by the financial and manpower resources available.

In the case of tourist expenditure and receipts data, organisations such as the International Monetary Fund (IMF) issue guidelines for the compilation of balance of payments statistics. But errors may occur where leakage results from tourist services paid for in overseas bank accounts and in extreme cases, where a black market exists in currency exchange. Edwards (1991) suggests that a regular programme of interviews with departing tourists and returning residents may assist in estimating levels of expenditure.

Despite the apparent problems which may exist with tourism statistics, Edwards (1991:72) argues that data on arrivals and nights spent for most destinations outside of Europe appear reasonably reliable.

Within Europe, data for both inbound and outbound travel are fairly satisfactory for the UK. Greece, Portugal, Spain and [the former] Yugoslavia all appear to have usable frontier arrivals data. The most serious problems are in core continental European countries such as France, Germany, Italy and the Netherlands for which there are no adequate volumetric measures of travel in either direction.

Accommodation arrivals and nights data are clearly gross understatements for many European countries ... often expenditure and receipts data appear better indicators. Outside Europe, the major problems are also in relation to high volume land flows, as between Canada and the USA (in both directions), from the USA to Mexico and from Hong Kong to China.

Therefore, in view of these potential constraints, Edwards (1991) advocates that researchers should compile a range of data from different sources which will not only highlight the deficiencies in various sources, but also extend the existing baseline data. Although Edwards (1991) provides guidelines for comparative tourism research using a range of data for different countries, trends in tourism data remain one of the main requirements for travel industry organisations. Edwards (1991:73) lists key issues to consider in examining tourism trends (*i.e.* Have arrivals or accommodation data been changed in coverage or definition? Have provisional data for earlier years been subsequently revised? Has the reliability of the data changed and how are changing tastes in travel products affecting the statistics?). Even so, the analysis of trends remains the fundamental starting point for most research studies in tourism. Having considered the issues associated with how tourism statistics are generated, attention now turns to the ways in which geographers analyse such statistics, and variations in tourism activity at different scales.

PATTERNS OF TOURISM

D.G. Pearce's (1995a) seminal study on the geographer's analysis of tourism patterns offers an excellent synthesis reflecting his international contribution to the methodological development of spatial analysis of tourism. By using geographical methodologies and concepts, D.G. Pearce (1995a) uses statistical sources and primary data on tourist activity patterns to analyse the processes and patterns associated with the dynamics of domestic and international tourist activity. This section can only provide a limited evaluation of the geographer's approach to analysis of the presentation of spatially oriented insights on modern-day tourism demand.

The WTO provides the main source of data for international tourism, collated from a survey of major government agencies responsible for data collection. While most international tourists are expressed as 'frontier arrivals' (*i.e.* arrivals determined by means of a frontier check), arrival/ departure cards (where used) offer additional detail to the profile of international tourists, and where they are not used periodic tourism surveys are often employed. WTO statistics are mainly confined to all categories of travellers, and in some cases geographical disaggregation of the data may be limited by the collecting agency's use of descriptions and categories for aid of simplicity (*e.g.* rest of the world) rather than listing all categories of arrivals.

In terms of the growth of international travel, documents the expansion of outbound travel with constant growth in the 1960s in an age of discovery of outbound travel for many developed nations. The late 1960s saw international travel expanded by new technology in air travel (*e.g.* the introduction of the Boeing 747 jumbo jet and the 737 as well as the DC10) which led to rapid growth until the oil crisis in the early 1970s. Growth rates varied in the 1980s, with 'shock waves' to the upward trend being caused by events such as the Gulf Crisis, but international travel has maintained strong growth rates, often in excess of 5 per cent per annum. In contrast, international receipts from travel have outperformed arrivals, with consistent rates of growth (with the exception of the oil crisis and Gulf Crisis) of 10 to 20 per cent which is indicative of the powerful economic effect of tourism for countries. However, China is the notable success story in terms of growth in receipts while a number of European destinations (*e.g.* the Netherlands and Belgium) have retained the volume of arrivals but their ranking of expenditure has dropped.

As the world's largest tourism markets by expenditure, the USA and Germany have retained their prominence in the top two rankings, whereas Japan has increased its importance as an outbound high spending market as have a number of other Pacific Rim nations such as Taiwan, Singapore and South Korea until the 1997 Asian financial crisis (Hall and Page 2000). As a result of the growth of major outbound growth and travel within the Pacific Rim region, a case study of the outbound South Korean market is now examined.

CASE STUDY: TOURISM DEMAND IN EAST ASIA PACIFIC: THE CASE OF THE SOUTH KOREAN OUTBOUND MARKET AND ACTIVITY PATTERNS IN NEW ZEALAND

Prior to the Asian financial crisis, Korea represented one of the major outbound markets in the Asia-Pacific region. Outbound travel grew from 484,000 in 1985 to 725,000 in 1988 to 3.1 million in 1994, which quadrupled in a six-year period up to 1994. By 1995, outbound travel had reached 3.8 million, representing 9 per cent of the national population of 45 million. Within New Zealand, inbound Korean arrivals increased consistently between 1989 and 1995 as the fastest growing market and remained the focus of industry attention until the Asian financial crisis (New Zealand Tourism Board 1995), despite any substantive and detailed research to consider the needs, aspirations and impact of this market in New Zealand.

Holiday travel has remained a major reason to visit, while females outnumbered males in holiday travel by 54.4 per cent: 45.66 per cent in 1994 and VFR by 63.5 per cent: 36.5 per cent, highlighting the trend towards housewives comprising the majority of outbound female visitors. Male visitors dominated in the purpose of visiting in relation to business travel (91 per cent), to attend a convention (87.7 per cent) and official travel (91.3 per cent). The age profile of the most common outbound Korean tourist was the 31 to 40 age group followed by the 21 to 30 age group, with a significant proportion of 'honeymooners' and single female office workers. According to the 1994 Nationals Overseas Travel Survey, shopping was a major leisure activity for Korean tourists, with an average spends of US$413 per person on purchases such as cosmetics, alcoholic beverages, electronic goods, clothing and toys. McGahey (1996) observed that 40 per cent of these purchases were for gifts.

THE KOREAN INBOUND MARKET IN NEW ZEALAND

According to New Zealand's International Visitor Survey (New Zealand Tourism Board 1995), the Korean market was estimated to have generated NZ$225 million of spending at 1995 prices, equating to an average spend of NZ$2253 per person of NZ$345 a day, the highest amount for any inbound market. In the 12 months ended March 1996, Koreans comprised 8 per cent of New Zealand's international visitor market, increasing from 2,018 in 1987 to 4,184 visitors in 1990 to 61,583 in 1994. The significance of this market was reflected in the New Zealand Tourist Board's (1995) optimistic forecasts for a further doubling of visitor arrivals over the next five years and a target of 114,000 arrivals. However, the size of the impact of the Asian financial crisis on Korea can be illustrated by the 78 per cent drop in Korean visitors to New Zealand in December 1997 compared with the previous year, with there being an expected 75 per cent drop in arrivals from South Korea in 1998 over the previous year.

In contrast to the age profile of the entire Korean tourist outbound market, the main age group of visitors to New Zealand was dominated by the visitors aged 45 to 64 years, predominately those aged 55 to 64. Yet among those visitors aged under 24 years, females outnumber males as unmarried office workers or tertiary level students are more likely to travel than their male counter-parts, since the former enjoy relatively more leisure time.

Since group travel tends to predominate among the inbound Korean market, the length of stay in New Zealand was conditioned by two key factors. First, it is a medium long-haul destination, and second, Korean holiday entitlement was still limited to under ten paid days a year and is not available in one block. Therefore, the maximum length of stay for most outbound Korean tourists was less than one week. According to research (New Zealand Tourism Board 1995), Korean tourists perceived the main appeal of visiting New Zealand as its unspoiled natural phenomena such as hot springs in Rotorua and volcanic areas such as Mount Tongariro.

This reflects the limited spatial activity patterns which most inbound Korean tourists were likely to experience, typically including arrival and departure through Auckland International Airport, with time spent in Auckland, Rotorua, Waitomo Caves, Taupo and returning to Auckland. The following results report the findings of a survey to understand the interrelationship between the time constraints of Korean inbound travel and the spatial distribution of such visitors beyond the limited knowledge base derived from the 442 Korean tourists included in the New Zealand International Visitor Survey of 1995/1996.

KOREAN TOURISTS' ACTIVITY PATTERNS IN NEW ZEALAND

Using a time budget methodology, a survey in July 1996 was employed to produce a systematic record of a person's use of time over a given period to hereby understand the sequence, timing and duration of the tourist's activities in relation to the location of the activities. The technique provides a systematic record of a person's use of time over a given period, typically for a short period ranging from a single day to a week. One of the fundamental assumptions in using this research method is that tourist behaviour and activities are the result of choices, a point illustrated by Floor (1990). D.G. Pearce (1987a) argues that there has been a comparative neglect of tourist activities by tourist researchers, compounded by the lack of available data. Where questionnaire surveys have addressed such issues, the results have often failed to provide a comprehensive assessment of tourist activities, both formal/informal and the relative importance of each. Thrift (1977) provides an assessment of three principal constraints on tourists' daily activity patterns, which are:

- *Comparability constraints* (*e.g.* the biologically based need for food and sleep);

- *Coupling constraints* (*e.g.* people need to interact and undertake activities with other people);
- *Authority constraints* (*e.g.* where activities are controlled, not allowed or permitted at a certain point in time).

Thus both Chapin (1974) and Thrift (1977) identify choices and constraints which will influence the specific activities and context of tourists' daily activities. The use of time budgets via diaries to record tourists' activity patterns has been employed in a number of contexts as research by Gaviria (1975), Cooper (1981), P.L. Pearce (1981), D.G. Pearce (1986) and Debbage (1991) indicates. Methodological issues raised by these studies highlight the problem of selecting appropriate temporal measures to record tourists' activities. P.L. Pearce (1981) used three main time periods (morning, afternoon and evening) with Gaviria (1975) selecting quarter-hour periods and Cooper (1981) using five time sequences. While the recording of activities by time is a demanding activity for tourists, D.G. Pearce (1986) argues that the main methodological concerns for such surveys are the type of technique to be used; the period to be covered; and the type of sample selected. In addition, Chapin (1984) argues that such studies may choose to use three main survey techniques, which are:

- *A checklist technique*, where respondents select the list of activities they engage in from a pre-categorised list;
- *The yesterday technique*, where subjects are asked to list things they did the previous day, where and when they did them;
- *The tomorrow technique*, where participants keep a diary on what they do, where and when they undertake them.

Although time budget studies may still be viewed as experimental in tourism research, they do offer great potential to gain a detailed insight into tourist activity patterns.

THE SURVEY

During three weeks in July 1996, a time budget survey was developed using the 'yesterday technique' and the time sequencing technique advocated by P.L. Pearce (1981) as part of a more detailed survey of inbound Korean tourists. The complete survey was designed to be completed by Korean tourists during their tour of the North Island of New Zealand and four sites were selected as distribution points for the surveys during the tourists' initial familiarisation point of their tour in Auckland and Rotorua. Two major hotels and two Korean restaurants were selected to provide a degree of close contract with Korean tourists in a familiar environment. Due to the highly organised nature of the Korean itineraries, a one-page diary was distributed at the key sites over a three-week period.

One immediate problem facing the use of the budget approach was in soliciting responses. While a Korean researcher approached the respondents on a random basis, it was essential to keep the survey to one A4 page to encourage participation. As a result, only time-budget questions could be included and key demographic data were omitted (a separate survey by the authors was undertaken examining demand issues among Korean tourists which did consider the profile of visitors).

However, from participant observation conducted during the data collection, it is apparent that the sample of 78 tourists who were prepared to participate in the time budget exercise were typical of the Korean tourist then visiting New Zealand, being largely aged 31 to 50, being of middle-class status, earning between NZ$40,000 and $60,000 a year and undertaking a multi-destination product.

ACTIVITY PATTERNS OF KOREAN TOURISTS

According to D.G. Pearce (1995a), few data are collected to examine circuit tourism which this market is following, since they adhere to a predetermined circuit pattern. Data exist in a New Zealand context on the touring patterns of international tourists which builds on Forer and Pearce's (1984) innovative study of coach tours by nights spent at key nodes and inter-regional flows.

Forer and Pearce (1984) established the Auckland to Rotorua and Taupo axis by examining tour group itineraries for package tours. While it is apparent that a great deal of continuity and similarity exists in terms of the Korean tour group itineraries which follow a series of linear routes, activity patterns of the tour groups and their specific time budgets remain largely unresearched. One immediate feature which emerges from the 78 completed schedules is that the activity patterns of the visitors closely follow the tour itineraries. The respondents were undertaking three commonly used itineraries developed by tour companies which comprised:

- *Itinerary* 1: Auckland to Rotorua and return to Rotorua (12 tourists).
- *Itinerary* 2: Auckland to Rotorua and Waitomo Caves and return to Auckland (39 tourists).
- *Itinerary* 3: Auckland to Rotorua and Waitomo Caves to Taupo and return to Auckland.

Both itinerary 1 and 2 record only a limited amount of free time, being the shortest tour schedules among inbound visitors to New Zealand. The typical itinerary commences at 07:00 and finishes at 18:00 to 19:00 hours, with sightseeing comprising the major activity (30 to 32 per cent), undertaken over two nights and three days. During the 53 to 59-hour period, respondents spent their time:

- Sleeping (33 per cent);
- Touring (30 per cent);
- Free time (14 per cent);
- Transfers (12 per cent);

- Eating/meals (11 per cent).

On the basis of these results, three types of Korean tourists could be identified based on time budget research by Ashworth and Dietvorst (1995):

- *Organised sightseeing oriented visitors*, who comprise the large majority of visitors, with a city tour in a chartered coach during the day, interspersed with shopping before or after meals and a limited amount of free time spent walking around attractions and taking photographs. Evenings were spent at the accommodation base to rest after the day's activities.
- *Shopping and conviviality oriented tourists*, where shopping activities were conducted near to the accommodation base in the morning. The age profile of this group was younger (typically under 40 years of age), in search of specialist markets, tourist attractions and not venturing far from the accommodation base. In the evening, this group spent their leisure time at a wide variety of fun-related facilities (*e.g.* at a pub, gambling at the Casino in Auckland or at a night-club). In Rotorua, this group spent most of their free time at Korean pubs in the central tourist district.
- *Health and sports oriented tourists*, comprising the majority of the senior group (aged 50-plus) and a number of business travellers who pursued largely 'private' leisure activities. While no 'typical' activity patterns could be discerned during the day, with some preferring walking or going shopping, the time spent on these activities was much less than the two former groups. In the afternoons, sports activities dominated (*e.g.* golf and fishing) and in the early evening they frequented health facilities followed by relaxation for the remaining part of the evening.

While the results from the Korean case study indicate that removal of travel restrictions in 1989 has significantly increased outbound travel, there were significant 'pull' factors promoting Korean travel to New Zealand (*e.g.* immigration policy, no-visas agreement, new air services and 15,000 Korean residents living in Auckland promoting VFR traffic) which can be related to the motivational literature and the unique attractions available in New Zealand. The analysis of tourist activity patterns shows that in urban areas, Korean visitors do not venture far from their accommodation base. This limits the flow and distribution of visitors, with a tendency for bunching and concentration at key nodes around Auckland, Rotorua and Taupo.

Concerns over a saturation of tourists at key attraction sites accentuates the problem of managing the geographical patterns of this short and concentrated experience of New Zealand tourism. Many attractions are unable to cope with the arrival of large numbers of tour groups simultaneously, as this highly organised and almost regimented form of tourism is posing significant strains on the visiting infrastructure. In this respect, a spatial analysis of activity patterns and time budgets illustrates not only the shape of existing demand, determined by tour operators and group leaders, but also the geographical interaction and time constraints under which these tourists visit New Zealand have clear spatial implications for the type of tourism experience they require in time and space.

- Developing tourism from new markets in East Asia Pacific highlighted the fickle nature of tourism as an economic activity: a currency crisis led the Korean outbound market to New Zealand to decline dramatically.
- Packaged tourist itineraries have a strong influence on the activity patterns of tourist groups. This conditions the geographical patterns of consumption in time and space for tour groups.
- Even within tour groups, time budget research identified the diversity of motivations in relation to the reasons for undertaking a tour.
- Within urban areas, the Korean visitor has a tightly defined spatial search area which constrains the flow and distribution of their activities in time and space.
- Specific research tools such as time budget surveys, when linked to spatial patterns of activity, can yield a great deal of important information for tourism planners and commercial operators about the tourists' use of time and space.

PATTERNS OF DOMESTIC TOURISM

According to the WTO, domestic tourism is estimated to be up to ten times greater in volume than international tourism and yet comparatively little research has been undertaken on this neglected area of tourism activity. D.G. Pearce (1995a: 67) argues that this may be attributed 'to the less visible nature of much domestic tourism, which is often more informal and less structured than international tourism, and a consequent tendency by many government agencies, researchers and others to regard it as less significant'.

This problem of neglect is compounded by a paucity of data, since it is not a straightforward matter of recording arrivals and departures. It requires an analysis of tourism patterns and flows at different spatial scales to consider spatial interaction of tourists between a multitude of possible origin and destination areas within a country as well as a detailed understanding of inter-regional flows. Where government agencies and other public sector organisations undertake data collection of domestic tourism 'the results are not often directly comparable, limiting the identification of general patterns and trends'. For this reason, the innovative research undertaken by D.G. Pearce (1993b) is worthy of attention here since it comprises one of the few systematic analysis of domestic tourism in a country, which in this case is New Zealand.

As D.G. Pearce (1995a: 67) rightly acknowledges, 'there are still few examples of comprehensive inter-regional studies where the analysis is based on a complete matrix of both original and destination regions ... [since] few appropriate and reliable sets of tourism statistics exist which might be used to construct such a matrix'. Nationwide surveys are undertaken which are weighted to reflect the population base. One of the few comprehensive studies which yielded an origin-destination matrix is the somewhat dated New Zealand Domestic Travel Survey (NZDTS), established in 1983 (New Zealand Tourism Board 1991a) and recently updated.

THE NEW ZEALAND DOMESTIC TOURISM SURVEY

Domestic tourism data are harder to collect than those for international visitors, simply because no frontiers are crossed or formal registers required. Domestic travel estimates can thus only be made by factoring up from representative surveys of the population. As with all surveys, sample size and representativeness are critical, so that a manageable (and affordable) sample size of a thousand or so will give reasonably accurate figures for national trends but is useless at a regional level. The domestic travel surveys of the 1980s carried out by the NZTP were based on a sample of 12,000 interviews.

This gave confidence limits of +/" 0.9 per cent at the 95 per cent level and so was extremely reliable for national estimates. Even so, the authors of the research noted that potential error limits increase very quickly as sample sizes reduce and particular care should be taken in interpreting results for small subgroups of the sample. They went on to remind us that when a large proportion is being sampled and the sample result is projected, the sampling error is magnified also, and that a sampling error may run into very large numbers when expressed as a projection, even though, expressed as a percentage, it may appear to be quite small. The implication of this is that even regional statistics derived from a national survey may be quite inaccurate.

In 1999, New Zealanders are estimated to have made 16.6 million trips with at least one night away, comprising a total of 52.9 million nights; they spent NZ$4.1 billion on overnight trips. In addition, they made 44.3 million day trips of more than 40 km each way and spent a further NZ$2.8 billion on them (Forsyte Research 2000). As well as easily equalling the expenditure of international tourists, albeit in local currency, domestic travellers provide the essential base for most tourism infrastructure. These domestic tourism figures were derived from a major 1999 study carried out by Forsyte Research on contract to the former Public Good Science Fund. The primary focus of the research was to determine the direct economic impact of domestic tourism in New Zealand. A secondary objective was to measure domestic travel patterns for both overnight and day trips for 1999, to a level that allowed regional analysis. This was the first study of its scale since the last of the domestic travel survey series, noted above, carried out by AGB McNair in 1989/90 and the first to measure day trips in addition to overnight trips. Prior to this, the only recent research was a pilot survey carried out by Simmons (1997). The Forsyte sample was substantial, at 17,037, and provides high-grade data.

In all, almost 70 per cent of domestic travel in New Zealand was to the North Island, or within it. Canterbury, and then Otago, were the major destinations in the South Island. Regional flows, in net person nights, show a more interesting picture. The North Island is a net exporter of some two and a half million person nights to the South. Within the North Island, Auckland and Wellington are the main deficit regions, exporting a total of almost nine million person nights. The major beneficiaries are Northland, Waikato and the Bay of Plenty. In the South Island, the main beneficiaries are Otago and Nelson, followed by Marlborough and the West Coast. Canterbury is the only deficit region.

About half of all travel (46 per cent) is for holidays and leisure, with an average duration of 3.8 nights, and one-third (35 per cent and 2.9 nights) for visiting friends and relatives; a further 12 per cent is business travel, with an average stay of 2.5 nights. Of course, the economic impacts will not fall in direct proportion to the type of travel. Accommodation used is, overwhelmingly, the private home of a friend or relative or a borrowed second home. Motels are the commonest form of commercial accommodation with a total of 14 per cent; hotels attract only 7 per cent, many of whom would be business travellers (Forsyte Research 2000; Hall and Kearsley 2002).

Overall patterns of expenditure are split between the two islands broadly proportionately to visitor numbers, but the average amount spent per night varies considerably by region, with Wellington and Auckland the highest and Northland, Gisborne and Marlborough the lowest. As a result, Auckland has the largest total receipts at over NZ$700 million, followed by Waikato, Wellington and Canterbury. In total, the North Island receives almost NZ$2.8 billion and the South NZ$1.29 billion.

Even the least earning region, Gisborne, receives nearly NZ$47 million, although in Gisborne's case there is a small net outflow. In terms of regional flows of income, the North Island is an exporter of money, to the value of NZ$212 million, to the South. Auckland shows the largest net deficit by far ("NZ$453 million). In the South Island, every region is a net beneficiary, so that domestic tourism is a major economic sector and a powerful agent of income redistribution on a regional basis. In aggregate, a quarter of all expenditure is on accommodation and just over a quarter is on food. Shopping of all types consumes one-fifth of expenditure, while transport, recreation and alcohol account for about 10 per cent each. Business travel is getting on for three times the cost of other trips per night, and is heavily weighted towards travel and accommodation costs when compared with other sectors, both proportionately and in real terms. VFR travel is slightly more demanding of travel expenditure than are holidays, but accommodation costs, not surprisingly, are considerably less.

The analysis of behavioural issues in recreational and tourism research indicates that 'in behavioural terms then, there seems little necessity to insist on a major distinction between tourism and leisure phenomena. Therefore, it should follow that a greater commonality between the research efforts in the two areas would be of advantage' although different social theoretical approaches exist towards the analysis of recreation and tourism phenomena. As a result, Moore *et al.* (1995:79) conclude that 'there is little need, if any, to take a dramatically different approach to the behavioural analysis of tourism and leisure'. One needs to view each activity in the context of the everyday life of the people involved to understand how each is conceived. There is a clear distinction within the literature between what motivates recreationalists and tourists, and comparative studies of similar groups of people and the similarities and differences between these motivations has yet to permeate the research literature. While geographers have focused on recreational and tourist behaviour in relation to demand issues, the analysis has largely been quantitative, site specific, and has not adapted a comparative methodology to examine the recreation-tourism continuum.

10

Group Travel, Tourism and Human Resource Management

Most of the tourism activity also involves economic costs, including the direct costs incurred by tourism businesses, government costs for infrastructure to better serve tourists, as well as congestion and related costs borne by individuals in the community. Community decisions over tourism often involve debates between industry proponents touting tourism's economic impacts (benefits) and detractors emphasizing tourism's costs.

Sound decisions rest on a balanced and objective assessment of both benefits and costs and an understanding of who benefits from tourism and who pays for it. Businesses and public organizations are increasingly interested in the economic impacts of tourism at national, state, and local levels. One regularly hears claims that tourism supports X jobs in an area or that a festival or special event generated Y million dollars in sales or income in a community. "Multiplier effects" are often cited to capture secondary effects of tourism spending and show the wide range of sectors in a community that may benefit from tourism. Tourism's economic benefits are touted by the industry for a variety of reasons. Claims of tourism's economic significance give the industry greater respect among the business community, public officials, and the public in general. This often translates into decisions or public policies that are favourable to tourism.

Community support is important for tourism, as it is an activity that affects the entire community. Tourism businesses depend extensively on each other as well as on other businesses, government and residents of the local community. Economic benefits and costs of tourism reach virtually everyone in the region in one way or another. Economic impact analyses provide tangible estimates of these economic interdependencies and a better understanding of the role and importance of tourism in a region's economy.

Tourism's economic impacts are therefore an important consideration in state, regional and community planning and economic development. Economic impacts are also important factors in marketing and management decisions. Communities therefore need to understand the relative importance of tourism to their region, including tourism's contribution to economic activity in the area. A variety of methods, ranging from pure guesswork to complex mathematical models, are used to estimate tourism's economic impacts. Studies vary extensively in quality and accuracy, as well as which aspects of tourism are included. Technical reports often are filled with economic terms and methods that non-economists do not understand. On the other hand, media coverage of these studies tend to oversimplify and frequently misinterpret the results, leaving decision makers and the general public with a sometimes distorted and incomplete understanding of tourism's economic effects.

How can the average person understand these studies sufficiently to separate good studies from bad ones and make informed choices? The purpose of this bulletin is to present a systematic introduction to economic impact concepts and methods. The presentation is written for tourism industry analysts and public officials, who would like to better understand, evaluate, or possibly conduct an economic impact assessment. The bulletin is organized around ten basic questions that either are asked or should be asked about the economic impacts of tourism.

ECONOMIC IMPACT ANALYSIS

A variety of economic analyses are carried out to support tourism decisions. As these different kinds of economic analysis are frequently confused, let's begin by positioning economic impact studies within the broader set of economic problems and techniques relevant to tourism. These same techniques may be applied to any policy or action, but we will define them here in the context of tourism. Each type of analysis is identified by the basic question(s) it answers and the types of methods and models that are appropriate. Benefit cost analysis and economic impact analysis are frequently confused as both discuss economic "benefits".

There are two clear distinctions between the two techniques. B/C analysis addresses the benefits from economic efficiency while economic impact analysis focuses on the regional distribution of economic activity. The income received from tourism by a destination region is largely off-set by corresponding losses in the origin regions, yielding only modest contributions to net social welfare and efficiency. B/C analysis includes market and non-market values (consumer surplus), while economic impact analysis is restricted to actual flows of money from market transactions.

While each type of economic analysis is somewhat distinct, a given problem often calls for several different kinds of economic analysis. An economic impact study will frequently involve a demand analysis to project levels of tourism activity. In other cases demand is treated as exogenous and the analysis simply estimates impacts if a given number of visitors are attracted to the area. A comprehensive impact assessment will also examine fiscal impacts, as well as social and environmental impacts. Be aware that an economic impact analysis, by itself, provides a rather narrow and often one-sided perspective on the impacts of tourism.

Studies of the economic impacts of tourism tend to emphasize the positive benefits of tourism. On the other hand environmental, social, cultural and fiscal impact studies tend to focus more on negative impacts of tourism. This is in spite of the fact that there are negative economic impacts of tourism (*e.g.*, seasonality and lower wage jobs) and in many cases positive environmental and social impacts (*e.g.*, protection of natural and cultural resources in the area and education of both tourists and local residents). An economic impact assessment (EIA) traces changes in economic activity resulting from some action.

An EIA will identify which economic sectors benefit from tourism and estimate resulting changes in income and employment in the region. Economic impact assessment procedures do not assess economic efficiency and also do not generally produce estimates of the fiscal costs of an action. For many problems economic impact analysis will be part of a broader analysis. Environmental, social, and fiscal impacts are often equally important concerns in a balanced assessment of impacts. An economic impact analysis will assess the contribution of tourism activity to a region's economy.

The basic questions an economic impact study usually addresses are:

- How many jobs in the area does tourism support?
- How much tax revenue is generated from tourism?
- How much do tourists spend in the area?
- What portion of sales by local businesses is due to tourism?
- How much income does tourism generate for households and businesses in the area?

An economic impact analysis also reveals the interrelationships among economic sectors and provides estimates of the changes that take place in an economy due to some existing or proposed action.

The most common applications of economic impact analysis to tourism are:

1. To evaluate the economic impacts of changes in the supply of recreation and tourism opportunities. Supply changes may involve a change in quantity, such as the opening of new facilities, closing of existing ones, or expansions and contraction in capacity. Supply changes may also involve changes in quality, including changes in,
   - The quality of the environment,
   - The local infrastructure and public services to support tourism, or
   - The nature of the tourism products and services that are provided in an area.
2. To evaluate the economic impacts of changes in tourism demand.

Population changes, changes in the competitive position of the region, marketing activity or changing consumer tastes and preferences can alter levels of tourism activity, spending, and associated economic activity. An economic impact study can estimate the magnitude and nature of these impacts.

3. To evaluate the effects of policies and actions which affect tourism activity either directly or indirectly. Tourism depends on many factors at both origins and destinations that are frequently outside the direct control of the tourism industry itself. Economic impact studies provide information to help decision makers better understand the consequences of various actions on the tourism industry as well as on other sectors of the economy. For example, increased air pollution standards have been opposed in some regions due to the predicted economic consequences of the closing of plants that cannot meet the new standards. Tourism interests counter these arguments with estimates of the potential gains in income and jobs in tourism industries that depend on good air quality and visibility.
4. To understand the economic structure and interdependencies of different sectors of the economy. Economic studies help us better understand the size and structure of the tourism industry in a given region and its linkages to other sectors of the economy. Such understandings are helpful in identifying potential partners for the tourism industry as well as in targeting industries as part of regional economic development strategies. Issues such as economic growth, stability, and seasonality may be addressed as part of these studies.
5. To argue for favourable treatment in allocation of resources or local tax, zoning or other policy decisions. By showing that tourism has significant economic impacts, tourism interests can often convince decision-makers to allocate more resources for tourism or to establish policies that encourage tourism. Tax abatements and other incentives frequently given to manufacturing firms have also been granted to hotels, marinas and other tourism businesses based on demonstrated economic impacts in the local area.
6. To compare the economic impacts of alternative resource allocation, policy, management or development proposals. Economic impact analyses are commonly used to assess the relative merits of distinct alternatives. The economic contribution of expanded tourism offerings may be compared for example with alternatives such as resource extraction activities (mining, timber harvesting) or manufacturing. Impacts of alternative tourism development proposals may also be evaluated, *e.g.*, tourism strategies that emphasize outdoor recreation, camping development, a convention facility, or a factory outlet mall.

Tourism has a variety of economic impacts. Tourists contribute to sales, profits, jobs, tax revenues, and income in an area. The most direct effects occur within the primary tourism sectors—lodging, restaurants, transportation, amusements, and retail trade. Through secondary effects, tourism affects most sectors of the economy. An economic impact analysis of tourism activity normally focuses on changes in sales, income, and employment in a region resulting from tourism activity.

A simple tourism impact scenario illustrates. Let's say a region attracts an additional 100 tourists, each spending \$100 per day. That's \$10,000 in new spending per day in the area. If sustained over a 100 day season, the region would accumulate a million dollars in new sales. The million dollars in spending would be distributed to lodging, restaurant, amusement and retail trade sectors in proportion to how the visitor spends the \$100. Perhaps 30per cent of the million dollars would leak out of the region immediately to cover the costs of goods purchased by tourists that are not made in the local area (only the retail margins for such items should normally be included as direct sales effects). The remaining \$700,000 in direct sales might yield \$350,000 in income within tourism industries and support 20 direct tourism jobs. Tourism industries are labour and income intensive, translating a high proportion of sales into income and corresponding jobs.

The tourism industry, in turn, buys goods and services from other businesses in the area, and pays out most of the \$350,000 in income as wages and salaries to its employees. This creates secondary economic effects in the region. The study might use a sales multiplier of 2.0 to indicate that each dollar of direct sales generates another dollar in secondary sales in this region. Through multiplier effects, the \$700,000 in direct sales produces \$1.4 million in total sales. These secondary sales create additional income and employment, resulting in a total impact on the region of \$1.4 million in sales, \$650,000 in income and 35 jobs.

While hypothetical, the numbers used here are fairly typical of what one might find in a tourism economic impact study. A more complete study might identify which sectors receive the direct and secondary effects and possibly identify differences in spending and impacts of distinct subgroups of tourists (market segments). One can also estimate the tax effects of this spending by applying local tax rates to the appropriate changes in sales or income. Instead of focusing on visitor spending, one could also estimate impacts of construction or government activity associated with tourism. There are several other categories of economic impacts that are not typically covered in economic impact assessments, at least not directly.

For example:

- *Changes in prices*: Tourism can sometimes inflate the cost of housing and retail prices in the area, frequently on a seasonal basis.

- *Changes in the quality and quantity of goods and services*: Tourism may lead to a wider array of goods and services available in an area (of either higher or lower quality than without tourism).
- *Changes in property and other taxes*: Taxes to cover the cost of local services may be higher or lower in the presence of tourism activity. In some cases, taxes collected directly or indirectly from tourists may yield reduced local taxes for schools, roads, etc. In other cases, locals may be taxed more heavily to cover the added infrastructure and service costs. The impacts of tourism on local government costs and revenues are addressed more fully in a fiscal impact analysis.
- *Economic dimensions of "social" and "environmental" impacts*: There are also economic consequences of most social and environmental impacts that are not usually addressed in an economic impact analysis. These can be positive or negative. For example, traffic congestion will increase costs of moving around for both households and businesses. Improved amenities that attract tourists may also encourage retirees or other kinds of businesses to locate in the area.

INDUCED EFFECTS

A standard economic impact analysis traces flows of money from tourism spending, first to businesses and government agencies where tourists spend their money and then to:

- *Other businesses*: Supplying goods and services to tourist businesses,
- *Households*: Earning income by working in tourism or supporting industries, and
- *Government*: Through various taxes and charges on tourists, businesses and households

Formally, regional economists distinguish direct, indirect, and induced economic effects. Indirect and induced effects are sometimes collectively called secondary effects. The total economic impact of tourism is the sum of direct, indirect, and induced effects within a region. Any of these impacts may be measured as gross output or sales, income, employment, or value added. Direct effects are production changes associated with the immediate effects of changes in tourism expenditures.

For example, an increase in the number of tourists staying overnight in hotels would directly yield increased sales in the hotel sector. The additional hotel sales and associated changes in hotel payments for wages and salaries, taxes, and supplies and services are direct effects of the tourist spending.

Indirect effects are the production changes resulting from various rounds of re-spending of the hotel industry's receipts in other backward-linked industries (*i.e.*, industries supplying products and services to hotels). Changes in sales, jobs, and income in the linen supply industry, for example, represent indirect effects of changes in hotel sales. Businesses supplying products and services to the linen supply industry represent another round of indirect effects, eventually linking hotels to varying degrees to many other economic sectors in the region. Induced effects are the changes in economic activity resulting from household spending of income earned directly or indirectly as a result of tourism spending. For example, hotel and linen supply employees supported directly or indirectly by tourism, spend their income in the local region for housing, food, transportation, and the usual array of household product and service needs. The sales, income, and jobs that result from household spending of added wage, salary, or proprietor's income are induced effects.

By means of indirect and induced effects, changes in tourist spending can impact virtually every sector of the economy in one way or another. The magnitude of secondary effects depends on the propensity of businesses and households in the region to purchase goods and services from local suppliers. Induced effects are particularly noticed when a large employer in a region closes a plant. Not only are supporting industries (indirect effects) hurt, but the entire local economy suffers due to the reduction in household income within the region. Retail stores close and leakages of money from the region increase as consumers go outside the region for more and more goods and services. Similar effects in the opposite direction are observed when there is a significant increase in jobs and household income. Final demand is the term used by economists for sales to the final consumers of goods and services. In almost all cases, the final consumers of tourism goods and services are households. Government spending is also considered as final demand. The same methods for estimating impacts of visitor spending can be applied to estimate the economic impacts of government spending, for example, to operate and maintain a park or visitor centre.

REGIONAL MODELS

An input-output model (I-O model) is a mathematical model that describes the flows of money between sectors within a region's economy. Flows are predicted by knowing what each industry must buy from every other industry to produce a dollar's worth of output. Using each industry's production function, I-O models also determine the proportions of sales that go to wage and salary income, proprietor's income, and taxes. Multipliers can be estimated from input-output models based on the estimated re-circulation of spending within the region. Exports and imports are determined based upon estimates of the propensity of households and firms within the region to purchase goods and services from local sources (often called RPC's or regional purchase coefficients). The more a region is self-sufficient and purchases goods and services from within the region, the higher the multipliers for the region. Input-output models make a number of assumptions.

The basic ones are that:

- All firms in a given industry employ the same production technology (usually assumed to be the national average for that industry), and produce identical products.
- There are no economies or diseconomies of scale in production or factor substitution. I-O models are essentially linear—double the level of tourism activity/production and you double all of the inputs, the number of jobs, etc.
- The model doesn't explicitly keep track of time, but analysts generally report the impact estimates as if they represent activity within a single year.
- One must assume that the various model parameters are accurate and represent the current year.

I-O models are firmly grounded in the national system of accounts, which relies on a standard industrial classification system (SIC codes) and various federal government economic censuses, in which individual firms report sales, wage and salary payments and employment. I-O models will generally be at least a few years out-of-date, although this isn't usually a major problem unless the region's economy has changed significantly. An I-O model represents the region's economy at a particular point in time. Tourist spending estimates are generally price adjusted to the year of the model. Multiplier computations for induced effects generally assume that jobs created by additional spending are new jobs, involving new households in the area. Induced effects are computed assuming linear changes in household spending with changes in income. Estimates of induced effects may be inflated due to the violation of these assumptions. Induced effects tend to account for the vast majority of the secondary effects of tourism, and therefore should be used with caution.

MULTIPLIERS EFFECTS OF TOURISM

Multipliers capture the secondary economic effects (indirect and induced) of tourism activity. Multipliers have been frequently misused and misinterpreted in tourism studies and are a considerable source of confusion among non-economists. Multipliers represent the economic interdependencies between sectors within a particular region's economy. They vary considerably from region to region and sector to sector. There are many different kinds of multipliers reflecting which secondary effects are included and which measure of economic activity is used (sales, income, or employment).

For example,

- The Type I sales multiplier = direct sales + indirect sales direct sales.
- The Type II or III sales multiplier[1] = direct sales + indirect sales + induced sales direct sales.

Multiplying a Type I sales multiplier times the direct sales gives direct plus indirect sales. Multiplying a Type II or III sales multiplier times the direct sales gives total sales impacts including direct, indirect and induced effects. The multipliers defined above are called ratio type multipliers as they measure the ratio of a total impact measure to the corresponding direct impact. Comparable income and employment ratio type multipliers may be defined by replacing sales with measures of income or employment in the above equations. Ratio multipliers should be used with caution.

A common error is to multiply a sales multiplier times tourist spending to get total sales effects. This will generate an inflated estimate of tourism impacts. The problem is that tourism spending or sales is not exactly the same as the "direct effects", appearing in the multiplier formula. Tourist purchases of goods (vs. services) are the primary source of the problem. To properly apply tourist purchases of goods to an input-output model (or corresponding multipliers), various margins (retail, wholesale and transportation) must be deducted from the "purchaser price" of the good to separate out the "producer price".

In an I-O model, retail margins accrue to the retail trade sector, wholesale margins to wholesale trade, transportation margins to transportation sectors (trucking, rail, air etc.) and the producer prices of goods are assigned to the sector that produces the good. In most cases the factory that produces the good bought by a tourist lies outside of the local region, creating an immediate "leakage" in the first round of spending and therefore no local impact from production of the good. Before applying a multiplier to tourist spending, one must first deduct the producer prices of all imported goods that tourists buy (*i.e.* only include the local retail margins and possibly wholesale and transportation margins if these firms lie within the region). Generally, only 60 to 70per cent of tourist spending appears as final demand in a local region. While all tourist purchases of services will accrue to the local region as final demand, only the margins on goods purchased at retail stores should be counted as local final demand. The ratio of local final demand to tourist spending is called the capture rate.

Capture rate = local final demand/tourism spending in local area. Capture rates, like multipliers, will vary with the size and nature of the region as well as the kind of tourist spending included. One must therefore be cautious in taking a multiplier or capture rate cited in one study and using it in another. Another way of calculating a multiplier (generally the preferred approach among economists) is as a ratio of income or employment to sales. This kind of multiplier is sometimes called a Keynesian multiplier or response coefficient.

- Type III Income multiplier = Total direct, indirect, and induced income direct sales
- Type III Employment multiplier = Total direct, indirect, and induced employment direct sales

This income (employment) multiplier produces total income (employment) impacts when multiplied by the direct sales. One must still be careful in distinguishing between tourism spending/sales and direct sales effects. Some studies may embed the capture rate in the multiplier, expressing the ratio in terms of tourism spending rather than direct sales.

The economic impacts of tourism are typically estimated by some variation of the following simple formula:

Economic Impact of Tourism = Number of Tourists × Average Spending per Visitor × Multiplier

The formula suggests three distinct steps and corresponding measurements or models:

1. Estimate the change in the number and types of tourists to the region due to the proposed policy or action. Estimates or projections of tourist activity generally come from a demand model or some system for measuring levels of tourism activity in an area. Economic impact estimates will rest heavily on good estimates of the numbers and types of visitors. These must come from carefully designed measurements of tourist activity, a good demand model, or good judgement. This step is usually the weakest link in most tourism impact studies, as few regions have accurate counts of tourists, let alone good models for predicting changes in tourism activity or separating local visitors from visitors from outside the region.
2. Estimate average levels of spending (often within specific market segments) of tourists in the local area. Spending averages come from sample surveys or are sometimes borrowed or adapted from other studies. Spending estimates must be based on a representative sample of the population of tourists taking into account variations across seasons, types of tourists, and locations within the study area. As spending can vary widely across different kinds of tourists, we recommend estimating average spending for a set of key tourist segments based on samples of at least 50-100 visitors within each tourism segment. Segments should be defined to capture differences in spending between local residents vs. tourists, day users vs. overnight visitors, type of accommodation (motel, campground, seasonal home, with friends and relatives), and type of transportation (car, RV, air, rail, etc.). In broadly based tourism impact studies, it is useful to identify unique spending patterns of important activity segments such as downhill skiers, boaters, and convention and business travellers. Multiplying the number of tourists by the average spending per visitor (be careful the units are consistent) gives an estimate of total tourist spending in the area. Estimates of tourist spending will generally be more accurate if distinct spending profiles

and use estimates are made for key tourism segments. The use and spending estimates are the two most important parts of an economic impact assessment. When combined, they capture the amount of money brought into the region by tourists. Multipliers are needed only if one is interested in the secondary effects of tourism spending.

3. Apply the change in spending to a regional economic model or set of multipliers to determine secondary effects. Secondary effects of tourism are estimated using multipliers or a model of the region's economy. Multipliers generally come from an economic base or input-output model of the region's economy. In many cases multipliers are borrowed (often improperly) or adjusted from published multipliers or other studies. One should not take a multiplier estimated for one region and apply it in a region with a quite different economic structure. Generally, multipliers are higher for larger regions with more diversified economies and lower for smaller regions with more limited economic development. A common error is to apply a statewide multiplier (since these are more widely published) to a local region. This will yield inflated estimates of local multiplier effects. Multipliers can also be used to convert estimates of spending or sales to income and employment. Simple ratios can be used to capture how much income or jobs are generated per dollar of sales. These ratios will vary from region to region and across individual economic sectors due to the relative importance of labour inputs in each industry and different wage and salary rates in different regions of the country. Be aware that job estimates are generally not full time equivalents, making them difficult to compare across industries with different proportions of seasonal and part time jobs. Income or value added are generally the preferred measures of the contribution of tourism to a region's economy.

THE TYPICAL APPROACHES FOR AN ECONOMIC ASSESSMENT

At the simple, "quick and dirty" end of the spectrum are highly aggregate approaches that rely mostly on judgement to determine tourism activity, spending and multipliers. Such estimates can be completed in a couple hours at little cost and rest largely on the expertise and judgement of the analyst. At the other extreme are studies that gather primary data from visitor spending studies and apply the spending estimates to formal regional economic models for the area in question. In between are a wide range of options that employ varying degrees of judgement, secondary data, primary data, and formal models.

Different levels of detail and corresponding expense (time and money) and accuracy are possible for each of the three steps—estimating tourist volume, spending, and multiplier effects. Four typical approaches illustrate the levels of detail that are possible and the associated methods to sales estimates. With sound judgement in choosing the parameters, the MGM model can yield reasonable ballpark estimates of economic impacts at minimal cost. This approach, however, provides little detail on spending categories or which sectors of the economy benefit from either direct or secondary effects. The aggregate nature of the approach also makes it difficult to adjust recommended spending rates or multipliers to different applications. The Bureau of Economic Analysis's (BEA) RIMS II user handbook illustrates how to apply published multipliers to estimate economic impacts. This approach starts with visitor spending (from survey or secondary sources) divided into a number of spending categories and makes use of sector specific multipliers to estimate the direct and total sales, income and employment effects. Multipliers from the BEA's RIMS II models are used to estimate secondary effects. Multipliers are reported for 39 sectors for each state in the second edition of their report.

This method uses margins to properly account for retail purchases of goods and makes use of disaggregate sector-specific multipliers for each state. Multipliers for sub-state regions are not as readily available, but can be acquired from BEA or other sources. Secondary effects cannot be disaggregated to individual sectors using the BEA approach.

The MI-REC/IMPLAN System: Stynes and Propst have developed a fairly complete micro-computer-based system for estimating economic impacts of recreation and tourism. The system combines spreadsheets for estimating spending with the IMPLAN input-output modeling system. IMPLAN uses county level data to estimate 528 sector input-output models for regions down to account level. IMPLAN generates a complete set of economic accounts for the region including multipliers and trade flows. MI-REC spreadsheets estimate visitor spending within up to 33categories based on the number and types of visitors attracted to an area. Spending is then bridged to the IMPLAN model sectors to estimate direct, indirect and induced effects in terms of sales, income and employment. Users may estimate spending via visitor surveys or use the MI-REC database of spending profiles, compiled from previous studies. The system also includes price indices to easily update spending data to a current year.

Two other systems for estimating economic impacts of tourism should be noted. The TEIM or Travel Economic Impact Model developed by the U.S. Travel Data Centre has been widely used to estimate tourism and travel impacts at state and national levels. A more recent development is the satellite accounting approach developed by the World Travel and Tourism Council.Both of these systems are primarily designed for estimating the overall economic significance of tourism at national or state levels. They are not readily applied to estimate the impacts of particular policies and actions at the local level. The TEIM relies on national travel surveys to estimate trip volume and spending on a state-by-state basis. Local estimates of impacts are obtained using simple allocation formulas to distribute statewide impacts to counties and cities within the state. These local estimates do not account very well for the distinct types of tourism activity or spending patterns in different sub-regions of a state. The WTTC effort also focuses on national and statewide accounting of tourism's economic significance. Their satellite tourism account identifies the contribution of travel and tourism to gross national product (GNP) or gross state product (GSP). Using the standard national system of accounts, they identify the portion of sales, taxes and investment attributable directly to travel and tourism. The WTTC system does not use multipliers or attempt to estimate secondary effects. It does, however, capture a great deal of travel-related economic activity, not covered by visitor trip spending, such as durable goods purchases (boats and RV's), construction and investment in tourism, and government expenditures.

An economic impact study involves four basic:

1. Define the problem
2. Estimate the change in final demand (tourism spending).
3. Estimate the regional economic effects of this change
4. Interpret, apply, and communicate the results

The most important part of any study is the first step—clarifying the nature of the problem being addressed and intended uses of the results. Before launching an economic impact study, be sure this is the kind of study that is needed rather than one or more of the other kinds of economic analyses. Stynes and Propst (1996) identify seven factors that should be specified as part of defining a problem for an economic impact assessment:

- Define the action to be evaluated. Begin by clarifying the action or actions involved in the problem. Actions may include construction, government investment, changes in marketing, management, or policies, or changes in the quality or quantity of tourist facilities. If evaluating impacts of existing tourism activity, be sure to define what is to be included as "tourism".
- Identify the change in the amount and kinds of recreation/tourism activity resulting from the action. The action must be defined precisely enough in step one to be able to estimate the changes in the number and types of visitors to the area and/or their spending patterns. As a general rule, the analysis should be with vs. without the action rather than simply before vs. after. Thus, if tourism has been growing by 5per cent per year and a new promotional programme increases this to 10per cent this year, only half of the 10per cent growth can likely be attributed to the promotional programme. Identifying the net changes in activity that are attributable to an action can be a complex and difficult task. Assessments of economic impact, however, rest

firmly on such estimates, so attention to these details is very important. In situations of some uncertainty, we recommend evaluating impacts using a range of estimates in order to establish rough confidence intervals around your estimates. Evaluating a range of alternatives also helps to evaluate the sensitivity of the results to your initial estimates of changes in activity levels.

- Identify the kinds of spending to be included. Tourism may impact the local economy through visitor trip spending, durable goods purchases, government spending, or investment and construction. Which to include in a given analysis depends on how the problem is defined, and again, on attributing given spending changes to the proposed action.
- Identify the study region. Perhaps the most important, yet often neglected part of a recreation and tourism impact assessment is the definition of a study region. The region defines the area for which impacts are desired, as well as the portions of visitor spending that are relevant. An impact assessment evaluates the impacts on households, businesses, and organizations within the given region. Spending that visitors make outside of a study region either at home or en route are not included in assessing impacts of spending on the designated region. For an economic impact analysis, the study region should be large enough to constitute a viable economic region. Since little economic data exists below the county level, the county is generally the smallest region one should consider for a tourism impact assessment.
- Identify key economic sectors and desired sectoral detail. The proposed action and anticipated uses/users of the results should suggest the key sectors that will be impacted. Recreation and tourism activity typically impact the lodging, restaurant, amusements, retail, transportation and government sectors most directly. In the problem definition stage consideration of impacted sectors helps to identify relevant categories of spending. The desired sectoral detail plays an important role in structuring the presentation of results. In some cases only an aggregate measure of impacts may be desired. In other cases, clients may be interested in which particular sectors are most heavily affected and will want estimates of sales and jobs broken down by sector. If formal input-output models are used, impacts may be estimated in considerable sectoral detail. This is not possible if an aggregate spending estimate or multiplier is used.
- Identify the most important measures of economic activity. Tourism impacts may be reported in terms of visitor spending, business receipts/sales/production, wage and salary income, proprietors income

and profits, value added, and employment. The direct effects are the most important and are captured well by estimates of visitor spending. Simple ratios can be used to convert direct spending or sales to the associated income and jobs. Input-output models and multipliers are needed only if one is interested in secondary effects.

- Identify the tolerable levels of error in the results. Although confidence intervals and estimates of error are rare in economic impact studies, this doesn't mean they are not important. You should have at least a ballpark idea of how much error you can tolerate in the analysis, as this will dictate how much effort and expense you must put into it. The more accuracy you demand, the greater the requirements to gather up-to-date local data on visitation, spending and economic activity. These data allow you to fine tune the spending estimates and input-output models or multipliers. Such fine tuning will require time, knowledge, and money that must be weighed against the benefits of the improved estimates. Estimates of impacts are based on three components: visits, spending, and multipliers. You should try to balance the errors across these components.
- What are some questions to ask when evaluating or interpreting a tourism economic impact study? Evaluating, interpreting and applying an economic impact study requires a clear understanding of the findings and at least some knowledge of the underlying concepts and methods. Judging the accuracy or quality of a study can be based on the reputation of the author or the quality of presentation, although a careful evaluation of the methods that were used is the best approach. Here's some questions to ask when reading or evaluating a tourism economic impact study.
- *Impact of what?* The report should identify the action being evaluated. An economic impact assessment is most useful when evaluating the effects of a particular action or policy. If so, the action and assumptions about alternatives should be spelled out in presenting a with vs. without scenario. If the study reports impacts of existing tourism activity, identify how tourism is defined (if at all). What kinds of tourism activity and spending are included? Which trip expenses are included? Does the study include all visitor spending or only spending of tourists who live outside the local region? Does the study address impacts of visitor trip spending, durable goods purchases, operational expenses of a programme, or construction and investment?
- *On what region?* The study region should be defined (preferably with a map). It should be viable both economically and as a distinct tourism destination area. Spending that is included should be restricted to spending in this region and multipliers should represent the given

region of interest. A short profile of tourism and economic activity in the region provides useful background for an economic impact study.

- *Sources and quality of the data:* The report should identify the sources of the data for estimating visits, spending, and regional economic multipliers/models. The methods that were used to estimate impacts should be clear. Judgements of the quality of the estimates must be based largely on an understanding of the data and methods that were used. A more disaggregate analysis reporting spending within at least six categories, visitors for two or more distinct segments, and multipliers and results broken down by sector will generally be more accurate and meaningful than a study that only uses aggregate data. Disaggregation is particularly helpful when adjusting secondary data taken from government reports or other studies to a new situation. The fundamental question is whether the visit estimates, spending profiles and multipliers adequately represent the intended population and study area.
- *Quality of methods:* There are a number of issues to watch for in evaluating methods.
- *Visits:* Has the study clearly defined which visits/visitors will be affected by the proposed action, separated local visitors from tourists, and identified which visitors would be lost or gained due to the action (with vs. without the action)? Are secondary sources of visitation reliable? If models are used, how good are they and do the assumptions hold for the intended application? Has the study handled potential double counting problems in estimating visits?
- *Spending:* How accurate are the spending estimates? Do the spending averages or totals seem reasonable? If spending averages are taken from a secondary source, evaluate the source, as well as how well these averages may apply to the intended application. What year does the spending represent? Has the data been price adjusted to the current (or model) year? If spending data come from a visitor survey, evaluate the survey methods-how was spending measured, what was the sample size, the response rate, soundness of the analysis? Are variances and confidence intervals reported for the spending estimates? Are visitors divided into distinct segments to reduce variances? Also make sure the units for which spending is reported match the units for visits, *i.e.*, the study doesn't multiply a per party spending average times the number of person visits. If adjustments are made in units of analysis, evaluate the assumed or estimated average length of stay or party size assumptions.
- *Multipliers:* If "off-the-shelf" or borrowed multipliers are used, investigate the source. Does the study clearly define what type of

multiplier is being used (Type I, Type III, income, sales or employment, ratio or Keynesian) and use the multiplier appropriately? In particular, watch for studies that multiply tourism spending by a multiplier taken from an input-output model. They should adjust for the capture rate either by reducing spending, only using retail margins on goods purchased by tourists, or using a "tourist spending" multiplier that takes the capture rate into account. If an input-output model is used, the report should summarize where it came from, what year it represents, the levels of sectoral aggregation, and the basic assumptions of the model.

- *Communication and reporting of results:* The study should communicate the study results in terms that are understandable to the intended audience. For most audiences, a summary and glossary of economic terms is helpful. Most readers will not fully understand terms like indirect and induced effects, Type I and Type III multipliers, and input-output models. Formal definitions of the measures of sales, income, and jobs that are reported are also needed to clarify what each of these terms include and the measurement units. For example, is income only wage and salary income or does it also include proprietors income, rents and profits? Study limitations and errors should be indicated.

STUDY COST

The costs of a tourism economic impact study can range from $500 to $50,000 and more. Costs will depend largely on the size and scope of tourism activity to be covered, the size and complexity of the study region, how much primary data are to be gathered and the level of accuracy and detail desired. The greatest and perhaps most significant cost will be the technical expertise of the analysts involved.

Tourism economic impact studies require considerable technical judgement of specialists and a mix of corresponding skills:

- Knowledge of tourism
- Expertise in conducting tourism surveys, particularly spending studies
- Regional economic modeling skills, including knowledge and access to economic data bases, multipliers and input-output modeling systems
- Communication skills

The cost of conducting economic impact studies has dropped substantially in the past ten years due to improvements in microcomputer programmes for estimating spending and regional economic models. The three principal components of an economic impact estimate (visits, spending, and multipliers) each involve different costs and somewhat different skills. The costs and needed skills will vary considerably depending on whether primary or existing data are to be used. If levels and types of tourism activity are known and spending averages and multipliers may be taken from secondary sources, a complete economic impact assessment can be conducted in less than a month and in many cases for under $5,000.

You are paying primarily for the time, judgement and skills of the analyst. A small visitor spending survey may add another $5,000. For a more complete analysis of secondary effects using a

formal input-output model, figure another $2,000-$5,000. Increase the cost estimate if several distinct alternatives are to be evaluated or multiple regions are involved. There will generally be scale economies in these situations with additional impact analyses costing less than half of the initial one. Costs will increase significantly if the number and types of visitors must be estimated using a general visitor survey or a demand model. Large scale spending surveys and custom input-output models based on primary data will also increase costs considerably. In many cases, the tourism activity and visitor spending data needed for an economic impact analysis can be gathered in a general visitor survey or market study. Spending averages for particular tourist segments can be estimated by having a portion of the general survey respondents complete an extra page of spending questions. Armed with good estimates of the number and types of visitors and their spending patterns, one can complete an economic impact study at little additional cost.

The principal motivations for a business or region to serve tourists are generally economic. An individual business is interested primarily in its own revenues and costs, while a community or region is concerned with tourism's overall contribution to the economy, as well as its social, fiscal and environmental impacts. A good understanding of tourism's economic impacts is therefore important for the tourism industry, government officials, and the community as a whole.

Tourism economics is unfortunately a technical area, involving concepts, methods, and models that are unfamiliar to most non-economists. In this bulletin I've attempted to define the key concepts and explain the basic methods for estimating the economic impacts of tourism, hopefully in as "non-technical" a way as the subject allows. Understanding the concepts and methods is critical to interpreting, evaluating, and applying economic impact results. This bulletin should be read along with one or more economic impact reports that can be used as examples and opportunities to test your grasp of the issues.

At the risk of oversimplifying a complex topic, let me conclude with the five pieces of advice, most frequently give to people who ask about tourism economic impacts. First, tell them that the most important information for estimating tourism impacts is a good estimate of the number of tourists. This requires clearly defining what one wishes to include as "tourism" and the region of interest. Secondly, recommend that tourists be divided into distinct subgroups (segments) with distinct spending patterns and likely reacting differently to various policy and marketing actions. In particular, local customers should be distinguished from visitors from outside the region and day users from overnight visitors.

Thirdly, focus most of your effort on estimating the direct effects of tourism, usually as tourist spending in the area. Multiplier effects are not nearly as important in most cases, as their use in tourism would suggest and multipliers tend to introduce complexities that most users of the results do not fully understand. Even if multiplier effects are important to the study purpose, remember that any errors in estimates of the direct effects will also be multiplied by any multiplier. Fourth, if you must use multipliers be sure you understand them.

E-COMMERCE TOURISM

Tourism is growing fastest in the developing countries, where it is a major component of most economies. Tourism is one of the world's largest industries, and it is a natural partner for the Internet, where it is also the world's largest on-line industry. Community-based tourism (CBT) has been shown to foster local development in developing countries, particularly in the poorer rural areas. At the same time, Information and Communication Technologies are being deployed within poor communities in developing countries and are beginning to demonstrate their potential for inducing local development. This paper describes an action research initiative for introducing electronic commerce for community based tourism (e-CBT) in three Asian rural communities in order to reveal its potential for community development.

E-CBT targets an important and growing market segment in the developing world, consisting of individual travellers for whom travel is an essential component of their life-style and who seek new and authentic experiences that are not directed towards a mass market. The proposal describes strategic partnerships between a University in Hong Kong and three other Asian universities who will work with local communities and tourism authorities for the eventual propagation of the development benefits of e-CBT among wider rural populations in their countries.

The WTO forecasts that international arrivals are expected to reach over 1.56 billion by the year 2020. The total expected tourist arrivals by region shows that by 2020 the top three receiving regions will be Europe (717 million tourists), East Asia and the Pacific (397 million) and Americas (282 million). East Asia and the Pacific, South Asia, the Middle East and Africa are forecasted to record growth at rates of over 5per cent per year, compared to the world average of 4.1 per cent. By 2010, WTO forecasts that the Americas will lose its number two position, behind Europe, to East Asia and the Pacific, which will receive 25per cent of world arrivals.

Tourism offers huge opportunities for developing countries to increase incomes from the growing number of arrivals that land on their shores. However, it has been recognized that many tourism policies developed from central governments without local involvement fail to cater for the sensibilities and aspirations of the communities that tourists visit. The conference on Community Based Ecotourism in Southeast Asia agreed that local communities should have the right to self-determination and to decide whether to accept or not accept the policies that affect their livelihood. As tourism is essentially a micro-enterprise, tourism lends itself to local entrepreneurial activity, and community-based tourism has emerged as a mechanism for fostering locally based tourism operations, as opposed to those whose financial interests are often located away from the tourist destination.

Moreover, as Information and Communication Technologies (ICTs) are beginning to be deployed in rural communities for the purpose of fostering local development, communities are able to implement electronic commerce in support of their CBT operations, and engage in e-CBT. Furthermore, it will be shown that the Internet is not only a natural partner for tourism, it also a natural partner for the market segment that e-CBT should target. With more than 600 million people on-line by September 2002, and more than 60per cent of them residing in Europe or North America, even small and remote communities with an Internet connection can address huge global markets.

The purpose of this paper is to introduce the concept of electronic commerce for community based tourism, e-CBT, as a mechanism for local development. E-CBT involves the operation of local tourism activities which are promoted across the internet by a community using a community based telecentre, which provides community access to information and communication technologies. The concept is presented as a method for fostering rural development in developing countries. Tourism is a principal export for developing countries and the least developed countries (LDCs). It is growing rapidly and is the most significant source of foreign exchange after petroleum. There is a general shift of tourism arrivals towards developing countries. Growth rates of international tourism receipts during the 1990s were, on average, 50per cent higher in the major developing country destinations than in comparison with the major developed country destinations. By far the largest single developing country international tourism destination is China.

The People's Republic accounted for US$10 billion in international tourism receipts in 1996, receiving 22.7 million international visitors, experiencing 19per cent annual growth rates of receipts since 1980. Together with earnings generated by the Hong Kong Special Administrative Region, China's 1996 receipts surpass US$20 billion. In 2001, China ranked fifth in the world's top tourism destinations, measured both by the number of international arrivals and by international tourism receipts. Yet in terms of Gross National Income per capita, China ranks 108 out of 173 countries in the World Bank's statistical indicators for 2001. China, Thailand and Indonesia together generated 40per cent of all international tourism receipts accruing to developing countries in 1996.

The World Tourism Organisation says there is a strong economic case for promoting tourism in developing countries, suggesting that affirmative action and pro-poor policies are able to go beyond trickle down and multiplier affects by unlocking opportunities for the poor within tourism (WTO 2002). Success in poverty alleviation through tourism depends, says the WTO, partly on effective community-public-private partnerships that serve to reduce financial leakages and increase economic linkages to the local economy. Financial leakages occur where a disproportionately low percentage of tourism revenues stays in the local market, and they reduce the development impact of tourism. Linkages with the local economy foster revenue retention from tourism activities, and they depend on quality, reliability and competitiveness of local products. WTO suggest various steps that can be taken to increase the benefits to the local economy in tourist destination areas, by;

- Facilitating local community access to the tourism market,
- Minimising the financial leakages from the local economy,
- Maximising the linkages of tourism to the local economy,
- Building on and complimenting existing livelihood strategies through employment and small enterprise development,
- Ensuring that tourism products contribute to local economic development not just to national revenue generation.
- Tourism is a principal export for 83per cent of developing countries and it is the principal export for one third of them.
- Developing countries had 292.6 million arrivals in 2000, an increase since 1990 of nearly 95per cent. The 40 least developed countries had 5.1 million international arrivals in 2000; they achieved an increase of 75per cent in the decade.
- 80per cent of the world's poor, those living on less than US$1 per day, live in 12countries. In 11 of these countries, tourism is significant and growing
- The developing countries are attracting an increasing share of global international tourist arrivals up from 20per cent in 1973 to 42per cent in 2000.

The developing countries and particularly the LDCs secured a larger increase in the income per international arrival between 1990 and 2000 than did the OECD or the European Union countries. The LDCs secured an increase of 45per cent between1990 and 2000 and the developing countries nearly 20per cent. This compares with18per cent for the OECD countries and 7.8per cent for the EU.

In 2000, tourism ranked third among the major merchandise export sectors for both developing countries and LDCs. If petroleum industry exports are discounted (and they are significant in only three) tourism is the primary source of foreign exchange in the 49 LDCs.

COMMUNITY BASED TOURISM

Community-based tourism provides alternative economic opportunities, which are in essence in rural areas. Community-based tourism is regarded as a tool for natural and cultural resource conservation and community development and it is closely associated with ecotourism, sometimes referred to as community-based ecotourism.

It is a community-based practice that provides contributions and incentives for natural and cultural conservation as well as providing opportunities for improved community livelihood. It has the potential to create jobs and generate entrepreneurial opportunities for people from a variety of backgrounds, skills and experiences, including rural communities and especially women.

Community-based tourism has been implemented in many developing countries, often in support of wildlife management, environmental protection and/or development for indigenous peoples.

Community tourism should;

- Be run with the involvement and consent of local communities. (Local people should participate in planning and managing the tour.)
- Give a fair share of profits back to the local community. (Ideally this will include community projects (health, schools, etc).)
- Involve communities rather than individuals. (Working with individuals can disrupt social structures.)
- Be environmentally sustainable. (Local people must be involved if conservation projects are to succeed.)
- Respect traditional culture and social structures.
- Have mechanisms to help communities cope with the impact of western tourists.
- Keep groups small to minimise cultural/environmental impact.
- Brief tourists before the trip on appropriate behaviour.
- Not make local people perform inappropriate ceremonies, etc.
- Leave communities alone if they don't want tourism. (People should have the right to say 'no' to tourism.)

Community based tourism occurs when decisions about tourism activity and development are driven by the host community. It usually involves some form of cultural exchange where tourists meet with local communities and witness aspects of their lifestyle. Eco-tourism also emphasises observation and learning by the tourist, alongside economic and cultural conservation, and the delivery of benefits that ensure long-term sustainability of communities and natural resources. In Nepal, the Tourism for Rural Poverty Alleviation Programme began in 2001, jointly funded by the United Nations Development Programme (UNDP), the UK Department for International Development (DFID) with advisory services from SNV (Stichting Nederlandse Vrijwilligers) a Dutch development organisation.

Operating in six remote locations, the programme employed social mobilisation and tourist awareness programmes in villages to empower local communities to manage their own tourism development. In Vietnam, the International Union for Conservation of Nature and Natural Resources (IUCN) or World Conservation Union, is operating a community based tourism pilot in Sa Pa, a highly visited area with colourful ethnic minorities. Funded mainly by the Ford Foundation, the goal of the project is to assist local stakeholders to achieve an environmentally, culturally and socio-economically sustainable form of tourism, establishing mechanisms that support the active participation of the community in tourism decision-making and implementation.

The Nam Ha ecotourism project in Lao PDR uses community-based tourism as a vehicle to integrate environmental and cultural conservation with sustainable socio and economic development. Working closely with local villagers, limits were set on the number of trekking tourists allowed each year so as not to overwhelm the communities and to ensure that tourist incomes supplement rather than replace other economic activities.

Typically, with community-based tourism, the community runs all of the activities that a tourist engages in; lodging, food, guiding and craft sales. Benefits include; economic growth in rural regions; the distribution of tourism revenue, which can foster improved welfare and equity in the industry; improved resource conservation by local people; and diversification of the regional and national tourism product.

Intertwined with community-based tourism in developing countries is the concept of pro-poor tourism. In most counties with high levels of poverty, tourism is a significant and/or growing component of the economy. Governments and aid agencies acknowledge that whilst economic growth is essential for poverty reduction, of itself, it is insufficient to ensure a significant reduction. Growth that is specifically pro-poor is a pre-requisite for significant progress towards agreed targets for poverty reduction.

Tourism has many characteristics that make it potentially pro-poor:

- It is a diverse industry, which increases the scope for wide participation,
- The customer comes to the product, providing important opportunities for linkages(*e.g.*, souvenir sales),
- It is highly dependent on natural capital (wildlife, scenery) and culture, assets that some of the poor have in abundance, even if they have few financial resources,

- Tourism can be more labour intensive than manufacturing,
- A higher proportion of benefits (jobs, trade opportunities) go to women.

Pro-poor tourism is defined as tourism that generates net benefits for the poor. It maximises the potential for eradicating poverty by developing appropriate strategies in co-operation with all major groups, indigenous and local communities. Benefits may be economic, but they may also be social, environmental or cultural. Pro-poor tourism is not a specific product or sector of tourism, but an approach to the tourism industry. The core activity is to increase access of the poor to economic benefits. Pro-poor tourism strategies unlock opportunities for the poor; whether for economic gain, other livelihood benefits, or participation in decision-making.

Early experience shows that pro-poor tourism strategies do appear able to 'tilt' the industry at the margin, to expand opportunities for the poor and have potentially wide application across the industry. Poverty reduction through pro-poor tourism can therefore be significant at a local or district level. Moreover, the poverty impact may be greater in remote areas, though the tourism itself may be on a limited scale. Most examples of community-based in tourism in developing countries qualify as pro-poor tourism as they are designed to foster development at grassroots levels.

EFFECTS OF TOURISM TAXATION

The analysis reveals that, unlike the traditional outcome of a deadweight loss associated with higher taxes, increasing taxes on tourism can be welfare improving. Tourism is being targeted as a growing source of tax revenue by governments across the world. However, tourism taxation can have significant effects on welfare, which should be taken into account when taxes are levied. Little research has been undertaken on the welfare effects of tourism taxation and, given the special characteristics of tourism as an export sector, direct application of the literature on commodity taxation and export taxation to tourism taxation is not appropriate. This paper examines the welfare effects of tourism taxation on residents of a tourist destination country within a partial equilibrium framework, in the context of fixed and variable prices.

It is also found that the higher the proportion of tourism demand in total demand, and the more inelastic tourism demand is relative to domestic demand, the higher will be the welfare gain. Tourism's role as one of the fastest growing economic activities in the world makes it a key target for taxation. As a major source of foreign currency receipts, tourism appears to be the salvation for governments faced with budgetary constraints and pressures to decrease their reliance on income tax and tariffs as sources of revenue. On the other hand, taxes on tourism have proliferated and there are now calls from international bodies and tourism businesses and consumers for reductions in the range and levels of taxes on tourism. Although the revenue gained from tourism taxation can be used to benefit the public by such means as increasing the provision of public services, it may also reduce welfare and act as a disincentive to tourism demand. Given the increasing importance of tourism taxation in both developed and developing countries, greater understanding of the economic underpinnings of tourism taxation and its effects is necessary, so that modeling of tourism taxation can be undertaken and appropriate policies for tourism taxation can be formulated. Tourism taxes thus have a direct effect on domestic consumption and hence domestic welfare.

Moreover, trade policies such as import tariffs aimed at the tradable sector also affect the tourism sector, with the tourists paying the domestic price instead of the world price. Most importantly, the burden of a tax on the tourism sector falls on both domestic residents and foreigners (tourists). Therefore, the burden of a tourism tax is a combination of the burden of an export tax and a domestic tax. Formal analysis of the welfare effects of tourism taxation is undertaken in section 4, and the fifth section of the paper includes some parameter values in the equations for the welfare effects in order to determine the results of tourism taxation in alternative contexts

TAXING THE TOURISM SECTOR

In practice, the tourism sector can be taxed either by taxing the businesses in the tourism sector or by taxing the tourists directly. Both methods may be implemented either via the general tax system of the economy or through special tourism taxes. The World Tourism Organisation (WTO, 1998) has identified 40 different types of taxes applied to the tourism sector in both developed and developing countries. They are given in the tourism tax typology.

Additional taxes relating to tourists' use of the natural environment and general taxes that also fall on tourists have also been included. Of the 45 taxes, 30 are directly payable by the tourists and 15 are levied on tourism businesses. Five broad sectors involved in tourism taxation can be identified, namely airlines and airports, hotels and other accommodation, road transportation, food and beverages and provider of tourism services. The practicality of taxing each of these sectors is highlighted below.

- *Airlines and airports:* In long haul destinations, international transport occupies a major part in the total cost of holiday packages and hence taxing this sector should, in principle, be lucrative. However, although this is an option for developed countries, this is beyond the reach of most developing countries because they normally do not own an airline company or if they do own one, it is often unprofitable. Revenue may, instead, be generated from airport-related taxes.
- *Hotels and other accommodation*: This is normally the most important

revenue generator of the tourism industry and is also easier to tax. However, the practicality of taxing the accommodation sector also varies between developed and developing countries and tends to be more problematic in the latter. The hotel sector is often highly subsidised or receives investment and tax incentives from the government in developing countries, with the aim of attracting foreign and domestic investment to the sector. The motivation is twofold, first to expand the sector as a part of a policy to expand the tourism industry and second, to protect the sector because it is a relatively unstable one due to its highly seasonal nature. The contradicting implication is that the easiest and major target for tourism taxation is most likely to be freed from taxation.

- *Taxis, food and beverages and tourism services:* These sectors are relatively easy to tax in industrialised countries but form part of fragmented small business sectors and do not normally contribute a major proportion of tourism revenue. They include such sectors as entertainments, handicrafts, jewellery and other souvenirs. In most developing countries, these activities form part of the informal sector or of the hard-to-tax formal sector and it is difficult to raise much revenue from this source. Ecotourism tax is a relatively new form of taxation that destinations such as the Balearics levy in an attempt to counter the environmental damage caused by mass tourism. Carbon tax and landfill tax are more general environmental taxes on the level of carbon emissions and wastes respectively, but are borne by tourists as well.

Although gambling (in-shop and racing) is not legal in some countries mainly due to religious opposition, casinos are socially accepted in several countries. Tourists are involved in gambling and casinos, and hence bear the tax associated with those activities. The tax can be levied on the suppliers rather than tourists as in the case of the UK where the betting tax that was initially levied on the gamblers is now levied on the gross profit of bookmakers.

TAXING TOURISTS

Since taxing tourism businesses is not always a lucrative way of raising tax revenue, much tax revenue from tourism is generated from consumption taxes and special tourism taxes applied directly to tourists' consumption. Consumption taxes take the form of general sales taxes or value added tax (VAT). Sales tax/VAT is levied in almost all countries, regardless of the tourism taxation policies.

Therefore, in the presence of this type of sales tax, tourists are being taxed without any deliberate tourism tax policy on the part of the government. In the spirit of optimal taxation, some countries discriminate between domestic and tourism consumption, such that the latter is taxed at a higher rate or an additional tourism tax is applied to tourists' consumption. However, this entails administration problems in enforcing and monitoring such taxes. Special tourism taxes are generally levied directly on tourists and they can take several forms.

Common forms include taxes on hotels and restaurants, passenger services, tourist transport, entry/exit taxes and hotel accommodation taxes. The last tax is the most common and, as the name suggests, hotel accommodation tax is simply a tax on the tourists' expenditure on accommodation. The rate levied usually depends on hotel class and the season. It is relatively easy to collect, although discrimination across hotel classes sometimes creates administrative problems. In countries such as Jamaica, it is levied at a flat rate amounting to around $4-12 per night, and in other countries it is an ad valorem tax, which differs across countries: for example, 13per cent in South Africa, 12.5per cent in Senegal and 7.5per cent in Grenada. Entry/exit taxes include those on airport departures, which are fixed amounts that have to be paid when leaving the country, on airport embarkation, which is paid on entering the country, and the visa fee.

These taxes are usually levied at a flat rate and are relatively small in amount: for example, the airport departure tax has been within the range $1-6 in Singapore, Indonesia, Malaysia, Philippines, and Thailand, and was set at $10 in Malawi, Tanzania and Zambia.

CONTROVERSY

The WTO (1998) posits that the nature of the tourism sector makes it a target for tax revenue not only because tourism taxes are easy to collect and easy to administer but also because international tourists are rarely voters in the destination country they visit. Most of the arguments in favour of taxing the tourism sector are based on the fact that tourism products are consumed jointly with unpriced natural amenities and public goods.

Unpriced natural amenities include the sun, sea and wildlife, while public goods can include security and health services. As Gray (1982) argues, "the question of public goods, their supply and their pricing, is relatively more important in tourism than in many other industries, in part, because of the needed role of the government in asset preservation and, in part, because of the greater role of the government in the normal routine when foreigners reside temporarily within its own borders."

The main reasons for tourism taxation can be considered under the following categories. Besides providing law and order, under which contracts can be enforced and property rights protected, so ensuring that the private sector is operating efficiently, one of the main roles of the government is to provide 'public goods'. The technical definition of public goods comprises the following: indivisibility, ie. commodities are not divisible into units that can be sold individually; non-excludability, ie. no one can be excluded from benefiting from the product; the free-rider problem, where it is difficult to charge users an appropriate fee.

Common examples of public goods include national defence and street lighting. The distinctive characteristics of public goods makes it difficult to provide them via the private sector because there is no price mechanism that controls the market. They can be provided only by the government, which uses its right to tax to generate the resources necessary to supply them. Domestic taxpayers usually finance the provision of such goods. The influx of tourists imposes an extra cost on the government relating to the provision of items such as greater security and an improved environment. As non-residents, tourists do not pay to finance these extra costs.

A tourist tax will, therefore, serve to redress the balance and impose the burden on those who are responsible for them. There are often user charges for some attractions, such as parks and safaris, but in other cases, such as street lighting and public security, enforcing payment is difficult. In such circumstances, taxing the may be the only way of 'charging' them for the public goods they consume.

Higher government revenue can increase welfare by such means as financing improvements in public services. Furthermore, it may help to reduce the burden of income taxation on domestic residents, and it may also be an alternative policy for countries that want to reduce their dependency on trade taxes while, at the same time, not imposing an additional burden on domestic residents.

The WTO (1988) estimates that 'tourist countries' obtain around 10-25per cent of their tax revenue from the tourism sector. In some small specialised tourism countries such as the Bahamas, over 50per cent of government revenue is generated from the tourism sector. In Mauritius, about 12-15per cent of tax revenue is collected directly and indirectly from the tourism sector. The tourism sector is an unusual sector for revenue generation. Bird (1992) believes that developing countries tend to under tax their tourism sector, failing to exploiting fully the economic rent emerging from the sector.

Such rent results from less than perfectly elastic demand for their tourism products, due to the differentiated nature of their natural amenities. The degree of inelasticity of demand depends, in part, on the degree of differentiation of the destination and affects the ability to tax. The greater the degree of differentiation of the destination, the more inelastic demand will be and, hence, the greater the scope for taxation.

Tourism product differentiation generally occurs in terms of types and quality of attractions (endowments), types and quality of goods and services sold in the country, geographical location and distance. Examples of attractions with very inelastic demand are the pyramids of Egypt, the Taj Mahal and the

Grand Canyon. Gray (1987) associates the demand for differentiated tourism products with 'wanderlust' tourism, involving seeing or doing something that is unique to the destination, as opposed to 'sunlust' tourism which refers to the sun, sea and sand destinations such as Mauritius and the Caribbean countries. 'Sunlust' destinations tend to have less inelastic demand because the tourism products tend to be less differentiated across countries.

Less than perfectly elastic demand implies that tourism gives rise to 'economic rents' which suppliers of tourism services may try to maximise and governments may attempt to tax. However, tourism is a composite product with multiple components, and each of the components can be taxed at a different rate. For example, Bonham *et al.* considered a room tax on hotel receipts in Hawaii and found that the tax resulted in an insignificant change in hotel revenue. Combs and Elledge found that a small ad-valorem tax room tax imposed on motels and other forms of tourist accommodation in the USA would have very little impact on the industry and would generate substantial revenue for the government.

However, an increase in taxation on one component of tourism can result in lower expenditure on another. In one of the first systematic tourism taxation studies, Mak and Nishimura investigated the effect of a hotel room tax on the length of stay of tourists in Hawaii. The results were that visitors' length of stay was insensitive to price changes and that an increase in the room tax would not reduce tourist arrivals in Hawaii significantly.

However, Mak and Nishimura also examined the effect of a hotel room tax on non-lodging consumption and find that tourists 'respond to marginal increases in price of lodging partly by reducing some of their non-lodging expenditures and partly by reducing their savings and/or spending at home'.

EXPORTABILITY

Taxation on tourism may be exportable in the sense that tourists bear the major burden of the taxation. The issue of tax incidence is important in this respect, as discussed in the context of the UK by Durbarry and Sinclair. One of the first studies that examined the tax incidence of tourism taxes explicitly was by Fujii *et al.*, who examined the incidence and the exportability of an ad valorem hotel room tax for Hawaii in a partial equilibrium framework.

Tax incidence refers to the distribution of the tax burden between the buyers and the hoteliers whereas tax exporting refers to the extent to which the burden of the tax is distributed between the residents and the non-residents. If the hotel industry is an enclave with a high proportion of foreign investment, then the distinction between tax incidence and tax exporting is minor because the incidence of the tax on the supplier is actually exported. Under a partial equilibrium framework, the incidence of a hotel room tax depends on the relative sizes of the elasticities of demand and of supply. Fujii *et al.* calculated the relative burden of the hotel tax on tourists and the tourism industry as the ratio of the supply and demand elasticities for accommodation. They estimated the demand function for accommodation and found that the price elasticities of demand were negative and significant, and also found supply to be less than perfectly elastic. Their results suggested that one-third of the hotel room tax was borne by the tourism industry and the rest by the tourists. They also showed that the hotel room tax was more readily exported than similar taxes levied on meals, drinks and entertainment and the general sales tax. Hence the exportability of tourism taxes is liable to vary between different components of the tourism product.

SUSTAINABILITY OF THE ENVIRONMENT

Many developing countries under balance of payments and foreign exchange pressure have targeted tourism as a means of development. In many cases, no proper management strategies have been formulated especially at the initial stage of the tourism development. Natural resources have been degraded to the point where environmental sustainability is threatened. Regulating the inflow of tourists and taxation are the two most popular tools used, or considered, to remedy the problem.

However, regulating the inflow of tourists may not be the ideal solution because it deliberately contracts the tourism sector and this may have negative repercussions on the economy. It should also be remembered that many countries are investing resources to expand the tourism sector, and therefore it would be contradictory to pursue these two policies simultaneously. Moreover, it is believed that unconstrained growth (not limiting tourist arrivals) is usually beneficial in the sense that it increases the level of per capita income, thus providing more funds for maintaining the environment and sustaining growth. On the other hand, regulation through taxation not only provides the government with revenue (if designed properly) but also targets only the activities and individuals involved in the environmental degradation process and is, therefore, an efficient way to tackle the problem.

Furthermore, with higher revenues, more resources will be available to sustain the development of the industry. The tourism sector does not only rely on the natural amenities in the country but also on public goods. A strong regulatory framework, such as maintaining high health and food preparation standards, is also important in the success of the tourism sector. Taxation can generate the necessary resources to provide these requirements. Of course, the tourism industry has no inherent right to have the taxes it pays ploughed back into the industry.

However, appropriate earmarking of tax revenue can help to sustain the tourism industry and also help to reduce and combat the associated degradation of the environment. The taxation issues involved in controlling environment degradation and sustaining tourism are similar. The basic method is to use the

Pigouvian tax, whereby the tax rate should correct for the divergence between the market price and the social marginal cost. Such taxes should be applied to all users, including both domestic residents and tourists, and should as far as possible be directed to the goods and services that generate the externalities so as to avoid inefficiencies.

If resources are to be exploited only to the economically desirable limit, then the social marginal cost (hence tax rate) should be set sufficiently high to include not only the opportunity costs to local residents in terms of environmental damage and congestion costs, but also the maximum possible rent extractable. On the other hand the price, hence the tax rate, should not be set so high as to hinder consumption of the product and tourist arrivals in the country. Congestion is an important facet of sustainability. High congestion, often caused by tourists themselves, reduces the quality of tourism services, which can lead to a reduction in arrivals, especially of high class and high spending tourists. The presence of crowds may detract from the enjoyment of tourists seeking solitude and privacy.

Discomfort in crowds, long queues at popular places, traffic congestion and an untidy environment will not only affect the quality of tourism services but also the quality of life of domestic residents. Tourism taxation may be used both to reduce the inflow of tourists and to compensate the local residents. However, many tourism activities are not priced, for example, sun, sea and sand, and if some are priced, the associated transaction costs relating to monitoring and enforcement are generally very high.

Thus, they are supplied at a zero fee to all users and the problem of free riders is difficult to avoid. In this context, regulatory processes such as parking fees near crowded beaches and taxes on car rental can be applied. An entry/exit tax, which is a fixed amount of money that tourists pay when they enter and leave the destination country, can also be used. An entry/exit tax is an easy way of extracting economic rents from the tourism services the destination country is selling because it is often a tax included in the airfare, unnoticed by many travellers. Sometimes countries discriminate between domestic residents and tourists, so that only tourists pay the tax. However, an entry/exit tax has some disadvantages.

First, by capturing rents from tourists, an entry/exit tax does not provide any incentive for tourism to reduce their demand for the specific good that is causing the externalities, as should optimally be the case. The tax will reduce the number of tourist arrivals. Hence not only the demand of the externality generating commodity will fall but demand for other tourism services will also fall because of the complementary nature of tourism demand. The economic benefits normally attached to expanding the tourism sector may then be constrained. Second, a uniform entry/exit tax does not offer first degree price discrimination in the sense that both low and high income tourists or short and long stay tourists pay the same amount of tax. This may discourage short stay tourists. Third, since it is levied mainly on foreigners, or at a higher rate on foreigners, it may fail to take full account of the full contribution of residents to environmental degradation.

Despite the advantages of tourism taxation, governments have been cautious about the magnitude of the taxes levied on the tourism sector because there are also negative effects associated with tourism taxation. A range of arguments has been levelled against tourism taxation, and some of the key arguments can be included under the following headings.

COSTS OF COMPLIANCE

Taxes levied directly on the tourism sector are sometimes difficult to justify. The amount of tax collected may be small but the tax can still have a substantial negative impact on the tourism sector, with repercussions on the overall economy. This happens especially with taxes levied directly on tourists, such as visa fees. It is not only the high fees required; there is often unnecessary bureaucracy (indeed discrimination between tourists of different nationalities) that can greatly raise the compliance costs for the tax payer and act as a deterrent to visiting the country.

This may contract tourist arrivals and affect other sectors related to the tourism sector. For countries where tourism comprises a major part of the economy, this can adversely affect the employment level and the balance of payments resulting in an overall contraction of the level of economic activity of the economy. The fiscal effects are likely to differ from country to country and from time to time, for three main reasons.

First, the effects depend on the policy of the government. If the government wants to maximise revenue, the tax rates will tend to be high. On the other hand, if the government wants to promote the sector, tax rates can be very low. In some case the government goes further by providing subsidies, such as subsidies for airport and parking infrastructure, and investment incentives to businesses. Second, the effects also depend on how important tourism is to the economy. Obviously, the higher the contribution of tourism in the economy, the higher will be the effects of tourism taxes on the government budget.

Thirdly, the number and types of linkages with other sectors in the economy and leakages from the economy that the tourism sector brings about are also important. As a general rule, linkages tend to increase government revenue and leakages lead to a reduction in revenue. The amount of revenue that is obtained from tourism taxation depends, in part, upon the value of the price elasticity of demand for tourism. If the price elasticity of demand is high, the effect of an increase in tax may be to decrease revenue.

In the case of tourist accommodation, all obtained demand elasticities for accommodation that were significantly different from zero. Hiemstra and Ismail reported a significant price elasticity of demand for the lodging industry based on a survey of the properties owned and managed by the American Hotel and Motel Association.

RETALIATION

Taxation generates revenue but, as in the case of trade taxes, it invites retaliation by other countries if they feel that the other government is unfairly treating their citizens. For example, Kenya and Tanzania introduced visa charges for UK citizens in retaliation to the application of visa fees by the UK on their citizens. Retaliation is always a threat and in most cases the eventual outcome is lower welfare for both countries. Tisdell (1983) showed how retaliation in the case of tourism taxes can lead to a lower economic surplus for both countries.

This is because the consumer surplus that the tourists from the leader country were enjoying in the retaliating country will disappear after the tax. The country with a more inelastic demand for tourism will lose less but, compared with the case without retaliation, both countries lose. However, if a developing country imposes, say, an entry tax on tourists who are mainly from developed countries, then retaliation will tend to affect the developing country to a lesser extent.

This is because the number of tourists from the developing country visiting the developed is fewer than the number of tourists from the developed countries who visit developing country.

WELFARE IMPLICATIONS OF TOURISM TAXATION

It is widely accepted in the literature that taxation should comply with three main principles: efficiency, equity and having a low disincentive to work effect. Tourism taxation may meet all three criteria or only some of them. The efficiency principle can be achieved because, unlike other taxes, tourism taxes can lead to an increase in welfare, thereby rendering tourism taxation more efficient than taxing other sectors.

The main reason why this occurs is that the presence of tourists increases the tax base for commodity taxation and hence higher tax revenue is generated. However, the welfare loss corresponding to a tax increase is not reflected in domestic welfare since utility of tourists is not included in the social welfare function. This is explained in more detail below.

The equity principle can also be achieved as some tourism products are classified as luxuries. Following the redistributive effect of taxation literature, taxing such products entails positive equity effects because they are consumed mainly by individuals from the higher income brackets. The disincentive to work effect of taxation is also considered to be an important criterion for good taxation principles. It is believed that taxation leads to a disincentive to work because the more a person works, the more tax the person pays, so that to avoid paying high taxes, people work less and take more leisure. This effect is more notable with direct income taxation, but Corlette and Hague demonstrate how commodity taxation can be used to circumvent the problem. They argue that goods that complement leisure more can be taxed at a higher rate. The intuition is that by taxing goods that are complementary to leisure, the price of leisure will increase.

Hence, people will be less willing to undertake leisure activities, thereby reducing the disincentive to work effect of taxation. Taxing tourism products reinforces the above proposition because taxing tourism is equivalent to taxing commodities that are complementary to leisure, thereby not only reducing the disincentive effects inflicted by the commodity tax but also reducing those introduced by income taxation, hence making the overall taxation system more efficient.

The latter two principles will not be considered further here but the focus of the analysis will be on the first principle and will concern the welfare implications of tourism taxation, based on the normative analysis of the taxation literature using demand and supply analysis.

A practical and common method of taxing the tourism sector is through consumption taxes. Consumption taxes can either take the form of special taxes designed specifically to tax the tourism sector, such as a hotel room tax, or can be levied through the general sales tax system. Tourism may be the only export sector that can be taxed using the domestic sales tax. This is because of the special nature of the tourism product as an exported commodity. In contrast to conventional commodity exports, foreign tourists who want to consume tourism travel to the exporting country; ie. rather than sending goods across boundaries, consumers move across boundaries to consume the product. Consumption of goods and services will thus have a non-tourism consumption and a tourism consumption component.

Therefore, in an economy where a sales tax already exists, the tourism sector is taxed even without any deliberate actions from the government. This is, of course, true unless there is price discrimination between local consumers and tourists in the sense that tourists are exempted from sales tax.

However, this happens rarely, especially in developing countries, and if price discrimination is present, it is generally in favour of the domestic residents rather than the tourists. It is widely accepted in economics that there is a deadweight loss (a reduction in social welfare) attached to almost all taxes.

Sales tax may not always be welfare diminishing in the presence of tourists. Taxing tourists using the existing sales tax can be welfare improving. The presence of tourists means higher demand and, thus, a higher tax base that will generate more tax revenue. On the other hand, part of the burden of this additional tax revenue is borne by the tourists and is not accounted for in domestic welfare. Therefore with higher tax revenue and a relatively lower reduction in domestic consumer surplus, the increase in the tax rate in the presence of tourists will have a lower deadweight loss, and in some cases a windfall gain may emerge. In this section, we examine this issue within a one commodity partial equilibrium framework. Although, the latter does not take account of general equilibrium effects, it provides a range of interesting insights about the possible sources and directions of welfare gains or losses. We consider two cases, the fixed producer price and the variable producer price case.

11

Indigenous Group Traveling and Service

Aboriginal tourism gives Indigenous people the chance to tell their story in their way, to share cultural insights, traditional practices and contemporary concerns with non-Indigenous Australians and international visitors. Indigenous communities view tourism as a means of both educating others about Indigenous culture, and creating employment and training opportunities at a local level. Aboriginal tourism experiences are varied, but a common thread is the inclusion of insights about the cultural knowledge, lifestyle and beliefs of Australia's Indigenous people.

Aboriginal tourism goes beyond the lifestyles and traditions of Indigenous people who live on homelands, out-stations and remote communities to include the urban experience of Australia's Indigenous persons. Rock art tours, politically themed art exhibitions, live theatre and stories from the Dreamtime told around a campfire are all expressions of Indigenous culture. The National Aboriginal and Torres Strait Islander Tourism Industry Strategy defines Indigenous tourism as including all forms of participation by Indigenous persons in tourism:

- As employers
- As employees
- As investors
- As joint venture partners
- Providing Indigenous cultural tourism products
- Providing mainstream tourism products.

In Aboriginal culture the significance of land is intimately bound in the spirituality surrounding the origins of landscapes, animals, plants and people. Traditional owners, or custodians, have a responsibility to look after the environmental, cultural and spiritual wellbeing of the land. This unique relationship and respect for the land is increasingly attracting visitors seeking to 'touch the earth'.

Another key element of Aboriginal tourism is cultural control, considered crucial to maintaining authenticity and preventing cultural exploitation and cultural appropriation. Intellectual and cultural property rights, along with copyright issues, are of particular concern to Indigenous. Authenticity is important to international visitors. The Wet Tropics World Heritage Area (WHA) was declared in 1988. It covers an area of 894 420 hectares and mainly includes tropical rainforest extending from Townsville to Cooktown in northeastern Queensland. It is managed by the Wet Tropics Management Authority (WTMA) based in Cairns, and the Queensland Parks and Wildlife Service (QPWS) is responsible for field management and permits for activities in the WHA.

There are twenty Indigenous language groups in or near the Wet Tropics WHA, which also includes Indigenous communities such as Yarrabah, south of Cairns, Mona Mona, near Kuranda, and Wujal Wujal, in the Daintree region. The involvement of Rainforest Indigenous communities is set out in Wet Tropics WHA legislation, the Wet Tropics Management Plan 1998, and in the key policy document Protection through Partnerships.

WTMA negotiates with Rainforest Indigenous groups on cultural protocols, planning, site management, infrastructure, walking-tracks, and joint management agreements. Three Indigenous community liaison officers are employed on contract by WTMA, to consult Indigenous groups on management issues.

Rainforest-based nature tourism and ecotourism is a major activity in the Wet Tropics WHA. In 1998, more than 210 commercial tour operators had permits to operate in the Wet Tropics region. Half of all Queensland nature-based tour operators are located in Far North Queensland, with the majority visiting sites in the Wet Tropics. The region has an estimated 2.8 million visitors per year. High-use areas include Mossman Gorge with 500 000 visitors and the Daintree with over 300 000 visitors per year.

Indigenous tourism ventures include Kuku Yalanji Dreamtime Walks in Mossman Gorge; Native Guide Safari Tours conducted by Hazel Douglas in the Daintree; Tjapukai Aboriginal Cultural Park in Cairns; Menmuny Museum in Yarrabah; Nganyaji Cultural Centre in Ravenshoe; and guided rainforest walks at Malanda Falls with Ngadjonjii elder, Ernie Raymont. Kuku Yalanji art and craft workshops, storytelling and Indigenous-guided rainforest walks are included at the Daintree Ecolodge.

New Indigenous tourism ventures in 2002 include Kuku Yalanji Coastal Habitat Tours marketed by Daintree Ecolodge; Bunda Dibandji Art Site Tour near Kuranda, a joint venture between Djabugay Tribal Aboriginal Corporation and Cedar Park Resort; and Gugubarabi Echo Creek Walk in the Tully Valley, a partnership between El Rancho del Rey and local Jirrbal guides, Robert and Ernie Grant. Other Rainforest Indigenous participation in Wet Tropics tourism includes employment as QPWS rangers, the construction of boardwalks, and cultural heritage signs in national parks. Tourism in the Wet Tropics WHA directly generates $179 million, while flow-on tourism expenditure in the local region is around $753 million. At present, Rainforest Indigenous groups do not receive any licensing income from tourism operations in the Wet Tropics and visitors do not pay park entry fees at popular rainforest sites such as waterfalls, lakes and rainforest boardwalks in National Parks.

Tourism use should contribute to the conservation and understanding of Aboriginal cultural heritage and help Aboriginal people as tourism industry participants to achieve economic and social benefits.

Apart from consulting with traditional owners about site management, there is limited Indigenous participation in the development and management of tourism in the Wet Tropics WHA. Indigenous cultural and land issues are addressed by the North Queensland Land Council representing Wet Tropics native title claimants, Indigenous land management agencies and by Indigenous community liaison officers. New cultural protocols will guide consultations with Indigenous peoples about permit applications in the Wet Tropics. Wet Tropics nature-based tourism strategy Indigenous involvement in rainforest-based tourism is a central part of the Wet Tropics Nature Based Tourism Strategy.

This tourism strategy for the Wet Tropics World Heritage Area of North Queensland aims to 'facilitate Aboriginal involvement in (nature) tourism and tourism management'. It also acknowledges that 'Rainforest Aboriginal people have native title rights and are partners in management of and participation in nature-based tourism in the Wet Tropics'.

The Strategy has policy statements on 'Rainforest Aboriginal People's Rights and Interests', including the cultural responsibilities of native title landholders, visitor site management involving traditional owners, and Indigenous involvement in nature-based tourism. This included participation, employment and training in tourism, interpretation of natural and cultural values and partnerships in tourism, such as cultural tours at Mossman Gorge.

The Bama Wabu Rainforest Aboriginal Association was listed as a key partner in Wet Tropics marketing guidelines, monitoring visitor sites, and setting accreditation levels for tour operators. Indigenous groups, though, were not involved in permit approvals for commercial tour operators in the Wet Tropics. This Strategy endorsed nature-based tourism in the Wet Tropics WHA that promotes Indigenous cultural heritage values and empowers Indigenous peoples as participants in the tourism industry. ATSIC, Bama Wabu and local Indigenous groups contributed to the policies and principles for the Wet Tropics Nature Based Tourism Strategy.

Consultation with traditional owners about site planning and management was required for most of the popular visitor areas in the Wet Tropics WHA. Rainforest Indigenous interests in tourism or cultural interpretation were also mentioned for eighteen visitor sites, including Mossman Gorge, Cathedral Fig Tree, Lake Barrine, Lake Eacham, Tully Gorge, and five scenic waterfalls: Murray, Josephine, Millstream, Blencoe and Wallaman Falls.

Other sites are under review with traditional owners about tourism concerns. The Strategy also states the need for assessment of the impacts of tourism on Indigenous cultural landscapes in the Wet Tropics. It does not address the specific programmes or training required for developing Indigenous tourism ventures at key visitor sites.

Wet Tropics Walking Strategy

The Wet Tropics Walking Strategy identified 145 managed walks in the Wet Tropics WHA region. Rainforest peoples were identified as key stakeholders with opportunities for walk management and cultural tourism. This Strategy acknow-ledged the cultural significance of walking tracks with many based on traditional trading routes through rainforest areas. Indigenous participation in this Strategy included employment through tourism operations, guided walks, track construction and maintenance. Negotiation on walking-track routes, protection of cultural sites, permits for commercial operations, and resources to fund Rainforest groups in track construction were highlighted. The Indigenous cultural setting was one of four key criteria used to assess walk experiences, focusing on Indigenous history, use, perceptions, names, cultural associations and stories about walkways.

Walkingtrack management by community rangers and Indigenous cultural walks were also identified for key rainforest areas such as Malanda Falls, Bare Hill, Wabunga Wayemba, Echo Creek Falls, Barron Gorge, and Murray Falls/ Kirrama Range. Some eighty per cent of the Wet Tropics WHA is claimable under native title legislation and sixteen claims covering 282 966ha have been lodged to date.Land-use agreements have been negotiated recently by WTMA with the Mona Mona and Wujal Wujal Aboriginal communities. Indigenous Land Use (ILU) agreements have also been reached with major tourism developments in the Cairns region. These agreements cover Skyrail Rainforest Cableway and Tjapukai Aboriginal Cultural Park, located on adjacent sites under a native title claim, with guarantees of employment for the local Djabugay people, protection of cultural heritage, and Indigenous approval of cultural presentations.

In 2002, the Mamu Aboriginal Corporation and Johnstone Shire Council, based in Innisfail, signed an ILU Heads of Agreement for a proposed new rainforest canopy walkway in the Wooroonooran National Park.

This Agreement also provides for Indigenous employment, protection of cultural heritage, and cultural tourism input at the Mamu canopy walk, during and after construction. The Queensland Ecotourism Plan 2003-2008 (Tourism Queensland 2002) also recognises the importance of negotiating native title claims in managing protected areas for ecotourism.

Indigenous Tourism in the Wet Tropics WHA

Kuku Yalanji Dreamtime Walks in Mossman Gorge won the 2002 Tourism

Queensland Award for Aboriginal and Torres Strait Islander Tourism, previously won by Tjapukai Aboriginal Cultural Park. However, this tourism venture operated by the Mossman Gorge Aboriginal Community depends on CDEP wages for guides and is not open on weekends. Indigenous tour operators also require QPWS permits in national parks and approval from WTMA to build new infrastructure such as visitor centres and walking tracks in the WHA.

Indigenous tours also compete with other rainforest day tours offered from Cairns, Port Douglas and Mission Beach, and mainly attract self-drive independent travellers rather than regular tour groups. Thus new Indigenous guided tours in 2002 are partnerships with established rainforest lodges in the Wet Tropics. There are other key issues for developing Rainforest Indigenous tourism in the Wet Tropics WHA. Tasting rainforest fruits (bush tucker) are part of an Indigenous cultural experience that may be constrained by seasonal availability, or environmental laws that prohibit taking or using natural resources in protected areas. One Indigenous tour operator in the Wet Tropics used to let visitors taste rainforest fruits, but a sign in the operator's vehicle now asks guests not to touch or eat anything in the rainforest. Telling tourists how (Rainforest) Indigenous peoples ate bushfoods and utilised the natural environment, as a past practice, seems to contradict the image of Indigenous culture as 'alive and authentic'.

Since 1990, Rainforest Indigenous peoples have sought to have the Wet Tropics officially re-listed by the World Heritage Convention for its Indigenous cultural values, along with current natural heritage values, in order to manage jointly the WHA. With this official cultural recognition, 'they would become equal partners rather than seen as "stakeholders"' in Wet Tropics' management, including tourism. Rainforest Indigenous groups did not consent to WHA listing of the Wet Tropics region, neither have they benefited economically from rainforest tourism in the area.

Funding for new tourism infrastructure such as rainforest walking tracks and cultural centres has been provided through the Queensland Heritage Trails Network. Ongoing funding for Indigenous groups to maintain and preserve Wet Tropics WHA values is required, drawn from an environmental levy on visitors. ILU agreements for major tourism projects such as Tjapukai, Skyrail and the Mamu Canopy Walk have generated Indigenous employment and protection of cultural heritage.

Allocation of commercial tourism permits to Rainforest Indigenous groups for key sites, with leaseback or licensing arrangements for tour operators, would also increase the economic benefits of tourism for Indigenous communities.

Putting the 'ECO' in Tourism

Bicycling on back roads. Trekking a 2,000-year-old trail. Crouching in the sand to measure a giant sea turtle. Sipping chai and savoring chapati prepared at a local Indian restaurant. However diverse the modern vacation, there's a common thread that ties each together: the traveller's thirst for discovery, passion for authenticity and interest in helping preserve and protect the planet.

"We're longing for gung-ho, do-something, learn-something, give-back-something vacations that will exhilarate us and leave us feeling good," write Daniel and Sally Wiener Grotta in The Green Travel Sourcebook, eloquently capturing the sentiment of the globe-trotting environmentalist. "We want vacations that will allow us to experience intimately the people and places we visit, while not inadvertently polluting the environment or contributing to an oppressive political regime, and perhaps make the world a better place."

Defining Green Travel

Ecotourism, or ecotravel, strives to do just that. "Ecotravel helps conserve fragile ecosystems, support endangered species and habitats, preserve indigenous cultures and develop sustainable local economies," sums up Megan Epler Wood, president of The International Ecotourism Society. "By looking at travel alternatives and making informed choices, you can minimize your impact and positively contribute to the conservation of natural environments, local economies and cultures." That's something the mainstream travel industry has yet to accomplish. In popular resort areas like Cancun and Hawaii, overbuilt waterfront hotels have contributed to beach erosion, flooding and the disappearance of natural wetlands, while generating mountains of garbage without adequate means of disposal. The rapid growth of the trekking industry in Nepal has increased pollution in Kathmandu and caused dangerous crowding and destruction of trails; logging for hotel building materials and cooking fires has led to deforestation, flooding and landslides as far away as Bangladesh.

More than 500 million people travel for leisure each year, making tourism the world's largest industry at $425 billion and climbing, according to the World Tourism Organization. Tourism provides 10 per cent of the world's income and employs almost one-tenth of its workforce. Ecotourism, although growing by 20 to 30 per cent a year, still represents less than one-tenth of the total tourism industry.Although "ecotourism" attempts to recognize the incredibly complex interactions among the environment, culture, economy and travel, it often eludes a clear definition. Guidelines are offered by such diverse groups as the United Nations Environmental Programme, Conservation International, the American Society of Travel Agents, Sierra Club and Mountain Travel Sobek. "Certified ecotourism" has recently been introduced in Australia, offering consumers a "Good Housekeeping"-type seal like those used for certified organic produce and sustainably harvested wood.

Touring with a Purpose

Ultimately, however, the responsibility for the impact of your travel rests not with a label, but with you. Be an activist—traveling the world as a dedicated ecotourist is not a spectator sport. "Ecotravellers ask lots of questions," says M.J. Kietzke, team coordinator of Co-op America Travel Links, which matches members requesting ecotravel with the operators or destinations that meet their needs.

"Because ecotourism is consumer driven," she says, "these questions help create a green demand for responsible travel options." If you choose all organized ecotour, ask about the trip fee. Besides responsibly sourced food and lodging, it can also help defray the cost of fieldwork, support local education or health programmes and leave economic dividends with the host community.

(Often, if paid to a nonprofit organization, the fees for service trips are also partially tax-deductible.) Ask whether you'll be visiting a place during the most heavily traversed time of year, contributing to overcrowding, and whether you'll be using mass transportation, to reduce pollution, and eating regional cuisine, to support local markets.

The answer to the most vital question, however, still hangs in the air: Can ecotourism help connect us with the rest of the world, and by doing so, actively make it a better place? There are many who believe it can. The following examples are but a sampling of the vast array of ecotravel options and operators, for all budgets and for all age groups.

Whether you have a few days or a few months, these ideas offer a glimpse into an amazing world, one we must either learn to protect or lose forever. Participants on Oceanic Society Expeditions need no prior scientific training, but their enthusiastic contributions will support the research that leads to environmental protection of marine life in Belize. This small, diverse Central American country nestled along the Caribbean Sea is still captivatingly wild. As of 1992, 90 per cent of Belize's forests were very much intact, and much of the reef system—the second longest in the world—was considered so valuable that it received World Heritage protected status.

Oceanic Society groups in Belize, under the guidance of top specialists in the field, alternate between conducting scientific research on dolphins—including observing their behaviour and recording their vocalizations—and taking naturalist-guided excursions, snorkeling in the pristine waters around Sergeants Caye, or birdwatching in the mangrove lagoons. To avoid tourist-saturated San Pedro on Ambergris Caye, the Expeditions are now based on Spanish Lookout Caye at the Belizean-owned Spanish Bay Resort.

The solar-powered resort offers its guests sun-washed cabanas over the water and native family-style cuisine in the main lodge. Evening slide shows and discussions about the dolphins, reef and mangrove ecology supplement the daily experiences. "These trips help us learn, grow and give back," says Elly Schaefer, a recent volunteer. Beginning in 2001, the dolphin project will move to the Blackbird-Oceanic Society Field Station at Blackbird Caye, and Spanish

Bay will host a project on coral reefs. For over 30 years, Mountain Travel Sobek has helped thousands of cubicled office workers transform themselves into modern-day replicas of Indiana Jones. Although this ecotravel doesn't scrimp on comfort and cuisine, environmentally sensitive practices like solar showers and leave-no-trace camping are part of the painstakingly planned cultural and wilderness experience.

Breathtaking describes both the spectacular landscape and high-altitude effects that come from trekking with Mountain Travel Sobek's ecotrip in the Annapurna Himal region of Nepal. The magical panorama includes some of the highest mountains on the planet, 20,000-plus-footers like Annapurna South, Annapurna I and III and Machapuchare, the so-called "Matterhorn of Nepal." A tattered topographic map will lead you along ancient, stone-stepped passageways and narrowly carved trails, through terraced rice paddies, rhododendron, oak and bamboo forests. The journey brings you, too, in close contact with the Gurung and Tamang clans, who have practiced sustenance agriculture in the region for centuries.

An active supporter of global nonprofits, Mountain Travel Sobek and the grassroots conservation work of white-water rafters led in 1993 to the preservation of the Tatshenshini River in Canada and Alaska as an international park, saving it from development as a giant, open-pit copper mine.

In the rainforests of Guatemala, slash-and-burn agriculture and other deforestation pressures continue to close in on the four-million-acre Maya Biosphere Reserve, which contains the popular Mayan temple complex of Tikal and the El Peru and Tikal National Parks. Conservation International (CI), along with USAID/Guatemala, the Guatemalan government, the National Council for Protected Areas and local conservation organizations, has set out to redirect development there in a more life-preserving direction.

The Mayan Trails, or Caminos Mayas, provides ecotravellers with the opportunity to explore both the cultural and natural heritage found beneath the forest canopy of Guatemala's Peten region. Three distinct trail systems await the ecotraveller: The Scarlet Macaw, El Mirador, and Zotz-Tikal. Hosted by communities along the path and guided by local experts, each offers a spectacular glimpse of flora and fauna—tropical birds such as Mot Mots, Macaws, Toucans and Trogons, and spider and howler monkeys—and the ancient Mayan ruins. Accommodations are at rustic campsites where guests rest in hammocks with protective mosquito nets, falling asleep to the late-night symphony of nocturnal rainforest life.

"The services, including meals, lodging, guides and horses or boats, are offered by the communities themselves," says Juan Carlos Bonilla, former coordinator for CI's Ecotourism Enterprise Development and Marketing Programme. "Conservation International is trying to build community-based, conservation-savvy entrepreneurship, not that big of a stretch."

Scotland is a hill walker's paradise. A journey there features rugged mountains, heather-covered moors, sparkling lochs, swift-flowing streams and cragged coastlines. The country's wilderness—from alpine flowers to colonies of Max shearwaters, guillemots, razor bills and Arctic terns—complements its ages-old castles and ancient Standing Stones.

Ecotravellers on the Wilderness Travel trip make their way through the highlands to the poignant Isle of Sky, rich in tradition and a spectacular landscape created by ancient volcanic activity. At a local pub, the Gaelic language still hangs heavy during discussion of the latest rugby match. After a spirited day of hiking, you'll find yourself warmly invited into this proud culture—perhaps for a "wee dram." A quaint country inn will welcome you to stop and rest for the night.

"Many of [our clients] see tourism as contributing to a more sustainable economy," says Barbara Banks, director of marketing and new trip development for Wilderness Travel. Rather than engage in destructive activities that may "benefit a region in the short term," she says, "the host communities can safeguard their land and bring money into the economy for years to come."

The sun-bleached and wind-swept slope on which Concordia Eco-Tents rests contrasts with the lush green landscape of the surrounding Virgin Islands National Park on the island of St. John. It's difficult to imagine that Maho Bay Eco-Tents, Concordia's sister resort, nestles among the forested terrain just a short drive away.

Concordia Eco-Tents is an ongoing experiment in the practical use of sustainable design. On St. John, where water is a precious commodity, owner and developer Stanley Selengut was inspired to create truly low-impact accommodations—a resort that brings people literally closer to nature. Guests collect their own solar-heated water in a cistern. Solar panels and wind generate much of the electricity that powers energy-efficient lighting and a small refrigerator. Floors and boardwalks are made with a recycled composite wood and each eco-tent includes a composting toilet with low-water flush.

"Living within the Earth's resources is something that we have to do to survive as a race," says Selengut. "There are a growing number of people interested in these problems, and we're probably one of the most popular resorts in the Caribbean because of it." Vistas of undeveloped coastline and sparkling turquoise water, accompanied by a constant breeze, certainly don't hurt either.

Great, fluttering butterflies, dragonflies the size of softballs, and huge spiders resting on shimmering strands of web, melt into the lush forest understory of the Gunung Leuser National Park in Sumatra, Indonesia. This steamy, tropical rainforest is also home to endangered orangutans, known locally as the "humans of the forest," and the subject of the Earthwatch expedition called Orangutan Health. Joining an Earthwatch expedition is an opportunity to both explore the world and assist the scientific community. Volunteers for the Sumatran project follow orangutans, making behavioural observations from close distances, in the hopes of learning how these lumbering primates use specific plants to heal themselves.

Situated at the edge of the park along the Bohorok River, the base camp is what you might expect from such a jungle adventure: a simple, clean bungalow with a bed and mosquito net, cold-water showers, Asian toilets and freshly made Indonesian dishes of rice, fish, chicken, vegetables and amazing tropical fruit.

The diverse projects and global presence of Earthwatch attracts volunteers from all over the world. The trips, which usually last several weeks, are organized by research focus, and the fee, which covers the meals and accommodations of volunteers, also directly supports the research of leading scientists in the field. On the Sumatra expedition, besides tough hiking terrain, high humidity and manic mosquitoes, the nearly two-million-acre park also harbors 130 mammal species (including gibbons, leopards and Sumatran rhinos) and 325 species of birds. So there's plenty to do when not observing orangutans. When travellers to any of the U.S. national parks venture forth from their cars for more than just a quick bathroom break, their experiences can be transforming.

Numerous wildlife interpretive programmes, which offer travellers valuable insights to area flora and fauna as well as the unique histories of the parks themselves, help put the all-important aspect of education in ecotravel. Grand Teton National Park in the U.S.

Rocky Mountains is one of the most majestic—high enough to support a dozen mountain glaciers, with 12 Teton peaks that reach above 12,000 feet. Grand Teton itself rises 13,770 feet above the bucolic valley of Jackson Hole, the Snake River threading the terrain below. Plant communities thrive there, from ribbons of riparian plants to sagebrush fiats, lodgepole pine forests, subalpine meadows and alpine stone fields. The nonprofit Teton Science School offers Wildlife Expeditions, a programme in which locally trained wildlife biologists teach people not only about the wildlife, but also wildlife viewing ethics and habitat preservation.

These specialized safari-style tours help visitors turn a casual trip to the park into a more intimate, ecologically friendly experience. "Often times, people approach wildlife, endangering themselves and disturbing an animal's natural behaviours," says Christy Bradburn, administrative coordinator for Wildlife Expeditions. "We teach people how to enjoy wildlife and understand their natural history."

Immeasurably rich in geography, ecology, culture and history, Bolivia is home to expansive cloud forests, unique salt flats, savannas and the snow-capped Andes, making it one of the most biodiverse portions of the Amazon region. Tread Lightly trips to Bolivia, completely set up through in-country operating partners, offer backstage views of the prehistoric ruins and indigenous villages of the mystical islands of the Sun and Moon in the expansive Lake Titicaca, at 3,810 feet the highest navigable lake in the world. Tread Lightly provides intimate cultural and natural experiences for ecotravellers to Latin America. It favours lodges that respect natural surroundings, carefully use water and other valuable resources, and employ alternative energy and waste-disposal techniques. Tread Lightly partners sponsor guide-training courses that provide rich careers for locals, helping preserve community integrity while increasing awareness for the environmental diversity and fragility of their surroundings.

Visits to Potosi and the magnificent capital city of Sucre offer ecotravellers an opportunity to enjoy Bolivia's unique cultural, as well as natural, attractions. Located at an altitude of nearly 13,100 feet, Potosi is one of the highest cities in the world and best known for the extraordinary quantities of silver extracted from Cerro Rico, "Rich Mountain."

Amidst a sea of cruise ships competing for the honour of biggest and most grandiose, the 100-passenger Galapagos Explorer II is putting luxury in a more intimate, and environmentally sustainable, context. "We want to be the most environmentally friendly ship in the Galapagos," says Freddy Espinel, hotel manager of the Explorer II. He proudly points to practices like on-board desalinization of water; its purification with ozone, rather than chlorine; composted biodegradable waste and recyclables flown to the mainland; and the use of only biodegradable soaps and detergents.

While the service is impeccable and on-board atmosphere inviting, the islands themselves are the real showstoppers. On excursions escorted by the ship's naturalists (trained by Galapagos National Park) visitors see firsthand the unique adaptations of island fauna, such as flightless cormorants, marine iguanas, giant tortoises and Darwin's finches. Opportunities for photography are rife, as is snorkeling with schools of brightly-coloured fish or hiking in search of the more perfect vista.

Small group size and tight Park Service control help protect the fragile ecosystem and ensure that even on this limited terrain more wildlife than tourists are encountered. The new interpretation centre on San Cristobal Island is well worth exploring, and after you return to the ship for some native Ecuadorian cuisine and to sail to your next destination, you can watch a slide show about the natural history of the archipelago, discuss with fellow shipmates environmental challenges faced by the islands, or browse through the science library on board.

Winding along the sweeping valleys and rolling hills of unglaciated southwestern and central-western Wisconsin, the Elroy-Sparta State Trail tempts both bicyclists and walkers alike. Interrupted occasionally by cavernous rock tunnels through which bikers pass, the trail showcases local history and wildlife as it crosses trout streams and weaves through farmlands and hardwood forests.

By staying in quaint bed and breakfasts, eating at family-owned restaurants and shopping for unique gifts or handmade Amish furniture along the 32-mile trail, visitors help preserve the area, support struggling agricultural communities and revive interest in natural corridors for wildlife and recreation.

The Elroy-to-Sparta trail is among the first of the U.S. rail-trails, recreational trails created from abandoned railroads, advocated by the nonprofit Rails-to-Trails Conservancy. Such trails provide a link among historic, cultural and natural sites, boost sagging local economies and, in some cases, completely revive economically depressed towns.

Playing hopscotch across the landscape, the number of trails has grown from 75 in 1986 to more than 1,000 today; they cover 11,000 miles.

Ecotourism operators and "free independent travellers" each share a commitment to tread lightly on the land and culture, and support the local economy at their destination. Ecotourism is not defined by the distance traveled, but rather how it's accomplished and what is experienced, so don't overlook natural attractions like rail-trails right in your own backyard.

After all, for most travellers, a fully satisfying journey can be one of less than 100 miles.

Eco-Cultural Tourism in India

There is an urgent and growing need for local/regional/national/international peace and security. This may be broadly ascribed to the increasing conflicts arising out of social, economic, religious and political factors. Peace and sustainability, considered as the indicators of development are threatened due to a myriad of conflicts and they are more visible than ever before in India. Tourism considered as a Global Peace Industry has greater potentials to reduce these conflicts. This paper analyses the threats to peace and sustainability and indicates that the newly emerging Heritage Eco-cultural Tourism holds the key for the promotion of peace and sustainability.

As we enter into the next millennium and the birth of a new global era, we are confronting the urgent need for local/regional/national/international peace and security more than in the past. This may be broadly ascribed to the increasing conflicts arising out of social, economic, religious and political factors. The widening gap between the haves and have-nots, have further accelerated these conflicts. Hence, we are seeking universal human rights and universal human progress and prosperity.

One powerful indicator of such a development is the fact that more people are traveling from more countries than ever before, making travel and tourism the worlds largest industry. Its growth is expected to continue with globalization and as people everywhere seem determined to exercise their right to travel and to make their world a more familiar place in the spirit of peace and friendship. Tourism itself has always been a peace-based industry and may be considered as a Global Peace Industry. In the face of current human population increases and worldwide ecological degradation, intact and healthy ecosystems are becoming the world's most sought-after tourism destinations. Culture and Heritage besides peace and harmony in such areas attract special groups of tourists, who demand quality products.

Peace and sustainability, considered as the indicators of development are threatened due to a myriad of conflicts—Social, Economic, political, cultural and Environmental. These conflicts usually confront multiple and diverse stakeholders such as state institutions, religious organizations, communities, indigenous ethnic groups, local institutions, private development and non-government organizations, international organizations, and many other players.

Wide differences in culture, knowledge, power, influence, and resources characterize these groups. Even though most conflicts essentially develop in a local framework, they are also frequently connected at regional, national and even international levels, transcending political and geographical boundaries including non-represented interests (*e.g.* future generations).

Such complexity explains, in part, the lack of sustained attention that conflicts receive. In addition, many conflicts in India are often dealt with unprofessionally and result in frustrations, violence, greater inequities, and negative impacts on quality of life, economic and social processes and in the natural resources themselves.

The most common methods of intervention in conflicts tend to be centralized, hierarchical, and sectorial, with a predominantly technical and adversarial (judicial) and at times political. Seldom do they achieve a reasonable level of satisfaction for all interested parties.

Hence, we are urgently in need of alternative paradigms for development—we are moving from the narrower 'reductionist', 'reactive' and 'bureaucratic' approaches to 'wholistic/Integrated or Systems' view of looking at issues, 'pro-active' policies and 'participatory' strategies. How quick and how effective we are in reorienting ourselves according to these shifting paradigms will determine our sustainable futures.

The word 'conflict' carries negative connotations. It is often thought of as the opposite of cooperation and peace, and is most commonly associated with violence or the threat of violence. This view of conflict is not always helpful. In many settings it should be seen as a potential force for positive social change—its presence a visible demonstration of society adapting to a new political, economic or physical environment. A potential non-violent approach to solve these conflicts at the least social/economic/Environmental costs may be through evolving alternative tourism strategies.

In the midst of growing tensions and worries everywhere "Getting away from it all," is understandably popular. With so many wonderful places in the world, prices of international travel falling, and the stresses and strains of everyday life increasing, more people are traveling. And as the population grows and incomes rise in many societies, the trend is steeply up. In 2000, international tourist arrivals reached an all time high of 698 million, an increase of 7.4per cent that was double the growth rate of 1999, according to the World Tourism Organization. Tourism sector employs 11 per cent of the global workforce—over 200 million people—either directly or indirectly.

The Tourism Sector in India

India's tourism potentials are immense—with a large variety ranging from rich cultural diversity, world-renowned historical, religious, heritage and architectural monuments, unique fairs, festivals, folklore and folk dances besides the costumes and customs to wildlife sanctuaries with exquisite flora and fauna. Besides, there are cool hill stations and long stretches of sunny beaches all round the peninsula.

The diversity is not only in climate but is all pervasive and as J. Nehru put it, "India is a land of contrasts—with the rural tranquility of simplicity and urban bustle, pomp and show". Added to this, there are plenty of traditional arts and crafts to carry back as souvenirs; Indian hospitality and variety induce tourists to make repeated visits. India's wide choice of adventure sports ranges from the daring to the exotic—trekking, camping, rock climbing, white water rafting, skating, air/water gliding, etc. In spite of such attractions, tourist arrivals in India are less than 1per cent of the world arrivals.

Tourism in India is different from other sectors by some special characteristics that include: A wider variety of stake-holders but with lack of communication and coordination. Uniformity of artificial structures in Tourism areas does not blend with the natural diversity of undisturbed areas. Inter-sectoral linkages and complexity with several intangible costs and benefits; conflicts leading to problems in analysis, monitoring and coordination; mixed priorities and conflicts, make cooperation and participation difficult. Research on tourism especially on policy and planning has been given low priority—as a result, it is poorly studied and understood as a sector in general and its Environmental and Social/Cultural impacts in particular; hence, we are confronted with fragmented and poorly coordinated policies, riddled with ad-hoc decisions for short term gains at the cost of long term sustainability.

Multiplier effect is prominent—can enhance poverty alleviation and alternative livelihoods; but is rarely understood by the planners and the implementing agencies. Seasonality in Tourist influx has implications for carrying capacity analysis and Tourism policy/planning/implementation, but rarely taken into account by the planners/policy makers Spatial and temporal dimensions—implications for Physical planning:

Positive and negative feed backs—implications for absorbing capacity, carrying capacity, Sustainability, and resilience; a typical tourism cycle would involve—Exploration/developmen/tconsolidation/stagnation/decline/ rejuvenation; however, negative impacts, on a cumulative basis destroy the resource base, affecting the natural, cultural, and Heritage attractions, culminating in declining tourism trends. Life supporting systems are impacted, culminating in debates on Ecological integrity Vs Economic security.

'Profit maximization' is the prime motto of Tourism enterprises (irrespective of whether they are private or Govt. sector undertakings) and hence, tourism is largely out of control for planners; some impacts are irreversible and hence tourism itself is affected due to degradation in Environmental health/quality. The Ecological impacts of tourism are more on Common Property Resources—air, soil and ground water, leading to tragedy of the commons as they are treated as 'open access commons'. Lack of know how and trained man power in Govt. agencies on Eco-cultural tourism lead to lack of appreciation and Govt. support for community based initiatives. Tourism industry is fundamentally dependent on the diversity and quality of the natural and cultural resources. Hence, it has grater reasons to conserve/protect the same. But are we giving adequate attention/priorities for natural and cultural resources while planning and implementing tourism projects in India? Though tourism is India's one of the largest foreign exchange earners and one among the fastest growing industries, the natural resource base that supports tourism is "heavily stressed" in and around the main tourist destination areas. In spite of the overwhelming technological and information revolution, we have trapped ourselves in a vicious circle of self-destruction by adopting the typical "boom and bust" tourism paths paved by the ill-conceived and unplanned/uncontrolled mass tourism, promoted for short-term profit maximization at the cost of degradation in Environmental quality. Ironically, this in turn, ultimately detracts the tourists and destroys the Tourism industry itself.

The question is whether we, in the blind pursuit of rapid Economic growth and earning more foreign exchange Q an afford to sacrifice the higher Environmental quality and our rich cultural Heritage upon which tourism so strongly depends. Though we have already learnt many bitter lessons, we tend to overlook them.

Changes in the physical, spatial, and socio-economic structure of a tourist area as well as the existence of several, sometimes burdensome, environmental/ social problems testify to the presence of these conflicts and the crying need for evolving appropriate strategies to sustainably manage the Environmental quality, and to improve the local livelihood opportunities.

However, the researchers as well as policy makers in India largely ignore the inseparable links between the Environmental quality (EQ), sustainability, peace and tourism and pay little attention to participation of local communities, by focusing only on setting up infrastructures, promoting marketing strategies and make only *ad hoc*/piece meal efforts to improve the EQ, sustainability and peace in the destination areas. This is self-evident from the "tell-tale symptoms" or "indicators" such as garbage dumps, foul smell, very high rates of pollution, over exploitation of natural resources, alienation of local communities, increasing conflicts and violence in several destination areas.

The industry has learned these bitter lessons only after the irreversible damages have already set in. Examples can be seen every where the mass tourism went out of control—starting from Ooty and Kodai lakes in the South to Dal lake in the North; from Kovalam in the South to Goa in the North; even our nation's pride Taj Mahal is not spared!

As a result, tourism has become a dirty word amongst many communities, environmental groups and human rights campaigners. This is really unfortunate as the tourism sector has greater potential to enhance local livelihoods, if it is properly planned.

The Ills of the Tourism Industry

Though tourism could lead to a variety of potential benefits, uncontrolled mass tourism, the most predominant form of tourism today, inevitably increases the already existing conflicts, besides creating new ones. Tourism's voracious appetite for basic resources—land, water and energy—has meant that the tourism industry and Government Agencies are increasingly finding themselves opposed over land rights and water rights by local people. Lack of access by locals to public beaches, violation by hotels of environmental regulations, and heavy-handed tactics by local authorities to free-up beach areas for hotels' use, have all been cited in legal disputes throughout the world.

For instance, three quarters of the sand dunes on the Mediterranean coast between Spain and Sicily have now disappeared, largely because of the construction of hotels and holiday flats. One of the most famous long-term tourism protests has been in Goa, India. With one five-star hotel consuming as much water as five local villages and one five-star tourist consuming 28 times more electricity per day than a local Goan, local discontent over resource-use is understandable. Thus, the modern world is characterized by mass concentrations of people, mass production, and mass activities. Diversity and beauty of land and life are more and more replaced by uniformity and ugliness. Human settlements in their mad rush for development have turned beautiful tree-clad landscapes into desolate concrete jungles, and fertile lands with diverse native vegetation are increasingly destroyed by monocultures. Tourism is no exception to this general rule.

The Green Signals

Over the last decade, understanding of these complex and interconnected issues by the world tourism industry, tourists, governments and communities has increased as indicated by the evolution of numerous alternative forms of tourism such as 'green' tourism, 'alternative' tourism, 'responsible' tourism, 'sustainable' tourism, 'eco' tourism, 'eco-cultural' tourism (ECT), 'eco-development' tourism, 'Heritage eco-cultural' tourism (HECT), 'community' tourism, "ethical' tourism, 'fair-trade' tourism and even, most recently, the particularly un-catchy, 'pro-poor' tourism (PPT).

Unfortunately, we, in India have not sufficiently re-oriented ourselves, to meet the future international market demand for these specialized forms of tourism. The concept of sustainable tourism should not be confused with ECT. According to WTO, all tourism activities, be they geared to holidays, business, conferences, congresses or fairs, health, adventure or ECT itself, must be sustainable.

This means that the planning and development of tourism infrastructure, its subsequent operation and also its marketing should focus on environmental, social, cultural and economic sustainability criteria, so as to ensure that neither the natural environment nor the socio-cultural fabric of the host communities will be impaired by the arrival/activities of tourists; on the contrary, enterprises, as well as the communities in which they operate, should benefit from tourism, both economically and culturally. Eco-tourism, a growing trend, is the most commonly understood term as tourism that focuses on an appreciation of the environment. In 1993 the World Tourism Organisation (WTO) estimated nature tourism generates 7 per cent of all international travel expenditure. More recent research reveals this is now much higher, accounting for 20 per cent of international travel in the Asia-Pacific region and some areas, such as South Africa, experiencing a massive growth in visitors to game and nature reserves, of over 100 per cent annually. Research by The International Ecotourism Society (TIES) reveals that coo-tourists are likely to be higher spenders on their holidays than 'ordinary' mass tourists. And high spending, nature-loving, responsible tourists are undoubtedly an attractive option for governments looking for ways of earning foreign exchange.

The recent Amman Declaration on Peace Through Tourism reflects many of the strategies discussed above and has recognised that peace is an essential precondition for travel and tourism and all aspects of human growth and development. Hence, it has recommended the development of tourism as a global vehicle for promoting understanding, trust and goodwill among peoples of the world through an appropriate political and economic framework.

The New Threats

The alternative tourism strategies, evolved in response to the concern for the Ecology, culture, Heritage and local livelihoods, have created both new opportunities as well as new threats. One of eco-tourism's first problems is one of definition. Although, there are several definitions, there is no certification system to abide by or international monitoring body. The term can be used by anyone at anytime for anything from a small-scale locally run rainforest lodge where the money goes to support a local community, to a large, luxury, foreign-owned resort which has little community involvement and uses masses of natural resources.

Eco-tourists may even visit areas of national beauty and wildlife significance without realizing that local people have been evicted from the area in order for eco-tourism to be developed, as has happened in East Africa, India, Southern Africa and many other destinations. Ill-conceived and/or ill-planned Eco-tourism, as practiced now by a majority of the business communities has caused serious, irreversible negative impacts in environmentally and culturally sensitive areas, even in countries that are well known as eco-tourism destinations like Belize or Costa Rica.

The Malaysian-based Third World Network working with the Thailand-based Tourism Information Monitoring team (TIM-team) cite examples throughout Asia, including the eco-tourism policy promoted by the tourism working group under the Greater Mekong Sub-region (GMS) development scheme, led by the Asian Development Bank, which covers a vast area across Burma, Cambodia, Laos, Thailand, Vietnam and Yunnan/China. They are riddled with several problems relating to accusations of 'human zoos' being created and financial exploitation of hill tribe villages by outside tour operators.

Besides, the increasing link of eco-tourism to the multi-million dollar biotechnology industry through bio-piracy in key eco-tourist sites like rainforests, and the use of eco-tourism by the World Bank's Social Investment Project to support massive development projects, some involving logging operations are becoming common in many developing countries. The revolution in information and communication technologies would enable both the promoters and the tourists to exploit the hidden potentials ECT in a region, more efficiently than ever.

However, the lack of discipline of government and the escalating demand for growth will undermine efforts to create sustainable eco-tourism economies that are small but beautiful. Under extreme conditions of land grabbing and unplanned structures, it may create concrete jungles, surrounded by degraded vegetation, thus destroying the once tranquil zones. Hence, we have to be extremely careful while promoting ECT.

Despite these problems, an International Year of Ecotourism (IYE) was declared by the United Nations for 2002. This will be co-ordinated by the WTO and UNEP and a range of activities held, including a World Ecotourism Summit from 19-22 May 2002 in Quebec, Canada plus various regional conferences. Oliver Hillel, the UNEP tourism programme co-ordinator sees the IYE as a chance to "assess what eco-tourism is, or can be, rather than only a promotional event for UN member governments, for the private sector and for recipients of development aid." It is clear to many that nature-based tourism is presently seen as one of the most lucrative niche markets, and powerful transnational corporations are likely to exploit the IYE to dictate their own definitions and rules of eco-tourism on society, while people-centred initiatives will be squeezed out and marginalised.

While the commitment of the tourism industry in India to tackle these complex issues seems limited, a few smaller operators are keen to work closely with local people in order for the communities to support their business and out of an honest desire to protect environments and optimise benefits to local people. However, such small operators lack the know-how to tackle the issues involved. As a result, alternative tourism strategies for which India has a greater potential, make up a very small proportion of overall tourism facilities.

The Potential Alternatives

In any outdoor tourism activity, human experience, knowledge, expectation, and socio-cultural contexts interact with environmental elements and environments as entities to produce an outcome that affects both the humans and the environment.

Thus, sustainable tourism development depends in many important ways on the proper handling of the relationships between Tourism and the Environment. Sustainability, Peace and Environmental quality occupy the central table in the wake of global terrorism.

Greater sustainability of the tourism would mean more regional products, less noise and emissions, lesser solid wastes and appropriate sewage treatment measures, creation of jobs, lesser social conflicts/violence by learning to live in harmony and higher quality of life for the local populations well as improved quality of holidays for the guest. The conventional mass tourism, by its very nature cannot cater to these demands. Hence, alternative tourism strategies are emerging. Sustainable tourism is defined as "Tourism that meets the needs of the present tourists and host regions while protecting and enhancing opportunity for the future. It is envisaged as leading to management of all resources in such a way that economic, social and aesthetic needs can be fulfilled while maintaining cultural integrity, essential ecological processes, bio-Diversity and life supporting systems (soil, air and water)".

Thus, it has the inbuilt mechanism for promoting peace and harmony among the tourism stakeholders. A related alternative is Eco-cultural Tourism (ECT). ECT activities are offered by a large and wide variety of operators, and practiced by an even larger array of tourists. While there is no single universal definition for ECT, its general characteristics can be summarized as follows:

All nature-based forms of tourism in which the main motivation of the tourists is the observation and appreciation for admiring, enjoying and/or studying nature as well as the traditional cultures and Heritage (both past and present) prevailing in relatively undisturbed or uncontaminated natural areas

It contains participatory, interactive, educational and interpretation features. It is generally, but not exclusively organized for environmentally, socially conscious small groups by specialized and small, locally owned businesses. Foreign operators of varying sizes also organize, operate and/or market ECT tours, generally for small groups.

It minimizes negative impacts upon the natural and socio-cultural environment. Heritage Eco-cultural Tourism (HECT) is a newly emerging type of alternative tourism. When Heritage of the destination areas can be exploited along with the local Ecological and cultural attractions, we have a case for Heritage Eco-cultural Tourism. Heritage embraces magnificent natural, indigenous and historic landscapes (natural or man-made), wildlife and healthy, intact ecosystems, historical elements (that has helped to shape the regional/ national identity), cultural elements and human values, shaping regional, national, global identity; it also incorporates a strong connection to 'place'; that is, people come to the place by choice, they are somehow transformed by it, and they choose to identify themselves with it even if they don't live there. This may be because of the outstanding universal value of the areas visited from the point of view of science, conservation or natural beauty.

Historical places, objects and manifestations of cultural, scientific, symbolic, spiritual and religious values are important expressions of the culture, identity and religious beliefs of societies. Their role and importance, particularly in the light of the need for cultural identity and continuity in a rapidly changing world, need to be promoted.Tourists are actively seeking such lost values. They come hoping for a profound psychic or spiritual experience in some quiet corners of the destination areas. Hence, we have greater responsibility to conserve the cultural Heritage areas.

The following are the key potential benefits of HECT:

- Protection and active conservation of natural and built heritage resources, justified by their own intrinsic value for posterity and the revenue which visitors contribute.
- Enhancement of the natural and built environment to meet rising quality standards necessary to sustain modern travel and tourism.
- Reconstruction for visitor usage of urban environments and environments degraded by the industrial practices of former extractive and manufacturing industries.
- Establishment of attractive environments for tourism destinations, for residents as much as visitors, which may support other compatible new economic activities, from agriculture and fishing to service and manufacturing industries.
- Creation of economic value and protection for resources which otherwise have no perceived value to residents, or represent a cost rather than a benefit- livelihood opportunities—micro-enterprises?

- Opportunity to communicate and interpret the values of natural and built heritage and of cultural inheritance of residents of visited areas.
- Effective management of visitors within an environment so that it can support long-term economic development and repeat visits.
- Research and development of good environmental practices and management systems to influence the operation of travel and tourism businesses as well as visitor behaviour at destinations.

Opportunities, through the direct customer contacts that all travel and tourism businesses have, for operators to communicate and interpret the values of natural and built heritage and culture to visitors, thus helping to create a new generation of responsible consumers

The available knowledge indicate that the following may be considered as the major criteria for selecting HECT sites:

- *Geography*—proximity to mass-tourism sites; sufficiently closer for easy accessibility but adequately away from motorable roads and other human disturbances.
- *Climate and Ecology*—microclimates/habitats conducive enough for the tourists without any need for artificial comforts
- *Rarity and Uniqueness*—Ecosystems like mountains, rivers, mangroves, coral reefs and islands endowed with unspoiled beauty, unique culture and Heritage.
- *Infrastructure*—only reasonable—to the barest minimum but with desirable conditions—hygienic ethnic food (locally produced/prepared), protected water supply, natural ventilation and local architecture.
- *Diversity*—higher habitat/community/Ecosystem/cultural (food, cloth, architecture, crafts, festivals etc.)—diversity and purity—potentials/ opportunities for viewing/appreciating more attractive species/cultures as well as Heritage elements; Potentials for a variety of nature/ adventure tourism activities such as camping for wildlife observation, traditional healing camps, caving, bird-watching, trekking, rock-climbing, mountain biking, skating, para-gliding, wind-surfing, funky jumping, canopy walkways, white water rafting, snorkeling, scuba diving, recreational fishing
- *Unpolluted/relatively undisturbed areas with higher Environmental quality*—in contrast to polluted/degraded landscapes/seascapes
- *Minimum health/safety risks*—to avoid costly demands from the tourists
- *Opportunities for Environmental Education and interpretation*—for all the stake-holders
- *Opportunities for generating and sustaining new livelihoods*—to cater to the demands of the tourists—*e.g.* Apiculture (the science and art of raising honey bees), agriculture, horticulture, floriculture,

community dairy/piggery/poultry, preparation of Ethnic foods, rich diversity of arts and crafts.

- *Community cooperation*—to make and enforce their own decisions on eco-tourism development.
- *Presence of dedicated NGOs*—for catalyzing cooperation.
- *Cooperation of other stake-holders*—Govt. and other institutions—their policies, programmes and goals.
- *Marketing opportunities*—potentials for targeting different types of eco-tourists (hardcore, dedicated, mainstream and casual); marketing linkages and potentials.

The HECT will enable the tourists as well as the local communities to find ways to live sustainably, and in peace with nature, Cultural Heritage and intact, functioning ecosystems. More importantly, we will be reconnecting ourselves with our forgotten treasure of the diverse culture and Heritage of the bygone era.

In this process, tourism will promote peace and sustainability by closer mutualistic interactions between tourists and the local communities. Among the several organizations that could be involved in the promotion of HECT, mention must be made of UNESCO (World Heritage sites programme) and the International Institute for Peace through Tourism at international levels and the Indian National Trust for the promotion of Arts and Cultural Heritage (INTACH) at the national level. The Indian Tourism Development Corporation and the State Tourism Development Corporations have to recognise the potentials of HECT and reorient themselves to the tasks ahead.

Broad guidelines for promoting HECT strategies may be modified and adopted from UNEP that has prescribed Environmental codes of conduct for tourism and Gonsalves' (1991) paper on guidelines for alternative tourism for the third world.

The adoption of the Global Code of Ethics for Tourism, the Green Globe programme, the ECOTEL Certification awarded by HVS Eco Services, Certification Programmes for Sustainable Tourism and Eco-tourism, Exemplary Practices by Canadian Tourism Commission, The National Eco-tourism Accreditation Programme of the Eco-tourism Association of Australia and the Australian Tourism Operators Association and equitable community participation in tourism are a few other such initiatives to name, globally.

Recently, Mastny (2002) from World Watch Institute has provided policy guidelines with examples for sustainable tourism. The recently emerging pro-poor tourism approaches, have to be ideally integrated into HECT.

Bibliography

A C Mittal and B S Sharma: *Human Resource Management*, Vista International, Delhi, 2006.

A K Mishra: *Human Resource Management*, Shree Publication, Delhi, 2008.

A.P. Rastogi: *Travel Agency Operations*, Aman Publication, Delhi, 2007.

Amrita Bhagnani: *Travel Agency and Tourism*, Abhijeet Publications, Delhi, 2012.

Ashim Gupta: *Travel Agency and Tour Operations: Concepts and Principles*, Centrum Press, Delhi, 2012.

Avdhesh S. Jha and Ghuran Jha: *Human Resource Management*, Sumit Enterprises, Delhi, 2011.

Avdhesh S. Jha and S. Bhargava: *Human Resource Management*, APH Publication, Delhi, 2010.

B. Narayan: *Human Resource Management*, A.P.H. Publication, Delhi, 2010.

Biswajeet Pattanayak: *Human Resource Management*, PHI Learning, Delhi, 2000.

Dipak Kumar Bhattacharyya: *Human Resource Management*, Excel Books, Delhi, 2012.

Gurpreet Randhawa: *Human Resource Management*, Atlantic Publication, Delhi, 2007.

Iain Henderson: *Human Resource Management*, Universities Press, Delhi, 2009.

Jagmohan Negi and Gaurav Manoher: *Travel Agency Operations : Concepts and Principles (With Examination Questions)*, Kanishka Publication, Delhi, 2003.

Jogendra Mehta: *Human Resource Management*, Aadi Publication, Delhi, 2010.

Jyotsana Singh: *Human Resource Management*, Centrum Press, Delhi, 2011.

K.S. Negi: *Travel Agency Management*, Wisdom Press, Delhi, 2011.

L K Singh: *Management of Travel Agency*, Isha Books, Delhi, 2008.

Lalita Sharma: *Travel Agency and Tour Operation : Concepts and Principles*, Centrum Press, Delhi, 2010.

Manohar Puri and Gian Chand: *Travel Agency and Tourism*, Pragun Publication, Delhi, 2006.

Margaret Inman, Nuala OSullivan and Adrian Murton: *Human Resource Management*, Viva Books, Delhi, 2011.

Margaret Inman, Nuala OSullivan and Adrian Murton: *Human Resource Management*, Hodder Education, Delhi, 2011.

Mohinder Chand: *Travel Agency Management : An Introductory Text*, Anmol Publication, Delhi, 2003.

Naga Raju Battu: *Human Resource Management*, Discovery Publishing House, Delhi, 2006.

P. Jyothi and D.N. Venkatesh: *Human Resource Management*, Oxford University Press, Delhi, 2006.

P.K. Gupta: *Human Resource Management*, Dreamtech Press, Delhi, 2010.

R G Menon: *Travel Agency Management*, Arise Publication, Delhi, 2007.

R. Kaushik, U.Kaushik and S. Arora: *Human Resource Management*, Pointer Publication, Delhi, 1999.

Rajesh Kumar and Santosh: *Human Resource Management*, Shree Publication, Delhi, 2011.

Shanmukha Rao Padala: *Human Resource Management*, APH Publication, Delhi, 2011.

Surendra Jain and Sonia Bhargav: *Human Resource Management*, Knowledge Book, Delhi, 2010.

V S P Rao: *Human Resource Management*, Excel Books, Delhi, 1998.

Index